DERREN BROWN

HAPPY

Why more or less everything is absolutely fine

Acclaim for *Happy*:

'Witty, useful and beautifully written . . . this book grapples expansively with the most profound questions any of us face.'
Sunday Times

'Brilliant. Really brilliant and just crammed with wisdom and insight. It will genuinely make a difference to me and the way I think about myself. I'm going to recommend it to everyone I know.'
STEPHEN FRY

''Til now, we've known Derren Brown as a supreme illusionist and magician. Now he surprises us with a new and brilliant identity: as a philosopher. Not just any philosopher. Brown takes philosophy back to its truest task: that of helping us to live and die well. His book is deeply informative, moving, wise and full of love. It sets out to change lives – and it will. Derren has pulled off a properly implausible trick: that of making the deepest ideas relevant, humane and urgent.'
ALAIN DE BOTTON

'Brown tries to resurrect the original Stoic ambitions here: not just to live well but to die well, too. His book is thoughtful, insightful and ultimately, well, helpful.'
Sunday Times Books of the Year

'In this wise and perceptive book Derren Brown has conjoined personal experience, profoundly sensible psychology and the magic of philosophy to produce a really excellent account of how to be happy – really, maturely, properly happy. This is a wonderfully educative – and enjoyable! – book, and should be on everyone's reading list, always.'
A.C. GRAYLING

Derren Brown began his UK television career in December 2000 with a series of specials called *Mind Control*. Since redefining the genre of magic for intelligent, modern audiences, he has become synonymous with the art of psychological manipulation. His TV shows have become must-see events. Amongst a varied and notorious career, Derren has played Russian roulette on live television, convinced middle managers to commit an armed robbery in the street, led the nation in a séance, stuck viewers to their sofas, successfully predicted the National Lottery, motivated a shy man to land a packed passenger plane at 30,000 feet, exposed psychic and faith-healing charlatans, and hypnotised a man to assassinate Stephen Fry. On top of this he tours the UK every year with a sell-out stage show.

He has published three previous books: *Tricks of the Mind*, *Confessions of a Conjuror* and a book of his paintings, *Portraits*.

HAPPY

Why more or less everything
is absolutely fine

Derren Brown

CORGI BOOKS

TRANSWORLD PUBLISHERS
61–63 Uxbridge Road, London W5 5SA
www.penguin.co.uk

Transworld is part of the Penguin Random House group of companies
whose addresses can be found at global.penguinrandomhouse.com

First published in Great Britain in 2016 by Bantam Press
an imprint of Transworld Publishers
Corgi edition published 2017

A CIP catalogue record for this book
is available from the British Library.

ISBN
9780552172356

Typeset in 11.5/13.25pt Bembo by Falcon Oast Graphic Art Ltd.
Printed and bound by Clays Ltd, Bungay, Suffolk.

Penguin Random House is committed to a sustainable
future for our business, our readers and our planet. This book
is made from Forest Stewardship Council® certified paper.

For the Piglace

THINGS ARE NOT ALL AS
GRASPABLE AND SAYABLE AS
ON THE WHOLE WE ARE LED TO
BELIEVE; MOST EVENTS ARE
UNSAYABLE, OCCUR IN A SPACE
THAT NO WORD HAS EVER
PENETRATED

From *Letters to a Young Poet*, Rainer Maria Rilke

For Your Eyes and Minds

Part One: Beginnings

Part Two: Solutions

☺

He is ubiquitous. At once irreproachable and black-eyed sinister, he cheers us for a moment before we sense a sneer. He is the rubber-stamp guarantee of congeniality, designed for contagion: a morale-boosting initiative for a life assurance company in the 1960s, disseminated into the world in the form of fifty million black-on-yellow badges. The hallmark of seventies' psychedelia and eighties' electronic dance music, his is the glazed ecstasy of the narcotically compelled. Today, he is such a familiar currency in electronic communication that the modern iconoclast's first break with convention is a decision *not* to use him.

In England, the smiley or his sideways colon/parenthesis cousin provides a familiar sign-off where an X would seem too intimate; and in an age of typed communication, where tone of voice is not conveyed, it is important shorthand. 'I am happy; now you should be happy.' It reports that no offence has been meant, that one's intentions are entirely benign, and the warm lubricant of assured conviviality will smooth any further communication. But within it lies the troubling behest to be cheerful, and the childish contours of this exhortation's grinning emblem tell us that nothing should be simpler. Yet the desire to be happy, to obtain happiness, to claim our *right* to be happy, remains the most enduring and conspicuously self-defeating aspect of our modern condition.

Part One: **Beginnings**

1

Once Upon a Time

A while ago, my long-term friend and collaborator Andy Nyman told me the following story.

Andy, an actor with a strong fan base, had emerged from the stage door after a show to find waiting for him a lost-looking, nervous young girl, perhaps fourteen years old, barely able to make eye contact. Her mother, who was clutching a small camera, stood next to her. The mother asked if her daughter might get a photograph with him. He happily agreed, and the girl wordlessly stepped forward and wrapped an arm tightly around his torso. He could feel her trembling at his side as they posed. He grinned dutifully, and as the mother took the picture, Andy sensed that the girl had neither smiled nor properly faced the camera. He asked to look at the picture on the camera's viewing screen, and there he was, looking the picture of happiness, while the poor soul next to him had indeed been caught with her eyes half shut and expression indistinct.

'Do you want to do that again? You weren't smiling,' he asked the girl.

The mother answered for her: 'Oh, she always looks terrible in pictures.'

My friend was taken aback by her words. 'Don't say that!' he protested, in defence of the daughter.

The girl spoke up for the first time: 'Oh, it's okay, it's true.'

In that brief exchange over a photograph, there also appeared to be a snapshot of a life: one of wretched self-esteem for the girl, and its apparent maternal origins. Instead of helping to encourage and nurture her child at all times as we would hope, the mother, it would certainly seem, is instead helping to perpetuate a crippling lack of self-belief. The damning word in the mother's remark is 'always', because 'always' tells us there is a pattern, a story at work. And stories affect us deeply.

When I perform my day job as a kind of magician, I work with people's capacity to fool themselves with stories. A good magic trick forces the spectator to tell a story that arrives at an impossible conclusion, and the clearer the story is, the better. Normally, everything you need to solve the puzzle happens right in front of you, but you are made to care only about the parts that the magician wants you to. When you join up *those* dots, so misleadingly and provocatively arranged, you are left with a baffling mystery. A good magician might make the trick *mean* more, by elevating it beyond the mere disappearance or transposition of some props. If it can be made to feel somehow relevant to *you*, rather than a mere display of skill, then the story is likely to have more import and the trick more impact.

If magic exploits our capacity to continuously, unconsciously modify events in the ongoing world to form a story, even at the expense of everything we know to be possible in the universe, then we are indeed master editors, tirelessly working to communicate to others and ourselves a meaningful tale. We turn the memory of a holiday or a meal into something entirely wonderful or completely appalling, depending on the story we have decided for ourselves of a successful or failed event. We adjust details and selectively remember what fits into our preferred narrative. When a relationship ends, we may one day recall all the good times we shared with that person, and the next day all the bad. These stories shift and change.

We are, each of us, a product of the stories we tell ourselves. Some of our stories are brief and inconsequential, allowing us to get through our day and make sense of other people: 'I'll do this and head to the shops and get that done, and then I'll be able to completely relax this evening.' Or, 'She was snappy because really she's worried that I'm putting other people before her. She does that because she's insecure.'

These are neat narratives that allow us to arrange complicated reality into a satisfying and tidy parcel, and move on with our lives. Without them in place, we would see only a mess of details. If we were unable to form meaningful patterns, our lives would become overwhelmed.

Other stories, like the one we sense the girl at the stage door is learning from her mother, become deeply ingrained and in many ways define who we are. We tell ourselves tales about the future: 'Oh, I'm an awkward misfit who looks terrible and always will.' Or, 'I'll never have a fulfilling relationship.' Other stories are about the past: 'I'm like this because my parents treated me in a particular way.' Or, 'I'm an unlucky person – always have been.' Yet our entire past, which we feel (in many ways correctly) is responsible for how we behave today, is itself just a story we are telling ourselves in the here and now.

We join the dots to tell one tale when we consider how, for example, we came to this point in our career, another when we consider how we developed our psychological foibles or strengths. It is hard to think about your past without tidying it up into a kind of story: one in which you are cast as the hero or victim. Invariably we ignore the regular dice-rolls of chance or random luck; successful high-flyers are typically prone to ignoring the interplay of blind fortune when they credit their career trajectories to their canny business sense or brute self-belief. We tell the story we want to tell, and we live out those stories every day.

Some of these stories are consciously constructed, but others operate without our knowledge, dictated by scripts handed to us by others when we were young. We can carry around the psychological legacy of our parents for our whole lives, whether bad or good. Where they have unfulfilled wishes and regrets, these are commonly passed to us as a template for storytelling. Many of these templates make it hard for us to feel happy: 'You must achieve impressive things to be happy/loved.' Or, 'You must sacrifice your own happiness to make others feel better: that is the measure of your worth.' Similar insidious directives can also come from the Church, our peers, classmates and teachers, the cumulative effect of the news media we encounter daily or any number of ideologies in which we find ourselves enmeshed. With these overarching stories or templates in mind, we repeatedly arrange our lives in such a way as to let events and others reinforce the same familiar message, like a child's fable. Again and again, many people play out the same story: that they surely cannot be easy to love; that love and admiration are dependent on career success; that others will always disappoint us. 'The greatest burden a child must bear is the unlived life of the parents,' wrote the legendary psychoanalyst Carl Jung. Whatever we have taken from them, the founding story of our lives, imposed on us by a mother and father who in turn inherited a faulty script from their own parents, *isn't even ours.*

This book is at heart about how we might take control of those stories, with a view to living more happily. Two thousand years ago, a Roman slave called Epictetus, a prominent figure in the ancient school of Stoic philosophy, which remained the most prevalent school of thought for five hundred years before Christianity exploded into the world, gave voice to the notion: 'What upsets people is not things themselves but their judgements about these things.'[1] In other words, it is not events out there that cause our problems but rather our reactions to them: the stories we tell ourselves. This mite of ancient wisdom is the source of many modern-day self-help and therapeutic methods of varying substance, including neuro-linguistic programming (NLP), cognitive behavioural therapy (CBT) and the sixties' mantra of 'Change your head, don't change the world.' Shakespeare gives us the same thought through Hamlet: 'There is nothing either good or bad, but thinking makes it so.' Later, in the nineteenth century, Arthur Schopenhauer (pictured overleaf), a philosopher with whom we will spend time in this book, echoed the maxim less snappily:

> If we leave out grave misfortune, less depends, in the good things as well as in the bad, on what befalls and happens to us in life than on the way in which we feel it, and thus on the nature and degree of our susceptibility in every respect.[2]

1 Epictetus, *Enchiridion*, 5
2 Arthur Schopenhauer, *The World as Will and Representation*

A true Stoic would frown at the exception of 'grave misfortune', but let's dwell a moment longer on Epictetus's extraordinary thought.

Perhaps the first mark of emotional maturity is to realise that there is an enormous gulf between the events of the world and what we do with them. Out There and In Here are two very different kingdoms, and other people are not accountable for how we feel. No one, however ludicrously they behave, has the right or the direct means to affect your self-control or dignity. No one need annoy us so much that we in turn become a source of annoyance to others. In fact, the Stoics have some powerful advice about how to appreciate and maintain a distinction between the outer and inner worlds, and therefore how to reduce our levels of anxiety.

When we grasp that we do not *need* to react unhappily to events in the way to which we are accustomed, and thus begin to question our relationship with those aspects of the outer world, we can apply the same understanding more deeply to our *inner* world and the story we tell ourselves every day about who we are. That can change too. It is, after all, a fiction. I came across a nice analogy in David McRaney's book *You Are Not So Smart* that has stayed with me:

> When a movie begins with the words 'Based on a True Story,' what crosses your mind? Do you assume every line of dialogue, every bit of clothing and song in the background is the same as it was in the true event on which the film was based? Of course you don't. You know movies like *Pearl Harbor* or *Erin Brockovich* take artistic license with facts, shaping them so a coherent story will unfold with a beginning, middle, and end. Even biopics

9

about the lives of musicians or politicians who are still alive are rarely the absolute truth. Some things are left out, or some people are fused into single characters. The details, you think when watching, are less important than the big picture, the general idea.

If only you were so savvy when it came to looking back on the biopic in your head.

We are trapped inside our own heads. Our beliefs and understandings about the world are limited by that perspective. Schopenhauer wrote, 'Every man takes the limits of his own field of vision for the limits of the world.'[3] Of course, then, we mistake that story we've constructed of our lives as the truth.

Interestingly, we are prey to an analogous error every waking moment of our lives. You have a blind spot in your vision where you can't see anything. We all have one. You can find it by extending your right arm and pointing the thumb straight up in front of you. Close your left eye and look straight ahead with your right, level with but a little way to the left of that thumb. Now slowly move the thumb from side to side, keeping it level with your gaze, until part of it disappears. Experiment long enough and you'll find your blind spot, if you haven't already tried something similar as a child. Remove the thumb and the blind spot is still there, but you won't be aware of it, as your brain is filling in the gap like a Photoshop clone tool, in order to provide a seamless viewing experience.

Look around your environment now. You are editing what you see; your eyes will probably dart from one point

3 Arthur Schopenhauer, *Studies in Pessimism*

of interest to another. There is an *infinite* data source around you, but you are selecting, deleting, cloning and generalising from that source in order to provide a working model of your environment in which you can effectively function. You simply can't take it all in at once, so you decide what might be important and largely make up the rest. We err on the side of caution, thus an unexpected movement will attract your eye in case it signifies a threat; while at a deeper level we will assign undue weight to a look or tone of voice from another person because it confirms for us some ingrained fear.

Even at this immediate visual level, we are missing a huge amount of information, preferring to go with an easy summation of our environment. We can look for our keys and not see them right in front of us if we don't believe they're there. When it comes to telling stories, it's easier to see this editing process at work in other people than ourselves. When someone tells you about an argument they were involved in, do you not administer a dose of scepticism? You know you're hearing only *their* version of the events. They've turned something complex into a neat story (usually one that leaves them suspiciously blameless). You know there will be a lot more to it that's been left out: how frustrating or antagonistic they may have been themselves; how the other person may have been misunderstood. You know that events have been exaggerated and simplified so that the person can get their point across.

Do we ever think to take the same sceptical view of that one story that affects our life the most? Would we consider applying the same wry detachment to the private tale of who we are? How might we even gain the necessary vantage point to consider our stories when we are tucked away within them? We will look at ways of gaining that perspective, but if we don't consider how to view it for what it is, the negative aspects of that story will trap us. Feelings of anxiety and helplessness can become all too familiar. And, as we'll discover, overt optimism tends to leave us defenceless and flailing too.

Here's a way you can see that negative storytelling take root within five minutes. Try a little exercise, in the form of solving some anagrams. Ready? Each word I will give you below is an anagram of another word, so you must try to unscramble each example to form another word that can be made from its letters. They're not supposed to be difficult, and you should be able to solve each in five or so seconds. If you don't unscramble it in that time, move on to the next one.

Here we go with the first one. Rearrange the letters to make another word. Solve this before you move on to the next, or limit yourself to five seconds' effort before continuing.

1. WHIRL
(Give yourself five seconds . . .)

Did you get it?
Here's another one to unscramble. Five seconds' limit again:

2. SLAPSTICK

Easier? More difficult? Last one:

3. CINERAMA

Done?
How many did you solve?

If you were to attend a class run by Charisse Nixon at Penn State Erie University, and if you happened to sit on the left-hand side of the room, you might be handed that list of anagrams to try to solve. Unbeknownst to you, your fellow students across from you on the right-hand side were handed another list of anagrams – TAB, LEMON, CINERAMA. Note that in each list the last word is the same. Now here's the ruse: the first two words on *your* list – WHIRL and SLAPSTICK – are unsolvable anagrams. They can't be unscrambled. So, apologies for wasting ten seconds of your valuable time here. The first two on the list handed to the *other* people are easily solvable: BAT and MELON are simple enough to decipher. But of course you all presume you have been given the same words. Nixon asks people to raise their hands when they have solved the first word. You see a lot of hands go up – you may not realise they belong only to the students on the other side of the room – and you feel frustration that you couldn't unscramble WHIRL. What have they seen that you haven't? Now you're told to try the next word and raise your hand when you've got it. Again, you can't see any solution. Other hands go up – the same hands as before, of course. Your frustration increases. You feel stupid and rushed. You've already given up.

And now the third word.

Did you solve it when you tried a moment ago?

CINERAMA can be unscrambled fairly easily – to form AMERICAN. But did you spot it? Most likely not. Especially not if you were trying this in Nixon's classroom. And neither did the others sitting on your side of the class.

But the students on the right-hand side got it. All their hands went up again. The right-hand side solved the anagram; the left didn't.

13

Nixon uses this neat experiment to demonstrate a phenomenon called 'learned helplessness'. Sitting over on the left, struggling with a task that is supposed to be easy, and seeing others raise their hands to acknowledge their success, you feel like a failure. That becomes your story: 'I can't do this. I shall fail at this task.' So you give up, preferring to repeat the story you have learnt: 'I can't do this exercise.' And the result is that you cannot unscramble CINERAMA: something that you would otherwise be very likely to do. Meanwhile, those on the right-hand side, enjoying their first two successes and feeling good about themselves, comfortably solve the final anagram.

As Nixon points out, there are social implications for this learned helplessness. She has a deep interest in the problem of bullying in schools and finding practical ways of optimising children's development. If a child becomes a victim of aggression and feels helpless, he or she is less likely to try to stand up to bullying in the future. And likewise for most of us: when we feel from previous experience that we're 'no good' at a task, we act out that helpless role when we are faced with it again. And bullying is not always overt or conscious: a mother's repeated disparagement of her daughter's looks can easily have the same effect.

The good news is that we can give ourselves permission to change our story. To act differently. To remind ourselves that we are not characters in a movie based on a true story, whose personalities are clearly defined and predictable. We, unlike them, can act out of character.

In a programme I made on the subject of placebo, an actor playing a doctor injected volunteers with what they believed to be a wonder drug, which was followed up by a course of pills. Each group of participants was formed of people with specific problems or traits, who were told that the drug was made to dramatically improve their particular situation: for example, a group of people suffering from debilitating anxieties was told it would remove the capacity for fear; a separate band of smokers was assured it would banish the desire for cigarettes, and so on. In each case, the participants were told they need make no effort themselves – the drug would do all the work.

The results can be seen in the 2012 Channel 4 show *Fear and Faith, Part One*. Nick, a chap with a crippling social anxiety, goes on to break up a fight in a pub and brilliantly overcomes his fears. Dan, who had a fear of heights so paralysing that he couldn't walk over a tiny stone bridge in his village, stands proudly on the edge of a viaduct with a drop of hundreds of feet beneath him, arms extended, soaking up his transformation. And smokers stop without any discernible effort. Nicky, who had tried every patch and method to give up previously, had been rewarded only with stress and failure. Following the placebo, she finds herself no longer thinking about cigarettes and can't believe how effective the magic medicine has been.

The injections and pills of course were fakes – the injection was saline and the pills contained only icing sugar. The dramatic transformations of the volunteers came about because they gave themselves permission to act differently. The idea of this drug coursing through their veins was enough to make them change their stories about who they were: 'I am no longer the person with this problem, because a new medicine is solving that for me.' Perhaps most astonishing was the story of one chap who suffered from dermatitis so badly that he hadn't been able to wear his wedding ring for years. At work he had to wear special gloves. For legal reasons we couldn't tell him the drug would cure that condition – we were only permitted to say it would cure hay fever and similar allergies – and we were all astonished when he reported that the 'Rumyodin' (if you wish to rediscover faith in your anagram skills, you can unscramble the name I gave the drug) had cured his skin condition too. It was truly remarkable.

The initial administration of the drug via injection was followed by homework: they had to report to us all the positive changes they were noticing. Naturally, this task would encourage them to live out their new story each day. This is 'confirmation bias' at work: one of the most reliable cognitive snares to which we are prone. Confirmation bias occurs when we notice things in the world that support our beliefs and pay less attention to things that contradict them. People fall into this trap when they notice the times their prayers have been 'answered' but explain away or ignore the many more times they haven't. Similarly, we operate under its influence whenever we notice the annoying habits of someone we dislike, more than her pleasant ones. Confirmation bias provides daily all the evidence we need to keep the storyline we've created for our life continuing in the same vein and looking like the truth. In the *Fear and Faith* programme, we were harnessing confirmation bias to focus the participants on new, more helpful stories. The result was that the dramatic changes in these people's lives, once their old stories were interrupted and sent off in a new direction, happened *effortlessly*.

This book is the result of many years of interest in what makes us happy, what happiness means, and how we might find more of it for ourselves. Over recent years, my television shows have involved unwitting subjects who have found their inner heroes and learnt to engage with lives they were letting slip by unlived. But the neatly packaged ideas that constitute such small-screen viewing material belie a much richer fascination with what constitutes a happy life. And for me, this question is brought into focus by the regular influx of deeply unhelpful messages we receive about what happiness *should* be.

You may consider yourself happy enough already or very unhappy; you may have strong ideas about what the good life should be about, or perhaps you've never thought about it. There is, sadly, a wealth of self-help literature and societal pressure regarding the pursuit of happiness, which can be deeply counter-productive and lead simply to more anxiety. Many of the routes to happiness and success with which you may be familiar – such as positive thinking, self-belief and setting goals – can be, as I hope to show you, disastrous to follow.

I am going to draw on some of my favourite thinking from the last two millennia, most of which will come from a time when philosophers – literally 'lovers of wisdom' – were concerned with how we might best live. For some time now, philosophy and psychology have existed as very separate disciplines, the latter more concerned with observing or fixing pathologies than studying how we might most happily live out our short lives. Then, recently, visionaries in both fields have again found common ground. Martin Seligman and a wake of other 'positive psychologists' have attempted to redress the balance by looking at what empirical psychological research can teach us about flourishing. Psychologists, they feel, have the opportunity to best equip themselves with solid, reliable research into what makes us happy, and then to pass that on to those who need to hear it, rather than leaving it to self-help gurus (who normally have only flimsy anecdotal support for their claims). Meanwhile, in the other camp, public philosophers such as Alain de Botton have sometimes risked derision to publish books or establish institutions designed to take a dry and analytical field back to its humanitarian roots. They have dared to remind us how the great thinkers of history might help us navigate our modern world contentedly and with minimal trauma.

I will try to glean from these twin disciplines the most helpful and effective ideas about how to flourish and live most happily. I will favour those ideas that work well for me. But on that note – perhaps you baulk at the very idea of anyone with the advantages of financial success and mediocre fame offering thoughts on happiness. I can hear the complaint of 'It's all very well for some' sounding from you and other shoppers as you disparagingly skim this volume's back cover in remainder and charity bookshops across the country.

These are not simply the thoughts of a man trying to shed a measure of guilt after being paid handsomely for his fatuous peacockery. The practical advice and ways of thinking that I offer here are from intellectual giants and astonishing thinkers. Furthermore, the ideas I shall present articulate the priorities I instinctively had in place well before my career took off, at a time when I was claiming what was then called housing benefit and trying to scrape together a living as a table magician. And as we'll discuss later, fame and success do very little to affect one's level of happiness. It seems that there can be *some* financial element at play, in that we report feeling less happy when we earn under a certain 'comfortable' amount. However, when we earn over that figure, more money does *not* make us incrementally happier. That magic number seems to vary greatly according to what study you read, depends on the cost of living wherever the study was carried out, and is rendered even less meaningful when you take on board that the type of job you do makes a huge difference to your happiness. According to a recent Cabinet Office report, for example, clergy reported substantially greater levels of happiness on an income of about twenty thousand pounds at the time, in contrast to lawyers who tend to be notably unhappy and earn much more.[4] So while it remains clear that having *less than you need* is a source of unhappiness, having *more than you need* does not make you happier.

Let us then be willing for a while to entertain the notion that the story we tell ourselves of our lives is a confabulation, a fiction. Ultimately, we will need some sort of story in place, for without one we would lack any coherent sense of identity. But perhaps for a while we can gently reconsider our personal tale and see whether it can be shaped more effectively through a little editing and polishing, or at least be open to improvement. We need not do this with a view to drastically altering our identity – although changes might be profound. As a light briefly flares between the eternities of darkness that precede and follow us, our concern is to make sure that we enjoy its fugitive consolation. And we can start by ridding ourselves of the most pervasive myth of them all.

☺

4 Joanne Evans, Ian Macrory and Chris Randall, 'Measuring National Well-being: Life in the UK: 2015,' Office for National Statistics

2

The Problem With Being Positive

I have just, uncomfortably and without joy, finished reading an extremely popular self-help book called *The Secret* by Rhonda Byrne. It stands out as a particularly tragic example of self-defeating misinformation, in a genre generously populated by hopeless handbooks and vapid visions of how to live well and prosper. I imagine it owes much of its success to the esoteric promise of its title and its suggestion of worthwhile, arcane knowledge, which Byrne explicitly (and inexplicably) describes as being revealed to such bygone luminaries as Plato, Einstein and Beethoven.

If you don't know the book, or don't share Byrne's keen-eyed insight into the psychological motivations of our genius forebears – a perspicacity that has so far eluded their most eminent biographers – let me explain. *The Secret*, I understand, first appeared in the form of a film, which I shall go to my grave without watching, along with straight porn and the greater part of Kung Fu cinema. According to Byrne, the film provoked a deluge of life-changing testimonies from viewers who within days of watching it and putting its message into practice found unexpected cheques cascading on to their doormats with quotidian aplomb. It's unclear who was sending these cheques, and whether, as one imagines, they might have been due anyway, but nonetheless the viewer or reader who grasps and puts into practice Byrne's 'Law of Attraction' can expect at the very least a surprising if undeserved financial turnaround in his or her life.

The two-step Law of Attraction (the Secret) runs as follows:

1. You are 'the most powerful magnet in the universe . . . and this unfathomable magnetic power is emitted through thoughts'. Being magnetic, your thoughts attract more of the same things back into your life. So if you think negatively, you will attract negativity and bad luck. Instead, you should decide on what you want in your life (such as a new car), and act as if you already have that thing, filling your mind with positive feelings about it.

2. 'What most people don't understand is that a thought has a frequency. We can measure a thought.'[5] That frequency vibrates in the universe, which responds by *actually sending us the new car*. The cosmos 'will start to rearrange itself to make it happen for you'. She goes on to explain: 'This is really fun. It's like having the Universe as your catalogue. You flip through it and say, "I'd like to have this experience and I'd like to have this product and I'd like to have a person like that." It is You placing your order with the Universe.

5 Rhonda Byrne, *The Secret*

It's really that easy.'[6] The car, or the desired thing, will turn up. The film version of *The Secret*, I understand, shows a lady avariciously eyeing up a necklace in a shop window, sending out a desire for it to the universe, and a moment later it appears around her neck. So you get the idea – it's pretty explicit.

We cannot truly trace Byrne's 'Secret' back to such places and figures as Babylon and Plato as she promises, despite how impressive such references might be to an audience that knows no better. Its origins are more pedestrian. It is a rehashing of the nineteenth-century New Thought Movement, founded by a philosopher and inventor called Phineas Parkhurst Quimby, who first extolled the all-healing power of positive thinking to America. The very notion of the system being a 'Secret' is, of course, purely a marketing stratagem; there is nothing revelatory or particularly interesting about any of it.

In the nineteenth century, America was in the grip of Calvinism, a harsh puritan variant that insisted on extensive and unforgiving self-examination coupled with punishing hard labour. It had been introduced by seventeenth-century settlers and, according to Barbara Ehrenreich in her excellent attack on American positive thinking, *Bright-Sided*, laid the ground for a revolt. The New Thought Movement, mentioned above, which was to spawn America's oppressive positivity, emerged as an antidote to the mental self-flagellation of its pietistic, sententious forebears. With New Thought, God was seen as an all-powerful Mind or Spirit, and man as part of that perfect force. Everything, we were told, was already as it

6 Ibid.

22

should be, and humanity only needed to learn to harness the power of this all-encompassing Mind/Spirit to exercise control over illness and the physical world. This is the true wellspring of Byrne's 'Law of Attraction'.

We will see several times in this book that when a movement arises to oppose a current culture, it often inherits the telltale structure of its predecessor. Thus the New Thought Movement brought with it an oddly censorious approach to positivity inherited from the Calvinists:

> If one of the best things you can say about positive thinking is that it articulated an alternative to Calvinism, one of the worst is that it ended up preserving some of Calvinism's more toxic features – a harsh judgmentalism, echoing the old religion's condemnation of sin, and an insistence on the constant interior labor of self-examination.[7]

Eventually, twentieth-century advances in medicine were to render redundant most of the New Thought's 'think yourself better' approach to health, at least for a while. While the celebration of thinking positively remained ingrained in American culture, it is the modern faith healers and televangelists, I would suggest, who have since most fiercely reclaimed the power of the Spirit to heal the body. Religion – or more precisely the hijacking of religion to perpetrate a scam – can treat the advances of medicine with disdain, exploit the suspicion and fear engendered by such unpleasant treatments as chemotherapy,

7 Barbara Ehrenreich, *Bright-Sided: How Positive Thinking Is Undermining America*. In the UK this book is called *Smile Or Die: How Positive Thinking Fooled America and the World*

and in doing so enforce the simple message of You Can Be Healed Through Faith Alone.

We have seen the prescriptive message of positive thinking come to surround many health issues. Ehrenreich details her own frustration with not being able to express her anger over having breast cancer in a culture which insists that she should only be 'brave' and report how life-affirming the experience has been. And the business world's fetishising of self-belief and quashing of naysayers, she goes on to argue convincingly, was a substantial cause of the 2008 financial collapse.

In this book, I'm going to suggest an alternative to positive thinking that is far more effective in making us happier. To understand it, we're going to look in some detail at ways of thinking that developed in ancient Greece and Rome. So let's start with Byrne's claim of her system having foundations in that most extraordinary era.

The only aspect of the 'Law of Attraction' that might take us back to the ancients is that of secret muttered formulas or magic words. Pythagoras, of geometry fame, was a very early magician-philosopher cited boldly by Byrne as part of her line-up of Those Who Shared The Secret. He seems indeed to have been the first to realise the psychological power of incantations. But along with many of the other philosophers Byrne and similar gurus cite as support, he was an ascetic figure, who gave up riches and wealth for a life of poverty and purity. In fact, his teachings couldn't be more removed from Byrne's bunkum. Iamblichus, a later classical thinker and biographer of Pythagoras, points out that the philosopher stressed the importance of *acknowledging the boundaries* of what we could achieve and of *resigning* ourselves to 'vicissitudes out of our control'[8]. Byrne's bizarre attempt to claim this sort of intellectual basis for *controlling* the universe is risible – yet, as we'll find, there is much to be mined from the genuine thoughts and reflections of these philosophers, if we take some time to actually read what they said.

Many people do attest to the success of *The Secret*, and I'll explain a little later why it may seem to work. Meanwhile, it would be lovely to assume that Byrne is well meaning and that the scheme is harmless, but the scale and success of her project means she can be fairly held to account for peddling this information to so many, and for the casualties created by her scheme. So does it cause any harm? Is it not merely a benign, if hilariously deluded, instruction to think more positively? And if so, surely that's a good thing, right?

An unwavering belief in the power of positive thinking can, surprisingly, be every bit as destructive as spending your life steeped in the gloomiest outlook. While we are looking at predominantly American ideas, let's take a detour to an eccentric domain that shares some surprising characteristics with the Law of Attraction. An even more egregious example of deception, it will illustrate why a scheme such as *The Secret* can lead to disaster.

Believe in yourself, blame yourself

In 2010, I travelled to Dallas with a TV crew and a scuba-diving instructor called Nathan. We were making a film about evangelical faith healing. Nathan had been trained in order to pass as a healer himself and was equipped with

8 Iamblichus, *Life of Pythagoras*

a back story detailing his supposed years of ministry in Uganda (which explained why there was no record of his alter ego 'Pastor James' working in England). We visited a few hoary old frauds who were peddling their version of the Prosperity Gospel, frighteningly popular in that part of the world. This message of wealth and riches can also be traced back to the same New Thought Movement that was rehashed in *The Secret*, but it really took off in the 1950s with the healing revivals of the United States. This interpretation of the Gospel tells us that as good Christians we are as entitled to financial wealth as spiritual wealth – in fact, both are part of the same vision that God has for us. It is based on the usual cherry-picking from scripture and some self-serving readings of verses such as Malachi 3:10:

> Bring ye all the tithes into the storehouse, that there may be meat in mine house, and prove me now herewith, saith the Lord of hosts, if I will not open you the windows of heaven, and pour you out a blessing, that there shall not be room enough to receive it.

'Give and ye shall receive.' The instruction has mutated, through the work of pastors such as Kenneth Copeland, into the notion that you, the congregant, must give money 'in faith' to your pastor, and in return God will give you back that amount hundredfold. There is no veneer of pretence that the money you give your pastor is going to buy Bibles or help the orphaned. The pastor takes the money forked out by his usually impoverished congregation beyond their means (what better test of faith than to give more than you can afford?) and quite openly spends it on houses, jets and bling; his very wealth is demonstrated as evidence of his favour with God. And the congregations are bizarrely happy to fund his expensive tastes, ever hopeful that their reward will come.

I was stunned by the transparency of the process. How can this scam be maintained? Why would people continue to give when God isn't keeping his apparent promise?

We decided to film undercover during the healing services of a minister called W. V. Grant. He is a well-known pastor in Dallas and runs his church in a charmless former car salesroom optimistically renamed Eagle's Nest Cathedral. In the nineties, he spent time in prison following that most common of evangelical crimes: tax evasion. If you've ever wondered why so many dubious institutions are so eager to claim church status and call themselves a religion, the answer is simple: if you're a religious institution, most of your income will be tax-exempt. Some of Grant's income was taxable, and when he didn't declare $375,000 of it, and admitted during a secretly filmed conversation that he had spent $100,000 from church members as a down payment on a $1.2 million house, he was fined and sentenced to sixteen months in jail. He emerged the next year to a dwindling congregation and now peddles his wares on Interstate 30.

We assembled that evening at eight o'clock in a meeting room at our hotel in Fort Worth. Our plan of action was drawn out on a flipchart. It showed the seating layout of the Eagle's Nest and where we would be positioned. We listened and giggled and were repeatedly warned that this was a dangerous operation. There were strict guidelines laid down by the legal team at Channel 4. There were frightening health and safety issues: this was a dark underside of southern-state culture. We had already found ourselves close to arrest when driving around Copeland's

church earlier in the week. We were dealing with highly defensive and wealthy people, and we were in Texas. There would probably be guns.

Nathan was kept away – he had his own act to be working on. The crew and I were loaded with hidden micro-cameras and microphones to capture what we could. Secret filming is an inefficient business: for every half-hour of clandestine close-ups of clavicles and ceilings and empty space, you're lucky if there's ten seconds good enough to use. I had a tiny camera in my tie, and Jennie, my long-time friend and make-up artist, was armed with a pen-cam. Other members of the production team and crew were to be dotted around at strategic places in the congregation with similar equipment, which allowed us to get useful lines of sight for filming.

I had heard that Grant would often relate people's private information to them during his services – something generally referred to as 'The Word of God'. The Lord would show him a person's name or ailment, and this would normally segue into a healing. It sounded like a variation on the same trick a phoney medium or a psychic might perform; one that normally relies on having people write down information beforehand in the form of a prayer request or similar. If you attend a psychic's performance and hear her reveal amazingly accurate details to members of the audience, you can be pretty confident that they have either written down details in the foyer for a seemingly unrelated reason, or have previously been in touch with the psychic or her team, telling them everything they need to know in the hope she can put them in touch with a loved one. The psychic or healer's team can then pick out the best information to use and feed that information to the performer through an earpiece or via crib sheets hidden, for example, amongst the pages of a

Bible. All that then remains is for the performer to attribute his bursts of seemingly miraculous insight to the Lord, or the spirits, or whomever people think they're paying to hear from.

And it's an easy trick to unearth. Suspecting this ploy, I told our crew to offer false names and ailments if they were asked to fill out a card before the service.

We pulled up in our van into the desolate car park surrounding the erstwhile car salesroom. Jennie fiddled with what was left of my hair, and we checked our cameras. Splitting into couples, we made our way inside. I went in with Jennie.

Cheerful songs and a hearty welcome awaited us in the otherwise soul-destroying interior. A small band was playing and perhaps half of the thirty or so who had already arrived were standing in their seats, arms raised, warming up for the main event. We smiled and tried to look as benign and believing as we could. Barely five steps into the room, a woman approached us with some prayer cards and pens and asked us to fill them out for their records. We duly did, lying about who we were and why we might need divine assistance. David, our series producer, offered the pseudonym 'James Lee' and a complaint of a gammy leg.

As the congregation assembled, it quickly became clear that these were people on a very low income. Many of them must have been there for the first time, as a lot of these cards were being handed out. This suggested a quick turnover of flock. Perhaps not much satisfaction was to be had under the pastoral care of the doctor. Paranormal investigator James Randi examined Grant's practices in his 1987 book, *The Faith Healers*. About Grant's degrees, Randi wrote:

. . . even Grant's college degree is phony. He claims
that he obtained it from "Midstates Bible College"
in Des Moines in 1972. He displays the diploma on
his office wall. But Midstates wasn't then and isn't
now accredited with the Iowa Department of
Public Instruction, as all parochial and public
schools are required to be. It wasn't recorded with
the secretary of state's office in Iowa as a corpor-
ation; nor was it listed in the county recorder's
office. It didn't even show up in the telephone
directory.

The service started with a few notices delivered by the
woman who had handed us the cards, and Jennie and I
responded with the beaming delight and displays of
ecstasy that we felt were required. We also did our best
not to catch the eye of any of our fellow crew members.
Few things remain as dear to me as seeing our blonde
bombshell production manager standing, eyes closed,
arms raised, receiving her Lord in quiet ecstasy. We could
not hide the fact that there was an unusually high quotient of English people in the congregation that night, and
so we had prepared a back story regarding a convention
we were attending, in case our abundant presence was
commented upon.

The question was almost permanently in my mind –
'Are all Grant's staff in on it?' Is there an inner and trusted
sanctum of confidants – a core team of scam artists?

Grant soon emerged through a small door at the side
near the stage and appeared before us. He was congenial,
portly and heavy of jowl. Not unlikeable, certainly. As
expected, he was smartly dressed, bejewelled, but not as
electric a character as we might have hoped. His manner
was more avuncular, and he addressed his flock as old

friends. He told tales of his many healings – always careful to credit the Lord with the miracle and modestly dismissing his own role in the proceedings. He sang, though not well, and when he did, I put my foot on Jennie's and held it there to make it harder for both of us to maintain our devotional countenance without laughing. It was huge fun.

After who knows how long – these services continue for hours – Grant walked down amongst us and spoke to an African American man near the front. The dubious reverend assured this congregant that he had a problem with his liver and that the Lord was *growing him a new one*, right now. Much delight and praising sounded from the gathered. The man seemed more bewildered than impressed. Other similar moments followed, where people were simply told they had ailments and that they were being cured. 'This is *lazy*,' I thought. No evidence was being offered that any of this was hitting home for the people receiving this very weak display of healing – they were barely given the chance to acknowledge what he was saying. If they offered any words of agreement, they just seemed bamboozled into doing so.

Then, to my deep joy, he pulled out David, our series producer. He had some fun with David's accent, clearly enjoying the fact he had an international audience that night. David played his part well, and in the middle of their conversation, Grant received a word from God. 'I'm getting five letters, a J . . .' he said, sounding like any psychic pretending to flounder for information they already know. 'James? Is that your name?'

'Yes! That's my name!' David replied and, hearing the name from the prayer card, we knew Grant was busted and our trip had been worth the effort.

A collection was taken. Grant said that the Lord was

telling him that two people could give two hundred dollars that day, and that one person could give two thousand. Perhaps someone did, but no one looked like they could afford anything like either of those figures. We gave our donations – signed off and supplied by our production manager – and I bought a CD of Grant singing a selection of Christmas classics.

The next week, we returned. We wanted to get more from Grant. After the nerves surrounding our first attempt, we were more relaxed. Too relaxed, as it turned out.

I called my then partner back in London and asked him to obtain whatever software he would need to record the online transmissions of the service, as we needed to use their footage; our own, as expected, had turned out to be worse than shoddy. We arrived, filled in fresh prayer request forms and sat down as on the previous occasion. This time, after similar initial formalities and a few songs from a terrific warm-up guy, we were treated to a 'sermon' by a visiting pastor. Whereas Grant was soft-faced and jolly, here was a pig in a suit. Flushed, fat and sweating, this foul man told us how he had prayed for so-and-so, who had the *next day* obtained a brand-new Cadillac and a forty-thousand-dollar ring. Again and again, we heard how his congregation and others for whom he had prayed had hit the financial jackpot. There was no pretence of love or pastoral interest; this was a cheap salesman doing his gross pitch for the poor and needy. He spat and shouted his avaricious filth to those who knew no better; the one true Lord Mammon was invoked, and the true, bloated, porcine face of the whole business was revealed to our horrified crew.

Following this wretched performance, Grant walked amongst us as he had on the previous occasion, and this time he pulled Jennie from the crowd. We thought she might act as bait: Jen is a hottie (of the naughty secretary variety) and was giving Grant every flirty signal she could. He stood her in front of the faithful and began to list a series of conditions from which she apparently suffered. The Lord did not hold back. Judging from the multiple diagnoses, it was a miracle Jen had been able to get out of bed, let alone hold a successful career together. Always a trooper, she nodded undiscerningly to his free-flowing and dramatic pronouncements.

Following the Lord's diagnoses and manifold healings of my friend, Grant asked me to step out into the aisle. I had, he divined, trouble with my leg. I had disingenuously mentioned on my prayer card that week that I suffered from a damaged calf muscle, hoping that if he was reading them for information, he might try the leg-lengthening trick on me. It's one of the hoariest and most shame-faced of fraudulent ploys, and can be seen all over YouTube, performed by 'street healers' and some of the major names in the business. The ruse consists of sitting a person in a chair, holding their legs out together and parallel to the floor, and finding a moment to surreptitiously slide the heel of one shoe a little off the person's foot. Attention is then called to the *other* leg, which, because of the difference in shoe positions, now appears to be a few inches shorter. The believer's 'short' leg, it is proclaimed, is the source of all their leg trouble and pain. The healer calls upon the healing power of Jesus and slowly slides the loosened shoe back on to the other foot, whilst proclaiming loudly to those who are gathered that the 'short' leg is miraculously stretching out to its full length. Healed.

My joy was unbounded when Grant asked me up on to his stage. He seemed keen that these new English people in his congregation go back to their home country spreading word of what the Lord was doing through him. As he brought me up, he called to the congregation, 'See how he walks with a limp?' which of course, to my knowledge, I did not.

He sat me down and had me extend my legs. He held my heels and, as he turned to address the audience (a standard magician's move to misdirect attention from some subterfuge; the YouTube street healers usually beckon the camera over to cover the same moment), slipped the heel of my upstage, left shoe from my foot. I had worn slip-on shoes, which I knew would make the job easy for him should the opportunity arise. Without caring for my own distinctly underwhelming experience, he invoked the Lord, cajoling Him with the tempting carrot of cross-Atlantic PR, and pushed my shoe slowly back into place. After months of investigating this particular nugget of religious fraud, teaching it to our fake healer and trying it on friends, here I was, my twin trotters resting in the podgy palms of a once-incarcerated evangelist, having the same trick performed on me. And thanks to our hidden crew and cameras, as well as Grant's own streaming feed, we would catch him at it quite beautifully.

Legs healed (or, perhaps, if I may, *heeled*, but I suspect I may not), he declared my non-existent limp now gone and had me run around the congregation to prove my new clean bill of health. Of course one does what one is told, aware that everyone else is being unfairly provided with evidence of a miracle. But it was not the time to cause trouble or complain that he had just been fiddling with my footwear. Everyone was well and truly on his side. I looked grateful and returned to my seat.

Throughout my healing and the entire service, I was filming as much as I could on my tie-camera. Those little spy-cams have a fixed wide lens, but I was manoeuvring it as I could to try to get the best shots. I saw that Grant had what appeared to be filled-out prayer cards lying openly on his lectern, so I tried to get as close to the front as I could when we were invited up to receive his blessing, in case I could get a clear shot of them. I also thought that footage of Grant blessing me straight down the barrel of my neckwear would be fun for the final programme. So I adopted a pose with my hands clasped to my chest underneath the tie, in such a way that I could angle it upwards to get the necessary shot of the elevated Grant. I also made myself conspicuous: some members of the congregation were happy to stand and turn around and watch the action when Grant was receiving word from the Lord, even leave their rows, so I did the same, to try to get a useable shot. On reflection, I was unaware that the pig-faced pastor, watching everything from the stage, had the perfect opportunity to pay me close attention.

We knew that in the past, people had been caught filming and detained. Clear signs on the doors prohibited any such recording of the events inside. We had no back-up story if we got caught, just an agreed exit strategy for the rest of the crew.

I had returned to my seat, and was stood singing next to Jennie, once more angling myself to get a shot of the doctor in between two people in front of me. Grant was lending his own professional voice to our own, with its distinctive affected vibrato, letting us continue here and there on our own while he consulted his papers and cards on stage. I once again reached for my tie and shifted it to secure what I hoped would be a useable shot.

At that point, the fat pink pastor shifted himself from his seat, walked over to Grant, who was singing at the time, and whispered something in his ear.

Grant listened attentively, then beamed too widely: a

wordless display of 'everything's fine' in response to the words from his colleague. I knew we were rumbled.

Jen and I continued singing but had both seen the exchange and Grant's mock show of ease. We had to abandon our mission and escape without being caught.

We stood, asked the people sitting between our seats and the centre gangway to excuse us and walked out into the aisle. Our scattered colleagues took the cue and did the same. We calmly walked up the aisle and left. The message had got back to the van that we were making an emergency exit, so as we walked out, it screeched round into the car park and we jumped inside. And sped off. With another screech. It was fantastic.

Grant is a small fry compared to the really big names in the business. Pastor Benny Hinn, at the time of writing, is at the top of that particular game, apparently earning something like $100 million a year, tax-free, in donations alone. Some months before, I had snuck into one of Hinn's few events in London with my co-writer to watch the famed televangelist at work. The scale and energy dwarfed Grant's gentle style and diminishing congregation, and allowed Hinn to work without sleight of hand. Hinn's crowds are brought to an adrenaline-fuelled frenzy, which effectively blocks pain. Thus without any shoe-pushing or prayer cards, he can create the effect of healings entirely through suggestion. I borrowed his techniques for my 2015–16 stage show *Miracle*. To my knowledge, I am the first travelling healer to lay hands and cure the sick in the name of the Lord whilst simultaneously declaring his atheism and the absence of any such Divinity at work.

At a certain point in Hinn's and other healers' proceedings, people are invited to the front if they feel pain relief following the healing in the room. Stewards usually filter these people before bringing a select few up on to the stage. Thus 'invisible' conditions, including arthritis, cancer, drug addictions and AIDS, are supposedly healed, while the more manifest maladies (Down's syndrome, a missing arm) are ignored. At some of Hinn's larger rallies, there are hospital beds behind the cameras, right at the back; those who need healing most are rarely noticed, let alone receive what they have come for.

The most disturbing aspect of the healing scam – aside from the fact that these top names provide no after-care for the wake of unhealed and disturbed people they tell to throw away their pills and then leave behind – is that the blame for the ultimate, inevitable failure of the healing is placed squarely on the shoulders of the victim. Clearly we cannot blame God or his appointed pastor when our symptoms return, so we are told to blame ourselves and our own lack of sufficient faith. If you did not receive healing, or were blessed with it for only a short while before the cancer returned with full force, it is because you did not approach God (or his pastor) with enough belief (for 'belief' we can confidently read 'money'). Perhaps you did not give more than you could afford when the buckets came round: *that* would have been a sign of true faith. Or perhaps you hung on to those pills when Dr Jesus has shown you that you don't need them. Or perhaps you're just not a good-enough Christian. Somewhere, somehow, you're to blame. But by now the healer has moved on to the next city, and if you try to contact his staff for assistance, they're not interested.

I heard many stories of unfortunate souls who fell prey to this tragic spiral of self-blame. I spoke to a pastor with cerebral palsy whose mother had years before plunged her family into debt as she petitioned God to cure her child. The Lord's healers were not interested in allowing her son on stage with a condition so obvious to the eye. Another pastor I met, who also now warns against the dangers of these healers, was so ensnared by the need to show no compromise to faith that he let his daughter die rather than give her the medicine she needed. If the death of a child is the foulest thing that can happen to a person, imagine how much worse it must be when you know you sat by and slowly let it happen.

I met Ole Anthony, the founder and president of the Trinity Foundation in Dallas, which is dedicated to exposing these fraudulent healers. He told us the story of a thirteen-year-old girl with multiple sclerosis. She had seen a television testimonial from someone who had apparently pledged a thousand dollars to the healer behind the advertisement and been cured of the same condition. Of course, the person giving the testimonial was an actor, but the girl didn't know this. She believed that she too would be cured if she could get a thousand dollars to this healer. So she borrowed the money and paid it across over the course of a year. When she hadn't been healed – in fact, of course, her condition had worsened – she called up the pastor's people to ask why. She was told it was because she had secret sin in her life. Her response, now at fourteen years old, was to douse herself in petrol and self-immolate.

How does this relate to *The Secret*? In the same way that these victims of faith healers are told that *they* are at fault if the healing doesn't happen, so Byrne tells her readers that they are to blame when the universe fails to provide its riches at our request:

> If it doesn't work, this is your fault for not having
> enough faith or thinking positively enough: You

39

must believe that you have received. You must
know that what you want is yours the moment you
ask. You must have complete and utter faith . . .
Every negative thought, feeling or emotion is *block-
ing* your good from coming to you.[9]

Once this important caveat is internalised, the system is
perfect, and potentially tragic. Of course it amounts to an
instruction to fool yourself, and to continue to fool yourself for as long as you can, while Byrne and her notions
about how life works are exempt from blame. In fact, *any
questioning of the system* would be in itself evidence of a lack
of faith; not only must one self-deceive but one must also
remain fearful of any rational enquiry. A sort of neurotic
bravado must be maintained, and to admit to oneself that
it could be defective would be to assure the instant failure
of the magic.

The result is a destructive cycle of self-condemnation.
Byrne's system would be bad enough if it simply reneged
on its promises, but, like the promise of the healers, it is
particularly foul for placing the blame for its inevitable
failure on its poor victims.

Her secular harnessing of the power of faith is, of
course, more benign than the healers'; my comparison
may seem rather histrionic. Yet her adherents are explicitly instructed to plan blindly for success and to buy things
they can't afford to attract greater riches. Any hint of self-
doubt, they are assured, will deny them the luxuries that
the universe promises. The same toxic principle is absolutely at work, even if the issue of physical health is not
explicitly at stake. Although the focus on acquiring luxury
goods makes its victims seem less sympathetic than the

9 Rhonda Byrne, *The Secret*

afflicted who are failed by healers, we must remember that *The Secret* will hold a particular appeal to the poorer and less educated, whom we cannot glibly blame for wanting to reap its promised rewards.

Doesn't it work?

By this point, some people who have had experience of *The Secret* will want to insist that *it works*. A few days ago, for example, I was listening to a man who worked in his wife's coffee shop openly laud the many virtues of Byrne's system. His wife had visualised herself owning such a café, and sure enough it had appeared. So what is happening there?

Well, indeed, why *not* decide you'll open a coffee shop? Sometimes a blast of focused single-mindedness can do us good. Clearly there are lessons to be learnt from planning for success. That's *true*. The problem is, *The Secret* is based on something *false*, and so by its nature its promises will eventually collapse. And because it over-promises, it won't allow you to differentiate between what's helpful (true) and what isn't. Consider the important information the faith healers keep to themselves. They cannot cure anything *organic* (anything involving physical change to some tissue or organ of the body). Some people will feel pain relief; that is all. The rest is showmanship. All claims to have cured cancer or any-thing else are simply false. And the money you give makes no difference to anything. Any improvement is unlikely to last after the show is over. The bouncing around they make you do on stage to demonstrate your 'healing' can even make your condition *worse*. And above all, that cycle of self-blame in which you are likely to find yourself once you've gone home and calmed down is based on a lie. In reality, *God isn't doing anything to you, and it's* not *your fault when the symptoms return.*

Likewise, Byrne hides from us a fact you'd think was self-evident: the universe is *not* rearranging itself to supply what we want. We are just focusing our ambitions and thinking more positively about them. Yes, that can sometimes be helpful. However, as we would know if failed businessmen could sell their biographies as well as the successful ones, blind faith is more commonly a recipe for disaster than for triumph. And nothing in *The Secret* lets you see how to distinguish between the two. So for every advantage there is a danger, and rather than teaching you how to navigate safely away from self-delusion, Byrne and the healers encourage only greater and greater investment.

How wonderful to visualise owning a coffee shop and then have this come to fruition after a year or so. How *not* wonderful to be one of the many more people who will have invested without caution (as Byrne tells us to) and failed. How *not* wonderful to be lied to (that the universe rearranges itself around your wishes) and to orient your life around such a glossy and deeply infantile prevarication. It's a cheap lie, which feeds upon one of our most prevailing wishes: that we can control things outside of our control, like the forces of fate. Magicians and scam artists have tapped into the same primal urge for millennia. *Of course* decide to open a coffee shop if that's viable, and *of course*, where helpful, be single-minded; however, your determination will be interacting with random fortune, not a listening, caring universe; the project may well come to nothing, and it's good to be prepared for that. There is much you can do with a clear, positive vision, but there are important limits. This book you are now reading will encourage clear-sightedness and the application of a prudent pessimism.

Once you put Byrne's Law into practice, it is your natural confirmation bias that ensures you will notice any evidence for the Law being true and ignore or explain away contradictory indications. Rather like the placebo patients watching out for evidence that their drug had worked, we are all hard-wired to maintain our beliefs this way. You successfully open a coffee shop according to the instructions revealed in *The Secret* and there's all the proof you need that the system works. It's a delicate matter for someone to pull apart what's true and useful from all the misinformation that might well lead to future embarrassment or financial collapse.

What 'provided' the coffee shop? Your focus and single-mindedness, your seeking of opportunities, and a large amount of luck. The 'amazing coincidences' that happened along the way only appear so because of the thinking traps into which you fall: you have paid special attention to everything that has supported your belief in the Law of Attraction. You require a miraculous story to defend a magical system, and you have sought that out, that's all. The question is not 'How do you explain THAT?' but 'Why am I paying attention to that?' Because the system isn't magical, because *there is no system*, you shouldn't have faith in it. Otherwise next time it may fail you and leave you crushed. Something worthwhile has happened, certainly. But understanding what has *really* happened will set you in better stead next time. It may save you from becoming an adherent to a nonsensical belief system, and it will help maintain your self-respect. It can also, importantly, *preserve your overarching happiness* by keeping you rooted in reality. A coffee shop might make you happy and be a worthwhile goal, but what might ultimately make you even happier is understanding that there is *more* to happiness. The café might not work out; if your happiness depends on it, you've overinvested. If there is a secret to happiness, it isn't that the universe is a catalogue from which we can order a new car or coffee shop. The real secret might be to accept the indifference of the universe and delight just as much in the coffee shop *not* appearing. This odd but undeniably true thought, as well as the balance of pessimism that it entails, is the thrust of this book.

It's hardly controversial to suggest that systems like *The Secret* and the performances of faith healers are born from a place of greed. These are promises guaranteed to sell books, secure donations or fill stadia. The belief systems they sell do *not* come from a place of respect; they do not arise from an understanding of what helps *you*. If they did, their peddlers would let you know the fuller picture. The healers would tell you that your pain is subjective: in some cases you may have the capacity to suffer less if you think differently about your condition or realise that you don't have to *identify* with your suffering. *You* are responsible, not this curious God that demands money and heals only certain invisible conditions. *That* is a respectful, honest message. Likewise, Byrne could tell us that if you don't believe you're ever going to amount to anything, then you probably won't; it is worth developing healthy levels of confidence and self-belief if you lack them. Sometimes, focused energy is a very helpful thing, but it doesn't guarantee any results. And you should be prepared for when things don't work out. Plan for success; prepare for failure. And the universe doesn't care either way.

No one wants to buy a book that proclaims such a measured, modest message from its cover. To sell big, you have to over-promise. This, in contrast, is a book written from a place of respect. It won't sell as well as books that make extravagant claims, but it does propose some thoughts that are *true* as well as, I hope, extremely helpful. That combination, ultimately, makes them the only kind worth having.

We are so embroiled in the rhetoric of self-belief that to apply any qualifications to the mantra of 'Go on! You can do anything!' seems to be actively denying people their chance of happiness. Yet when we warn, 'This may not work out', we are being, at heart, very supportive. We are asking the person to set aside, for a moment, their single-minded, emotive image of happiness (opening a coffee shop). We are reminding them that their *overarching* happiness is in fact independent of a successful café venture. We are not naysaying. We are pointing to a potentially deeper level of happiness and saying, 'If this doesn't work out, as it may not, *irrespective of your enthusiasm*, there is more in life that can make you happy. Don't attach too much to this one goal.'

That is a truly considerate message, though we are unlikely to want to hear it.

Goal-setting

Most of us would scoff at the idea of Byrne's universe showering us with jewellery and lovers at our request, or the dangerous claims of faith healing. But this nineteenth-century, anti-Calvinist attitude of blissfully directing some cosmic Spirit to attend to our well-being still ubiquitously and insidiously trickles down to us through our modern obsession with goal-setting. Again, to be clear, there is little doubt that if a person lacks any motivation or engagement with his or her life, then focusing on a healthy target to reach may provide a useful spur. But goal-setting has become for many a way of life, synonymous with worthwhile achievement and personal progress. It starts

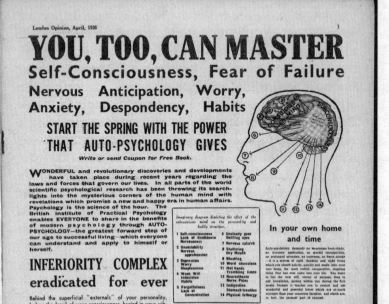
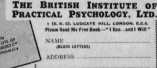

when we are young: we choose *these* subjects for GCSE in order to study *these* ones at A level, in order to go to *this* university, to study *this* subject, to get *this* job, to get this promotion and work our way up *this* corporate ladder, to what? Meanwhile, our lives are relegated to something that happens, to borrow from Schopenhauer, *ad interim*: in the meantime; unattended.

The eccentric world of faith healing, as well as the more familiar hokum of *The Secret* and the modern obsession with single-minded goal-setting, all fall prey to the same principle of self-blame we have been discussing. We are told by self-styled self-help gurus, and the folk wisdom down into which their proclamations have trickled, that we must clearly visualise for ourselves the specifics of a successful future and progress along the direct path towards those goals. Any number of books – with titles like *Goals: How To Use Goal Setting To Get Everything You Want Fast* and *Goal Setting: Discover What You Want In Life And Achieve It Faster Than You Think Possible* – offer to show you the simple secret formula for guaranteed success, and bring us close to Byrne's misleading vision. Goals, we are told, are to be Specific, Measurable, Achievable, Realistic and Time-Targeted (S.M.A.R.T.). Once we have committed ourselves to such an ambition, and have found the route to achieving it, we can then move, sometimes Faster Than You Think Possible, to getting there. What on earth is wrong with that?

A lot, I would suggest.

Firstly, we tend to grossly misunderstand what will make us happy. This book hopes to address the common misunderstandings and provide some more effective alternatives. From a starting point of ignorance and mis-information, we commonly choose the wrong goals. Locked within our neat little stories of who we are and how we would like that story to continue, we aim for a point on the horizon that advances the narrative in the direction we see fit. For some, it is to be a millionaire by a certain age. For others, to be the biggest and best at their job. Very commonly, these goals are driven by a vision of financial success that we aim to realise within the next few years or by a certain age. At all levels, the drive to achieve the brightest kind of success is seen as the most natural and robust path to take in life.

I see no reason to decry financial success as long as we don't confuse it with happiness. I've mentioned already that once we earn over a comfortable amount, money does not make us happier. We might get richer, but we don't become more content.

I can testify to this fact. I am no more or less happy than when I was in my years in Bristol post-university, claiming housing benefit in between very occasional magic gigs. We will talk later about success and fame, but for now it is absolutely the case that for the vast majority of people wealth does not significantly affect levels of happiness, despite how things might appear.

The psychological reason for this can be expressed simply – your happiness levels are largely defined by the balance of your personality. How happy you are by default is largely set. Now, there is more to the story of course, and the aim of this book is to explore some of the powerful, transformative possibilities that are open to us. But money does not affect this core aspect of your character: if you are prone to unhappiness when poor, you are very likely to be prone to unhappiness when rich. The vital changes to our happiness do not come from outside circumstances, however appealing they might seem. Some external conditions, such as having an accessible network of friends, do statistically make a difference in levels to which people report being happy. Yet it is not upon these trappings that we would choose to be dependent if we are to explore what might make us truly happy. Indeed, unless one has a helpful philosophical grounding, these external variables are unlikely to make a profound difference, or might even make things worse. This book will look at what that 'helpful philosophical grounding' might be. As Joseph Campbell wrote about middle age, 'There is perhaps nothing worse than reaching the top of the ladder and discovering that you're on the wrong wall.'

So we establish a goal, which may well be misguided, because we tend to make incorrect judgements about what makes us happy. What then? We now strive towards that specific, planned-out success, and here we encounter our second problem with the fetishising of goals. We invest too much and too specifically. If we stay true to our plan, we will need to sacrifice other aspects of our life to reach our intended destination. We forget that nothing happens in life independently of other things. You may find yourself a partner and get married as intended but then suffer the loss of other dreams that you now regret abandoning. You may become a millionaire by thirty-five but at the expense of your personal relationships. The goal has proven too specific, too isolated; upon reaching your destination you realise with companionless regret that this solitary and lonely place was too remote and too much has been left behind.

Or if the journey's end is not so lonely, or if success is reached without too much sacrifice, what then? The enjoyment of arrival is usually short-lived; the happiness envisioned and rehearsed for years is unlikely to last. Why? Because it does not arrive quite as satisfyingly as suspected; because we quickly get used to it; above all, because when one arrives *one is still oneself*, with whatever tendency towards dissatisfaction or restlessness that may bring. So what next? Set another goal? Other dreams have been forgotten; one must start anew. After we achieve our goals, we are forced to *disidentify* with them. Sometimes this can be painful, and perhaps more commonly so for men, who tend to equate success with achievements and standards external to themselves. When work ends – through retirement or downsizing – many people become depressed, because their sense of self was too closely tied to such ends. A line misattributed to Plutarch and more accurately credited to *Die Hard*'s Hans Gruber runs as follows: 'When Alexander the Great saw the breadth of his domain, he wept for there were no more worlds to conquer'.

And this comes only if we're lucky, if the goal is reached. What if we fail? When the universe and fortune have not played according to our hopes, and we have sacrificed much to the pursuit of something that has now proved elusive, there is the double anxiety of humiliating failure and the same confusion as to what to do next.

To avoid failure, the faith/self-blame process demands a constant renewal of investment. Blind faith in the desirability and achievability of the goal (and a fear of its collapse) has us abandon all sense in its pursuit. Like the attendees of the healing rally, we put in more than we can afford, proud to call ourselves faithful. And thus we might continue, as this hubris compels us forward and deeper into places from where it may be difficult to return. We have come to identify ourselves with the goal, we have become committed to pursue it at all costs rather than admit defeat.

Determined to retain a positive outlook, we remove naysayers from our lives, as the self-help industry instructs us. This may make for a proud slogan for social-media profiles – a snappy, self-assured 'Ignore the h8ers' – but it can be a dangerous folly. By removing or ignoring the sources of honest feedback, we create a neat means of fuelling the downward spiral of self-deception. When we proudly denounce those who would undermine our self-belief, we emulate a model of strength we have been sold principally through the biographies of successful, strong entrepreneurs. We equate persistent commitment and the ability to laugh at one's detractors with a recipe for success. But this is a lie. We believe it because we are told it through many channels, but its source springs from a powerful select few who boast about their life stories *as they perceive them*.

These life stories are of course a formalising of the fabricated narratives we discussed in the first chapter. These are overwhelmingly the self-serving rationalisations of people who, upon becoming successful, now wish to feel that they have rightfully earned their status and the respect of others. So they look back over their journey and filter through it for evidence of their deservedness. The perpetual and overwhelming play of random chance is glossed over, and in its place a hero's journey is invented. And very often that story is one of adhering to a vision, no matter what, and having no time for those who would get in the way or did not share the hero's Herculean self-belief.

This success story is a fiction. And we know it is a fiction, because it is also a recipe for *failure*. To persist with a belief in an end goal, to ignore the cries of others who tell you that your aspiration is unrealistic, to proudly commit yourself to a maverick scheme against all the odds – this is the story of financial *ruin* far more often than it is one of success. This might sound counter-intuitive. Yet what could be more conducive to financial disaster than blindly ignoring all advice? What more reliable recipe for professional miscarriage than a conviction that one knows best when one doesn't? Many more will fail than succeed through blind self-belief.

But we don't read books of entrepreneurial failure, only the triumphs, so we cannot learn from those tales of dogged self-belief anything of value. In fact, we can be fairly sure that such single-mindedness may as likely lead to disaster. We may glean inspiration from tales of down-trodden persons who find improbable success through perseverance, but we cannot presume to draw from this uplifting genre any conclusions of real utility.

The diagonal

The success stories of the rich are misleading because they trumpet the notion that the random events of the external world can be subsumed under the driving will of the dynamic goal-setter. But is this true? Arthur Schopenhauer describes, I think, a more accurate dynamic, in his *Counsels and Maxims*:

> Events and our chief aims can be in most cases compared to two forces that pull in different direc-tions, their resultant diagonal being the course of our life.

This is an image that will run throughout this book. The nineteenth-century philosopher is saying: you do not have the control over your life that you might like to believe. You will of course have certain aims, pulling you in one direction. However, life is constantly pulling back in the other. Irrespective of how much 'you believe in

yourself', the forces of life (or the universe, or fate) will continue to do their own thing. They operate independently of your wishes. You may put everything into opening a successful coffee shop and making your fortune, but a sudden recession will scupper that plan with no respect for how S.M.A.R.T. your goal was, how positive you felt about it, or how beautiful your vision board was. You may dream of having a certain life, but financial crashes, illness or any number of similar inconveniences have no respect for your fantasies. Nor do the actions or successes of other people that may scupper your plans. Most of what happens in life is entirely out of your control, and while blind self-belief might disguise that fact for a while, it will eventually prove an anaemic opponent to brute reality.

Here is a graph showing the good life as it's sold to us:

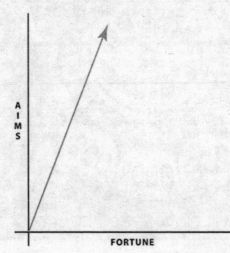

Here, on the other hand, is a diagonal drawn from Schopenhauer's more realistic interplay of aims and fortune: a true reflection of how life actually works:

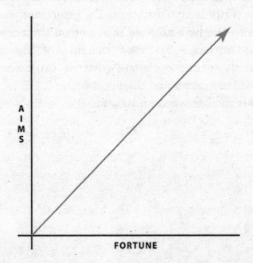

It is a clear image and an antidote to the self-satisfied rhetoric of many who share what they presume to be the secrets of their success. We do not have the control over events that we like to imagine would allow us to succeed through self-belief. In truth, we aim in one direction, events pull us in the other, and the line of our life is drawn along the middle.

Schopenhauer also uses the game of chess to give us another image of how our goal-setting might be unrealistic. When playing chess, we start out with a plan, but our plan is affected by the inclinations of the other player. Our plan must modify itself constantly, to the point that, as we carry it out, several of its fundamental features are unrecognisable. To stick blindly to the same goals would be to deny that a second, independent player was at the board.

We are told to live our lives by focusing on the future and by believing in ourselves at all costs. The result, too often, is waste and frustration. By projecting ourselves always into the hereafter we miss out on the present, on knowing ourselves and the richness of the current moment. By trying to control what we can't, we all but guarantee frustration and disappointment.

Is this the life we wish to lead?

☺

3

Wanting

To get to the root of why ambition and goal-setting don't quite deliver the happiness they promise, we need to look a little more deeply at how we tend to *desire*. 'Get what you want' remains a mantra of modern living, as if we each had the birthright to accumulate whatever we think will make us happy. We have seen that the 'Get' part of the instruction is more complicated than we like to admit: there's no guarantee life will come up with the goods, or, if it does, that the goods were the ones we wanted. Our planning does not reflect the reality of life; it can root our concerns too rigidly in the future while life slips by; it may leave us feeling empty when we get there. So now we'll look more deeply at the 'Want', as there is much about our capacity to desire that promises happiness but delivers disappointment. Once we understand some important aspects of how and why we want things, we can rebuild a new relationship to desire that can greatly increase our happiness.

You and I are both desiring creatures at many levels. Right now I desire to write this page and hopefully you desire to read it. We carry out almost all of our actions in order to fulfil some future goal that we desire – perhaps, for example, you start quickly skimming this page because you want to get up from the sofa in order to go to the kitchen to assemble a snack because you are hungry. The desire to eat creates a chain of smaller desires, some of which may be more intellectual than emotional in nature, but all are designed to ultimately satisfy a need. We are slaves to these desires in one form or another.

We know, of course, that after we've fixed ourselves a snack from the fridge, we will be hungry again some time thereafter. But this thought does not trouble us as we assemble muffins, Marmite and butter. It is part of an endless chain of desires: we will eat, then, after a while, desire to eat again.

The problem arises when we fail to see the same process in operation regarding our less essential desires. I am currently, as I write this chapter, soon to move house. The place I'm moving into has undergone extensive developments for the last seven months. I don't remember ever being as excited about anything as the prospect of moving into this new home. It seems to me that getting to live in this place, after the builders have finally left and the work is complete, is a picture of ultimate happiness. Living *there* is clearly going to make me much happier than living *here*.

Now, I am lucky in that where I live now is also very lovely. I am aware that it is in large part the promise of a change of environment that is causing the excitement – the move from a familiar sort of lovely to a shiny, exciting, new form of lovely with new surrounds to explore and many exciting, fresh things that I can't enjoy here. *Here* is less appreciated as I see it every day and it rarely offers anything new. *There* will be a feast of novelty. But for how long? I realise that the new place, despite the wonderful improvements it boasts, will soon seem every bit as familiar. I am unlikely to be a happier person there than here. That *may* not be the case, as a house move may create a change in lifestyle that genuinely makes a difference to how happy I feel. There are some great places near the new house to have breakfast, which fills me to the lip and rim with a pleasure I can't imagine will ever entirely dissipate. But most likely, the initial burst of delight at living there will soon subside to resemble whatever level of pleasure I feel where I am now.

Welcome to the hedonic treadmill. Ancient philosophers such as the Stoics and Epicureans – and we will look more closely at them later – were very aware of it, though the term was first coined in the 1970s[10] and later developed by a psychologist called Michael Eysenck in the nineties. It refers to the cycle of desire-fulfilment ('hedonism' means 'the pursuit of pleasure'): we want something, we perhaps get it, we feel good for a while and then return to whatever default level of happiness or sadness we enjoyed before. Nothing really changes.

Presumably every thoughtful and reasonably affluent person has considered this truth at some point whilst considering upgrading his phone or laptop. This level of desire is where we see the treadmill in action. I *desire* at the time of writing the sixth incarnation of the Apple Macintosh portable Internet-enabled smart telephone, but I know it won't really make me any happier. After a short while – roughly equivalent to the time it takes me to explore its new features and get used to its new shape and weight – I will feel exactly the same about it as I do

10 P. Brickman and D. T. Campbell, 'Hedonic Relativism and Planning the Good Society'

about my current one. Clearly Apple know this and keep developing new models at such a pace that will make my non-ownership of the newest and best painfully obvious to me, adding a negative reinforcement to the process. There is the pleasure of the new model *and* the displeasure of knowing mine does not have certain features being enjoyed by everyone else. How pathetic. What does it mean to decry mindless consumerism when I know I will run out and mindlessly snap up the new one just because I can?

William B. Irvine, a philosophy professor at Dallas University, is the author of *On Desire: Why We Want What We Want*. Upon exploring the subject for this book, he found himself particularly drawn to the teachings of the Stoics and decided to become one. Stoicism was a hugely popular school of philosophy amongst the ancient Greeks and Romans, and was eventually subsumed into Christianity. Stoics thought very hard about what the good life might mean, and they had a lot to say about desire. Their ideas are going to form a large part of this book. He adopted the ancient teachings of prominent Stoics such as Seneca, Epictetus and the tiny handful of others who left their thoughts behind, and now lives as a Stoic. His subsequent book, *A Guide to the Good Life: The Ancient Art of Stoic Joy*, is a terrific manual for applying the philosophy to life, by a rare and fascinating man. Having met him when I spoke at Stoicon, a London conference promoting Stoicism, I can attest that he is utterly delightful, embodying a quiet warmth and openness not immediately recognisable as 'stoic' in the ordinary sense of the word.

In *On Desire*, Professor Irvine offers the following thought experiment:

Suppose you woke up one morning to discover that you were the last person on earth: during the night, aliens had spirited away everyone but you. Suppose that despite the absence of other people, the world's buildings, houses, stores and roads remained as they had been the night before. Cars were where their now-vanished owners had parked them, and gas for these cars was plentiful at now-unattended gas stations. The electricity still worked. It would be a world like this world, except that everyone but you was gone. You would, of course, be very lonely, but let us ignore the emotional aspects of being the last person, and instead focus our attention on the material aspects.

In the situation described, you could satisfy many material desires that you can't satisfy in our actual world. You could have the car of your dreams. You could even have a showroom full of expensive cars. You could have the house of your dreams – or live in a palace. You could wear very expensive clothes. You could acquire not just a big diamond ring but the Hope Diamond itself. The interesting question is this: without people around, would you still want these things? Would the material desires you harbored when the world was full of people still be present in you if other people vanished? Probably not. Without anyone else to impress, why own an expensive car, a palace, fancy clothes, or jewelry?

Irvine continues to suggest that, alone in this imagined world, you might try these luxuries for a while but would soon, for example, find a dwelling that was easy to maintain rather than live in a palace, obtain clothes that were comfortable rather than expensive, and would probably lose all interest in your appearance. The thought experiment shows that we choose our lifestyles – our houses, our clothes, our watches – with other people in mind. One way or another, we project a style designed to make others admire or envy us. That style may not, of course, be about what's strictly fashionable. We all have some sort of image we like to project, and whether that image is trendy, tweedy or just a mess, there will be *something* we're identifying with and choosing to show the world. We cannot really criticise the fashion victim for being a slave to convention when we are living according to an equally well-defined alternative protocol, however heretical or hipster or highbrow it might be. We have all drawn our style references and aesthetics from somewhere. And if we say we never give any conscious thought to what we wear, the chances are very high that we at least dress a lot like others in our peer group. We've all seen friends walking along the street sporting minor variations on the same wardrobe.

Irvine's thought exercise shows that our desires would diminish drastically if we didn't need to impress anyone. Our requirements would probably become limited to what we might think of as 'natural' or essential desires: food, water, shelter and so on. This does not sound like a particularly pleasant existence or a lifestyle we would choose, but we would certainly be liberated from a desire to impress others. We might find this notion – that we spend so much energy and time seeking the approval of our peers – quite eye-opening.

The Stoic Seneca knew this well. The playwright, statesman and philosopher (pictured overleaf) lived in Rome in the first century AD. He was tutor and advisor to Emperor Nero, who eventually instructed him to commit suicide: a command that he duly followed. Seneca wrote many letters to a young friend, Lucilius, containing advice on how to live well (history has not left us details of Lucilius's replies or the number of times he frantically changed address). The older man talks of attending an elaborate entertainment where conspicuous riches had been piled up to impress guests.

> 'What else is this,' he said to himself, 'than a stirring-up of man's cravings, which are in themselves provocative of lust? What is the meaning of all this display of money? Did we gather merely to learn what greed was?'[11]

It's a line I now try to use more often at parties. Perhaps it sounds puritanical to today's ears, but the point is a worthwhile one: the things we desire really do little other than fuel further desires and teach us what greed is. In the accumulation of material things, no deep satisfaction is to be found, other than fleeting pleasure and the temporary delight of impressing others. Both of these are short-lived (before we return to our default level of happiness), and ultimately *controlled by other people or things*. We choose whom to impress based on how impressive they seem to us, and if they fail to be convinced by our attempts, then we tend to feel anxious. This is neither a healthy nor a happy cycle.

We envy others; we desire some superfluous object in order to impress them; we obtain (or fail to obtain) that status symbol; those others are likely to feel a similar envy; they in turn seek out a similar status symbol for themselves; we continue the pattern of acquiring further

11 Seneca, *Letters from a Stoic,* Letter CX

Gio. Batis. de Poilly Sculp.

objects to keep the wheel turning. None of this relates to happiness, but if we don't *think* about happiness, we can easily throw ourselves into this perpetual default cycle, which feels more like an addiction to bursts of pleasure amidst a general tone of dissatisfaction and envy.

Worse, we feel this envy towards – and occasionally from – those closest to us. Our friends suffer most from it. We are far more likely to feel envy towards a work colleague than we are towards a celebrity. Envy is fuelled by a sense of entitlement and a perpetual comparing of ourselves to our peers. David Hume, a great eighteenth-century philosopher, wrote in his *Treatise of Human Nature*:

> It is not a great disproportion between ourselves and others which produces envy, but on the contrary, a proximity . . . a great disproportion cuts off the relation, and either keeps us from comparing ourselves with what is remote from us or diminishes the effects of the comparison.

Thus most people would not begrudge Madonna her placement at the top of the Forbes celebrity rich list for 2013 (though her peers well might), but they may seethe quietly at a colleague's pay-rise or a friend's new house.

This insidious envy that fuels so many of our desires is not then a product of the differences that exist between the strata of rich and poor. Instead, it is born from comparisons we make *within* our particular level of prosperity or success, where everyone is living in more or less equal comfort. Sociologists refer to 'reference group theory': the idea that in forming our self-identity, we compare ourselves to those in our peer group. Our cognitions, perceptions, attitudes and conceptions of ourselves are all tied in with those to whom we liken or contrast ourselves.

Driven as we are to form these self-evaluations, the groups with which we choose to identify will dictate whether we decide we're doing well or falling short, and are thus a vital component of our feelings of well-being.

Moreover, this process is amplified by a strong cultural presumption that we all have the same right to greater riches and standing if we wish for them: in other words, that we are all inherently equal. But this is a uniquely modern thought.

Rarely, before the seventeenth century, was it questioned that vast differences of wealth and status existed between different levels of society. A serf did not expect to elevate himself to become a landowner; the social brute knew his place. People got on with their lot in life, and aspirations were almost non-existent by today's standards. Enlightenment philosophers such as John Locke then started to question the role of government, and a powerful new idea was born: that governments might exist in order to bring happiness to their people. This astonishing notion helped to incite the American Revolution of 1776, and the new nation cemented such principles into its Declaration of Independence: 'We hold these truths to be self-evident, that all men are created equal, that they are endowed by their Creator with certain unalienable Rights, that among these are Life, Liberty and the pursuit of Happiness.'

Thus happiness and social equality were formally united for the first time, and most of us in the West would say that this was a good move. From the start, affluent Americans enjoyed the fruits of the democratic revolution and the old model of noble gentry and ignoble citizens was derided as a grotesque relic of an immoral past. God had turned a blind eye to social inequality for centuries;

now there were to be no serfs on His turf. Everyone in America was free to aspire socially and financially as they wished.

We have been left a contemporary commentary on the psychological effect of this curious new situation. Alexis de Tocqueville was a French historian who travelled to America in the early 1830s to investigate the functioning of politics and society. In America, unlike Europe, workers believed that they could earn their way, through labour, to a life of the same luxuries enjoyed by their employers. But de Tocqueville also found that this democratisation – and the emerging middle class it was producing – created a sense of entitlement and envy not present in the European model. His words below echo Hume's:

> When inequality of conditions is the common law of society, the most marked inequalities do not strike the eye: when everything is nearly on the same level, the slightest are marked enough to hurt it. Hence the desire of equality always becomes more insatiable in proportion as equality is more complete.[12]

The promise of equality teases and frustrates us, and thus envy brews. Whereas previously the underclasses were content with their lot, now the new poor feel betrayed. Betrayed by the system and by those around them, but also by their own aspirations. As we've seen previously, modern America's obsession with positive thinking, and therefore the fetishising of desire, has only exacerbated this potential for a very modern unhappiness.

12 Alexis de Tocqueville, *Democracy in America*

Though Schopenhauer was by all accounts a gruff and pessimistic character, he nonetheless wrote about desire and happiness in the *Parerga and Paralipomena* of his later years, picking up on the same point as Hume, that 'the great possessions of the rich do not worry the poor', adding, 'on the other hand, if the wealthy man's possessions fail, he is not consoled by the many things he already possesses. Wealth is like sea-water; the more we drink, the thirstier we become; and the same is true of fame.' He also highlights the relativity of a person's feeling of satisfaction: it 'rests not on an absolute but a merely relative amount, namely the relation between his claims and his possessions'. In other words, it is not what we own that satisfies us but rather what we have *in relation to* what we feel is possible and attainable for ourselves. That is the tension that causes dissatisfaction. Luxuries beyond that horizon (a billionaire's fleet of private jets) are not likely to seriously interest us. Schopenhauer of course recognises the advantages of having money: he notes that it is uniquely ready to meet a large number of our needs by transforming itself into the specific thing that we require.

Schopenhauer also draws from another great ancient Greek philosopher who concerned himself with happiness: Epicurus (not to be confused with the Stoic Epictetus, whom I've already mentioned). Epicurus saw human needs as divisible into three categories, and Schopenhauer clarifies Epicurus's classifications:

1. *Natural and necessary needs* – which cause pain if not satisfied. Essentially food and clothing, which are easy to satisfy.
2. *Natural but unnecessary needs* – such as sexual satisfaction – which are more difficult to satisfy.

3. *Neither natural nor necessary needs* – such as the latest gadget, other luxuries and personal fame – which are without end and difficult to satisfy.

In other words, the more *necessary* a desired thing is – such as food and shelter – the more readily we will usually find it is available *and* the more easily we will be satisfied. On the other hand, the entirely superfluous things we desire, whether they be gadgets, fame or wealth, are much more difficult to secure and very rarely satisfy us. There is always more or better to be had.

Such unnecessary things, of course, constitute the vast majority of our desires. And once we realise that satisfaction is relative, we see that we may never achieve it as long as a notable disparity continues to exist between what we feel is worth attaining and what we actually possess. Unnecessary desires are 'without end' because that disparity will always push us forwards to desiring more and therefore towards further dissatisfaction, and they are 'difficult to satisfy' because they either come at a great cost or because of their never-ending and self-perpetuating nature. This is why people who live in simple circumstances often surprise us with how happy they are.

We commonly spend our lives focused on the future: usually this carrot dangles before us in the form of a career ladder. It is easy to follow the carrot and harder to think about what might *truly* make us happy. We follow the former, not realising that we will never reach it to savour it, or that even if we do, we might find that particular carrot isn't even edible. We look for happiness in places that are supposed to offer it, but parties have a habit of being disappointing, and the promotion or new car does not quite yield the joy we expected. The places and things that insist most loudly that they will make us happy rarely do. Joy alone, says Schopenhauer, has declined to be present at the festival. It prefers to arrive quietly and alone elsewhere, unceremoniously and unannounced. Meanwhile, we search for happiness in distractions.

Travel is one such distraction. We have all had the experience of looking forward to a holiday, of looking at photographs on a hotel's website in order to choose a destination and imagining ourselves there, swimming in that sea or lying on that beach. The prospect is idyllic, and often making that trip will be a means of dealing with stress or discontent. The reality of the holiday, though, is often very different from its prospect and, by comparison, disappointing to one degree or another. Socrates, the first philosopher to turn knowledge into a tool for questioning our lives and finding ways to live better, explained why: when you travel (or for that matter attend a party), *you always take yourself with you.*

This is a wonderful thought expressed in Richard Linklater's beautiful 1995 film, *Before Sunrise.* The film, the first of a trilogy, is pure joy for lovers of cinema, and follows Jesse, a young American man (played by Ethan Hawke), and a French girl called Céline (Julie Delpy) as they meet on a train and spend one night walking around Vienna and falling in love. The night is magical, their situation is tragic, and we see that melancholy and beauty so often must go hand in hand. At one point, Jesse says to Céline:

> It's just, usually, it's myself that I wish I could get away from. Seriously, think about this. I have never been anywhere that I haven't been. I've never had a kiss when I wasn't one of the kissers. You know, I've never gone to the movies when I wasn't there in the audience. I've never been out bowling, if I

70

wasn't there, making some stupid joke. That's why so many people hate themselves. Seriously. It's just they are sick to death of being around themselves.

You, with your usual thoughts and predilections and capacity for dissatisfaction, find yourself on that sandy strip of paradise or in that turquoise sea, and you realise you have brought all of those disappointing aspects of yourself along with you. The rest is just a backdrop. Seneca highlighted the core point: 'You need a change of soul, not a change of climate.'[13] This inevitable problem with using travel as a means of 'getting away from it all' has been developed at length by Alain de Botton in his book *The Art of Travel*, and it also applies to other promised lands. We might think that we'll be finally happy when we get a job with a certain company, or begin a relationship with a certain person, but when we get there it's still *us* looking out, with all the frustrations and distortions that might bring. When we reflect, we notice:

> That the image we had before us of a bright and happy future either excluded us altogether, like the over-saturated images on the resort website, or contained a strange smiling version of ourselves that was not really us at all.[14]

This all sounds very dreary – how might we find hope amidst this hopelessness? Unexpectedly, it is precisely at the heart of this dilemma that we find the answer to the conundrum. And we must first do away with the notion that happiness is something straightforward, a simple *thing*

13 Seneca, *Letters from a Stoic*, Letter XXVIII
14 Alain de Botton, *The Art of Travel*

to which we are entitled. Happiness is a chimera: it is imaginary and deceiving in many of its forms. Like the rainbow which so commonly symbolises it, happiness is an optical illusion that retreats or hides itself the closer you approach.

But the news is not bad news: happiness, if you think about it in the right way, is quite achievable. So far we have only looked at the problems that beset us when we try to obtain it. Now let's discover some practical solutions and forget about chasing rainbows.

☺

Part Two: **Solutions**

4

The Considered Life

Perhaps I've convinced you that many of the things we are assured will bring us happiness are unlikely to, and that a key to achieving whatever this state might be is to harness the stories we tell ourselves *about* ourselves. In this chapter, we'll look at how we can start to own our stories and feel a sense of authorship.

Perhaps the biggest and most important step for becoming happier, then, is the first: realising we need a plan. Then we must find *which* plan stands up best to the realities of being alive. There is quite a marketplace of beliefs and philosophies to choose from, and it is hard to know which ones live up to their claims. It seems to be the case that many people who search for a consolidating philosophy tend to be eternal 'seekers', never quite comfortable in their own skin and every few years adopting a fresh external source of guidance or following some new charismatic leader. We certainly don't want to become one of those lost unfortunates.

In the same way an architect needs plans and an understanding of overarching structure when she comes to build a house, it would be madness for us not to pay attention to the foundations and overall vision of our lives. I do *not* mean the typical plans of the ambitious goal-setter (such as 'I will be a millionaire by thirty'), as such plans tend to relate to what we might accumulate for ourselves; what we hope to *have*. Instead, we are looking for a blueprint, a template, a considered piece of draughtsmanship to which we can refer when we come to make choices about who we *are*.

As I am not an adherent to any particular philosophy but have come, through reading and experience, to find the thoughts of certain schools and thinkers very helpful, I will not be offering a complete one-stop package here. I don't think it's ultimately helpful to adopt single labels as some kind of identity. Also, many of the ideas that suit me may not remotely suit you. I do, however, think the ideas I shall set out in this book are profoundly helpful, and that even if only certain parts speak to you or assist you, it will have been worth the read.

So, setting aside for now where we're heading, let's take a look at the importance and pleasure of living a considered life. I am talking about engaging with and owning our life stories; of being able to step back far enough to see them for what they are; of finding a way of living that has come from due thought rather than a passive immersion in the tangles of everyday distractions. Our philosophy can be highly flexible and subject to great changes, but the important point, I believe, is to have one, and one that enables us to live more fully. It does not need to be easily describable in its entirety, or clearly attributable to any philosophical school; although it should stand up to scrutiny and enquiry, being thought through and considered. It must give us a solid foundation without limiting us by insisting on a set of beliefs. If we don't assume more conscious authorship of our stories, others will write them for us, and we will invariably find ourselves fundamentally bored or anxious and prone to any number of complaints from within.

One way of achieving this authorship would be through undertaking extensive (and expensive) psychoanalysis. Under the guidance of a professional, we would be led to understand our unconscious drives and engage more with our personal stories. Our dreams would be examined, the deep messages of our early years discussed and revealed, and our pathologies and anxieties reinterpreted as clear signals that specific parts of our self are not being honoured. When we shut off something important within us, we are likely to experience it later as a psychological tension of one form or another. This kind of deep self-improvement is helpful and fascinating. It is neither cheap nor quick, although as Alain de Botton has pointed out, if we see it as the psychological equivalent of a gym membership, we might consider it worthwhile. Invariably, we associate the need for psychoanalysis with mental disturbance, as if therapy were a shameful thing to undertake. Yet we are all disturbed to one degree or another, all somehow repressed and to varying extents shut off from our true selves: this is the human condition and precisely what we should address to increase our quotient of happiness. The relevant question is whether these disturbances own us or whether we contain or manage them. Either way, the analogy with physical training holds: you don't need to be suffering from physical under-development to benefit from the gym.

So deep analysis would certainly offer up one way of engaging with our stories. It isn't the only way, and of course will remain for many too strange and expensive a luxury to undertake. But without *any* means of identifying and engaging with our stories, we might quickly find ourselves at the mercy of whatever voices happen to be loudest around us. These may come from the Church; from forms of cheap spirituality; from our immediate peer groups. But most pervasively they will come at an early age from our caregivers. The greatest burden a child must bear, we remember from Jung, is the unlived lives of its parents.

We might, worse, choose how to live based almost entirely on a reaction *against* the way we have been treated by people and thus hand over control of our life force to the transgressors of our past. Or we might not give any thought to such matters and just feel, if questioned, that our life is defined primarily by the job we perform every day. This may be a job we don't enjoy, and so we leave the 'living' part for weekends or holidays. The trouble with this familiar pattern is that these spurts of actual free existence tend to be still defined by the work that fills up the rest of life. The weekend partying is excessive because it's the only way to redress the balance after a stressful or depressing week, and a brief week's respite on a warm beach is only a matter of recharging before the next bout of intense application at our desks. And so we continue, rarely questioning whether there might be any break to the cycle, subjugating our own deep demands to the daily dictates of others, and thus slog through a huge chunk of our lives.

Leading a considered life is about getting our story right for ourselves. It's as simple as that. If we, at any point in our lives, can look at what we're up to and feel that everything is more or less in its place, and that our story is on the right tracks, we will have a good basis for happiness.

How, without the aid of an analyst, might we get it

right? How can we live a life that we will, even in our last days, be sure to deem our best effort? What of the things we enjoy, the things that make us happy now – what if they turn out to be our biggest regrets? It is an extraordinary thought that we could line up the things that bring us pleasure now and spend our life exploring these activities one after another and still come to the end deeply regretting the lifestyle we chose. And, perhaps, so what if we do? Why should the anticipation of future introspective thoughts triggered by illness in the final few months of our lives dictate the choices we make now and for decades ahead? Is it not potentially just as disastrous to live one's life with the goal of dying happily and without regret, just to find that our regret is that we did not live for the moment while we could?

Two selves

To take charge of our stories, it is helpful to take on board an interesting perspective only now being fully discussed in the realms of psychology through the work of Daniel Kahneman: that we cannot talk about happiness without distinguishing between two selves that both operate within us: the *experiencing* self and the *remembering* self.

When we look back over our lives and decide if we have had a happy time in this world, it is the *remembering self* that is making that judgement. However, it may be that some of those choices we made, which satisfied the future remembering self, were not at the time the most *enjoyable* experiences and therefore did not provide particular pleasure to the *experiencing self*. For our purposes, Kahneman's separation of those two selves seems to correlate with what we might intuitively understand to be the separation of happiness and pleasure: the former comes from a judgement we make, a sense of things being or having been right or as we would like them to be, and tends to be retrospective; whereas the latter relates to what we are being made to directly feel right *now*. Thus you might choose to spend an afternoon attending to a sick relative rather than go to a theme park with friends, choosing the least 'pleasurable' option and leaving your *experiencing* self less fulfilled. But this choice might furnish your future *remembering* self with a better story of how you spent your afternoon and even contribute to a wider sense of happiness regarding what you do with your life.

To illustrate the difference between these two 'selves' (of course they are two levels of processing rather than actual entities), Kahneman and his colleagues carried out a telling experiment, which he describes in his popular masterwork of cognitive exploration, *Thinking, Fast and Slow*. Participants were asked to hold one hand in water, which was uncomfortably cold but tolerable. Their free hand controlled arrows on a keyboard to indicate how much pain they were experiencing. This would of course amount to an ongoing communication from the experiencing self. They were asked to keep their hand in the water for a full minute at this temperature and then they could remove it, whereupon they were given a warm towel.

Then, seven minutes later, they were invited to carry out a second version of the same exercise with the other hand. This time the temperature endured during the first minute was identical to the first session but was followed by a slight raising of the temperature by one degree, which most participants would register as enough to cause a slight decrease in the pain. This session then continued for an extra thirty seconds at this marginally more comfortable temperature.

Seven minutes after that, they were invited to repeat the test one more time. This time they were offered a choice. They could repeat the first version (sixty seconds of discomfort) or the second (ninety seconds of discomfort but with the last thirty slightly less painful). Despite the fact that the first version involves less pain for the participant, 80 per cent of volunteers opted to repeat the second version rather than the first. Why would they choose the longer session over the shorter one? Because of the difference between what Kahneman calls 'decision utility' and 'experienced utility'. In other words, we don't make decisions based on our experiences. We make them based on the *stories* of our experiences. And we don't form our stories based on an accurate reflection of experience. We form them like novelists, and we look for a good ending.

The crucial difference is that the second session, with its extra period of a slightly more bearable thirty seconds, leaves us with a different story to tell. In this version, we emerge from the experience feeling a modicum of relief, and therefore our story is of an event that 'got better'. The shorter, sharper first version leaves merely a tale of pain. Although the experiencing self will report extended discomfort in that second longer session, the participant will remember it as more comfortable, because the ending is different. And as Kahneman points out, we care a lot about endings when we consider stories. They tend to define the character of the whole tale. He mentions a student who had listened to a recording of a symphony and was hugely enjoying the experience until the end, when a scratch on the disc ruined the finale. The whole experience was ruined for the student. His remembering self ignored the almost entirely positive experience of his experiencing self (which had enjoyed the music until that final moment): the bad ending had scuppered everything.

When writing a stage show, one normally concentrates disproportionately on the finale, as while the ongoing emotions of each scene cater to the experiencing self, it is the finale that is most pertinent to the remembering self's story of how much fun it had and how satisfying the whole experience has been. Hence the tendency of many modern commercial musicals to employ the tactic of the 'mega-mix' at the curtain call: the whole cast takes part in a fun refrain of the catchiest number or – Christ help us – comes out into the audience to get everyone dancing. You are forced to leave with a smile on your face and believe you enjoyed what until that point might have been a pretty mediocre show.

Interestingly, the remembering self is not particularly concerned with how long pain or pleasure have lasted: the fact that the second cold-water session was thirty seconds *longer* is ignored in its decision-making. Our capacity for storytelling allows us to misremember the extent of pain or pleasure we felt during an experience. We then make our decisions based on that misinformation. While Kahneman prefers not to say which self we should favour, leaving that to philosophers, I take the view that it is this remembering self with which we should be more concerned. Kahneman gives examples that support this preference: would you go on a holiday knowing that all memory of it would be wiped from your brain (and camera) the moment it was over? Probably not. Mere pampering to the experiencing self is not enough; we want memories too.

It seems that our experiencing self is something we share with our fellow beasts, whereas the kind of self-consciousness that makes us uniquely human lies within the complex, story-forming realms of the remembering self. Though we should not forget some animals' capacity for self-awareness. A classic, and rather entertaining, experiment has demonstrated its existence: a coloured mark is secretly placed on the forehead of an animal, and the animal is then placed in front of a mirror. If it responds to the reflection by trying to scratch or reach the mark on its own body, then we must take it that it can somehow conceive of itself.[15] Presumably, though, this conception does not operate at the same level of cognitive complexity involved when we think about, for example, how to spend an upcoming weekend or whether we want to attend a particular party.

Most importantly, we rely on our remembering self when we consider those stories we have internalised about ourselves; we join the dots in such a way that gives us our sense of identity. It is the remembering self that is a large part of what makes us human: a product of our highly evolved brains.

My encouragement, then, to lead a considered life (before we look at some suggestions as to what that might entail) is an appeal to acknowledge what Kahneman calls 'the tyranny of the remembering self'. We don't need to treat it as oppressive, but we can acknowledge that it has the upper hand. To live well and happily necessitates that

15 Neural evidence has also emerged to suggest that rats can project themselves into the future. When they have to make decisions as to which way to go through a maze in order to find food, they tend to stop at these 'choice points' and deliberate. The parts of the brain related to choice-making are activated: they are indeed considering future possibilities. A team from Warwick University has suggested that this means the rats must be able to distinguish between a real and imagined (future) self; in other words, they may well have a primal self-awareness, which is more than we have previously credited them with.

we engage with this side of ourselves. If we don't engage with our stories, taking our cue from passing pleasure, we pander only to our bestial experiencing self. This has an attention span of about three seconds, and its reports are quickly superseded by those of its story-loving, identity-forming superior. We might enjoy plenty of experiences along the way, but they will not tend to correlate with any particular feeling of happiness.

Regaining authorship

What is the experience of an unconsidered existence? We resemble the motif of Sam Mendes's film *American Beauty*: a thin plastic bag flitting and sailing on the currents of life. We may find ourselves in happy or sad places, but we are at the mercy of constant influences from without that pull or nudge us this way or that. This is the antithesis of a life where *our centre of gravity is rooted within ourselves*. In the centred life, work, health, family and friends may still make their demands, but we can acknowledge and entertain those forces without feeling them impose directly upon our core selves. We are missing out if we feel that happiness is a result of lucky circumstance rather than something rooted immovably in us. For it to be solid, our happiness would not rely on fortuity or what we happen to *have*. It would be fundamentally about who we *are*.

Ideally, it would reside quietly in the epicentre of our emotional lives, an area before which we can raise the drawbridge and from time to time close off from outside threat. We are well advised, then, to do what we can to make that a place of peace and self-sufficiency, and not to extend our general tendencies towards fear and panic into that hallowed space.

Let's return to the nineteenth-century German

philosopher Arthur Schopenhauer. His primary work, *The World as Will and Representation*, was published in 1818 when he was thirty. He became a university lecturer at Berlin, where his lectures clashed with those of Hegel, a celebrated philosopher whom Schopenhauer loathed. No one came to his lectures and he refused to change his time slot, resulting in him having to abandon his career. His fuming criticism of his academic colleague still makes me laugh:

> If I were to say that the so-called philosophy of this fellow Hegel is a colossal piece of mystification which will yet provide posterity with an inexhaustible theme for laughter at our times, that it is a pseudo-philosophy paralyzing all mental powers, stifling all real thinking, and, by the most outrageous misuse of language, putting in its place the hollowest, most senseless, thoughtless, and, as is confirmed by its success, most stupefying verbiage, I should be quite right.[16]

Schopenhauer was sued by a seamstress who shared his lodgings after he pushed her down the stairs for talking too loudly on the landing. He indignantly dragged out the litigation for five years. Meanwhile, he lived alone and followed a set routine every day. Up at seven, bath, coffee, write till midday, flute practice, lunch out at the inn, read at home till four, daily walk (which always lasted two hours, irrespective of weather), head to the library to read the London *Times*, then perhaps take in a concert or the theatre before returning home early to bed. He carried out this identical routine every day for twenty-seven

16 Arthur Schopenhauer, *On the Basis of Morality*

years. His only companionship came from a stream of pet poodles, which he kept throughout his life, giving each the same name, 'Atma'. This word refers to the first principle of Hindu philosophy, namely the essence of an individual; an appellation that in each case transcends the individual poodle and elevates it to the fundamental reality of poodledom.

He was by all accounts a grumpy man, which comes as no surprise, given that he was referred to as the philosopher of pessimism. But his work is a far richer and more uplifting wellspring of ideas than that word suggests. Schopenhauer gives us an image of what is left if our centre of gravity is not located securely within us. He points to pain and boredom as 'the two foes of human happiness'[17]. When our stability relies principally on external factors, we shuttle back and forth between the two. We avoid pain, seek comfort, and become bored. To counter that boredom, we may choose to engage in distracting or competitive activities that bring new forms of stress into our lives. Some enjoy the diversion of sport but injure themselves or suffer the pains of competitiveness. Others visit the casino and lose more than they can afford or develop gambling addictions. If we start to feel empty, we might crave extravagance and try hard to impress others, which (for the reasons we have seen) tends to produce misery. Without a solid sense of self, we can't help but swing between these unpleasant extremes.

You may remember Schopenhauer's image of the $x=y$ diagonal that shows how we truly navigate life. This graph conceit echoes that of the modern sociologist Mike Csikszentmihalyi. From his extensive discussions with

17 Arthur Schopenhauer, *Parerga and Paralipomena, Vol 1, Personality; or, What a Man Is*

people from all walks of life, he discovered there is a state of 'flow': a 'prime state' that brings together the chess player, the surfer, the artist, and others who can lose themselves in an activity and later testify that it is their happiest frame of mind. Csikszentmihalyi's graph is of 'skills' along the x axis and 'challenges faced' along the y:

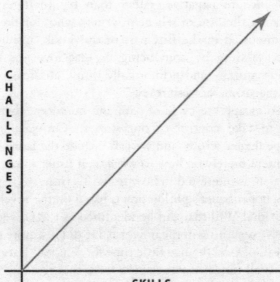

When an activity allows us to steer an $x=y$ diagonal, we find ourselves happily in this 'flow' state, avoiding the tedium that arises when our skills outweigh the challenges we face, as well as the anxiety that follows when our obstacles become too great for us. Once again, then, we note the twin pitfalls of pain and boredom, the enemies of our happiness. Both commentators on the human experience give us a memorable and useful picture of the relationship between the internal and external spheres.

Perhaps it was Schopenhauer's morose temperament that caused him to see the human experience as a battle between pain and boredom, but I think he can be misjudged. Most of his writing stands as a handbook for escaping the base and unpleasant forces in life and finding greater happiness. And it is more rewarding to read such advice from a philosopher whose initial presumptions about life are negative, rather than try to digest the Pollyanna rhetoric of self-help writers who, for the reasons discussed in the first part of this book, insidiously induce anxiety by convincing us that love and hope should naturally and primordially infuse all areas of life with the aroma of fresh roses.

To escape the cycle of pain and boredom, then, we need to take control of our stories. 'Ordinary men,' Schopenhauer wrote (and we can include the ladies too), 'are intent merely on how to *spend* their time; a man with any talent is interested in how to *use* his time.'[18]

Schopenhauer's philosophy is based on the revelation of a primal Will that can be identified as the power that propels everything in the universe. He did not quite mean the Will of God (he had little time for religion) but rather an eternal, fundamental driving force that remains when all individual subjectivity, perception and experience are cleared away. Unchecked, it drives us to base things: when we live in any civilised society, we sublimate the Will that would otherwise have us murder, steal and fornicate at whim. He believed that to lead a happy and considered life, we should seek to use our intellect in a way that allows us to rise above our instincts and this pertinacious Will. A considered life is one in which we aspire to aims other than the procreation and fame that the Will amply

18 Arthur Schopenhauer, *Parerga and Paralipomena*

encourages, avoiding the swing from pain to boredom and back that would carry us passively through life like a plastic bag in the wind.

A considered life also informs and improves that otherwise fickle thing: our self-image. We don't pay much *conscious* attention to the mental picture we carry around of ourselves, but it dictates so much of how we feel about our strengths and weaknesses. It's part of the story we tell ourselves about how we are and how we are likely to behave in any situation. That self-image is, though, just that: a picture we make in our heads. The trouble is, we often conjure up unhelpful images that make us feel bad or inadequate. We have, since we were very small, internalised the messages we have heard about ourselves from our caregivers regarding our worth, and of course (as Schopenhauer points out) we pay more attention to bad feelings than good. Thus we might be terrific listeners with a disarming honesty that makes most people feel very comfortable in our company, while we ourselves are convinced we are merely awkward misfits, unable to play the kinds of social games everyone else seems to enjoy.

The considered life – in which we take back authorship of our narratives – gives some structure to that self-image and resists its distortion by others. It is not to deny our weaknesses by developing an unrealistic faith in strengths we don't possess. Witness any number of TV talent-show hopefuls who, after dispatching their tuneless misadventure in the most unlovely way, meet their unanimous rejection from the judges with a baffled incredulity that is entirely their own. It's a rule in life that the more certain we appear about something, the less we know about it. It has a name – the Dunning–Kruger effect – and it is at work every time someone tells you with absolute certainty how things are in the world. The sign of the true expert is his modest awareness of how much *more* there is to know; how complex and nuanced the subject at hand insists on remaining. The kind of self-image we may be best advised to seek, then, is *not* of ourselves as beautiful winners (as we are often told we should), but one wherein our strengths and weaknesses are realistically appraised with neither self-aggrandisement nor abnegation, and our share of inevitable failings looked upon with kindness and good humour.

It is rarely effective to form a defiant self-image that blindly rejects all external influences. In opposing influences, we are still reliant on them to define our behaviour. If we proudly walk on the left-hand side of the road merely because everyone else walks on the right, then in order to maintain our apparently 'independent' stance we'd be forced to cross the road if everyone else decided to switch sides. Despite our attitude, we would be deferring authorship to other people. Choosing a lifestyle that makes a statement of non-conformity (or a rejection of parental expectations) might work as a temporary rite of passage to a more independent place, but in as much as it relies on the 'enemy' to know what to reject, it remains tied to and dependent upon the opposition. It may give the illusion of authorship, but 'fuck you' is too much about the 'you'; its centre of gravity is external. It's also, in the longer term, a very *unhappy* stance.

By contrast, a considered life is one in which we deeply engage with our own story. That means we need to identify what our story is and then know how to move it forward. If we don't – if we swing between pain and boredom, or merely defy those who would dare to tell us what to do – we shut off important channels of development (and, therefore, life). We are often most aware of this at work: the jobs that we chose in our twenties no longer appeal to us in our thirties or forties, once we've grown up and changed in all our other areas of life. We might hope for a promotion, but a step upwards will not comfort our soul if what it yearns for is a sideways leap into new adventures.

The career 'story' is usually established for us early on, with its challenges and passages, aims and endings predictably laid out. It's a script that we follow. We think *within* that framework when we consider how to have a full career. To make a drastic change in middle age seems foolhardy and irresponsible, especially if one has a family to support.

The scripts that our parents tend to hand us work analogously. Here are their unlived lives: a framework for ours. From that script we intuitively learn what will make us worthwhile, loved and happy. *Be successful; be happy; help others;* or *destroy all competition.* Then, as we grow into adults, these life scripts will prove insufficient for us. They, along with other directives provided by other significant institutions or figures in our early lives, will inevitably prove too restrictive for a full life that honours what *we* need. And there's the problem: when we shut parts of ourselves off, they re-emerge as pathologies and anxieties, or reasons for therapy. We are owned by feelings of depression, loneliness or anger because we are not living out – and most likely cannot even identify – our *real* stories. Our authentic selves are not being honoured: they have allowed the toxic clutter and trauma of other peoples' messed-up stories to confuse our own from an early age.

Often today, those who suffer from mental-health issues are encouraged by well-meaning awareness groups to claim proud ownership of their troubled inner lives. So rather than feel stigmatised, a sufferer might seek dignity

by *identifying* with her depression. That proud identifica-
tion might be helpful in the short term (and certainly to
disparage people for suffering in these ways amounts to a
baffling breakdown of empathy), but where we allow
a condition to direct our own overarching narrative, such a
move may well prove every bit as life-denying over time.
Meanwhile, the life story we *should* be seeking out, identifying with and proudly proclaiming, has been obscured.
Our pathologies are not badges of honour but helpful
alarm bells: reminders from the psyche that we have
reached the edge of the path and need to re-orient to
move forward into whatever greatness might be on offer
for us. We can pay attention to our anxieties, ask where
they come from and of what difficult episodes in the past
they remind us, and treat them as deep messages to enable
us to reconsider our priorities.

How do we set about engaging deeply with our
stories? How, to return to the architect metaphor, do we
draw up the best plans? If our walls are severely cracked,
no amount of wallpaper will solve the problem. We can
jump in and start building with arbitrary enthusiasm, but
without advice from the experts we should expect to
experience problems along the way. When we make these
blueprints for our lives, we want to have the best advice
before us, so we can begin the adventure of building and
enjoy the challenges we might face. We can cherry-pick
from sometimes quite conflicting advice, as long as we
know that the different features will complement each
other and work together in the final structure. Some
people may be happy to hand over responsibility to a
single architect and have him do all the work and
decision-making. Religion offers this relinquishing of
responsibility, and for many it's very appealing. Most
'complete' solutions provide a framework that largely

removes the need to continue asking the kind of existential questions the considered life provokes. The answers have been provided for you.

No one system is perfect, and even if there were a perfect philosophy, who could perfectly apply it? As we explore some philosophical answers, we will try to keep an open mind and tolerate contradiction, honouring the fact that life is always more complex than any one system will suppose. And it is with the ancients that we will begin, as we look at how we might assume a greater level of authorship of our life stories.

The roots of self-enquiry

In classical times, philosophers could be found dotted around the Athenian marketplace expounding their approaches to life. Philosophy was concerned with how best to live, and there was no shortage of thinkers ready to pass on their wisdom. It was a thing of the streets. Today, philosophy has become highly academic, concerning itself more with matters of language, logic and metaphysics, rather than with the business of living well. It would be unusual now for a philosopher to feel it was his or her place to instruct students in such a matter as how to personally flourish or find happiness.

Meanwhile, most philosophical considerations on the subject remain tucked away in the works and words of Greek and Roman thinkers, which have only recently been brought back to relatively popular attention. In our age, the wisdom of the ancients has joined forces with the disease model of psychology to form cognitive behavioural therapy: a currently very popular model of psychotherapy rooted in Stoic thinking.

Neither, as I have previously said, has the adjacent

field of psychology offered much help in how to best live, concerning itself traditionally with pathology and how to fix things when they go wrong. 'Positive psychologists' have more recently had an impact, and empirical research has been carried out in a quest to discover what makes us happier.

The work of these pioneering psychologists is fascinating and valuable. We can imagine their empirical research as offering a *horizontal* image of happiness, with its wide data drawn from large cross sections of people. It is handy to know the ten habits of happy people, or how employers might create a flourishing workforce, and undeniably useful to remember that higher reported levels of happiness statistically correlate with having one or more close relationships or a spiritual belief. Sometimes, though, it can lack a note of deep instruction for us as suffering individuals trying to make sense of the world and get close to each other.

Philosophy (if it's psychologically 'resonant') tends to be better at filling that gap. It rarely concerns itself with empirical research, preferring instead what I see as a *vertical* approach: an opportunity for an individual journey of deep understanding (although this may then extend into a scheme for transforming society at large).

Unlike the modern self-help genre, which has taken on the responsibility of offering life advice, the type of philosophy we are discussing does not concern itself with the latest fads or get-rich-quick schemes; it is about lasting change and the creation of deep structure: a blueprint for life. Thus the disciplines of empirical psychology and philosophy may complement each other, and the weighing of one against the other will depend on, for example, whether we are making policy decisions that will affect areas of the population at large or revising our personal attitudes. With the renewed interest in how we might live most happily, and the establishing of institutions such as Alain de Botton's School of Life in London and abroad, it may be that philosophy and psychology are finding their way back together again after their time apart.

We are going to look back to the ancients for most of our philosophical ideas. Before the Church secured its millennia-long grip over thought, early philosophers were unfettered in their study of what it might mean to live well.

In his book *Philosophy For Life*, Jules Evans sets out four steps of the Socratic tradition: that is, the type of enquiry that grew from the time of Socrates, the first philosopher to bring the field away from early metaphysical discussions and take it to the people. Socrates was also the first to offer the advice 'know thyself', and said that the considered life was the only one worth living. The influence of this short, ugly, modest man, who wandered the streets of ancient Athens encouraging people to join him in conversation, has continued to this day. Although varied and conflicting philosophies have grown from his descendants, they have in common a method of self-enquiry which we can trace to Socrates and which we would do well to consider as we contemplate our own lives. Here are the four stages, set out by Evans, and upon which any presumption of change through philosophical consideration is based.

1. Humans can know themselves. We can use our reason to examine our unconscious beliefs and values.
2. Humans can change themselves. We can use our reason to change our beliefs. This will change our emotions, because our emotions follow our beliefs.

3. Humans can consciously create new habits of thinking, feeling and acting.

4. If we follow philosophy as a way of life, we can live more flourishing lives.[19]

As Evans points out, it is the fourth step that is most complex, because different people and philosophers have varying notions of what a 'flourishing' life might entail. And included in the rest of this book are some different options for what might constitute Step 4. Each is tantalising in its own way, and each will appeal to a different temperament. Unavoidably, I am biased towards those philosophies that sit best with my personality. My nature is a little on the introverted side, which is ideal for our purposes, as the vast majority of philosophers are and were too. More extrovert personalities might find themselves constitutionally unsuited to chunks of this book's advice, but as we all exist on a sliding scale between these personality types, we can all make use of the kind of philosophy we will consider. We can all use it to build the foundations of our inner home, from which we can best and most safely enjoy the light and breezy heights of the upper floors.

No effort or study will be required of you. I hope that some of the ideas will take root and affect you for the better. Perhaps you may wish to go and read more about or by a particular philosopher who seems to speak to you. All you need to begin living a considered and fruitful life, Seneca said, is to wish it. But we have left far behind the vacuous and misleading 'wishes' of the followers of *The Secret*. This is not a childish cry out to an indifferent universe or an infantile drive to have every shallow wish

19 Jules Evans, *Philosophy For Life: And Other Dangerous Situations*

fulfilled. It is instead the sincere desire to rid oneself of illusion, to live authentically, and through that to find how we might flourish most happily.

Milan Kundera made the enduring point in *The Unbearable Lightness of Being* that there is no dress rehearsal for life. This is life; this is it, right now. It is a powerful and motivating thought. Each moment you live passes and is gone, never to return. Life is too brief to not consider how to experience it at its best. This is not about bungee jumping or forming an extravagant bucket list. It can happen in the ordinary moments of your everyday life.

Life is short. We know this. But there is a contradictory thought, which I find every bit as exhilarating and which was central to the writings of the German nineteenth-century philosopher Friedrich Nietzsche. It is called 'eternal recurrence': an idea that he drew from Indian philosophy. Time is infinite, Nietzsche points out, while the chances of a world appearing exactly like our own is (though very, very small) *not quite* zero. This means that eventually, as we move through infinite time, a world exactly like ours will appear again. And, given that we have endless time to play with, *over and over again*. In that world, of course, there will exist a repeated version of you, living exactly your life each time. If time is eternal, every configuration of events that has already happened will at some point happen again, and that will include a reliving of your life by a future version of yourself. Nietzsche finds the idea at first horrifying. That horror, however, leads to his realisation that a person living a considered and truly affirmed life would be happy for it to be lived over and over again for eternity:

What, if some day or night a demon were to steal after you into your loneliest loneliness and say to you: 'This life as you now live it and have lived it, you will have to live once more and innumerable times more' . . . Would you not throw yourself down and gnash your teeth and curse the demon who spoke thus? Or have you once experienced a tremendous moment when you would have answered him: 'You are a god and never have I heard anything more divine.'[20]

Now, I don't know if the basis of Nietzsche's idea really holds up. For one thing, time may not be infinite (the universe as we know it will come to some sort of end), and even if a future version of ourselves lives out our life again, it will not be *us*, in the sense that we will not share a sense of personal identity with him or her. It needn't worry us *now*; for all you know, you may already be living out a life identical to someone before you, and it doesn't follow that either of you should be bothered by the fact.

But such technicalities aside, the thought is a compelling one. Would you live your life over and over again exactly as it happened? Is your centre of gravity *within* you, with your self-image sturdy and tenacious, or is it *outside* of you and woefully subject to the inconstancies of fate and the intimations of others? And when you reach the end of this life, will you feel you have lived a life worth living?

☺

20 Friedrich Nietzsche, *The Gay Science*

5

A (Very) Brief History of Happiness

It's a strange thought. We take it for granted that happiness is a birthright, a sign of a life successfully lived. We talk about being happy, or otherwise, as if it were the most natural thing in the world to understand. It seems so straightforward, that we're surprised to find we can't put our finger on what it really means. And it seems to come so undeniably from within, that it's a shock to find out that our understanding of happiness is a social and historical construct, akin to many other questions of ethics and morality.

So far, we've seen some of the problems inherent in the modern idea of happiness, and the importance of having some sort of control over our relationship with this fundamental aspect of life. Now, in order to understand how to improve our levels of happiness, we need to take a step back and see what such an idea amounts to. We need to get a sense of its contours, rather than merely apprehend it as a big, indeterminate mulch of ambiguous sentiments. Yet if it's in the nature of the beast that we can't clearly identify it, how do we begin such a process?

Alan Watts, the compelling writer and talker who popularised Eastern ideas in the West, begins his book *The Wisdom of Insecurity* with an image of trying to tie up water in a paper package. 'The trouble is,' he writes, 'to get the water into any manageable shape, and to tie the string without bursting the bundle.' The attempts of bright and dedicated people over the centuries to solve the problems of philosophy often seem to amount to an equally futile exercise. Being human is an extraordinary, complex and befuddling thing, and it would serve us to remember this as we look for ways to improve our lot.

If you have had the experience of travelling abroad and noticing customs that differ from our own, then you'll appreciate that one way to bring something intangible and largely unquestioned into sharp focus is to contrast it with other cultures where different fundamental presumptions are at work. It's hard to realise, for example, how eager we English are to avoid embarrassment, until one has travelled to other countries where such an idiosyncrasy is not embedded into life. I remember, when living in Würzburg in southern Germany, a friend telling me how he had been sitting at a bus stop, one leg crossed over the other in such a way that the heel of one foot contacted the plastic bench. An elderly lady, passing on the other side of the street, spotted this transgression. She crossed over the road, muttering admonishments in her curt Franconian dialect, raised her hand to the offending foot and slapped it. It was an extraordinary bit of business and highlighted our own presumptions about what we take to be acceptable behaviour from an old lady in this country.

If cultural comparisons might offer us a horizontal view of happiness in context, history can give us a vertical perspective. And as it is ultimately from history that I believe we can find the most effective answers to improving our happiness, this is the route I want to take in this chapter. Perhaps this is a dangerous path: I might lose some of my younger readers who baulk at the idea of history. Kenny, the college student of Christopher Isherwood's *A Single Man*, tells our hero, his professor George:

> All I'm saying is, the Past doesn't really matter to most kids my age. When we talk like it does, we're just being polite. I guess that's because we don't have any pasts of our own – except stuff we want to forget, like things in high school, and times we acted like idiots.

Like George and Kenny, we must ultimately 'drink to tonight'. But first let's toast the past and unsettle a few presumptions about this seemingly straightforward idea of happiness.

Our notions of happiness are a product of the age that we live in. I owe much of this chapter's chronicle to Darrin McMahon, who has detailed in *The Pursuit of Happiness* a fascinating history of this elusive concept. If you believe you are *entitled* to be happy, that this is a given for any human being, then read on. This notion of a right to happiness is a very modern idea and, as I have already said, the cause of much anxiety.

We have one brilliant man to blame for the muddle.

Socrates and Plato

Socrates, whom we have already met, has been revered in the West as the first thinker to bring philosophy into the everyday and raise the question of the considered life. He

102

took delight in asking questions of his fellow Athenians to see how they ticked, and through this technique had them question their presumptions and narrow-mindedness. Socrates presented the desire for happiness as something quite natural to humanity. That we desire happiness seems to be such an unimpeachable statement that it is difficult to take on board the notion that in identifying it and claiming it as natural, Socrates gave life to the very idea of the desire for happiness. Before him, we hadn't considered it as acutely. And his great idea has obsessed humanity ever since.

Prior to Socrates (he lived 469–399 BCE), we of course enjoyed ourselves, and pleasure often came in the form of Dionysian festivals. Dionysus was the god of wine and merrymaking, of ecstasy and debauchery. Today, he would preside over the club scene and its modern excesses.

In contrast to Dionysus, we can posit another god, his brother Apollo. The latter represents that rational, logical, high-minded part of us where 'each thing is coherent in itself, separate, clearly bounded and distinguished from everything else; everything is what it is, and not confused with anything else'.[21] Meanwhile, in the opposing, passionate, intoxicating realm of Dionysus, such clear individual identity gets lost. In his bawdy world, we are reconciled with both nature and our fellow man, and are 'on the way to flying into the air'.

These gods weren't used in this way to illustrate the twin poles of human experience until some two thousand years *after* Socrates, but still offer a noble way of thinking of our characters, as these two forces in our nature pull us one way then the other. Dionysus is our instinctive, animal side that sits in contrast with our mediating,

21 Friedrich Nietzsche, *The Birth of Tragedy*

careful self. Apollo is Edward Norton in *Fight Club*; Dionysus is Brad Pitt. Many of the conflicts within us can be seen as a result of these opposing urges pulling us in opposing directions, and an important part of life involves recognising and respecting the power and validity of both, rather than denouncing one and attempting to live entirely by the other.

They are at work in the way we impose order on chaos and randomness. These realms of heated chaos and cool logic fused together in the great Greek tragedies as audiences followed a hero trying to impose *order* (the Apollonian urge) on whatever random *fate* threw his way (the Dionysian drive). Here on the one hand are our aims, and here on the other is fortune. Does this sound familiar? You might recognise our $x=y$ diagonal as an honest assessment of what it is to live wholly.

We can also draw a parallel with Kahneman's bifurcation of the self into its experiencing and remembering counterparts. We can see the Dionysian element in his experiencing self as it instinctively suffers or enjoys the chaotic emotions caused by uncontrolled, fleeting experiences – or, if you like, by fate. Likewise, we can recognise the detached, cooler Apollonian tendencies of the remembering self as it imposes order on that chaos by forming a clear narrative. And of course those clear and precise Apollonian stories become part of our identity and inform our supposedly cool decision-making (giving Apollo at least the illusion of having the upper hand).

Meanwhile, back in ancient Greece, Eros, the god of love was hard at work. Socrates recommended that to live happily, we should elevate our relationship with this fickle deity. First, we should rise above an attraction to beauty in a particular person and allow ourselves to be drawn to a more general picture of beauty and finally to the Idea of beauty itself as an archetype, with little erotic regard for mere mortal examples of it. We should try to move, in essence, from sexual attraction to a kind of contemplation. This is where the idea of 'platonic' love or attraction comes from. Not, of course, to everyone's taste.

Socrates wrote nothing down. We know of him only through the writings of Plato (hence 'Platonic'), his famous protégé. While we attribute the process of asking astute and probing questions to the older man, many of the ideas that emerge from his discussions are inseparable from Plato's thought. Plato, then, had much to say about the elevated, elusive Idea of things (such as beauty) that existed beyond the specific material examples that are scattered around our world. Plato doesn't hold these Ideas to be imaginary things. In fact, he says, the Idea of beauty is part of a realm *more real* than the beautiful things we see every day.

How can he mean this? In his famous analogy, he describes the things and qualities of our everyday world as if they were shadows cast on a back wall of a cave. We look at the shadows and mistake them for *real* things, but we miss the fact that they are mere umbrageous shapes and silhouettes. Plato believed it to be the job of philosophers to direct our attention towards the light and reveal the *true* objects creating the shadows. Comprehending these true objects – his Ideas – constituted the most authentic way of living. 'The Truth is Out There', as Mulder and Scully told us, and it is embodied in simmering, sublime concepts quite external to our limited everyday experience. We have to get beyond our normal way of seeing to apprehend them.

Plato still informs our notion of truth. Seeing what's real as something separate from our mere experience is built into the foundations of our two major ways of seeking truth: religion and science. Religion (at least our understanding of religion as laid out by St Augustine in the early fifth century) gives us a structure where God, grace, as well as beauty, truth, knowledge, justice and any other concepts we might care to identify with Him, exist quite *independently* of our own mortal soul-searching. Religious ethics are not about finding truth in our own value system but about learning how to see beyond the blinkered vision of our knowledge and grow closer to God. That Divinity embodies uncorrupted versions of those qualities we encounter here on Earth in the form of pale imitations. Truth is Out There, not In Here.

Science, despite being squarely opposed to religion, operates on the same principle. Scientific truth is not about looking within ourselves. The process of good science concerns itself with finding ways to bypass subjective experience and human error to describe as accurately as possible the 'Truth'. Whatever it is, it coolly operates Out There, independently of our value systems and biases.

The alternative approach would be to look for 'truth' subjectively. This happens when people turn to their feelings as evidence and regard empirical data as irrelevant. The two approaches will clash, for example, when one person passionately claims that a holistic remedy 'works' because her experience of it was positive, while another points out that it doesn't work on *enough* people to justify its claims. Subjective truth also comes into play when we consider matters of ultimate meaning and authenticity: we are more likely to look within ourselves (and our personal stories) than we are to turn to the pages of a textbook.

Meanwhile, this notion of elevating ourselves above individual attraction to a beautiful person may strike us as oddly detached and somehow wearyingly typical of the lofty and arid airs we expect from a philosopher. We probably see no point, for example, in trying to avoid attraction to an individual by looking beyond his or her personal beauty to the larger notion of Beauty itself. Yet, if we bring this idea down to Earth, we might see some advantages to what is being recommended.

For example, we can recognise what it is we like about somebody (some aspect of their beauty, or their goodness, or intelligence, or wit) and admire it as a quality quite separate from that particular person, rather than confusing it with him or her. We can learn from it, perhaps try to develop it in ourselves and know how to recognise it in others. We may also appreciate that those positive qualities continue to reside in a person even when they are annoying us and seem to have lost all their redeeming aspects. An ability to see beyond the individual may be of great therapeutic value if we find ourselves infatuated with someone. We are far less likely to come to idolise a person if we can recognise that what we admire about them are qualities that exist separately from the particular (and therefore flawed) example that they constitute. An appreciation of something like the Platonic Ideas (also known as 'Forms') can help us shed feelings of envy or unhealthy hero worship. In the same way that the Platonic Idea of, say, tree-ness is different from and so much better than any particular tree we may see (which will have branches missing and other imperfections), so a person will never embody the qualities we perceive in them as perfectly as we might imagine. While the loss of self that we feel when worshipping another can feel intoxicating (and appeal to that Dionysian side of us), there is no doubt that it can bring much pain when the all-too-human qualities of the targets of our obsessions become crushingly apparent.

At least that is the idea. While it may help us to see qualities as separate from their examples, it's asking a lot for us to forego such things as individual attraction and ponder instead the concept of Beauty. And I'm not sure it would make us happier. Part of the fun of sexual attraction is the intensity of idolising the object of our affections. It can allow us to find all aspects of them – how they wear their shoes, the glimpse of a tattoo, their choice of hairstyle – wildly sexy. In terms of *pleasure*, there's no contest. But Plato can help us: if we wish to take the sting out of a crush, there is no better way than getting to know its object. It isn't long before a range of imperfections make themselves known and we realise we are not dealing with an ideal Form but a mere shadow cast on the wall. Once our idealised impressions of a person are loosened up in this way, we can make better decisions regarding what to do about them.

The important point to remember is that Socratic happiness was about self-questioning and about appreciating the reality of an unseen world that lies beyond the physical realm. We might glimpse it through a process of contemplation and self-realisation. Happiness was indistinguishable from a rising above, a *virtuous* elevation, a higher plateau. This idea would stick around and bother us for a very long time.

Meanwhile, we were about to turn 180 degrees to start looking inwards for great and virtuous qualities.

Aristotle

After Socrates' death, the idea of happiness and virtue was developed and expanded by Aristotle, Plato's most famous pupil. He tutored Alexander the Great (who grew up to conquer the known world) and was the first great – and maybe the *greatest* – biologist and taxonomist, classifying and studying an enormous range of plants and animals. All forms of life seemed to fascinate him. He studied in Athens under Plato, though would later become Plato's strongest critic.

Plato, as we've just seen, had set out his ethical system whereby such ethical notions as goodness, virtue and justice were identified as far-off, objective concepts, known to us only by their pale imitations that we are able to perceive here on Earth. No amount of human introspection could bring us closer to these eternal truths; instead, it was the job of philosophers to see beyond the subjective nature of human experience and point us towards the reality that lies beyond what we perceive. Such things exist quite outside of ordinary human discernment, and in fact the latter only gets in the way of the eternal truths that might otherwise be revealed to us.

Aristotle's approach was different from Plato's, and far less lofty. He was very interested in life, and living, and his approach to ethics had none of the cool detachedness of the Platonist apprehending these sublime Ideals out there on some heavenly plane. Rather than the Truth being Out There, he encouraged us to look *inwards* to find out what matters most. His approach to happiness was more down to earth, and he had no time for the vertiginous, mystical touches of his tutor. In Raphael's famous fresco *The School of Athens*, Plato and Aristotle take centre stage, the former pointing to the sky and the latter to the ground.

In 335 BCE, Aristotle set up his school in the area known as the Lyceum, in Athens. His adherents were known as Peripatetics, which means 'walking up and down' – this may have derived from the *peripatos* or 'walking ground' in the Lyceum, or more endearingly from the fact that Aristotle liked to pace back and forth while lecturing.

Aristotle was interested in how we might *be* good, rather than *know* goodness. Thus when he taught ethics, his aim was to improve the lives of his pupils at a practical, everyday level. Like Plato, he saw the natural aim of human life, and the best condition of the soul, as *eudaimonia*, which is roughly synonymous with happiness, or more accurately 'flourishing'. But he had a different way of getting there. What should we have in place in our lives to secure this state?

Plato did not have the common touch; Aristotle did to a greater extent, and his ideas are more intuitive to us today. He points to the fact that we judge something to be good if it does well *the thing that it is uniquely designed to do*. For example, we say a shoemaker is good if he or she makes good shoes. Likewise, a good arm or leg is one that is strong and supple, and does its job of lifting or running successfully; a good eye is one that sees clearly. Goodness and proficiency lie in the successful execution of the unique function of that person or thing.

Likewise, people should learn to best fulfil their nature. But what do human beings *do* when they are being particularly successful at being human? What is our unique and therefore proper function, and therefore, Aristotle would say, the key to our happiness? In other words, what separates us from other forms of life? Aristotle supplies us with the answer: *reason*. What, then, is the highest aim of this reason? To ensure happiness. Success at being human would amount to the best, or most *virtuous*, use of reason. Flourishing – Aristotle's take on happiness – is 'an activity of the soul in accordance with virtue'.[22]

22 Aristotle, *Nicomachean Ethics,* Book i

Buried therein is another new thought: that there is an aim (or a *telos*) to human life. The *telos* is a goal to which human life should point, and one that will bestow goodness upon being reached. Aristotle suggests we are to fulfil what is highest in our nature, and rather than doing this in the way that Plato encourages (through the contemplation of lofty, eternal Ideas), we should instead use our reason to work out the best thing to do in the circumstances in which we find ourselves.

In fact, rather than tell us that we must overcome popular opinion of what happiness must be, Aristotle was happy to grant weight to and address it in his system. Believing that 'if a statement is true all the data are in harmony with it',[23] common perceptions of what happiness should entail were included in his ethical instructions. He was more charitably disposed towards the role of everyday pleasures in making us happy, and encouragingly looks for *balanced* qualities to ensure an ethical life. Thus virtue, according to Aristotle, could be found in balancing extreme qualities with their opposites: finding the *mean*.

For example: courage taken to an extreme is foolhardiness; its opposite is cowardliness. A virtuous person treads the middle path. Between licentiousness and asceticism lies temperance; between shyness and shamelessness lies modesty. Temperance and modesty, then, are amongst our virtues. Excessive behaviours tend to be easier to exhibit than virtues, so in order to tread the middle path we must practise well, as a musician practises his instrument, and be on our guard against temptations, our biases and our unhelpful tendencies. There is a sort of muscle-memory to ethics: we learn to act in a way that is appropriate until it comes naturally.

23 Ibid.

Working from intuitive 'common sense', Aristotle thus built on Plato's ethics to form a longer list of cardinal virtues: justice, courage, temperance, magnificence, magnanimity, liberality, gentleness, prudence and wisdom.

So happiness is now to be found in virtuous activity of the soul carried out in accordance with reason. The best sort of virtuous activity, Aristotle still suggests despite the common touch of his approach, is that of contemplation. The ability to devote ourselves to intellectual pursuits is what makes us unique and therefore connects us to the gods, and thus contemplation is divine.

'Virtuous activity.' Virtue may seem to us to be a very outmoded concept. As, to many, does the concept of 'the soul'. This latter term we can mentally substitute with 'the innermost person', though I quite enjoy the no-fuss employment of 'soul'. This was an age when such a thing was meant without any implication of religious dogma, millennia of which since are unfortunately responsible for our uneasiness with the word today. Despite this, we are certainly every bit at home with the idea of our innermost self as we were in Aristotle's time.

'Virtue', however, appears to the modern mind's eye in only faint adumbrations of knightly incorruptibility. We rarely talk of people today in terms of their goodness or their virtue. We might describe someone as an 'upstanding pillar of the community', but such a cliché does not seem to touch upon the inner life of that person; in fact, it even has about it the whiff of potential scandal. But the original notion of virtue, since developed and debated by philosophers, religions and psychologists over the years, is quite different from the implications of courtly or virginal decorum it later absorbed during the Middle Ages. And here we first have it, spoken of rationally and pragmatically as part of a guide for living.

There is something powerful in the idea that we recognise reason as something unique in ourselves, something that separates us from the animals, and that our aim should be to bring that to its most virtuous completion. According to Aristotle, we can enjoy trivial pleasures, but these should only be in preparation for activities in accordance with virtue. He believed that human beings are meant for greater things, and that a certain joy comes from fulfilling what is best and most noble in our nature.

Perhaps Aristotle's vision for happiness seems like too much hard work. Most of the time we prefer to watch television or browse the Net to take our minds off our worries. These anaesthetics certainly seem to do the job, but what happens when numbing diversions are not enough? When we lie awake in the early hours, resenting some situation or other in our life? The experiencing self might have been happy with a few hours of gaming to distract it from the niggling annoyances left over from a work colleague's promotion, a partner's refusal to help with the dishes, or our useless display before someone we were eager to impress. Yet the remembering self forms an excruciating narrative in which we have let ourselves down or been unfairly treated. When others sleep, it of course likes to vividly replay those stories, enthusiastically alerting us to each and every agonising detail.

If we hope for something deeper in life than distraction, we might note that our remembering, story-forming self needs a narrative of happiness in the same way our experiencing self requires its pleasures. And here we might find that we sleep more peacefully if we see our lives as part of Aristotle's *telos*, as a work in progress, one in which we could view daily irritations as a kind of test;

one which teaches us virtue and where we can, step by step, and by considering the variables of each situation as it happens, move towards being a better (happier, kinder, more fulfilled) version of ourselves. We are in the realm here of the 'considered life' and the possibility of serenity that such a life can offer. People take longer-lasting pleasure from being kind to others than having others be kind to them; likewise, there is a deeper happiness to be had in knowing that your life is part of a story of flourishing than there is in merely pursuing entertainment.

Aristotle described his ethical system in his *Nicomachean Ethics*, which he wrote for his son. It's an engaging read, surprisingly immediate and accessible in a way that many of these ancient texts are. This was an era when ethical philosophy existed only to provoke real changes in real people, and the language used was not only agreeable but very often medicinal. Doctors would heal the body, and philosophers were there to heal the mind.

There are other qualities about Aristotle's approach that are worth noting here. Firstly, like Socrates, his method of teaching about the good life was to engage his pupils in a *discussion*. His was not the role of an authoritarian instructor. Instead, he encouraged discourse, and the students completed the ethical instruction by taking what they had learnt and contributing further to it by thought and application in their own lives. Through this dialectic, back-and-forth process, the classes could sift through and identify the most pertinent issues. Using an analogy of an archer before a target, Aristotle believed that ethical enquiry could allow us to see our target more clearly. The aim was not to *identify* the target as such, but to allow us to discriminate better and see more clearly. This approach sits well with the notion of pupils continuing their own instruction through engagement in rational argument and self-discovery. They might then come to identify differing targets for themselves, having developed the keen archer's eye through their study.

In particular – and this will be important later when comparing his approach to the other major schools – he felt that an attachment to things for their own sake was a healthy part of the good life. A certain amount of anger when, for example, a loved one is threatened, would be a sign of virtue: too much would be excessive, and to show none at all would suggest an effeminacy or spinelessness that was not a part of the noble life. Prerequisites for a good life included good health, a certain amount of wealth and a certain measure of intellect. This was a much more pragmatic and relaxed approach to attachment than would follow in subsequent schools.

Aristotle also felt strongly that virtue requires action; mere noble intentions are not enough. We are social creatures; a solitary life is not worth living. Our personal happiness, then, was linked to the welfare of the community. With a population consisting of individuals engaged with thinking and discriminating and working out for themselves the best way to live as social creatures, a flourishing, democratic society could be expected to grow. He saw his philosopher's task as one of defining, and defending, his vision of *eudaimonia* so that it could be used to guide social planning and create a happier society. Today, as our governments implement psychological 'nudges' to improve our diet and make us happier and healthier, we are engaging with an Aristotelian mode.

But did Aristotle do the job well enough? It is a testament to the power of his thinking that we do find some of his ideas rather obvious today. It means they've lasted this long and become part of our modern way of understanding. He was the first person of note in history to consider these questions and bring his answers together to form a system with anything like the level of detailed comprehension it has.

Yet, somehow, it seems to lack real transformative power, and I think the reasons for this are twofold, though related.

Firstly, Aristotle's system is unashamedly a celebration of *reason*. The application of rational thinking separates us from the animals and allows us to fulfil our unique nature: that thing for which we were designed. Mastery over our ignoble qualities – a major key to a flourishing, happy life – is to be reached through clear-sightedness (as one might need for effective archery), debate and education. It is, as the modern philosopher Martha Nussbaum describes it, as if our innermost self were a clear shallow pool, where our qualities and emotions are visible and readily accessible. This does not seem to connect with our modern understanding, in which we perceive our emotional realm to inhabit far murkier, deeper waters. We are not as susceptible to rational enquiry – least of all our own – as Aristotle would like to believe. His system, we might note as moderns, does not take into account the turbid domain of the unconscious.

A second grievance regarding Aristotle might be found in his elitist presumptions about *who* can be taught the route to the good life. A prerequisite was a suitably receptive character, which is why his Lyceum was open only to men, and men who had already received an education.

Just as a piece of land has to be prepared beforehand if it is to nourish the seed, so the mind of the pupil

117

has to be prepared in its habits if it is to enjoy and dislike the right things.[24]

This amounts to an elitist view of happiness; it is certainly not something that is open to everyone. How different this is from our modern sense of universal entitlement. Children, women, the uneducated and slaves were seen as a lost cause. Can that be right? Or should an effective route to happiness be, by its nature, open to all?

The next wave of philosophers certainly thought so. The good life needed to be thrown open to everyone. And many of Aristotle's presumptions – which might seem rather straightforward to us today – were overturned in the search for what offers the happiest life possible. And amongst the radical new systems that developed are some life-changing tools that we can embrace today as powerful alternatives to the woefully inadequate techniques of the modern self-help industry.

The Epicureans and Stoics

After Aristotle, philosophers seemed eager to break away from his elitist model and find ways of bringing happiness to more people. The twin schools of Epicureanism and Stoicism sought to do that and, as I've already mentioned, became hugely popular schools of thought for a long time. The rigour with which they approached the question of the good life has not since been surpassed, and it is from their world of thought that we are going to find many of our answers.

Epicurus, the founder of the first school (which bears his name), was a very early atomist, with no time for

24 Aristotle, *Nicomachean Ethics*, Book x

mysticism. He controversially believed that everything was made up of tiny particles flying invisibly through space. Happiness, he said, was a question of *tranquillity*, and good and evil were no more than a matter of pleasure and pain; to live well was about maximising the first and minimising the second. In fact, one could live by referral to a sort of rational calculus: would an act bring me more pain or pleasure? Thus, indulgence in fine food and drink might be what we associate with a modern 'epicurean', but original Epicureans rejected them. This was because such extravagance or intemperance was seen as tending to eventually cause more pain (hangover, illness, frustrated desire for further luxuries) than the fleeting pleasure they might provide in the moment. Epicureans lived a simple, ascetic life, believing that by limiting themselves to a few natural desires (such as friendship, bread and water), they would be far happier than those who finally bring pain upon themselves through entertaining greater needs.

Situated outside of Athens amongst the olive groves and shut off from the world by a surrounding wall, the Garden home of the first Epicurean community was an embodiment of its lack of interest in the outside world. Above the gate, a sign read, 'Strangers, here you will do well to linger; here, our highest good is pleasure'. Despite Epicurus's prolific literary output, he did not share Aristotle's vision of transforming society. Instead, he chose to opt out, and in some ways the Garden became a prototype for the hippie communes of the 1960s and other cooperatives that have existed since all over the world. And this combination of admission to women, physical seclusion and focus on pleasure gave his detractors grounds for accusations of licentiousness and general naughtiness.

Epicurus's teaching represents a major step forward from Aristotle in one particular area. Aristotle, as we know, treated human emotions as a shallow clear pool, fully accessible to the trained intellect and amenable to change through rational, dialectical scrutiny. Since the time of Freud, we have known that to be an incomplete image of how we operate psychologically. In Epicureanism, we see an early glimmer of something else: an appreciation of the unconscious. Aristotle presumed that his pupils would be able to articulate their desires and concerns; Epicurus, by means of contrast, required his new converts to open their hearts and talk through what they did and didn't understand, touching on the content of their dreams and quiet moments alone. This process sounds strikingly similar to what we would expect from a modern psychotherapy session. He also had his pupils use memorisation and repetition to absorb his teachings in their training, rather than encourage them to arrive at conclusions for themselves through the respectful, protracted debate encouraged in Aristotle's Lyceum. The use of these techniques points to an understanding of the mind's automatic and non-rational processes. Affecting change here is not about discussion and mere intellectual engagement; it is a question of internalising certain principles unquestioningly. Epicurus was keen for his pupils to have useful slogans at the ready so that they could deal with adversity or disturbance without recourse to detailed thought or study; again we see an early appreciation of a non-rational technique that infuses much of self-help today.

The Epicureans of the Garden chose to pursue pleasures and avoid pain. Yet pleasures were *rationally* chosen, so that they would not ultimately lead to misery. The point was to achieve happiness, which was identical to a life of pleasure and the avoidance of pain. This 'happiness' came in the form of tranquillity, or *ataraxia*. There was no need for the type of ethical enquiry one would find at

Aristotle's Lyceum; such 'cultivation', it was believed, could not do us any good. Where Plato pointed to a purified, shimmering ideal of Reason (we remember how he said that the concepts that touch us in our daily lives are tawdry reflections of a pure, idealised version of the true Ideas that exist on a higher plane), Epicurus tells us we have nothing more than our animalistic bodily senses to put to use. And if we pay attention to what they tell us, we will find that the good life, of the highest pleasure, also happens to be the simplest.

Stoicism – founded by Zeno of Citium and named after the Stoa, the covered walkway in the Athenian marketplace where this new philosophy was expounded – also saw happiness in terms of tranquillity and, like Epicureanism, its approach centred on ensuring the absence of pain. Stoics taught, along with the Epicureans, that we should limit our desires, and that perceived problems in life are due to errors in judgement about those problems. If we change our attitude, the pain of those external factors can disappear. This may sound familiar to modern minds acquainted with the notion of 'reframing' a problem as an opportunity, and it is one of the Stoics' most powerful and prevailing ideas. We will discuss how we can put such notions to good use later in the book.

Both schools of thought are ascetic to one degree or another in that they require a turning away from what might be seen as the common pleasures of life. The Stoics were, however, far more engaged in society than the Epicureans. The latter removed themselves from civil life and lived communally in walled 'gardens', whereas Stoics by contrast were active, politically engaged and far more concerned with being effective members of society. Later, Christians drew upon the Stoic ideal of the good citizen

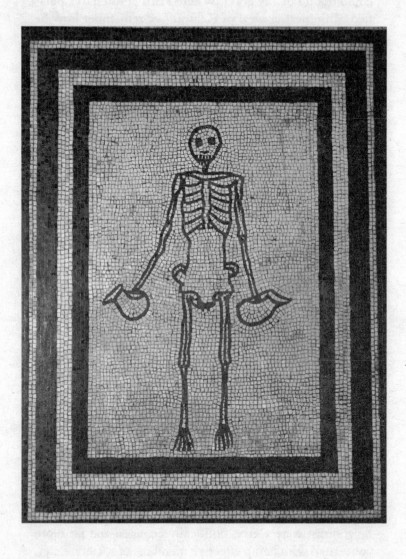

in their own ideation of the dutiful Christian as an active and productive member of the community.

Stoicism grew during a time of Hellenic wars and uncertainty, and its recipe for detaching from anxiety would have been very appealing. Strife, though, can take many forms, and the philosophy remains robust as an approach to dealing with the problems that fortune flings at us. Cicero, the great Roman orator and statesman, later translated Stoic teaching into Latin and ensured its popularity for centuries to come. The greatest names in Stoicism – Seneca, Epictetus, Marcus Aurelius – all come from the Roman period, by which point the school had left behind some of its early interest in the intricacies of logic and cosmology and become a powerful handbook for living in troubled times. More than any other ancient school of thought, Stoicism has proved enduring, and today many movements exist to encourage people to think deeply about it and apply it to their lives.

Although the Stoics and Epicureans offered their brand of happiness to all, it was still clear that few would reach any plateau of enlightenment. The Stoics spoke reverently of the 'sage', who was an embodiment of their wisdom and a role model for the journeyman in the art of tranquillity. For example, it was said a Stoic sage would be able to happily endure torture on the rack because he would think to himself, 'It isn't me they are harming, just my body.' While this sounds extreme, and indeed was seen as such by many in their day, there's no doubt that this kind of thinking has managed to keep some prisoners and victims of torture sane in modern times. In *Philosophy For Life*, Jules Evans talks to several people who have found themselves in such extreme situations and drawn on the principles of Stoicism to tolerate their crises.

Christianity

The semi-mystical, semi-fictitious figure of the sage was to figure in the next development in the story of happiness as Christianity exploded into the human story. Two huge shifts occurred with it that have affected views of happiness ever since. Firstly, as McMahon explains in *The Pursuit of Happiness*, the attainment of perfect happiness ceased to be a concern of the here and now and became something that would happen in the far-off future. In Heaven, or after the *parousia* (the Second Coming), happiness beckoned to us from just over the distant horizon. No longer was it to be measured in a lifespan; now it was the stuff of eternity.

Secondly, and closely connected with this first paradigm shift, we were told we should *suffer now* to obtain this happiness *later*. In fact, rather than avoid suffering as the Stoics and Epicureans taught, we were now instructed to embrace it as a sign of holiness.

It's hard to overestimate the impact that these new ideas have had on our culture ever since. They were seismic developments, and their legacy surfaced repeatedly over the next two thousand years. The cool rationality of the ancients was replaced by a more sensual, ecstatic vision of heavenly pleasure, and in a strange topsy-turvy twist, distress and pain were laid down as the route to get there. This was a powerful message to the suffering and an appealing promise to the meek and downtrodden.

Perhaps for the first time in history – at least since Socrates, who had first raised the question – we no longer had to *think* about how to be happy. The recipe for a meaningful life and all the reward we could wish for was now handed to us on a plate. Socratic questioning was redundant; we now need only believe in God, accept what we were told and live accordingly. Previously, reason had been seen as the greatest quality of the human being, and the key to our *telos*, our goal as a race. It had been celebrated as the feature that makes us unique on this Earth. Now, rational enquiry would become *dangerous*. Religious belief held sway, which meant all curiosity had to be reduced or silenced along with any other schools of thought. Thus a gulf sprang up between religious thinking and the way we normally try to find out what's true. The Romans would have been dazzled by this new deity that was immune to logic, defied rational thinking and cared only for what was in our hearts. Two thousand years later, we maintain a popular suspicion of the cool-minded. We recognise in any blockbuster film that the emotionally detached character with an English accent and a well-stocked bookcase (or clinical environment) must be the villain. He might 'mastermind' the destruction of many people for a supreme goal born from ice-cold logic. Characters typically played by Alan Rickman (or Anthony Hopkins, Tom Hiddleston, Ralph Fiennes, Peter Cushing, Christopher Lee, Benedict Cumberbatch, Tilda Swinton and many others) are the legacy of that new religion. The movie's hero, by contrast, will commonly 'follow his heart', choosing only love and self-sacrifice. As a rule he will exist alone, transform those around him, literally or figuratively descend into death and rise again transfigured. And if at the end he can fly off into the sky, he will. (We may owe *Superman* and *E.T.* to Jewish film directors, but there's no doubting that it's the Christian story we're being told.)

Despite the fact that religion claimed to provide the answers to the universe and dispense with the need for further rational enquiry, it was still the case that *within* the religion there was to be much tortuous discussion about what happiness could mean to the believer. The Christian

125

view of happiness was to undergo various developments from theologians over the next thousand years.

The first major evolution was to come through the work of St Augustine in the fourth century. He felt that the Stoics' man-made efforts to achieve happiness were an affront to our existence as mortals who are no longer at one with our Maker. We *cannot* be truly happy, because we desire a perfect unity with God that we are unable to achieve in this life. The idea that we could achieve true happiness through the sort of techniques taught by the Stoics was tantamount to heresy.

Why are we unable to make this connection with God? Because of the Fall. Augustine developed the doctrine of original sin and with it cast humanity as forever alienated from the Divine. Adam and Eve were thrown out of the Garden of Eden for disobeying God, and every person in every generation has paid for their transgression since, throughout the history of humanity, by being born inherently bad. Our inability to heal that eternally broken relationship with God means that our fate is predestined; whether we are eventually reconciled with God in the next life, or otherwise, is a decision He has already made before we were born.

Original sin is a profoundly toxic picture; I cannot imagine a more damaging story for a culture to create for itself than the idea that every one of its members is inherently evil. Of course it serves a purpose: as a piece of mythology it encourages us to strive for good and find unison with goodness. But more straightforwardly, it is one of those extraordinarily life-denying ideas that can only be dreamt up by religion. Remaining part of our cultural narrative, it has extended its tendrils into many familiar modern tales. Snow White, of course, ingests the forbidden fruit and loses her childlike innocence; we see

elements of the Fall today in the tortured stories of Kafka, whose characters awake already condemned to a primal, unspecified guilt. (His hero Gregor Samsa, of course, has an apple thrown into his side by an angry father.) It is a common trope in horror films and macabre stories; *The Exorcist*, *The Omen* and *Rosemary's Baby* come to mind as iconic movies born from guilt around sex and progeniture, which are ultimately inseparable from the notion of an ineluctable malevolence that grips us from birth. I could offer a long list of horror films that exploit this theme; at the time of writing, David Robert Mitchell's *It Follows* stands out as a recent and very effective example of the subgenre.

Original sin is explicitly at the heart of Hitler's demonising of the Jewish race, as a few excerpts from *Mein Kampf* illustrate:

> For the original sin committed in Paradise has always been followed by the expulsion of the guilty parties . . .
>
> The sin against blood and race is the hereditary sin in this world and it brings disaster on every nation that commits it . . .
>
> They ought to put an end to this truly original sin of racial corruption which is steadily being passed on from one generation to another.

We can even sense the vestiges of original sin in the way we tend to interpret Darwin's theory of natural selection. The underlying narrative of Augustine's doctrine, when removed from its specifically Christian context, is as follows: our beginnings are bestial, primitive and depraved, and we move gradually towards an exalted state of perfection. Likewise, natural selection, as we tend to see it, takes us from the lowly origins of our animal state 'to the very summit of the organic scale'[25]. We easily presume that a kind of ascendancy is at work through evolution, and thus Darwin's system is often (and unfairly) construed through the value filter of the Augustinian mode. Nazism, along with other movements that favour the strong over the weak (such as eugenics, racism, fascism and imperialism), are products of what became known by its opponents as *social Darwinism*, namely the profoundly questionable application of the biological theory to sociology and politics. Creationists, in fact, often point to social Darwinism as a logical consequence of natural selection, though this is an error. Ironically for these religious critics, the connection between the two emerges in large part due to the story of the Fall. It still, almost two thousand years after Augustine, echoes insidiously around us and ascribes a narrative of emerging supremacy to what should be a value-free biological theory.

At the level of individual human beings, the work of the pioneering psychoanalyst Sigmund Freud in the early twentieth century is also permeated with ideas of our unclean, destructive, aggressively sexual infantile stages developing into a 'healthy' adult ideal. We will catch up with Freud later in this chapter, but in the meantime we once again owe the idea of 'being born bad' to St Augustine. It has never been entirely cleared from our consciousness.

Aristotle reborn

The doctrine proved so oppressive, in fact, that it prompted later theologians to make careful efforts to find ways

---

25 Charles Darwin, *The Descent of Man*

whereby we *could* come to know happiness through our own earthly strivings. Such an idea, though, was in danger of being heretical, so these thinkers had to tread delicately.

The revolution took place in the thirteenth century, when the works of Aristotle (which had been preserved by Eastern thinkers throughout this time) were rediscovered and translated in the West. A Dominican friar called Thomas Aquinas brought back and 'Christianised' the pagan philosopher, making him suitable for modern pious reading. In the process, he revised Augustine's gloomy picture of a perpetually alienated, fallen human race by incorporating Aristotle's more optimistic vision and, ultimately, a place for happiness on Earth. This worldly happiness, which Aquinas called *felicitas*, was an imperfect version of the sublime euphoria that awaits us in the afterlife, which in turn he labelled *beatitudo*. To assist in our Christian journey on Earth, Aquinas gave us the theological virtues of faith, hope and charity, drawn from Aristotle's natural virtues.

Now Christian life allowed for a sense of striving and working towards a better life in God. As interest in Aristotle spread, so did the notion that happiness in this world could be at least partly attained by the efforts of humanity. The Aristotelian *telos* (the idea that human life moves forward towards a goal) had returned, and we could now look gladly forwards rather than only backwards to Adam's shame; there was now an acceptance of the idea that we might employ our virtue to move towards happiness. God was no longer the austere figure of pre-destination; He now bestows Grace, and allows us to experience *felicitas* in our lives while moving towards our true reward in Heaven.

The Renaissance

After this rediscovery of Aristotle, an interest in other classical authors developed and with it a new movement of humanism emerged. As long as it was understood to happen under the auspices of God's Grace, it was now acceptable to talk about people being able to shape their lives through human reason and intelligence.

How bizarre to imagine this as a new thought for the Western world to take on board, and what a fascinatingly elaborate means of getting there. Religion had thrown rational investigation out of the house; now the two were trying to find a way to peacefully cohabit. This was the great idea that led to the Renaissance of the fifteenth and sixteenth centuries: a wide series of cultural movements that swept the world, celebrating the dignity of man. Thomas Aquinas's suggestion that happiness could be (albeit imperfectly) enjoyed in this world was now being more boldly proclaimed, and thinkers and artists looked back to the pre-Christian, classical era of the Greeks and Romans as a golden age of reason and beauty. As Darrin McMahon elegantly points out, it was at this time that smiles began to appear on secular subjects in portraits. The *Mona Lisa*'s enduring twinkle from that era marks something of a watershed in developing attitudes towards happiness. Da Vinci was giving expression to humanity's beaming new self-confidence.

But it wasn't to last. It wasn't long before religion again led the backlash, but this time not quite as disastrously. Man, it seemed to the sixteenth-century monk Martin Luther, was becoming arrogant and heretical, considering himself free and impiously in charge of his destiny. Aquinas, it seems, had sown a dangerous seed, and Luther's Reformation movement was in part a return

to St Augustine's bleaker vision of the human race living under the dark shadow of the Fall.

At the same time, the Reformation brought us our modern emphasis on *personal faith* as a means of salvation, which was a reaction against the excesses of the Catholic Church and the implication that one could buy one's way into God's favour. Importantly, Luther declared our search for happiness – as long as it took place within an awareness of our sinful nature – to be righteous. Following Luther, faith and hard work now held the key to salvation, and we had finally rid ourselves of the love of suffering for its own sake.

The Enlightenment

So for a millennium and a half, well-being had been viewed as something indistinguishable from our relationship with God, the ultimate wellspring of happiness. It remained a tricky matter of theology interrupted by the cautious optimism of the Renaissance. The seventeenth century now steered us tentatively towards the humanist ideal once again, in readiness for the cultural eruption of the Enlightenment. John Locke, the English philosopher, put forward a controversial template for humanity, saying that we simply form our ideas through contemplation, comparing the human mind to a blank slate. It might seem uncontroversial to us today, but this thought – that we shape our thoughts and drives *ourselves* – did away with the need for original sin and the notion that moral momentum had its origin in God. As, indeed, did Locke's daring idea that we are propelled through life by nothing more than an impetus towards pleasure and away from pain, and that we should make our decisions by calculating the balance of both. There is an echo of Epicurus in this rational, materialist approach to making ethical choices. Our lives, Locke said, reminding us of that hedonic treadmill first recognised by the ancients, are coloured by an 'uneasiness' that leaves us always wanting something new.

God has been all but removed from the picture. We can quantify good by weighing up the practical results of our actions, without prayer or reference to Holy Scripture. Locke's view was potentially blasphemous, suggesting that all goodness was subjective and that there was no need for divine-inspired morality. Most likely for this reason he cautiously added a recommendation that in making our choices we should *prefer* the path to God and his promise of everlasting life, citing it as the best 'bargain' and economically the most sensible approach to happiness. But this feels like a half-hearted and impious addendum, and not surprisingly it paved the way for later thinkers to entertain the idea that we could enjoy happiness without *any* recourse to God whatsoever. Finally, after two thousand years, we were getting ready to release ourselves from the trammels of religion.

These extraordinary new thoughts culminated in the Enlightenment of the late seventeenth and eighteenth centuries. During this period, huge cultural changes swept across the Western world, celebrating the power of human reason and the possibilities of science. For the first time, rather than worrying about how to be reconciled with God, the question in the air was how to be *happy*. We could finally return to Socrates' project, started two thousand years before, since hijacked by religion and replaced by fear.

The answer to how we might find happiness was simple: through pleasure and through human effort. No longer did we need to look to God's plan; we could claim our destiny as happy individuals through our own work. Any mysticism surrounding the notion of happiness was firmly replaced by talk of pleasure and agreeable sensations. Coupled with this, we saw a surge in agriculture, the building of cities and the development of a consumer culture. People were living longer and were looking to spend more. Existence was no longer a struggle; life was plain sailing, and human reason was at the helm. One might dress in the latest fashions or walk in one of the many new pleasure gardens. London's Vauxhall, that modern den of Uranian merrymaking, still boasts its pleasure gardens from that time, and Tom Brown's *Amusements* from 1700 suggests a venue notorious for its intrigue: 'Both sexes meet, and mutually serve one another as guides to lose their way.' I note that when the gardens were leased in 1728 to the Tyers, a Ham Room was established there, serving the eponymous meat at a thinness of slice that was apparently proverbial. 'A journal of 1762,' according to Warwick Wroth in his *The London Pleasure Gardens of the Eighteenth Century*, 'complains that you could read the newspaper through a slice of Tyers' ham or beef.' Thackeray himself described the ham as 'almost invisible'. Times have changed: nowadays, sympathetic Londoners will know that the area confesses a density of meat to rival Smithfield Market.

This seismic shift in our relationship to happiness was the most important since Christianity replaced the ancients' celebration of reason with belief. And of course the Enlightenment signalled a return to the Stoic view that we could advance ourselves through our own effort.

It's one thing to proudly replace belief with knowledge, and Divine Grace with human endeavour; it's quite another to do away with the effects of two millennia steeped in the Christian narrative. What tends to happen when a culture suddenly turns in a new direction is that the old *variables* get replaced with new ones, while the deep *structure* of the old regime remains. It reminds me of when we move out of our parents' home, perhaps to go to university. We have spent our lives, until that point, feeling like a child. We have a clear place within the familial structure. Finally, we break away from that framework with some pride, feeling like independent adults for the first time. We proclaim our independence. Yet, as we head out into this new world, supposedly overturning and breaking away, we unconsciously look to recreate what we know. We look for new role models and authority figures to replace our parents. In the same way that we always take ourselves with us on our holidays, and suffer the disappointment of our unavoidable presence, so too do we move away from family but remain the same child. 'Everywhere you go,' the Zen saying goes, 'there you are.' And of course the act of rebelling against something is still dependent on that thing to define the terms of mutiny.

So in many ways the Enlightenment was a product of the religious model it so proudly overcame. The striving towards the rewards of Heaven was now replaced with the notion of progress towards a secular kind of salvation: discoveries of science that awaited us and which would lead us to a promised land. The old model was still recognisable, with God removed and reason placed firmly in the remaining gap.

It was only a matter of time before we would ditch Locke's careful proviso that the Christian path might be best for us. The job was eventually done by another English philosopher, Jeremy Bentham. He drew on Locke's ideas, dispensing with his religious clause, to found

Utilitarianism, which equated goodness with the ability to bring the greatest happiness to the greatest number of people. From this starting point, Bentham attempted to set out a rigorous categorisation of pleasures and pains, and thus to create a precise means of measuring the balance of both, taking into account such criteria as the duration, intensity and purity of each. This permitted us to identify the 'goodness' of any act. This confidence that happiness could be encapsulated in the precise language of science is typical of Enlightenment bravado. Before Bentham, other thinkers had made similar attempts. Francis Hutcheson, in his 1725 *Inquiry into the Original of Our Ideas of Beauty and Virtue*, arrived at a felicific calculus offering us a formula for happiness. McMahon offers it in his history:

$M = (B+S) \times A = BA + SA$; therefore $BA = M - SA = M - I$, and $B = (M - I)/A$. In the latter case, $M = (B - S) \times A = BA - SA$; therefore $BA = M + SA = M = I$, and $B = (M = I)/A$

Where B = Benevolence, M = Moment of Good, I = Interest, S = Self-Love, and A = Ability.

Although we can see in this Enlightenment period a general swing towards some of the broad tenets of the Stoics and Epicureans, the above misguided formula illustrates that much of the sophistication of ancient thought had been lost. Instead, troubling questions started to emerge: if all happiness is subjective, and goodness merely a question of calculating how much happiness a certain act might bring, then what of virtue? Is goodness really to be found in the mere balance of pleasure? With no divine breath to animate and steer us, is man

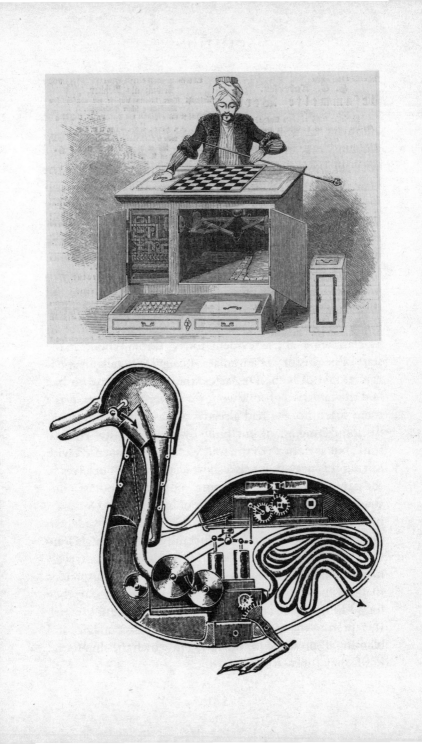

no more than a kind of automaton, a machine without a soul?

Not surprisingly, then, this was the era of the great automata, of Vaucanson's defecating duck and the chess-playing Turk. We became obsessed with mechanical life, with the power of clockwork and its ability to counterfeit creation. My own love of facsimile makes this a dear moment in history to me. My stage show *Svengali* drew from this era's *idée fixe*; its clockwork titular hero now resides in a secret room in my house, occasionally tapping out eerie messages for guests.

The questions left by the new godless vision of human potential and a new emphasis on public amusement found themselves conflated in the presentation of these uncanny entertainments, which would have had about them an air of blasphemy not as evident today. Gaby Wood, at the start of her history of automata, *Living Dolls*, tells an apoc-ryphal tale of René Descartes, the philosopher who had laid the tentative groundwork for understanding man as a mere machine. He had already said as much of animals, distinguishing mankind only by means of its 'rational soul', but as notions of the soul were being dispensed with during this period, it was a short leap to view ourselves in the same category of whirring, pumping, godless con-traptions as brute beasts. In Wood's anecdote, Descartes had been summoned by Queen Christina of Sweden to discuss philosophy and was reluctantly undertaking a long sea voyage to reach her shore. He was supposedly travel-ling with his daughter, but when the ship's crew, suspicious that they had never seen her, decided to seek her out, they found in her place an automaton, built to resemble a girl. Interpreting the machine as evidence of dark magic, and blaming its presence for the storm in which the ship found itself, they threw it overboard.

We had become godless in theory, but it would be a long while before we would trust such diabolical flaunting of irreverence. You may be faintly amused by the 'magical thinking' behind the sailors' ascribing of sinister powers to this inanimate automaton. Similarly today, non-believers might scoff at religious people who believe that sacred statues and other icons supernaturally connect them to the divinities for whom such objects stand as mystic avatars. But we are still prone to the same superstitious thinking. To appreciate this, try taking a knife and repeatedly stabbing a photograph of a loved one, and preferably one who has recently passed away. You'll soon appreciate the power of the graven image.

Perhaps it's no surprise to learn that once we had equated happiness with pleasure, compared man with machine, and located virtue in a series of felicific calculations, we started to feel something was missing in the new vision. We required, of course, a measure of spirituality, which we had dispensed too proudly along with the tyranny and superstition of religious authority. In the future, post-Enlightenment movements would seek to provide that absent component, which of course would largely amount to secular renderings of the cosmic answers that religion had previously provided. Again, I think of the young man leaving home for the first time and looking for substitutes for the authority figures he so proudly leaves behind. The language is different, but the yearnings are largely the same.

Thus, to continue with McMahon's overview, the French Revolution ostensibly sought to replace Christianity with a worldly substitute. Yet it combined, in its vision of happiness, aspects of the Christian model along with a Stoic emphasis on human effort. Like Marx's later model, it amounted to a communal vision, in contrast to the Enlightenment's usual focus on individual happiness. Draped in classical apparel, with its mobilisation of the underclasses and emphasis on a far-off vision of happiness, the Revolution had about it the indisputable air of its religious ancestry. The Kingdom of God was substituted by the golden vision of the new Republic.

So, prior to the Enlightenment, we might say we had tried to draw upon our own resources to achieve happiness, without being guilty of heresy in the face of God's plan. The secular revolution of the Enlightenment has since produced a number of attempts to *replace* God with a satisfying godless vision that might provide us with a sense of meaning and a new understanding of the old notion of virtue. This is not surprising, as it is the very nature of religion that it furnishes us with comfortable answers, and without it the business of finding meaning in life becomes more complex and personal. It is then not so much that we have a 'God-shaped hole' within us, as I was fond in my religious youth of insisting, but that there lurks within us something of Locke's 'uneasiness', a perennial desire for satisfaction that takes place at the metaphysical level as well as the everyday and material. We have a 'meaning-shaped hole' because we are story-forming creatures, and stories should not meander without a point.

America, meanwhile, had created a new culture of equality and aspiration based on the Enlightenment principles of life, liberty and the pursuit of happiness. As we've seen, the political commentator Alexis de Tocqueville was quick to point out the discontent and restlessness to which the hurried attempts to appropriate happiness were leading in that country. This was happening amongst people who found themselves on a playing field more level in terms of resources and opportunities than ever before. He wrote:

> In America I saw the freest and most enlightened men placed in the happiest circumstances that the world affords, it seemed to me as if a cloud habitually hung upon their brow, and I thought them serious and almost sad, even in their pleasures . . . It is strange to see with what feverish ardour the Americans pursue their own welfare, and to watch the vague dread that constantly torments them lest they should not have chosen the shortest path which may lead to it.[26]

Equality had ushered in its own set of frustrations. On a more positive note, the republicanism of the New World brought with it an emphasis on civic virtue and a moral sense of self-mastery and benevolence that Tocqueville applauded, along with a 'spirit of religion' that nonetheless encouraged an enjoyment of happiness and prosperity here on Earth. Virtue, rather than being unaccounted for, was coming to be identified with a kind of social welfare.

Moving on to the nineteenth century, John Stuart Mill, the English Utilitarian, lost faith in the idea of happiness as our ultimate human goal. What should replace it? What could be more valuable than happiness? His preference was for *liberty*, which might even come at the expense of our felicity. Instead of adhering to the pious, demanding Calvinism that had developed from Lutherism, and instead of blindly following the levelling spirit of capitalism that prevailed, Mill advocated

26 Alexis de Tocqueville, *Democracy in America*

that we concentrate on *self*-realisation and *personal* freedom:

> He who lets the world, or his own portion of it, choose his plan of life for him, has no need of any other faculty than the ape-like one of imitation. He who chooses his plan for himself, employs all his faculties. He must use observation to see, reasoning and judgement to foresee, activity to gather materials for decision, discrimination to decide, and when he has decided, firmness and self-control to hold to his deliberate decision . . . Human nature is not a machine to be built after a model, and set to do exactly the work prescribed for it, but a tree, which requires to grow and develop itself on all sides, according to the tendency of the inward forces which make it a living thing.[27]

Mill is advocating human potential, a vision of blossoming and spreading out, and the calling upon of our intelligence and dignity to realise it. His vision is not just a call to develop eccentricity. In one of my favourite passages of his, this development of the self is a call to enrich our race:

> It is not by wearing down into uniformity all that is individual in themselves, but by cultivating it, and calling it forth, within the limits imposed by the rights and interests of others, that human beings become a noble and beautiful object of contemplation; and as the works partake the character of those who do them, by the same process human

27 John Stuart Mill, *On Liberty*

144

life becomes rich, diversified, and animating, fur-
nishing more abundant aliment [nourishment] to
high thoughts and elevating feelings, and strengthening the tie which binds every individual to the
race, by making the race infinitely better worth
belonging to. In proportion to the development of
his individuality, each person becomes more valuable to himself, and is therefore capable of being
more valuable to others.[28]

Mill's vision for us is helpful when we feel that we are
unable to fit in, when we view our separateness with
embarrassment. It is a common part of human experience
to feel that we don't belong. In fact, it is often cited as the
greatest human concern. We may feel when around particular people that we have nothing to contribute, or have
that miserable sensation that everyone else shares some
fundamental part of normal human experience that we
lack. We try to fit in, and we neither convince ourselves
that we do, nor, we suspect, those around us. At those
times, what makes us different seems only to be the crushingly disappointing absence of what bonds everyone else
together. Mill says that this difference is something to be
celebrated. We may not have what they have, and this is a
very good thing. We should look to developing and
strengthening those parts of us that feel unique, not as an
aggressive stance against society but with the warm glow
of knowing that we can contribute more to it as a distinct,
idiosyncratic individual. And therefore, ultimately, be of
more use to the world.

I also find Mill's words to be of use when considering
relationships. Often we want our friends, partners and

28 Ibid.

people we love to be like us, because that allows us to feel validated and accepted. It is a powerful thing to find people in this world who share our values and instincts. But it is also important to celebrate the differences between our partners and us. Would we really want to be in a relationship where the other person reminds us every day of ourselves? Wouldn't it just be like having rich chocolate cake every day? Do we even especially *like* people who are very much like us? Don't we find ourselves cynical of their motives, believing we can see right through them?

Love seems to come without a template. We may think we know what we want in a partner and then one day find ourselves in love for very different reasons. In the same way that differing, developed individuals contribute to Mill's view of society and make it worth belonging to, so too the differences between people in a relationship can be precisely the substance of what makes it valuable. And then, rather than falling for that old fallacy of entering into a relationship thinking you will 'change' the other person to more comfortably reflect your values, you might see the qualities that separate them from you as precisely the features to celebrate. These qualities can complement our own: our laid-back approach to life can be challenged by the more active, dynamic ambition we might see in a partner, or vice versa. When the time comes, it will be useful to have them in mind as a role model. And to echo Mill: as our partners develop their own unique qualities, they can become of more value to themselves and therefore to the relationship as a whole.

There is another subtle but hugely important point here. According to Mill, happiness should *not* be our goal per se, and to chase it directly is a mistake. Instead, we should see it as a by-product, something achieved indirectly through the process of individual liberation from the levelling demands of society. Rather than directly seeking tranquillity or finding happiness through Christ, one might discover it as a by-product of a more personal emancipation. There is something of Aristotle in all of this: identifying our highest aim (liberty rather than virtue) through what makes us unique, and then working towards it, using reason and human faculties to steer the path. Liberate yourself, live freely, and find fulfilment and happiness through that process.

The Romantics

There is in Locke's solution more than a whiff of the Romantic Movement, which was in vogue at the time. The eccentric, glorious French philosopher Jean-Jacques Rousseau had, in the eighteenth century, laid the grounds of discontent with modern civilisation by denouncing it as a destroyer of the 'authenticity' of human beings. Flaunting a disposition of melancholy and non-conformity, the provocateur insisted that civilisation at once promised and undermined happiness, and, in appealing to a lost primitive lifestyle as being conducive to authentic living, planted himself firmly *against* Enlightenment thought. While the greatest Roman poets had hankered after simpler times and extolled a rural life free from cares, Rousseau imbued this vision with a golden haze and used it to denounce his society and show that in his original carefree state, man was perfectly content.

It is to Rousseau, then, that we are unconsciously indebted when we yearn to flee work and the stresses of society and spend time on a remote island, without Internet, commuting or phone signal, living plainly and rustically. It is thanks in part to his romantic

147

synonymising of a bucolic, bygone era with a lost state of happiness that today's bath products proclaim themselves to be simple, organic, natural and herbal, perhaps with overtly African or tropical overtones thrown in to impart some of their geographical claim on wholesomeness. They promise to transport us far from the evils of modern civilisation: a bubbly, perfumed antidote to the atrocity of the developed world. We spend far too much money on products that claim to 'detox' us (even though the very notion of 'detoxing' is a marketing myth).[29] Rousseau's sentimental suspicion of the modern world laid the groundwork for any number of present-day advertisers to exploit and develop our lingering intuition that 'natural' must equal 'good'.

Rousseau is concerned with that hedonic treadmill, or Locke's 'uneasiness': civilisation cultivates new desires, which in turn breed anxiety and further wants. A more primitive life, on the other hand, leads to fewer desires, which means less frustration and therefore more happiness. Rousseau's solution to our unfortunate state of being was his *Social Contract*, which set out a means of reshaping society that would reduce egoism, restrain wealth and limit desires. Unable to regain our primitive state of happiness, though, we must be remade as a new type of social animal. We can recognise in this solution a precursor to Communism, which Marx himself connected with the primitive, hunter-gatherer state of mankind.

The ghosts of old regimes linger in Rousseau's propositions. Firstly, he believes that we can obtain a clear thing called happiness through our endeavours, a thought which was of course a product of the very Enlightenment

---

29 Our kidneys and liver, our skin and lungs do all the detoxifying perfectly well for us, and there's nothing we can do to improve on that.

against which he was positioning himself. Once again, a reaction against a movement tends to inherit its structure. Secondly, Rousseau was saying that we had 'fallen' from a primordial state of savage Grace, which suggests once again the legacy of the Garden of Eden story. Something of the prelapsarian lingers in the Romantics' reverence for the childhood innocence they deem necessary for the attainment of true joy. Amazingly, Augustine's doctrine of original sin was still at work, in disguised form, nearly fifteen hundred years after he imposed it upon us, in this hankering after some lost state of unworldliness.

In his sentimental longing for happiness, his self-conscious treading of a different path, and a desire to return to nature, Rousseau led the Romantic movement in France, which was one part of a larger wave spreading across Europe. Around this time in Germany, Goethe's novel *The Sorrows of Young Werther* was published, in which a lovesick man chooses to kill himself. The book led to an epidemic of melancholy and suicide amongst young Romantics who identified with Goethe's hero. Such a melodramatic response to a novel might seem hilariously typical of what we imagine to be the tender, oversensitive souls of that period, but 'the Werther effect' is a recognised present-day phenomenon too. Celebrity suicides, well publicised in the media, often have a strikingly contagious effect. The famed *felo de se* of Marilyn Monroe, for example, was followed by an increase of 10 per cent in the national suicide rate of the United States (and this was long before the kind of perpetual news coverage and social media dissemination we have today). Many other examples support this. Interestingly, Kurt Cobain's suicide did not have this impact; the fact that journalists had taken heed and adhered to medical-issued guidelines about reporting suicides may have been responsible for the avoidance of the Werther effect.[30]

There is at the heart of Romanticism an urge to withdraw into oneself in order to then transcend the boundaries of that self and connect with nature and the larger order. The message of the Enlightenment, remember, had been that the advancement of scientific knowledge as well as personal pleasure (and its accompanying consumer culture) were the keys to happiness. But this left us with a gap that would prove too tantalising to ignore. Asking the question of what could be more important than such gratification, the Romantics' grandiose drive connected us once again with the mysteries of the universe and provided a form of transcendence to satisfy those who yearned for something deeper than pleasure gardens and shopping.

Immanuel Kant, the extraordinary Enlightenment philosopher, had laid down the thought that we could never come to know the *real* world which exists beyond our perceptions. Rational enquiry, he said, could never provide the path to understanding 'objective' reality, because the most our minds can do is set about organising and considering the world that we subjectively perceive. Science, it follows, only explores relationships *between* things. It is therefore limited to the language of time, space and the other organisational tools that we use to arrange our world of perceived objects and ideas. The accruement of such knowledge is our best way of organising that world in order to navigate it as well as we can, and make predictions of how the things in it should behave. But when science celebrates too loudly its claims to absolute *truth*, a lingering note of arrogance echoes

30 Zach Schonfeld, 'Did Kurt Cobain's Death Lower the Suicide Rate in 1994?', *Newsweek*, 4 April 2014

through the chambers of our romantic souls, and we feel that more must stir beneath.

The Romantics were determined to close the space between 'subject' and 'object' – that is, between the limited, perceiving human being and the true, real nature of things – and if rationality could not provide the path, a deep introspection and narcissistic exaltation of one's inner experience might do the trick.

Not surprisingly therefore, art was celebrated as a means to achieve this deeper connection. The job of art had been until this point to *imitate* life like a mirror in such a way that it might point us towards such worthy objects of contemplation as beauty and virtue. Now its task was to *create*, and to do so with the divine spark of originality. Opera houses and museums sprang up throughout Europe as secular cathedrals to Art. The artist himself gained a cultish repute of untouchable genius which lingers to this day. 'Criticism of poetry is an absurdity,' wrote the German poet and philosopher Novalis in the late 1700s. Music in particular, certainly that of Beethoven but emphatically that of Wagner, became a vehicle to stir the emotions and connect us with something profound. Subject was now brought into the realm of object; humanity to the feet of hitherto unknowable truth. Feelings were apotheosised as the path to revelation. The world had for too long imitated classical art and celebrated its strict rules and cold reason; now such bloodless behaviour was to be scorned.

As Schopenhauer saw it, art could free us from the tyranny of the Will that otherwise drives us to merely satisfy our base desires. Despite being a largely religious canon, J. S. Bach's extraordinary music of the earlier Baroque period had been in many ways a celebration of rationalism. It is quite extraordinary that only a hundred years later Wagner would produce such a hot-blooded and exquisitely melodramatic body of work that stands in such glaring counterpoint to his phenomenal predecessor.

Bach's music needs to be unlocked; its emotional content, when discovered, is somehow in and of itself, and uniquely musical. Much of it is deeply confessional. By contrast, Romantic music now seemed to create a broader emotional landscape: that of falling in love, spending a night on a bare mountain, suffering in turmoil or throwing oneself off a parapet. Instead of experiencing those things for ourselves, we are given music that stirs and excites the corresponding emotions within us. Thus the refrains of the Romantics are often more accessible, yielding their power more or less immediately. Those of us who prefer the earlier mode might even say this emotional mode became a mere *substitute* for experience, and that the unique, private experience of music was diminished.

Kant had pointed to the work that our minds carry out all the time to organise the world that we perceive. Locke before him had seen the mind as a blank slate, passively accepting that to which it was exposed: now, Kant has shown subjective experience to be hard at work, constantly constructing our reality. The fallout of the Enlightenment caused religion, too, to turn inwards and look towards subjective experience for validation. Since the mid-1700s, a Protestant Awakening had challenged ecclesiastical arrangements by emphasising personal experience as the route to salvation: conversion, faith, sin and sentiment became seen as all-important aspects of the Christian life. Now, with the 1835 publication of David Friederich Strauss's *The Life of Jesus Critically Examined*, a new discipline of biblical 'higher criticism' had struck at the heart of Christian belief, by subjecting the Good Book to historical analysis and finding it wanting. However, if it didn't stand up as history, the Bible could for many still retain its spiritual value as the stuff of myth. This in turn would encourage a new kind of sentimental-ised religious experience. Movements such as Comte's Religion of Humanity encouraged us to draw on our love for our fellow man and (particularly) woman, without this secular vision being soiled by Christian superstition. In Rousseau's widely read novel *Emile* he gives us the Savoyard Vicar, who too directs us to follow our heart in matters of spiritual truth. These were narcissistic times.

Before the Enlightenment, religious ecstasy was felt only by a few. For the rest, God (and therefore true hap-piness) had been a sobering presence, reminding us that we were innately alienated from true joy. Only our reunion with Him after our death could provide that joy in the euphoria of Heaven. Now, without God, the Romantics offered the mysterious and ecstatic to us all. We had reclaimed 'joy' and 'spirit' for ourselves through a direct communion with nature. We no longer needed God. We could each become God.

Marxism

It's now the nineteenth century, and one way or another we're still looking for salvation. God has been replaced with a variety of other means to get there, but happiness is still seen within the framework of a fundamentally reli-gious story: a human race alienated from its means of deliverance and becoming perfected over time, as it moves towards a far-off, shimmering Nirvana. The next major means of achieving happiness, and redemption from the encumbrances of society, was offered by the Marxists: *work* will set you free.

Marx, an atheist, still adhered to this religious template, promising salvation while describing it in the language of science. Here was a philosophy that provided substance and meaning for the common man in a way that most of the philosophies emerging from the Enlightenment could not. Perhaps you recognise once again the Christian principle of delayed gratification: suffer (or work hard) now and your reward hovers before you in the form of a distant golden utopia. Seen another way, the proletariat here is the Christ-figure, which must carry the burden of humanity in order to transfigure into the glorious apocalyptic saviour of the future.

Focus has again shifted from mere 'happiness' to the more meaningful concept of 'value', in an attempt to reconcile the alienation that Marx sensed between man and his God, his work and his fellow creatures. Rather than seek transcendence through a journey into the self (as the Romantics encouraged), the very notion of the self was now seen as dangerous, as it implied notions of property. The self was sublimated into the idea of community.

To Marx, a bourgeois society alienates its working class from rewarding or creative labour and robs it of its humanity. Socialists of the day argued for better working conditions, but Marx was concerned with a more profound liberation to overcome this alienation. Instead, the underclass needs to become conscious of its situation and potential, in order to then rise in revolt. Aside from its religious aspects, Marx's thought was in many ways rooted in that of one Georg Wilhelm Friederich Hegel, the German late-Enlightenment philosopher with a teleological view of history, whom Schopenhauer hated and lost his students to. To Hegel, the chapters of humanity's story are connected by violence and revolution. These charges are brought about by visionary revolutionary figures; champions who have sensed that the time is right for change. Marx's Hegelian heroic figure was the proletariat, which would rise to revolution as it became more aware of itself and its role in history. But rather than this merely continuing the cycle of one class replacing another, the sheer size and life-affirming nature of this revolution would be a paradigmatic victory for humanity itself.

Marx's scientific picture offered up a Utopia that finally seemed to answer Rousseau. Our ruinous, dehumanising society began for Rousseau with the fact that we must work. This leads to us reflecting on our social position, and creates feelings of envy and vanity. The division of labour follows; governments grow to protect the inequality and the unnatural rights of property. And it would be up to human beings to radically transform this situation as a part of the historical process.

One important new idea that emerged from Marx for our purposes is as follows: we saw work as an activity that was supposed to endow us with happiness and a sense of humanity. This was a strange new concept, and although it sprang up as a reaction *against* capitalism, there is no doubt that it is now part of the capitalist creed. How many of us talk proudly of working non-stop as if it were something to be admired? Or identify with our jobs more than anything else in life? To be unhappy in one's work today is often seen as having taken a serious wrong turning in life. Employment is no longer merely a means to an end, as it was in pre-Enlightenment days; it is now supposed to be a source of happiness in and of itself.

It seems so self-evidently preferable to enjoy your work, and to draw a sense of meaning from it, that it sounds bizarre to question the idea. Alan Watts, who gave us the image of trying to wrap up water with string, made the point that it is absurd to work at something you don't enjoy, purely to make more money to be able to live longer and continue doing something you don't like. And few would argue that there is tremendous benefit in finding work that brings us pleasure. But the moment we expect that we should do for a living what we enjoy, we unfairly cast those who do not have that advantage as failures. Perhaps because our first question upon meeting people tends to be 'What do you do?', and because this is taken to mean 'What do you do for a living?', we are used to being judged on the basis of our jobs. When we ask this question, we rarely think to enquire what the person's relationship to their job might be. Might they, for example, be indifferently employed, in order to create for themselves enough leisure time and a comfortable income to pursue their real interests? Perhaps you already dislike being asked what you do for a living because you feel the answer you have to give does you no justice. Why should the business of the firm you visit every day between certain hours be of any relevance when you are hoping to make an interesting personal connection with someone at a party?

We might prefer to ask a person the less career-specific 'What do you get up to?' or simply not enquire about work. Meanwhile, we can take comfort in the knowledge that for the vast sweep of human history it did not occur to people that they were supposed to enjoy their work. Our daily employment does not need to be our identity. It's a wonderful bonus to do what one enjoys, but it's not *necessary*. Far more important is knowing how to navigate the difficulties and disappointments in life and work, without setting up a romantic ideal of a 'perfect' job; it's no more helpful or realistic than that of a perfect partner.

Otherwise we are intimating that everyone who does not love his or her work has gone horribly astray; once again, the mantra of 'you can be anything' creates more pain than pleasure.

What counts is not the work but our relationship to it. Schopenhauer, refreshingly, ascribed far more importance to what one does with one's leisure. The ideal he describes (and he goes into some detail about how to sensibly store capital and live off the interest) is to be wealthy enough to have expansive free time and the intellectual capabilities to fill it with contemplation and activity in the service of mankind. It may not be our work but rather what we do with the rest of our time that gives us our true sense of worth. We might choose to identify far more with our hobby of paragliding, or the daily demands and rewards of trying to be a good-enough father or mother. In the meantime, we can stop asking people what they do for a living and recognise it for the meaningless and frequently discouraging enquiry that it is.

Meanwhile, Marxism may have arisen as a well-intended antidote to the material inequalities of modern economics, but as a surrogate religion it could at best only artificially satisfy our deep need for transcendence. In practice, it relied on oppression to enforce its ideology. Our current consumer-culture alternative may celebrate self-interest and therefore bypass the need for persecution, but it tends to be equally as unfulfilling.

Nietzsche

One man who would have defiantly rebuked Marx's vision was Friedrich Nietzsche, another towering giant of German Romantic philosophy. Rousseau's vision of happy savages being corrupted by the powerful in society was anathema to Nietzsche for similar reasons. He deplored the notion of 'slave revolt', rooted in the rising instincts of the rabble, or *ressentiment*. For Nietzsche, the urge of the mutinous underprivileged is only to *deny* the world that has oppressed them. It is their only option. He saw Christianity as the greatest denial of this kind: it advanced an ascetic idea which amounted to 'this hatred of the human, and even more of the animalistic, even more of the material, this horror of the sense, of reason itself, this fear of happiness and beauty, this longing to get away from appearance, growth, death, wishing, longing itself – all that means, let us dare grasp it, *a will to nothingness*, an aversion to life, a rebellion against the most fundamental prerequisites of life.'[31]

For Nietzsche, happier horizons would be reached through the *affirmation* of life, not its denial. The joyous and powerful hero we need is a future *Übermensch*, or Superman. Current humanity is merely a bridge to a future race that will show us our glorious ideal. 'Become who you are!' is Nietzsche's powerful imperative.

According to Nietzsche, Socrates had started us off on a dangerous path, causing us to value reason and enquiry over the instinctual, creative urge. The new type of hero he posits would connect us once again with the rich, intuitive realm of Dionysus; one to which Greek Tragedy had once connected us, but we have since left long behind. We can now push aside questions of whether this or that type of morality might be the correct one; dispense with petty ideologies such as utilitarianism or modern liberalism; forego the austerities of Christianity, and start making truth ourselves. Previous philosophers had enquired into human nature; Nietzsche now casts

31 Friedrich Nietzsche, *On the Genealogy of Morality*

aside all theories and demands we see the truth: that we are ourselves the authors of our nature, and must grasp that responsibility. Those who do will secure our future as a developed race.

Freud

The twentieth century saw the fairly abrupt end of Romantic sentimentality and replaced it with a rather more sceptical take on happiness. Whereas those before him had reclaimed the natural right to be truly happy – through self-examination, through nature or through work – Sigmund Freud saw such a goal as dangerously naive. The creator of psychoanalysis and the man synonymous with the discovery of the unconscious saw instead a 'natural *un*happiness' as the preferred aim. The modest goal of his revolutionary talking therapy was a removal of neurotic or 'unnatural' forms of unhappiness and a restoration of the patient (somewhat surprisingly to modern ears) to an ordinary balance of everyday *dis*satisfaction. Life is not supposed to be plain sailing.

According to Freud's model, we seek to satisfy various unconscious desires created during early childhood but unfortunately must submit to the demands of civilisation. This tension denies us the fulfilment of our true, animal-like needs, and we are pulled between the two opposing drives: our aims, and the demands of society. The resulting conflict leads to a necessary sublimation of those frustrated urges, which can mean for us the emergence of troublesome symptoms.

This might ring a bell. The conflict suggests once again the image of that $x=y$ line along a graph with '*pleasures desired*' along one axis and '*demands of reality*' along the other. A normal, healthy life of balanced happiness and unhappiness, of achievement and frustration, is represented along our $x=y$ diagonal. Freud then echoes Schopenhauer's similar, prefiguring words: 'Events and our chief aims can in most cases be compared to forces that pull in different directions, their resultant diagonal being the course of life.' [32]

Arthur Schopenhauer also spoke of the unconscious mind half a century before Freud officially revealed it, describing its relationship to the intellect thus:

> The intellect remains so much excluded from the real resolutions and secret decisions of its own will that sometimes it can only get to know them, like those of a stranger, by spying out and taking it unawares: and it must surprise the will in the act of expressing itself, in order merely to discover its real intentions.[33]

He was not the only one to point to this murky realm of 'real intentions' before Freud gave it a name. Friedrich Nietzsche also spoke of the unconscious.

Freud, probably disingenuously, claimed until late in his life never to have read either of these philosophers. Schopenhauer's pessimism and Nietzsche's optimism were both well acquainted with the automatic stirrings of the mind, and Freud's concept of the 'Id' (that instinctive self in which our primal processes are manifest) seems to be closely related to Schopenhauer's 'Will'. But it is Freud who has left us with the lingering story of those unfulfilled drives that motivate our desires and compromise our most tender-hearted and altruistic urges. Freud's

32 Arthur Schopenhauer, *Parerga and Paralipomena, Vol 1*
33 Arthur Schopenhauer, *The World as Will and Representation, Vol 2*

theories killed Dickens: easy sentiment in art was no longer plausible or interesting, and our modern tendency to root our problems in the past was born. The story of Oliver Twist today would be a very different, psycho-sexual tale hinged on the effects of an absent mother.

Freud himself – an effervescent prose stylist and pre-scient, revolutionary thinker – has since been somewhat denounced and his psychoanalytic theory labelled passé, even sexist. Psychoanalysis is today synonymous with a long-term, arduous process of self-exploration that has become the stuff of comedy:

> I was in analysis. I was suicidal. As a matter of fact,
> I would have killed myself, but I was in analysis
> with a strict Freudian and if you kill yourself they
> make you pay for the sessions you miss.
>
> *Woody Allen*

Particularly in America, a neo-Freudianism has emerged, shifting the emphasis from suppressed trauma within the individual to the ongoing relationship between client and therapist, and ultimately a greater emphasis on the here and now. Modern popular psychotherapist authors such as Stephen Grosz and Irvin D. Yalom have written beauti-fully about 'apprehending the world of the other', and both offer a very poignant insight into the subtlety and humility of the creative therapeutic intervention. To read their case histories and vignettes in such delightful and moving books as *Love's Executioner*, *Momma and the Meaning of Life* (Yalom) and *The Examined Life* (Grosz) is to be touched by the delicate, unassuming work of the long-term psychotherapist as he identifies and navigates the needs of his patient. There are demands that we all project into our interactions with others, and the books give a strong sense of the therapist's own journey as a 'fellow traveller'.

Much that is distasteful has grown from the therapeutic industry over the last hundred years. Reckless therapists have devastated lives by encouraging false memories of sexual abuse; a diagnostic frenzy has taken place at the expense of relating to the client as an individual; and any number of spurious, guru-led schools have emerged, offering worthless qualifications and basing their meretricious claims on anecdote rather than evidence. Meanwhile, we can remind ourselves: Freud's extraordinary legacy was to alter forever our treatment of psychological *dis*-ease and restore dignity to sufferers who at the time would have been simply incarcerated, castrated or left to die. Freud's consulting room provided a confidential place for a person to *talk*, frankly and probably for the first time, about sex and anguish, to be understood and find healing.

This in itself is a leap forward in the story of happiness, and perhaps for the first time in history a positive development that relates specifically to those who find themselves *un*happy. While many of Freud's approaches have been revised, we now live in a society where we can understand and appreciate that our troublesome urges and predilections might be the result of early trauma and come to understand ourselves and our complexities all the better. Likewise, we can gain a more sensitive understanding of others and think more carefully than ever before about the way we bring up our children. Freud's desire to understand the human condition has bequeathed to us a similar impulse to discern the functioning of people around us whenever they surprise us with seemingly irrational behaviour. Because of the popular dissemination of this extraordinary man's ideas (and, a little later, Carl Jung's) we feel we can grasp something of the human condition, and this connects us with the rest of humanity. Perhaps then, above all, Freud's legacy is one of empathy.

The unassuming claim of Freudian psychoanalysis has been somewhat drowned out amidst the hype that surrounds many forms of modern therapy. Any therapist offering to merely restore 'natural unhappiness' would not, we imagine, meet with success in the busy modern therapeutic marketplace. Yet it is so important to recall that $x=y$ diagonal. Aside from the relief Freud offered to the afflicted, he can also remind the rest of us that we are *all* troubled souls in one way or another, that the seemingly robust and successful types that we envy may, more than anyone, be assailed by feelings of self-doubt and failure. To allow for natural unhappiness in our lives and not berate ourselves for feeling it is to stand against the tyranny of the positive-thinking ethos that surrounds us daily. The gift of therapy is not just to cure the deranged but to point all of us to where we have lost authorship of our stories, bring those reasons to consciousness and thus show us the gentle path to healing.

We can think of Freud and Schopenhauer's images of the $x=y$ diagonal of life and remember that *this* is the reality of the human experience, and to shift that diagonal to denote a life in perfect accordance with one's wishes makes no sense or, worse, makes only temporary sense before a sharp downward swing restores equilibrium. If it was only the recent Enlightenment that created the presumption that we have some birthright to be happy, Freud reminded us of the more accurate picture. As this archaeologist of the psyche, who filled his London consulting room with a priceless collection of antiquities, skilfully sifted through the personal histories of his patients here and in Vienna, so too he restored for contemporary eyes the relic of a pre-Enlightenment truth: that we are not made for contentment.

Today

Today, we very much remain heirs to Romanticism in several areas relating to happiness. Above all, matters of love and spirituality remain swathed in an opaque, sentimental mist, which renders them immune to any kind of rational investigation. In our lonely age, where we seek connections perhaps more than ever before, we benefit enormously from opening those topics to intelligent discussion and myth-busting. (Alain de Botton's *The Course of Love* and Sam Harris's *Waking Up* are both excellent attempts to provide just that.)

Meanwhile, if Freud paved the way for our modern enthusiasm for diagnoses, we are now in the age of the happy pill. Allied to therapeutic intervention, and the enthusiastic diagnosing of conditions, it is now the case that medication (prescribed or otherwise) is playing a large part in our concept of happiness. As diagnoses of unipolar and bipolar depression become more widespread, demand for psychopharmaceutical solutions rises symbiotically. Kahneman's experiencing self finds itself the centre of attention, while our story-forming remembering half remains unnourished.

T. S. Eliot told us 'Humanity cannot bear very much reality.'[34] Now, more than ever before, we are presented with a coruscating array of narcotics and divertissements, which pander to the myopic, amnesic fancies of our experiencing self. Of course they have their place. They are

34 T. S. Eliot, *Four Quartets*

each helpful or amusing in the short term, and we would begrudge neither the beleaguered family man his PlayStation, nor the weekend bacchanal her occasional restorative. Life would be less colourful without such things, assembled by man to stimulate or calm the mind. But they are the very opposite of what we truly need at our core: mechanisms to help us engage with our deep stories. Without these structures, we merely swing between Schopenhauer's poles of pain and boredom. Xanax without therapy, or PlayStation without conversation, do little for us. Not only this: we also laugh at religion, that ham-fisted effort to articulate our deep need for meaning. We are no longer pointed towards the profound; we are distracted from it or too easily able to drown out its call. Yet life remains synonymous with growth, and the best growth comes from recognising the yearnings and crises of the spirit. Today's crisis is that we don't know how to honour our deep needs, and we mistake recreation for happiness.

The Romantic legacy, reinforced by any number of novels and films, encourages us to believe that we should seek out magical solutions to our feelings of isolation; that some magical 'other' is available to us in the form of a perfect partner, or perhaps a perfect job, to complete us and leave us perennially fulfilled. More than any other time in history we suffer from a sense of entitlement, and it remains attached to a warped image of what happiness should be. If Darrin McMahon is right, and happiness is now equatable with mere mood, then we have all but lost touch with our story-forming remembering selves. Chemicals are available to numb the hollow ache of emptiness, while the communal tales we once lived by to suffuse our lives with a sense of meaning are no longer accessible. Unhappiness is seen as a sign of failure, not a healthy symptom of our natural condition. Unarmed with an appreciation of the intrigues of wondrous tragedy, and having forgotten the importance of myth, we are at a loss to contextualise – and value – the disconsolate yearnings of the soul.

I think we will find far more helpful answers back at the start of this winding story. It's time to identify them and see how we might apply them to our lives.

☺

6

The Stoic Building Blocks

It is one thing to wish to live a more considered life; another to know how to get started. Although the journey will ultimately be your own, because it is *your* story over which you must find authorship, I think the ancients understood some important key principles that we can still embrace today.

The foundations of Epicurus

From his walled garden cut off from the city, Epicurus introduced us to the revelatory notion that to become happier, we need to reassess our attachments to things in the world. We need to *feel* differently about things that cause (or have the potential to cause) anxiety. We wish to live with as little pain and worry as possible. Epicurus has, in his way, discovered our unconscious mind and knows that we must change our *emotional* experiences; a purely intellectual, Aristotelian approach won't affect us deeply enough to make the changes we need.

This emotional reappraisal is central to improving

our happiness. If we are to live more felicitous lives, we should not bother greatly with the common approach, namely gathering for ourselves the popular trappings of success. Such an aim is difficult to put into practice and impossible to entirely fulfil. Instead, we should train ourselves – as and when we remember – to feel satisfied with what comes more easily. That way, we are far more likely to reach a point of relatively undisturbed happy contentment. If happiness lies in the relationship between what we *desire* and what we *have*, we are being encouraged to consider the first part of that equation rather than obsess over the second.

Of course we baulk at what sounds like merely 'settling for less': it goes against everything we understand about what it is to be successful, dynamic and in charge of our lives. At first glance, it suggests complacency and lack of vision. But we are not arriving at this philosophy out of laziness; as a considered choice, demanding less has the potential to be enormously enriching.

I remember muling in the foothills of the Atlas Mountains a few years ago, my gorgeous beast of burden guided by a local man, Mohammed. After we had explored the hills, he invited me into the small, simple Berber house that he shared with his wife, sister and eight other family members. Between them, his family seemed to own very few things. From what I could see, the list couldn't have run to much more than:

some prayer mats
a framed quotation from the Quran, which hung above a
    door
a teapot and cups and some mint tea
some items of crockery
candles and candle holders

a cupboard

a couple of rugs

some simple furniture and clothes

a handful of photographs of some pale tourists he had
    taken around on his mule

a mule.

As he poured me a sweet tea, I asked if he had ever been abroad. He laughed and pointed through a small square hole in the clay wall at the mountain range beyond and said, 'Why would I? I have everything here to be happy.'

I tried to contain the self-loathing that surfaced as I remembered my irritation that morning at the intermittency of the hotel Wi-Fi.

We remember Epicurus's thought: 'Everything we need is easy to procure, while the things we desire but don't need are more difficult to obtain.'

We live in an age where 'conspicuous consumption' (the purchasing of goods to display our economic success) and 'invidious consumption' (purchasing in order to make others envy us) are so commonplace we barely notice we're engaging in them. Advertisements generally work on the principle of creating in us a feeling that we lack something and then providing the means to fill it. The writer David Foster Wallace describes their goal as to 'create an anxiety relievable by purchase'.[35] The shiny toy will fill that need, whether it's to look or feel as good as the beautiful people who use the product in the ad, or to be free of some undesirable quality that up until that moment we didn't know we had.

I recently bought a Dyson fan, which clearly has its main appeal in its unusual, bladeless design. Rather than

35 David Foster Wallace, *Infinite Jest*

operate with the familiar turning propeller, it mysteriously generates air with a large stationary ring of plastic. To own one is to own a *talking point*; its advantage as far as I can tell lies not in any extra cooling effect but in the fact that it is a curiosity and will impress visitors to your home. The tagline on the box and used in the advertisements, however, is 'No Blades. No Buffeting'. 'Buffeting', it turns out, is the 'choppy air' (as described on the Dyson website) apparently created by traditional fans. By the use of this brilliant slogan, the advertisers have created an artificial deficit and in the same breath filled it. All these years we have been victims of domestic buffeting. Now, at last, breezy liberation. Transparent as this particular need-creation is, it seems to be there to distract and coddle people like me who are considering buying the fan for one reason: to impress others with a household oddity.

Conspicuous and invidious consumption are hallmarks of capitalism, and they have a powerful effect on us. Producers of goods saturate the market with their products and shout so loudly about them that we fail to hear the quieter voices pointing out serious concerns such as sustainability of resources and worker conditions. We blankly read on our phones a news story of safety nets being installed to prevent staff suicides at the plant where that same phone was manufactured, and then when the Wi-Fi fails again and we can't switch to YouTube to watch pets being 'shamed', we denounce it as a piece of crap.

Moreover, in recent years, it has become commonplace for these goods to be built with artificially short lifespans. It's strange to learn that in Livermore, California, one of the first light bulbs ever manufactured remains lit, *over a hundred years* after it was first switched on. In the earliest example of planned obsolescence, it took a group decision by light-bulb manufacturers in the 1950s to specifically limit the life of all subsequently made bulbs to a few years, in order to ensure that people would have to come back and buy more. That lifespan has been shortened further since then, and packaging might now carry the proud claim that a bulb will last 'for 200 hours' as if that isn't a barely discernible fraction of the burning time of which they could be capable.

We are driven to buying the latest computer, even though the tiny part that makes the new one more powerful could easily be slotted into our previous model. What has happened, at a psychological level so obvious that we never think about it, is that we have all but forgotten *what our tastes are*. We see the *illusion* of individual predilection being maintained, for example, in the array of different styles of iPhone cases available to us. We wonder which of the provided range of colourful or sophisticated sheaths best communicates to the world our unique character. Thus we lean towards the wood effect, or the Batman one (ironically sported, of course), or the vintage Union Jack. Meanwhile, it is much harder to honestly ask ourselves whether our lives would be improved were we not to be attached to our devices quite as umbilically, and how much misery they bring us alongside the various conveniences and amusements. Whether we might be more authentically *ourselves* if, with a pioneering and curious spirit, we occasionally left them at home.

It is naturally difficult to ask supposedly 'outside-of-the-box' questions when the boxes are so insidiously and thoroughly encompassing. And of course we worry we might 'miss out' or risk the derision that comes from being identified as an outsider (a derision which comes from being seen as a threat to a comfortable system and is always mixed with a dose of envy). I am reminded of Noam Chomsky's words: 'The smart way to keep people passive and obedient is to strictly limit the spectrum of acceptable opinion, but allow very lively debate within that spectrum.'[36]

The flourishing capitalist model creates and controls taste and leaves us all largely equivalent, each of us buying variations on the same theme and forgetting what we might have otherwise chosen for ourselves. A large part of the popularity of psychotherapy is explained by the fact that the demands of a consumer society have made us neglect our standpoints; we have allowed our centre of gravity to be shifted to a point outside of ourselves and have lost track of what we actually might want and like in our lives.

The development of astonishingly advanced but short-lifespan, almost disposable consumer goods such as mobile phones and computers (as well as the magnificent range of frantically upgradable software and applications we enjoy on them) is testament to the very powerful appeal of the *new*. *New* is exciting; *new* is intense; *new* promises to interrupt the monotony of that hedonic tread-mill (whilst spinning it endlessly) and distracts us from the fact that our lives tend to be, unless we choose to do anything about it, rather dull and predictable. We are hard-wired to enjoy the feeling of *intensity*, yet the films, novels and entertainments that cater to that desire do not quite give the soul the ongoing nourishment it needs.

We experience a similar intensification of desire when a new product comes out. We might rush to pre-order, enjoying a flurry of delight that is unlikely to be matched by the experience of the product itself. Time

36 Noam Chomsky, *The Common Good*

172

stands still and reality becomes heightened. We picture that product we cannot pre-order quickly enough in our hands before us, from a first-person perspective, and we saturate the mental image with intense colours and magnify its proportions: the visual language of immediacy and engagement.

This is an addictive, attractive high for the experiencing self. The advertising images that tend to mirror this first-person perspective and language of size and colour are designed to trigger this rewarding, intensifying capacity of our nervous systems. This capacity expands unfocused to define our lifestyles for better or worse in the case of rampant consumerism, thrill-seeking and extreme sports, or the uncritical pursuit of religious or mystical experiences. Pseudo-science is appealing because it is exciting and intense; science by contrast is slow and boring. But we are no longer children, tearing round the house with toy weapons, building imaginary worlds to keep us enthralled. Or if we are, we might expect to eventually crash and burn.

If we were the last person on Earth, we wouldn't bother with buffetless ventilators or ironic iPhone cases. When the desire to impress others is removed, we live a more authentically Epicurean existence. And again, we should not make the mistake of thinking that Epicurus would *deny* us such things as a fancy fan. Instead, he would have us not cultivate the *need* for such things in the first place, so that the pain of losing them when they are broken, lost or stolen would not compromise any enjoyment we might obtain from them in the meantime.

We are all attached to far too many unnecessary objects, and they affect our happiness as they each bring with them this risk of pain. While it might be too much to ask – and even undesirable – to adopt a strict Epicurean strategy and not aim beyond the simplest things in life, we might find it helpful to remember the benefits that this approach can offer. We could, if we find ourselves wanting to buy something we don't really need and can't comfortably afford, decide to reject it on Epicurean grounds. Buying it might feel good for a short while, but it could easily bring with it the potential for a pain that outlasts the brief pleasure it affords: that of getting it home and wishing we hadn't spent the money; of our anxiety that it might get damaged or stolen; even the guilt surrounding the admission that we look to such an object to give us a burst of happiness. To choose *not* to buy it even though we can afford it, on the other hand, might allow for some space for clarity: what do we *actually* like? What really suits *us*?

There is more to Epicurus's advice. He reminds us to *desire what we already have*, rather than to desire more and more unnecessary things: 'Do not spoil what you have by desiring what you have not; remember that what you now have was once among the things you only hoped for.' So he is not suggesting a purely negative process of resisting the lure of advertising and making sure we don't become too attached to unnecessary things. We can also re-evaluate the things we do have. If we are going to feel a little too attached to the idea of an iPhone, let's allow ourselves to nurture a sentimental attachment to our *current* one. Rather than take what we have for granted or greedily replace it as soon as we can, let's take a moment to reflect on the good fortune it has brought us. The day its map saved us from missing a friend's wedding. The dating app that matched us with our partner. Perhaps that extraordinary block of electronics has seen you through some troubled times and shouldn't be discarded the moment a marginally different shaped one is released.

You might come to value it more by choosing to leave it at home when you go out for dinner or a walk. Aside from the rewarding feeling of connection with the real world that you will feel (bolstered by the smugness of seeing everyone else fixated upon theirs), you will appreciate it more upon your return. The Stoics would have more to say about rehearsing the loss of the things you love, in order to remind yourself how much you value them.

Our aim here: some self-knowledge and contentment. This is not the same as complacency, as it requires at least a little work and self-examination. The end result of balancing our desires to sit more comfortably with what is available should be an increase in our sense of satisfaction and therefore our happiness. Keeping our desires simple makes us less fearful of what the ancients called 'fortune': with less to worry about, the unpredictable nature of life is less likely to bother us. If we only care about things which are truly necessary to us, we will be less affected by disasters.

Epicurus also encourages us to avoid unhealthy attachment in our relationships. He says: 'Those who possess the power of securing themselves completely from their neighbours, live most happily with one another, since they have this constant assurance'.[37]

This is a warning against neediness, which, according to the poet Lucretius (who brought Epicurus to a later Roman audience), is the destroyer of love. Neediness sets up another futile aim: we can never get enough from people towards whom we feel needy. They may provide on one occasion, but when they fall short of our inflated expectations the next time, we worry and quickly revert

37 Epicurus, *Principal Doctrines,* XL

to our previous insecure state. This kind of unnecessary attachment, 'unnatural' according to Epicurus's distinction, is therefore difficult to satisfy and endless in its desire.

Instead, if we were sure that we could – after a period of adjustment – get by happily enough *without* the relationship in question, we might find it easier to be less demanding and enjoy what the other person chooses to give. If we feel we could live sufficiently without our partners, this can greatly *improve* our relationship with them. When we are sure we could not survive without them, we are likely to bring a theme of intense jealousy or anxiety into the relationship. Once again, reviewing the nature of our attachments can reduce anxiety and increase contentment. Of course, merely *knowing* that we should be more self-sufficient seems very different from achieving such a state, particularly if we happen to be by nature quite neurotic. But in the meantime, an appreciation of the importance of these ideas is often enough to start the cogs whirring and encourage us to think and feel a little differently.

This encouraging of our self-sufficiency in our relationships also points to another aspect of Epicureanism that is both a weakness and a strength. They shut themselves away in their garden and were not concerned about the welfare of others. There is a natural reclusiveness and selfishness about the philosophy of the Epicureans. The Stoics, by contrast, were keen that we try to be the best citizens possible, and that notion has fed into the Christian model of civic duty with which we are still falteringly familiar. The Epicureans had none of that, and there's no doubt that at times the lack of social obligation is rather compelling. 'The tranquil man,' Epicurus tells us, 'is not troublesome to himself or to another' and should 'live unseen'.[38] This is likely to appeal to those of us who tend towards introversion, and I think that despite the misleading modern image of the gormandising hedonist, Epicureanism is a philosophy that best suits the diffident mindset. I like Susan Cain's description of us 'having a lower threshold for stimulation'.[39]

Even if we are relatively introverted, how might our emotions (usually so resistant to rational intervention) be so pliable as to succumb to teachings such as those of Epicurus? Surely it's one thing to agree that it would be better to feel differently about something, and quite another to experience a genuine transformation of our psychological response to it? We are all familiar with the experience of wishing we felt differently about some aspect of our lives. Surely if our emotions were that easy to control, we'd all be enjoying blissful relationships, without a care in the world? Epicurus encouraged rote learning and mantras to ensure success; the Stoics had richer answers to this conundrum.

Stoic virtue

Stoicism began around the same time as Epicureanism – around the third century BCE. Nowadays, rather like with 'epicure', the word 'stoic' has come to mean something related but different to its original sense: to many people today, it suggests someone dispassionate, cold and hard. But it is an unfair caricature.

While they shared with their Epicurean rivals the goal of achieving *ataraxia*, or tranquillity, the Stoics' vision

38 Epicurus, *Vatican Sayings*, I
39 Susan Cain, *Quiet: The Power of Introverts in a World That Can't Stop Talking*

of how to get there was *not* based on the pursuit of pleasure but rather that of *arete*, or virtue. However, this Stoic word does not quite mean *moral* virtue (as the legacy of medieval Christianity leaves us interpreting the word today) but rather refers to a kind of psychological robustness. Stoic 'virtue' has a subtlety of meaning rather lost on us, who might recoil from its righteous implications.

We should understand Stoic virtue by considering the phrase – 'a human being is unique by *virtue* of his capacity for reason'. That use of the word does not imply any ethical high-mindedness. Another way of phrasing that thought would be: 'A human being has virtue when he exercises his capacity for reason.' A Stoic would also have said, 'A house has virtue when it is well built and does its unique job as a house very well.' So deciding the virtue of a person or thing comes from first understanding what that thing's unique quality or purpose is in the world, and then seeing whether it is doing *that* as well as possible. *Our* unique quality is our capacity for reason, and if we exercise that well, the Stoics argued, we gain a psychological strength that protects us from disturbance. This continues on from Aristotle's thoughts about judging a thing by how well it does the thing it is uniquely supposed to do.

One interesting difference, then, between the Stoic and modern sense of 'virtue' is that the former is rooted in *intention* and the latter in *action*. When we think of virtue today, we might bring to mind instances of knightly behaviour, whereas for the ancients, the key to virtue was contained in one's mindset and is thus a little less easy to picture. Hence they commonly created visual metaphors to help us understand their points, and, continuing in the mode of Aristotle, these would often involve archery. Intention was the key: philosophy taught the Stoic student merely to aim the arrow clearly at the target. Whether or not the arrow reached the bull's eye was a matter for fortune and *not* a concern for the student.

As a law graduate, this allowing of intention to trump outcome rings alarm bells for me. Imagine if while driving your car, intending to bring a friend to the hospital as quickly as possible, you hit and killed a child. You would not expect to tell that story to friends and have them respond, 'Great, so good of you to get your friend some help. Well done – and no matter about the child, you didn't mean to kill it.' The things people actually *do* clearly matter to us enormously in everyday life, often regardless of intention, and certainly where harm has resulted. In their defence, the Stoics would most likely respond to this incident with the recommendation that you should report the accident, await your trial and, if necessary, patiently serve your time for manslaughter. On the one hand, you needn't feel terrible about what was not intended, but on the other, you would not expect to shirk responsibility if that is what the law of the land decreed. The important thing is that we act from a point of virtue (as opposed to pursuing pleasure), by which we mean psychological robustness.

There are some other important differences between the Stoics and the Epicureans. Firstly, as I've said, the Stoics did not shut themselves away; they were very active, often wealthy citizens, noblemen and leaders, interested (unlike the inhabitants of the Garden) in creating a just and virtuous society. They also did not rely on Epicurus's dogmatic approach to teaching. The Roman statesman and dramatist Seneca, one of the few Stoic writers whose work is extant, preferred to encourage the pupil to apply his thoughts and teachings to his own life. The philosophy itself was incomplete until conversation between a pupil and a friendly teacher had allowed the philosophy to creep 'bit by bit into the soul'[40]. Stoics also were keen on using reason as a training tool, which of course is a far more Aristotelian approach than Epicurean, the latter school being highly sceptical of giving reason any special place in our affections. Unlike Aristotle's Lyceum, but like Epicurus's Garden, Stoicism was open to both sexes and all strata of society. As with Epicurus, the Stoics had no time for fearing terrible gods: Seneca writes that it is 'stupid to pray' in order to achieve something virtuous in life, 'since you can obtain it from yourself'[41].

There are a few fundamental presumptions of the Stoics that we might want to consider as part of a life that aims to be considered and less prone to anxiety. These are core ideas within the structure of a more tranquil life, which, if we accept the leanings of classical thinkers, is equatable with a happier one. We are about to come across our first such building block, found again and again within the ancient records of these early thinkers. It is a thought of extraordinary power. Its potency is so great that it has survived two thousand years, has in modern times been hijacked and reclaimed by spurious self-help gurus, and to many of us steeped in that world it will now seem rather familiar. But customariness brings its own curse. Clichés go in one ear and out the other like water off a duck's back. Yet the original idea was once unheard of. It was then born, nursed and allowed to thrive for half a century by some of the greatest thinkers of the Western world, and nurtured with a rigour unknown to the self-styled, self-help luminaries of our age.

40 Seneca, *Letters from a Stoic,* Letter XXXVIII
41 Seneca, *Letters from a Stoic,* Letter XLI

Your judgements

Here, then, is our first building block, central to Stoic philosophy and to the tranquil life:

> 1. If you are pained by external things, it is not they that disturb you, but your own judgement of them. And it is in your power to wipe out that judgement now.[42]

These are the words of Marcus Aurelius, one of the greatest Roman emperors, taken neither from a public speech to motivate the masses, nor from philosophical teachings to be bestowed upon pupils. They come from his private journals and stand as a note to self from the most powerful man on Earth. Marcus ruled from AD 161 to 180, a time of near permanent conflict. His empire fought and defeated the Parthians in the east, as well as threatening Germanic tribes during the long Marcomannic wars. This great leader was known in his lifetime – and has been since – as a philosopher-king, and his 'blameless character and temperate way of life' were praised by the historian Herodian as evidence of his erudition. His collection of notebooks, known as the *Meditations* and composed while out on campaigns, remains one of the most abiding and touching sources of Stoic thinking.

Problems are created, Marcus is saying with the Stoics, not by events in the world but rather by how we interpret those events. That interpretation might involve a snap judgement or a more complex narrative that we tell ourselves, but it is this stage in the proceedings that leads to our problems. Hence the same event 'out there' in the

42 Marcus Aurelius, *Meditations*, viii. 47

world might affect someone else very differently from how it affects us. Likewise, *our* judgements about people are in truth responsible for how *they* seemingly 'make' us feel. Nobody, and nothing save our own judgements, truly 'makes' us feel anything.

When we think of the variety of anxiety disorders that abound, as well as the debilitating, often bizarre phobias that cripple otherwise very balanced people; when we consider the triggers in our own lives that can flip us into an angry or even depressed state with the reliability of a light switch, it would be understandable to hold out little hope for harnessing the level of control over our emotional lives that Marcus is suggesting. Yet we might also ponder how rapidly we *can* correct an unhelpful emotion in life when, say, new information comes to light. We might be miserable that our partner seems coolly indifferent to our upcoming birthday, until on the night in question we return home to find a surprise party has been thrown in our honour. Following the initial shock, the feeling of hurt that had haunted us for days is transformed into something very loving. Similarly, we might feel rejection following what appears to be uninterested behaviour of a friend, partner or work colleague, only to discover later that their behaviour was explained by the fact they had received terrible personal news. Our self-pity and resentment would quickly turn to sympathy and probably an embarrassed acknowledgement of how over-sensitive we can be. In these cases and countless more, we are correcting our beliefs about the target of our emotions (our partner, our friends, their behaviour) by allowing for new information to join the mix; a shift at the intellectual level has a near automatic effect at that of the emotions.

It is tempting to say that that so-and-so or such-and-such is *responsible* for the emotions we feel. The insulting way our boss treats us is the *reason* for our unhappiness at work. The fact we've lost our phone is the reason for our anger. And likewise, we are elated because our team has just won the match, or we've got a hoped-for promotion, or we've received triumphant examination results. Surely we are at the mercy of external events to produce our emotions? Our friend, to return to the example above, ignores us; surely it is right to say that *he* makes us feel bad. When his girlfriend tells us why he's been so taciturn of late, and we experience relief and sympathy, surely it's *her* that creates that shift of emotion.

But is that right? Another person in our place may not have been offended in the first place by our friend's nonchalance. Likewise, he might not be particularly angered by the loss of his phone or elated by the news of his promotion. He might even be *disappointed* by the promotion, if he had hoped for a different one. We cannot honestly state that events in the outside world *cause* the emotions we feel. We each react in our own way, and we do so according to a quality we all share, which takes us back to the beginning of this book. We tell ourselves stories.

If we are treated coolly or let down by a close friend, we might experience rejection or anger, or a mixture of both. Has the friend's behaviour automatically triggered that? Not quite. To move from perceiving the behaviour to feeling the emotion, we have to do a bit of work ourselves. We engage in a little internal storytelling first. We might quickly bring to mind a series of previous cases where the friend has acted in a similar way. We'll be sure to form that pattern in the way most likely to infuriate ourselves. We might imagine having a conversation with him, and we'll play that conversation out in such a way that he is as annoying and true to form as possible.

Moreover, the harshness with which we make these representations to ourselves will depend on our mood at the time. If we are already irritated by some other event, we will feel particularly unforgiving towards this one. Another time, another day, when we're in a better mood, our friend's behaviour might be forgivable, even delightful.

We're barely aware that we're forming this 'he's *always* like this and it drives me mad' story ourselves. We are so focused upon the unreasonableness of *his* actions that we won't think of looking at our own role in the proceedings. Moreover, there is likely to be a deeper, entirely unconscious story also being told, of which we won't be aware at all. Our friend's behaviour makes us feel small, or rejected, or unconsidered. Our anger is a frightened, defensive reaction against the way such feelings resonate with our history of analagous experiences. These low-level stories set the scene for our emotional lives, greatly affecting the way we join up the dots when we react to day-to-day events.

So let's acknowledge that when we find ourselves infuriated with people, irritated by our partners, annoyed, embarrassed, sad or scared, those feelings are in truth provoked by an exhausting little voice inside our head, and/or from the exaggerated pictures we show ourselves. The pictures or voice might refer to the past (if we're feeling bad about something that has happened, even a split second ago), or the future (if we're frightened of something that might happen, like a conversation or meeting we're dreading). These intermediary thoughts step in and interpret external events as a good reason to feel bad, mad or scared. In essence, we make a judgement about the event and then react to that verdict.

That judgement might be negative, in the way I've

described above, but it might also feel very positive: we might see a picture of the latest incarnation of our phone or car and feel a pleasant sense of desire for a new one. We might buy the car and feel a huge amount of delight. Although we know from the notion of the hedonic treadmill that these pleasures tend to be short-lived, nonetheless at the time, that internal voice might pipe up with, 'Oh God, that's amazing, I have to have one of those' when we see an advertisement. Proud mental images might abound of ourselves sporting the new phone or driving the new car: pictures that show us looking tall and rather luminescent, and people around us appearing very impressed. Again, we make a judgement: we create for ourselves a little narrative and respond to that. We work ourselves up, or indeed down.

This fights against a very different but well-received view of emotions, which is that they arise from some deep, animal, irrational place within us, quite separate from our intellectual faculties. This school of thought says that intellect is of the mind and emotions are of the body. We are *born* with our capacity for grief and anger and despair in place, whereas we *learn* reasoning through the society in which we live. This kind of thinking, while no longer exerting a strong influence in the field of psychology, nonetheless deeply affects the way we tend to talk of our emotions as very separate from reasoning. The Greeks, however, were not of this opinion, and their preferred model – that emotions stem from how we interpret events – now once again has the upper ground in modern clinical understanding.

For if, as the Greeks believed, our emotions are tied up with our thoughts and beliefs, if they are in essence 'cognitive' and will change and shift as those beliefs are modified, then we can see them as *fundamentally rational*.

We can in fact delve deeper and decide if certain emotions are reasonable or unreasonable, true or false and so on, depending on their logical relation to the belief being held. If on the other hand we adopt the model that *separates* intellect and emotion, then when David insults Jane, we would say that a primal response called anger is directly triggered in Jane and that her anger comes from a very different place to her rational thinking. Let's instead understand the anger as a response to Jane's own *judgement* or interior narrative about what David said.

Epicurus knew of these intermediary internal judgements when he spoke of changing our desires. This is why he cut to the chase and gave his followers slogans to memorise (such as 'He who is not satisfied with a little, is satisfied with nothing'[43]), making sure they had quick and easy techniques at hand to deal with the lure of unhelpful attachments. The key was to deal effectively with that internal voice as and when it arose, by habituating his followers to interject antithetical thoughts into their own internal narrative. Cognitive spanners could be thrown in the works.

Epicurus might have introduced it, but it was the Stoics who really embraced and developed this notion that emotions spring from rationally based judgements. They, the Epicureans and the Aristotelians, all shared this common ground of understanding, but the Stoics concerned themselves more than any other school with radically reappraising the role of feelings in order to create a life of increased tranquillity. Their starting point, as with the Epicureans, was the leverage gained by understanding that our emotional life was susceptible to reason.

---

43 Epicurus, *The Essential Epicurus: Letters, Principal Doctrines, Vatican Sayings, and Fragments*, translated by Eugene Michael O'Connor

Chrysippus, the third and probably greatest head of the Stoic school, asked, 'Where do we place our emotion?' Should we say it's in our stomach, in a mere flutter, and therefore equate our feelings with those of the animals who share such things with us? Surely not, he says; it must be located somewhere far more complex and uniquely human, a part worthy of the subtle and tangled feelings I have while, say, grieving. This emotion is clearly able to *evaluate and select*: reason looks like the right place to put it.

Whether or not Chrysippus's logic strikes us now as quaint, modern psychotherapeutic thinking has in a sense caught up with the presumptions of the ancients, and it is to the Stoics more than any other school that the debt is owed.

In Marcus Aurelius's world, wracked by violence and turmoil, this thought would have been a comfort. You may be at war and every day facing life-threatening situations, but it is ultimately up to you how you respond to those pressures. Stoicism emerged from troubled times, and the perennial conflicts of that era go some way to explaining its enduring popularity. Yet in our rather more peaceful age, we are no less aware of disturbances to what could be a very tranquil existence. Most of us may not regularly face physical attack, but we might still meet any number of very painful situations in our lives and find our fear or anger expanding to fill the same space. Stoicism remains a potent remedy for our modern lives and the myriad stresses and tragedies they may bring.

'Get rid of the judgment, get rid of the "I am hurt," you are rid of the hurt itself,'[44] Marcus notes. Is it so simple? At first glance it seems a dangerous recipe for

44 Marcus Aurelius, *Meditations,* iv. 7

repressing painful feelings. Just tell yourself you're fine and the pain will disappear? This does not tally with our modern preoccupation with expressing our negative emotions. If we are angry, we should talk about it or 'take it out' in some harmless way such as pillow-beating; certainly we shouldn't seek to pretend we feel fine.

The metaphor of 'letting off steam' comes from, not surprisingly, the time of the locomotive engine. Freud was fascinated by this invention, and for him it was a powerful metaphor for human emotion. By comparison today, our language for the brain is rooted in computer-talk and its language of 'reprogramming'. In Freud's time, too much built-up steam, not allowed to escape in some harmless way, was believed to create a neurosis. Today, it feels more 'modern' to talk about someone's brain 'processing' messages in a certain way or needing 'rewiring'. Steam and computer metaphors amount to the attempts of different eras to come to grips with something beyond their understanding by using a model of a technology dazzling and complex but just about graspable. The science fiction master Arthur C. Clarke gave us the law 'Any sufficiently advanced technology is indistinguishable from magic'[45], and these models have helped us form some comprehension of the endlessly bewildering complexities of the brain and its relationship to our emotional life. Yet the inevitable limitations of each metaphor mislead us in their own way. Electronic- and computer-speak encourage us to see our brains (and therefore each other) as reliable machines that must necessarily produce predictable results if certain data are inputted correctly. This may be no more helpful than the correlative analogue model

45 'Clarke's Third Law' from the 1973 revision of 'Hazards of Prophecy: The Failure of Imagination' in *Profiles of the Future*

of the motion-producing steam engine, as revolutionary to the nineteenth-century mind as the computer has been to ours.

'Venting' does not solve emotional problems as the metaphor of pipes, valves and steam suggests. In the mid-twentieth century, the human-potential movement encouraged us to cry, scream and beat 'boffers' (cushioned pads) to release our pain. The therapy rooms and encounter groups of the 1970s reverberated with the *thwump* of fist meeting cushion. More recently, Brad Bushman and team at Iowa State University effectively demolished the myth that this kind of activity helps us to feel better. In fact, their research shows it actually tends to make us *more* aggressive. Beating a pillow might legitimise our feelings of anger, encouraging us to relive them later, and we may become too attached to a venting activity that we feel should bring us catharsis and find ourselves searching for an assuagement that never comes.

There is much to be said about the Stoic approach to anger, so we will save it for a later chapter. But for now we can see the clear contrast between the discredited human-potential approach to emotional release and the Stoic position. The last thing the Stoics – or for that matter the Epicureans – would wish to do is *legitimise* negative emotions. Instead, we should acknowledge that it is our judgements, not the external event, which is creating the anguish. In taking responsibility for it, we can look for a way out of the pain.

Perhaps, as you read this, you might question the word 'external'. What about 'internal' events? What if we are injured? Or debilitated by physical or mental illness? Surely such a condition can cause all levels of suffering, but are we really then reacting to something 'out there', as we are when, say, we make a judgement about how to deal with damage to our property or a missed promotion? The Stoic response would be to still treat these events as externals, even if we feel that their point of origin is within us. We can still choose how to respond to an injury in the same way we can choose how we deal with a house fire. When the thick mire of clinical depression debilitates us, Stoicism may for some feel far from their grasp. While it may help a person deal with many of the anxieties that could encourage a downward spiral, I imagine it would be very tough to find the cognitive distance needed to acquire the necessary leverage when stuck in the thick of it. However, absorption of Stoic principles into life can still be of huge benefit to the uni- or bipolar sufferer, even if they are of limited use when, despite all efforts, the worst times descend.

It is, as Marcus tells us, always in our power to repre-sent events to ourselves in such a way they give us an advantage. Two thousand years later, we think of this as 'reframing': the reinterpretation of a negative event as something positive. Seeing the silver lining. Once again, the insipidness of the cliché robs the principle of its power. We tend to associate 'always looking for the positive' with a kind of smiling, Pollyanna vapidity (which might point to a neurotic refusal to acknowledge the disappointments of life). For that reason, perhaps, it tends not to strike us as something worthwhile we might employ to benefit ourselves but more as a kind of social lubricant, a way of avoiding difficult topics in discussion and appearing help-ful and friendly. If we touch on a problem in conversation and are met with something that begins 'Oh well, never mind, at least . . .', we are likely to feel that the other person has little interest in what we're going through.

Likewise, if we see Marcus's instruction as an encour-agement to merely 'look on the bright side', we also miss its potency. Marcus is reminding himself – and therefore us – that we are to take *responsibility* for those judgements we make and to reconsider our judgements in a way that helps us. That involves a profound shift in our relationship with all events in the world, and with our emotions. It is very far from being a rosy nudge to 'perk up'. The reason why this shallow pronouncement fails to hit the mark most of the time is that it clashes with our deeper convictions. We cannot effectively choose to feel more positive about an event that is bothering us unless we have first understood that it is our judgements, which are responsible for how we feel. An encouragement to see the positive in a situation will not be effective if it clashes with a deeper story we are telling ourselves.

Epictetus, the Roman slave who became one of the most prominent Stoic teachers, gives us the same important message as Marcus in his *Enchiridion*, or *Handbook*: 'Man is disturbed not by things, but by the views he takes of them.'[46] This truth is our starting point if we are to adopt Stoic principles. Epictetus later expands: 'If, therefore, any be unhappy, let him remember that he is unhappy by reason of himself alone.'[47] We might baulk at this when we are only too aware of people surviving childhood abuse or being horrendously persecuted for their beliefs, sexuality or their race. Should we really tell them to blame themselves for their pain? It sounds an appalling thing to say.

Stoicism, however, was born at a time when such violence was an everyday fact for many people and for similar reasons. If Epictetus appears glib, we do him a disservice. We can imagine how harshly he would have been

46 Epictetus, *Enchiridion*, 5
47 Epictetus, *The Golden Sayings of Epictetus*, CXXII

treated as a slave: we are told that his leg was deliberately broken by his master, leaving him lame for the rest of his life. His words are offered as a source of strength to those who are cruelly persecuted, not in ignorance of them. The Stoics even said that a Stoic sage (a semi-fictional role model for the seeker of virtue) would still, while being tortured on the rack, be able to smile and think 'This is happening to my body, but it isn't happening to *me*.' We may find this too far-fetched, as did many of the Stoics' contemporaries, but the reality is that for the person being tortured or abused, the kind of detachment that the Stoic message encourages might be the only comfort remaining. The message is not 'blame yourself' but to realise that whatever happens to you, it does not need to affect *you*, your core self, unless you choose to let it. Understood correctly, that is a powerful message of hope and a core survival skill for victims of oppression. Viktor E. Frankl's extraordinary memoir from the concentration camps, *Man's Search for Meaning*, is a moving testimony to this fact: 'Everything can be taken from a man but one thing: the last of the human freedoms – to choose one's attitude in any given set of circumstances, to choose one's own way.'

Stepping back from the immediacy of our emotions and realising that we are responsible for them is a very good starting point for living well. We might insist that the Stoic model is difficult to apply to severe depression or misses the point where gross social injustice occurs, but the overwhelming point remains that taking responsibility for your emotions (rather than insisting the rest of the world recognise them and respond with perennial sym-pathy) is by far the most effective path towards sustaining relationships, solving problems and therefore living happily. We all know people who live in a world where others are perpetually to blame, who are always in the right while everyone else acts wrongly around them. Some people seem trapped in a need to elicit sympathy from the rest of the world; they may constantly dramatise, exude self-pity and appear eternally wronged. These people rarely advance or solve their problems without therapy. Interestingly, if we try to help them, our most effective strategy is usually to help them gain some distance or perspective from their emotions: an echo of precisely this Stoic principle. After a certain point, merely sympathising with and echoing their grumbles tends to reinforce them.

If you are someone who easily feels wronged and tends to blame the world rather than take this kind of responsibility, then this first building block may cause you to stumble. You may feel angry about it and insist that *your* situation cannot be helped by such thinking. You may decide to interpret this notion of responsibility as an instruction to blame yourself, and haughtily insist that you certainly won't be doing *that*. But there is no Stoic directive to self-blame, to beat yourself up for causing problems. This part of their thinking is about *removing* pain, not adding to it or merely shifting it.

If you insist that you are purely the victim of your situation, or that the anguish you feel about something is entirely justified by the event in question, consider whether someone else you know might respond differently to it. Whether someone you know would find themselves in the same circumstances but be likely to deal with them in a more positive way. If you can imagine that, then you can notice that the key to your emotional response is not the events but the way you deal with them. The Roman historian and philosopher Plutarch – a Neo-Platonist but who drew frequently on the Stoics

– compared this to the experience of hating certain foods but realising that others can eat them quite happily. There is much relief to be drawn from the realisation that things *themselves* do not dictate our responses. Marcus writes on this subject in his *Meditations*: 'The same experience befalls another, and he is unruffled and remains unharmed; either because he is unaware that it has happened or because he exhibits greatness of soul.'[48] Moreover, the act of thinking of how someone else might respond to the same situation encourages us to mentally rehearse and surprise ourselves with a solution, which can of course make an enormous difference if we had previously felt stuck.

'Say to every harsh appearance – "you are an appearance, and not the only way of seeing the thing that appears,"' Epictetus tells us.[49] This trains us to distinguish between the 'appearance' (the thing that appears to us, or the event) and our 'impression' (the judgement we make about it). It is helpful to become familiar with seeing events in this way, as we have a tendency to need this teaching most when we feel at our lowest, when we are precisely least able to lift ourselves from a depressed state. We are all familiar with how, when we are in a bad mood, it is very difficult to pay attention to anything that doesn't reinforce our misery. For this reason, it's very hard to appreciate that our lowest plateaus have also most likely led to turning points in our past; often we need to hit rock bottom before we realise we have to make a change. But when we are feeling low, it is often near impossible to appreciate that this may be the start of a move in a positive direction. Realising that you are very unhappy with your

48 Marcus Aurelius, *Meditations*, v. 18
49 Epictetus, *Enchiridion*, 1.5

partner, for example, is a point that has to be reached before you make a change or find someone new. Hating your job and wanting to leave is a common catalyst for getting out and starting something afresh that will make life feel more fulfilling. But when we despair, we fixate on the negative. In *The Philosophy of Cognitive-Behavioural Therapy*, Donald Robertson quotes from Justus Lipsius, a Renaissance humanist whose works formed part of the revival of Stoicism for a Christian audience in the sixteenth century. Lipsius memorably compares our tendency to fixate on the negative to the behaviour of a fly:

> As flies and such like vile creatures do never rest long upon smooth and fine polished places, but do stick fast to rough and filthy corners, so the murmuring mind does lightly pass over the consideration of all good fortune but never forgets the adverse or evil. It handles and pries into that and often augments it with great wit.[50]

In one passage, Marcus tells himself to see those things that infuriate him as no more than the equivalent of sawdust and wood clippings on the floor of a carpenter's workshop. These things that obstruct us are the inevitable by-product of nature, and it would be mad to become enraged about them. This is typical of the Stoics' aligning of themselves with fate (that is, whatever the world throws at them), but it also should inform our first impressions and stop us from interpreting events in such a way that makes us feel worse.

Before we proceed to the next major building block of Stoic serenity, it is worth noting a minor point that may

50 Justus Lipsius, *On Constancy*

help us if we are to understand our emotional life in the way I am describing. There is perhaps one valid reservation we could raise in the face of the Stoics' idea that our judgements (or 'impressions') are the single *cause* of our disturbance. It's perhaps more accurate to think of them as a *constituent part*. For example, we are likely to have at some point in our lives crossed the road and narrowly avoided being hit by a car. The sudden screeching of the vehicle (especially when accompanied by the enraged bellow from the driver as he hurls some half-terrified, half-furious insult at us) is enough to make us respond automatically and emotionally before having a chance to really form any judgements about what has happened. In this case, it would seem wrong to say that our reaction of panic and the range of autonomic responses we would exhibit (rapid shallow breath, quickened heartbeat, a surge of adrenaline and so on) have come from any *judgement*, let alone one that we have, as Marcus tells us, the power to wipe out. Instead, it would seem that the shocking event really *has* triggered the response directly.

Of course in this case we could point to the evolutionary advantages of our nervous system and say that the reaction still comes from within *us*, as someone unaware of the collision they had just narrowly avoided (perhaps an entirely blind and deaf person) would not react at all. This is true but unimportant for our purposes; it is still the case that we are not making ourselves feel panic by the way we *choose* to interpret the events: there is simply no time for that. Does this sort of example undermine the Stoic claim? Not at all. Seneca was ready for it, distinguishing between the first automatic flush of emotion we feel as the near-accident occurs and what we choose to do thereafter. Albert Ellis, who drew heavily on Stoic principles in the 1950s to form his rational emotive behavioural therapy (a precursor to modern cognitive behavioural therapy) uses the car example to make the same point. We can expect to feel the fear at the moment of the near-accident, but we can then choose not to replay the event again and again in our minds and make ourselves feel terrible:

> Assuming that you don't, at the very beginning, have any conscious or unconscious thought accompanying your emotion, it appears to be almost impossible to *sustain* an emotional outburst without bolstering it by repeated ideas. For unless you keep telling yourself something on the order of 'Oh, my heavens! How terrible it would have been if that car had hit me!' your fright over being almost hit by the car will soon die.[51]

It's the *replaying* of the event that sustains the problem. Anyone who has been involved in this kind of scenario will know how hard it is not to keep reliving the event: such is the nature of trauma. Nonetheless, the Stoic approach allows us to understand what is happening and find a way out from the repeated self-infliction of emotional pain. Luckily, such extreme fight-or-flight autonomic responses tend to be triggered very rarely. And even when they are, we have it within our control to minimise the disturbance they inflict upon us thereafter.

We now have our first building block. We can pay attention to our responses to events and the stories we tell ourselves about them. We can check to see if we are increasing the pain caused by a negative event by

51 Albert Ellis, *Reason and Emotion in Psychotherapy: A Comprehensive Method of Treating Human Disturbances*

exacerbating things and searching for negative patterns, rather than simply accepting first impressions and events as they are. We can take responsibility for how we feel by realising that ultimately it is our after-the-event, ongoing *reactions* to what happens around us that are the cause of our problems. The point of this is *not* to blame ourselves. It is to begin to dissolve unwanted frustrations and anxieties in our lives. Once we stop blaming the world for our problems, we can achieve some control. Whether we see our judgement as a cause or a constituent part of our emotional pain, the same conclusion remains for us as for Marcus Aurelius. 'Cast out the judgement, you are saved. What hinders you?'[52]

It needs more, though. And the Stoics knew what was missing.

☺

52 Marcus Aurelius, *Meditations*, xii. 25

7

Relinquishing Control

So we are to take responsibility for the ways in which we respond to external events. It is those judgements that cause us problems, at least beyond the first flush of anxiety that a sudden danger may trigger, rather than the events themselves. If we avoid these 'disturbances' by not allowing events to upset our emotional life, then we might achieve the Stoic ideal, which is to live in the glow of a psychological fortitude that they called virtue. The Stoic sage – a semi-fictional role model for any student of Stoicism – has achieved this virtue so fully that he cannot act *un*-virtuously. From the right mindset can flow only virtuous acts. We are unlikely to reach his almost holy standard ourselves, but it is our attempt to do so that gives us the best sort of life and therefore the happiest. We may not spend our lives ceaselessly jumping for joy, but we will vastly reduce feelings of pain, anguish and disturbance as we continue along that $x=y$ diagonal: something that could constitute a remarkable transformation in our lives.

This is all well and good, but perhaps it still sounds a

little far-fetched. The second building block will give us a huge helping hand in making sense of these bold ideas. Again, it is a thought of staggering potential, and one which is not entirely unknown to us today, coming to us as it does in the diluted form of a faintly pious, withering cliché. But its potency is great. Here it is, this time from Epictetus: I paraphrase the powerful notion that opens his *Handbook*.

2. Don't try to change things you cannot control.

With the first building block in place, we might now appreciate a little guidance on how to use it. How can we best apply our understanding that our responses are the key to securing tranquillity?

Epictetus expands:

> Work, therefore, to be able to say to every harsh appearance, 'You are but an appearance, and abso-lutely not the thing you appear to be.' And then examine it by those rules which you have, and first, and chiefly, by this: whether it concerns the things which are in our control, or those which are not; and, *if it concerns anything not in our control, be prepared to say that it is nothing to you.* [my emphasis][53]

If something is not under our control, we can recognise it as such and decide that *it's fine as it is.*

The mindful application of these two building blocks is enough to release us from the anxieties that beset us daily. So let's consider this second lesson in detail; it's a truly magnificent thought.

53 Epictetus, *Enchiridion*

Epictetus is saying that we should only concern ourselves with things that we can control. All else should be
of no interest. Putting aside for the moment instances of
social injustice that may greatly bother us even though we
are not involved in them, this division into what is and
what is not under our control is known as the 'Stoic fork'.
For me, I prefer to place an imaginary line down the
centre of my vision, and when an issue is causing trouble,
I check to see on which side of the line it falls.

What does Epictetus suggest belongs on either side of
the line? He tells us on this first page:

Under our control are our thoughts and actions.

Not under our control is everything else, including fame,
power, the behaviour and thoughts of other people, our
property and our reputation.

Under Our Control	Not Under Our Control
Our thoughts	What people think
Our actions	What people think of us
	How people behave
	How well people do their jobs
	How rude people are
	Other people's habits
	Other people's success
	How well other people listen to us
	How much our partner behaves as we wish him/her to
	What our partner fears or finds stressful
	Everything else

We have already looked at the things that lie *within* our
control, namely our thoughts and actions, and how we
take charge of these by distinguishing between 'appearances' and 'impressions': between external events and our

interpretations of those events. But now we have a huge coda to that thought: *nothing else matters.* How other people behave towards us, for example, is of no real interest, as their behaviour is 'external' and not within the realm of our thoughts or actions. If our partner is stressed and acts rudely, that's ultimately his or her business and not ours. We don't have to be upset about it; *it's fine.* It's all good; let it go.

Can it be that easy? What if others behave in such a way towards us that they impede our progress or make life intolerable? There are clearly points of subtlety and complexity that must be addressed if Epictetus's argument is to convince us. Remember, though, that only the (probably fictional) sage encapsulates this thinking *perfectly.* It is enough for the rest of us to do our best to incorporate this thinking into our daily lives as we can. But is it worth it? Does it work?

The idea is strong enough to have stuck around for two thousand years as a perennial piece of wisdom. We know of it today as the Serenity Prayer, attributed to the American theologian Reinhold Niebuhr, from a 1943 sermon:

> God, grant me the serenity to accept the things I
>   cannot change,
> The courage to change the things I can,
> And wisdom to know the difference.

It has lost some of its power through its quaintness. The pious language masks a mighty statement of self-affirmation, first formulated by a Roman slave, long before Christianity took hold.

Relationships and other areas of control

If we are to try to reappraise our inappropriate urges to control what does not lie in our domain, we should look at some areas where this impulse can lie hidden yet cause great damage.

When we try to control something over which we have no authority, we will of course fail, and we set ourselves up for frustration and anxiety along the way. No amount of effort on our part will ever secure the kind of power we would like to wield, if the target of our endeavours does not fall under our sway. It's simply wasted effort that leads inevitably to disappointment.

Perhaps we see this most clearly in the dynamics of romantic relationships, especially at their start. When we fall in love, we unconsciously bring to the fore everything we learnt about ourselves from our parents when we were children. Those areas where our caregivers were (as fallible human beings) stuck, or where their lives were in part unlived, will have impacted upon us like a script that, to one extent or another, sets out what we should seek or avoid in the world. We will learn strengths from them, but we will also, without realising, internalise particular fears and needs: our own personal ways of feeling a bit scared. Unhelpfully, these needs will feel to us entirely normal and rational.

They will resurface when we later enter a significant relationship, as we project them on to our new partner. Although we profess to be in love, and to have lost ourselves in this other person, we are barely (at this early point) doing them the justice of considering them an actual human being. They begin as a projection of our needs; we hope that he or she will be the perfect match, the magical 'other' who will satisfy us. Like the projections we make upon our misplaced goals that we think will guarantee us happiness, it is an enterprise doomed to failure. Our partners will never entirely fit in with our plans for them, and neither should they.

It is only when we stop projecting our needs – which first means becoming conscious of them *as* needs – that we can release the other person from the tyranny of our expectations. Meanwhile, each partner will try to make the other conform to his or her own deeply ingrained demands, and as this proves less and less successful, the need to control is likely to grow. The least stable partner will tend to project the most, thereby commonly setting the agenda for the couple. Both may find themselves living the script set down by the past experiences of the needier partner. If one partner fears, for example, that he is not loveable and will eventually be abandoned (a lesson learnt from early home life and enforced by a string of unstable relationships), he will most likely seek out evidence from the other that confirms that fear. Any hesitation from his partner to commit to marriage, or to declare their love as impossibly everlasting and infinite, is nervously leapt upon as evidence of a wavering commitment. Because those needs are unconscious, they are most powerful, for it is the shadowy, unacknowledged parts of us that wield most control. Particularly if the other partner is more prone to a fear of being swamped than of being abandoned, it may well be that very note of anxiety that makes him or her retreat.

The emotional outbursts and manipulative questioning of a partner who fears abandonment are panicked forms of control, which become more necessary and frantic as their fantasies are eroded. If we find ourselves doing this, we may be trying to keep the doomed projection of the 'perfect' partner intact, but unconsciously we are seeking to self-sabotage and prove our private abandonment theory correct. Thus the hidden childhood script seeks to confirm and repeat itself over and over again, and we may find ourselves in a string of such doomed relationships. We are likely to blame those partners, while remaining unaware that our private fear-triggers may be the true common denominator.

These forms of control will of course come from both sides. They are part of the natural dynamic when two partners grow from the fantasy position of seeing each other in magical terms to a real-life appreciation of the wholeness of the other. The fear of being overwhelmed can lend itself to as many control games as that of abandonment, as an 'avoidant' partner unconsciously arranges aspects of the partnership to keep the other safely at bay. There is no clear right and wrong, no worthwhile question of blame, just the intricate dance of two human beings living out their own internalised scripts. Ideally, as such needs are highlighted, we would allow our partners to guide us to a more conscious understanding of whatever shadowy authorities rule from the depths of their own personal history. And rather than control our partner to pander to our needs, we might begin to celebrate him or her as an entire, separate human being, one with some disappointing peculiarities it is up to us to navigate, accommodate, forgive.

Commonly, when we feel out of control, we try to establish control over *something*: the urge is almost overwhelming. Feeling uneasy in conversation at a dinner party, we arrange the scattered objects before us on the table at neat right angles; when having to deliver or accept bad news, we calmly straighten the folds on our clothing. At the severe end of the scale, we note the unhappy situation of those afflicted with eating disorders and/or the need to self-harm.

After relationships, food is probably most commonly subject to our need for control: a neurotic impulse that comes from an avoidance of deep dialogue with the self. We project our needs on to food in the way we do with our partners; many people overstuffing to feed a spiritual hunger or denying themselves in order to establish a secure area of jurisdiction (and along the way commonly demonising this or that ingredient or compound such as sugar or carbohydrates). Modern spirituality is often shrouded in an obsession with controlling food. Popular online holistic source The Living Centre encourages us: 'Many spiritually minded people receive intuitive messages to delete certain foods or beverages from their diet . . . They develop sudden adverse reactions to ingesting these substances'.[54]

Meanwhile, important research into the comparative auras of buns vs chapattis (before and after being placed on plates) has been carried out by The Spiritual Science Research Foundation and yielded the following results:

> It becomes clear that the bun absorbs negative and stressful vibrations in the environment and the *chapati* emits positive vibrations and destroys negative vibrations in the environment. Therefore it is more beneficial to eat the *chapati* than to eat the bun.[55]

Ironically, the paranoia provoked by this kind of pseudo-science, as well as the promise of instantaneous transformation and rescue proffered by many of its

54 www.thelivingcentre.com/cms/spirit/spiritual-nutrition-feeding-the-body-nourishing-the-spirit
55 www.spiritualresearchfoundation.org/spiritual-life/research-on-vibrations-emitted-by-bread-and-chapati

purveyors, point only to a worthless, shallow spirituality that has everything to do with graven images and projection, and nothing to do with the truly worthwhile spiritual project of becoming more conscious of our inner world. The only internal rumblings we are likely to respond to are those of an increasingly delicate stomach. It is worth remembering that when we have suffered from trauma in the past, we can become very sensitive to symptoms of pain and discomfort. As we do our best to navigate in the present the sometimes painful echoes of our pasts, it is often helpful, and perhaps with the gentle guidance of a professional, to recognise the surface appeal of frenzied control and address what neglected part of ourselves would most truly benefit from our attention. Still others look to control the tension release of inflicting physical pain on themselves, or the spiralling minutiae of their behaviour and thoughts. The need to manage and regulate – to feel authorship when we are not experiencing it where we should – does not easily go away. It's a fascinating and too often debilitating part of our natures, and those who are gripped by it are always deserving of our empathy.

So let's look a little closer at what those things are that do not fall under our control. The feeling of letting them go is enormously liberating, so we want to make sure we can confidently reap the benefits without doing ourselves (or others) a disservice by ignoring anything that's important. Epictetus's statement amounts to saying that the impressions we form about external events – and the actions we base on those impressions – are the only domain where we should apply effort and think about control; otherwise, all else falls on the other side of the line and should not be of concern.

A clear and common example of this is how we deal

with the sting of jealousy we might feel when a colleague talks excitedly about his promotion while we ourselves are frustrated with not moving ahead in our own career. As we've already seen, we only feel envy towards people who are roughly equal to us in terms of status, so we needn't feel surprised to find we can harbour such a negative emotion towards a co-worker. But we can, in the same breath, acknowledge that his success is *fine*. We have no control over our colleague's professional life or the happiness he gleans from it. If we dwell negatively upon his promotion, we may even find ourselves trying to 'fix' the feelings it provokes through put-downs or other similar behaviour, and in the meantime we are going to make ourselves miserable.

The key to why this works is that when we let things go that we can't control, *nothing bad happens*. The situation can't get any worse, and generally we get to feel an awful lot better. For me, the relief I feel when I remind myself that a source of annoyance is *fine*, is *none of my business*, is akin to the surge of joy that would fill my lungs as a child when I realised it was a Saturday and I didn't have to go to school. Thus the thought itself, if allowed to deeply settle, provides its own clear reward.

Any number of situations arise where the power of *it's fine* can make itself felt. Someone you know exhibits some behaviour that deeply irritates you. Now we have a way of dealing with it: we can identify that it isn't within our control and tell ourselves *it's fine* and none of our business. Even if that instruction *it's fine* takes a while to truly make itself felt in our bones, we have a clear target that we are aiming for. We should not exacerbate things by ruminating on their behaviour or, for that matter, tell others how much they annoy us because they are *always* like that. We need to let that feeling of *it's fine* sink in.

Depending on the depth of our annoyance, we may not feel the calming flood of its cool waters immediately, but we can make sure their path is kept as free from obstruction as possible.

Consider the alternatives: that we harbour resentment, bury aggression, or anxiously try to change events or take revenge. All these reactions will make matters worse. Plus, so much of our anxiety can come from not knowing *what* we should do. The simplicity of *it's fine*, even if it's a journey to get there, undoes all of that vexed toing and froing.

Partly in control

Alternatively, in the case of our colleague's promotion, we might choose to renew our attempt to secure our *own* desired preferment. While this sounds like a perfectly good response – 'Don't worry about what your friend is up to, focus on getting ahead yourself' – we now hit an interesting conundrum. Whether or not we get a promotion: is *that* under our control? On which side of the line does that fall? Should we try to control it and face anxiety if we don't succeed, or pay no attention to it and lose any drive to get ahead in our work? If we unpack this puzzle, we realise that it is confusing not because Epictetus's bifurcation is too simplistic but because the scenario justifies closer attention. There are some aspects of securing a promotion that are under our control and others that are not. The same might be said for achievement in many areas of life. We wish to be successful: is that under our control or not? It's *both*. If we are to take Epictetus's wise advice on board and see how it might help us with this quite common circumstance of having only partial control of the things that concern us, we have to spend a moment distinguishing between what *is* ours to take charge of and what *is not*. Then, simply, we only bother about the part that is. Magically, the overall results will then tend to improve.

Epictetus has already given us the guideline for sorting through this: only the parts that concern *what we think and do* are worthy of our attention. The rest of it we can ignore. So in the case of hoping for a promotion, we *are* in control of how well we work, the time and effort we put into our jobs and, to an extent, making sure that our endeavours are visible to the people who might choose to reward us. Moreover, if we set about exercising this control with the thought 'I will work as well as I can and furthermore make sure that my good work is visible', we can make sure we achieve exactly that. We will look more at the wisdom of this approach and its relationship to fame and public success in a later chapter.

We are *not*, however, in control of whether or not our boss chooses to offer us the advancement we would like. He will have his own pressures and his own preferences, which have nothing to do with us. We cannot control these. If we try to, we are fighting a losing battle. So that part we have to let go. We can make sure that our attitudes and actions are in line with what would be needed for a promotion, but we should not try to control matters beyond that point. And it's no coincidence that when people do seek to control the external event rather than just their own thoughts and actions, their efforts tend to backfire. Trying, for example, to win over your boss in an attempt to secure the promotion would most likely be misguided: he may well see through your thinly veiled efforts and react against them.

At the 2012 Academy New Member Reception, Bryan Cranston was asked if he had advice for his fellow actors. His answer is informed by Stoic thinking and thus has relevance far beyond the confines of how an actor might best approach auditions:

> The best advice for fellow actors is this: know what your job is . . . An actor is supposed to create a compelling and interesting character that serves the text and to present it in the environment where your audition happens, and then you walk away. That's it. Everything else that happens is out of your control, so don't even think of that, don't focus on that.
>
> You're not going there to get a job. You're going there to present what you do. You act. And there it is. And walk away. There's power in that . . .
>
> It's also saying 'I can only do so much', and then the decision of who might get a job is so out of your control that . . . it makes no sense to hold on to that . . .
>
> Once I adopted that philosophy, I never looked back, and I've never been busier in my life.

William B. Irvine, the modern Stoic who offered us the last-person-in-the-world thought experiment, neatly encapsulates this question of control with a sporting metaphor.[56] When we play a game of tennis, we are only partially in control of the outcome. If we fixate on the thought 'I must win this game', then we are trying to control something that we cannot. Our opponent might be better than us. He or she might start to beat us, and then we would feel like we were *failing*. We'd

56 William B. Irvine, *A Guide to the Good Life: The Ancient Art of Stoic Joy*

feel disappointment and anxiety. *Failure* is a disturbing feeling.

Instead, we can enter the game with the aim of 'I will play this game as well as I can.' Now we can make sure that we do that: how well *we* play is under our control. We may not win, but we can successfully play to the very best of our abilities as we intended. If our opponent starts to beat us, we are not failing. And again, it's no coincidence that we will almost always play better when we approach a game with this attitude. We will feel less anxiety and pressure, and are far more likely to remain focused and comfortable. Our game improves.

It's interesting that this Stoic ideal greatly reduces the likelihood of a feeling of failure. We should never aim to achieve anything that is out of our control, therefore we can always feel *in* control of the outcome. We may not play the game of tennis to the best of our ability, but at least all the variables involved in that task are under our power. If we don't play as well as we hoped, we'll know why and can correct it next time; this is not the same as pinning all our hopes on winning and then having them dashed by fortune when our opponent thrashes us. There is no anguish in the Stoic approach and plenty in the other.

Epictetus is showing us not only how to perform better but also how to circumscribe bad feelings when things don't go as well as would have been ideal. This is a far more delicate approach to 'no failure' than we would expect from the roaring motivators of modern times. These, as we have seen, tend to presume that by self-belief and goal-setting (visualising ourselves winning and so on) we can claim full control over our achievements and therefore fortune itself. However, as we now know, this blind optimism rarely thinks to distinguish between what is and what is not in our control, and instead relies on rhetoric and the inculcation of sheer faith to have us believe that *everything* is under our sway – even the universe itself – if only we believe and desire strongly enough. This does not reflect the reality of life, or that $x=y$ diagonal along which we meet with the daily offerings of fortune.

Another area where our misplaced efforts to wield control tend to backfire is that very human concern, known to many but not to all, of wanting people to like us. Normally, when I meet new people, I want them to think well of me. If someone within that group is quiet and does not clearly signal that they approve – a response I arbitrarily equate with how much they laugh at my jokes – then I sometimes find myself persevering in an attempt to win over that person. At this point, I am stepping outside of what is in my control. I step up the gags, pay them too much attention and most likely overwhelm them. I make a dick of myself by trying too hard.

If, instead, I were to pay attention to the Stoic fork and did not try to control what was beyond my domain, I might think 'I will be the nicest and friendliest person I can be around people.' Beyond that, how *they* choose to respond to me is their business, not mine. And I wouldn't then find myself mentally reviewing my behaviour late at night, regretting a stupid comment I made and scolding myself for being an idiot.

So there we have it: an unexpected corollary of Epictetus's advice. If we ignore everything over the other side of that line – everything that we do not control, everything other than our own thoughts and actions – we tend to remove anxiety and even achieve more success. And by reminding ourselves, as and when pressures arise, to distinguish between the component parts of what we can and cannot command, we start to live our lives in the glow of tranquillity: one that the classical philosophers tell us is a realistic and achievable model of happiness.

Indifferents

The Stoics referred to these external things as 'indifferents'. If we ultimately attach no importance to them, we can be sure that if they disappear from our lives, we won't suffer too great a pain of missing them. 'Permit nothing to cleave to you that is not your own,' Epictetus says, 'nothing to grow to you that may give you agony when it is torn away.'[57]

Because indifferents exist in the realm of external things, it follows not only that we cannot control them but also that we may lose them one day. Our property, our house, all the things we value fall on that far side of the line. We may lose our job and have to sell our home; we may lose or break our possessions and have to do without. Their continued existence in our lives is not guaranteed, and to act as if it is, is akin to a misguided presumption of control. Therefore we must relinquish that feeling of authority and let go of the attachment we might feel. Two powerful, positive consequences result from practising this non-attachment: we learn to value those things more by appreciating their transience in our lives, and we are more prepared for the moment we lose them.

The Stoics took this non-attachment towards indifferents very seriously. Seneca recommended that we mentally rehearse *losing* everything we have – family and property – to learn to value them more and be ready for

57 Epictetus, *Discourses*, iv.1.112

when fortune strikes and they are taken from us. In fact, he went so far as to say we should, every now and then, purposefully go without the luxuries in our lives and live for a day here and there as a pauper, estranged from people and things that bring us comfort, in order to soften the blow should we ever find ourselves destitute.

This was the situation somewhat forced upon Steven, the protagonist in *Apocalypse*, a two-part programme I made for Channel 4 in 2012. A young man who by all reports took what he had for granted, he became the unwitting participant in an enormous stunt where the family and life he knew were taken away from him. The idea was to rekindle his appreciation for them both. After a period of controlling his news sources, and having his friends and family play their parts, we had him believe the world was about to end through a collision with a huge meteor. After being stranded in a controlled environment and witnessing our sequence of pyrotechnic destruction, he was put to sleep (he had been chosen for his high levels of hypnotic susceptibility) and woke up alone in a post-apocalyptic world. His journey through our zombie re-envisioning of *The Wizard of Oz* had him discover the qualities of courage, selflessness and decisiveness that he lacked, and ultimately taught him to value that existence he had previously paid little attention to. This correlated with the thinking that should be familiar to us from the Epicureans: *learn to desire what you already have, and you will have all you need.*

There is an ironic twist here: by undoing our attachment to external things and people, we can value them more. The word 'attachment' might be misleading: surely we must be attached to things to really value them? Surely we wouldn't want to care *less* about our loved ones? Perhaps feeling less attached would undo some of the eventual misery of losing them, but are we being seriously asked to distance ourselves from our loved ones to protect ourselves from future loss?

No. The Stoic route to valuing things is to accept that whether they come or go from our lives is not under our control. This understanding allows us to enjoy them *even more*, because we know that we will not have them in our lives forever. We can look at the things and people we value each day with the knowledge that we will most likely lose them at some point, and love them all the more for that. One day your best friend may move away, and you may never see each other again. Loved ones may die or become estranged. Your partner, despite your promises to love each other forever, may one day leave you. In fact, it is inevitable: through death or choice, your closest relationships will end.

Remembering this invites us to express our feelings to those we love *now* while we can, to never take them for granted, and to not regret, when it's too late, that they never knew how important they were to us. And we will mitigate the future shock and despair that might otherwise hit us if we lose them for good. In an extraordinary passage from his *Discourses*, Epictetus gives us this advice:

> Remind yourself that what you love is mortal, that what you love is not your own. It is granted to you for the present while, and not irrevocably, nor for ever, but like a fig or bunch of grapes in the appointed season; and if you long for it in the winter, you are a fool . . . Henceforth, whenever you take delight in anything, bring to mind the contrary impression. What harm is there while you are kissing your child to say softly, 'Tomorrow you

216

will die'; and likewise to your friend, 'Tomorrow
either you or I will go away, and we shall see each
other no more'?

Presumably we are to speak such words quietly to ourselves rather than directly to our children and friends.
Either way, it might strike us as a little morbid and unnecessary. But perhaps this is a matter of degree: to *fixate*
upon the mortality of our children or the transience of
most friendships would bring its own form of anxiety and
defeat the Stoic purpose. But an occasional reminder of
how lucky we are to have the gift of these relationships in
our lives can only do us good. This must come from considering the sobering thought that they will one day come
to an end. If we knew these treasured relationships would
last *truly* forever, to trip and dance through the Garden
Immortal and never die, what effort would we make and
for how long? Why buy flowers when they will never
leave? Why value time spent together when you have
infinite repetitions ahead of you? Would you still fall
asleep with interlocked forms and whisper 'I love you'
every night for the rest of time? Would you continue to
surprise each other with breakfast on any of eternity's
mornings you chose, knowing that the rapture of either
activity would be quickly lost in the tiniest flickering
instant of infinity's interminable drudge?

To treasure something is to hold on to it carefully,
realising that it is precious and risks being lost or taken
from us. It is only the finite nature of our relationships
that gives them their meaning. Bittersweet transience
lends context and value. It is intoxicating in the first six
months of love to pledge ourselves for the rest of our lives.
It is also brave and deeply caring to accept, at least quietly
to oneself, that this may prove untenable, or that a lifespan

may not turn out to be the generous stretch of time we imagined. That knowledge might then flood us with a more steadfast kind of love that values the present rather than venerating an imagined future and, unlike the inflamed delirium of its early incarnation that flickers and wanes, grows only brighter with bounded time.

The Stoics added an important qualification to this notion of indifferents, which might come as a small relief to us if we find the idea of 'non-attachment' towards the comforts of home, income and family difficult to swallow. Unlike the Epicurean school, the Stoics did not call for a life of horticultural quarantine and simple carbohydrates. We remember they were active in the community, politically engaged and often very successful, to the extent that their detractors often accused them of hypocrisy. How might one balance apathy towards 'externals' or 'indifferents' with the accumulation of wealth or exerted efforts to bring about social change? The answer lies in their sub-category of 'preferred indifferents'.

At the time that Stoicism emerged as a school, the Cynic movement constituted a well-known philosophical alternative. Zeno of Citium, the founder of Stoicism, had in fact begun his philosophical life as a Cynic after moving to Athens and seeking out the wisest people he could find in the tradition of Socrates. The Cynics famously made a great show of their contempt for the trappings of ancient Greek society: Diogenes, their leader, was content to masturbate in the street. When an admiring Alexander the Great offered him anything he might desire, he replied only that the famed king move out of his sunlight. Early Stoicism, which was as much concerned with trickier notions of free will and logic as it was with ethics and the good life, took its cue from the Cynics and ruled harshly on the notion of attachment to external goods. But later

Stoicism softened a little in this regard as it became increasingly popular.

Thus it became permissible to *prefer* certain external things such as wealth, family and social position, as long as one didn't become *attached* to them. Stoics do not have to eschew these comforts in the way the Cynics did, as their aim is merely to gain psychological robustness (virtue) through not needing or attempting to control anything in life beyond their thoughts and actions. Marcus Aurelius wrote admiringly of his adopted father, that he was able to enjoy great wealth 'without arrogance and without apology. If [riches] were there, he took advantage of them. If not, he didn't miss them.'[58]

If, then, we can afford nice things or find them bestowed upon us, we should not feel bad about enjoying their presence in our lives. However, all the previous instructions still apply in full force: we are to keep a check on our relationship to external goods. Regarding the desire to accumulate more luxuries, we should keep a check on our 'impressions' of such 'appearances' (how those external things affect us) and make sure that we remain, as much as possible, in charge of our emotions. The dangerous alternative as the great Stoic Chrysippus expressed it, is that we let our emotions direct us as if we were running downhill and unable to stop. We can *prefer* to have a comfortable home, a healthy income and a loving family. We may also *prefer* to push for change in the world where we see injustice. But a Stoic will be prepared for such projects to fail or be terminated by fate, through mentally rehearsing worst-case scenarios and, above all, taking care not to believe he is in control of such things in the first place. Fortune will always continue on her

58 Marcus Aurelius, *Meditations*, i. 16

own path, providing one day and denying the next; the Stoic does not fight fate but quietly separates his business from hers.

The Stoics and fate

We're going to reclaim for ourselves the notion of Fate. Often today, when we use the word, we're referring to 'how things will turn out' in the future. As we've seen, the Stoics use the term to mean *how things are at any particular moment*. Although they imagined it as a force, we don't need to think of fate as meaning any more than the circumstances in which we happen to find ourselves. This relationship to fate is a fascinating aspect of Stoicism.

Although they strongly felt, like the Epicureans, that we should not live in fear of the gods, the Stoics were not atheists. Their notion of the gods was broadly pantheistic and is worth briefly explaining. To the Stoics, the gods and fate were one and the same, sometimes described as a fiery force that runs through the universe, otherwise known as the *Logos*. We might recognise this term from its later Christian context: when God breathes His Word into Creation, we find this mystical force described in Genesis by this term Logos. The Logos, or God's Word, is His *intention*, and thus the universe is at one with God's great plan. The Stoic notion (adopted by the Christians) is not dissimilar: it suggests a cosmic *intention* that runs through all things. They sometimes describe this force as Zeus, but we should not anthropomorphise in the way we do the Judaeo-Christian Breather of the Biblical Word. Instead, we can think of *circumstance* that propels itself forward. To the Stoics it is the life force of the universe itself and inseparable from it. Schopenhauer would, centuries later, touch on a similar universal propulsion with his extraordinary conception of the Will.

We are not being told that things 'will all work out for the best'. Unlike the equivalent Christian thought of 'God moves in mysterious ways, His wonders to perform', there is no pretence that Zeus is arranging things to work out in the most *favourable* way possible. There is no need to engage in tortuous theological gymnastics to explain why, for example, God has allowed babies to be born with horrible diseases, or a shooting or natural disaster to take place in the site of a blameless church. Fate is not looking out for us, and we don't have to pretend it is.

Externals are *indifferent*. Let's not mince words: if we are ill, or a loved one dies, this is ultimately a matter of no importance to fate and the machinations of the universe. The fiery Logos *could have* arranged things whereby you would be in great health and the loved one would still be alive and well, but that would be *of no more importance* than the current, less pleasant situation. The well-being of ourselves and others may be to us a 'preferred indifferent', and thus something to be enjoyed or secured where convenient, but it is ultimately an indifferent because it does *not* occupy that realm of actions and thoughts that is uniquely our concern. Things will not necessarily work out for the best. External events will proceed as planned without our involvement, and that knowledge can encourage us to treat them as they occur with a Stoic, qualified indifference.

This approach to fate is both brilliant and vulnerable to criticism. It yielded some of their most creative thinking, as they responded to detractors who could not agree with their claim that everything that happens is destined to be that way. The Stoics were early espousers of determinism: namely that all events, including our own actions, are ultimately determined by causes external to the will. This is generally seen as the opposite to holding a belief in free will, and the resulting debate has raged for two millennia and achieved vertiginous levels of complexity.

Critics attacked the Stoics' idea that if everything happens by fate, then all events are due to antecedent causes. If that were true, it would make no sense to praise or blame anyone for their actions, as they would not themselves be responsible for their behaviour or the impulses that led to it. In fact, how can it make any sense for us to be in control of our thoughts and actions if the Stoics are right and our mental and physical lives are pre-determined every step of the way? What does it mean for something to be our decision, for something to be 'up to us', if our apparent free decision is the inevitable conclusion of a series of prior events rolling up to this moment in history? Certainly it could make no sense to blame or praise someone for their actions or intentions. And, we might conclude, why should any of us bother doing *any-thing* if all outcomes are predestined? If your recovery or non-recovery from an illness is written in the stars, why should I bother getting you medical help? For Epicurus and others, these points made a nonsense of the doctrine of fate.

Chrysippus, the great Stoic academic, responded to this criticism by describing a cylinder rolling down a slope. The initial push needed to start it rolling is (to use Chrysippus's term) an 'auxiliary' cause of its movement and corresponds to the presentation made to our minds of some external event. In the real world, this auxiliary cause might be the approach of a lady of the sexy variety to a married man at a party. This is the equivalent of the cylinder receiving a push.

But what happens next? The direction the cylinder takes is not just determined by the external nudge; it also is a direct result of its own shape. This 'inner' quality of the cylinder is responsible for its continued motion – Chrysippus calls it a 'perfect' cause – and corresponds to the way we choose to assent to, or refuse to assent to, the possibilities presented to us in the world. Our man may choose to resist the temptation of an extra-marital affair or not, and this expression of his 'inner', moral constitution is as responsible as the presence of the woman for the direction he takes, and therefore allows us to blame or praise him as we see fit.

It's a creative response, but it feels like a dodge. It still begs the question: is our man responsible for his 'inner' impulses and assents? Elsewhere, Chrysippus takes an almost Aristotelian stance and says that well-educated and healthy constitutions will allow us to respond to external 'appearances' in a robust and virtuous way, whereas the ignorant will know no better than to succumb. Confusingly, he states in *On Nature and Soul In Animals* that these matters of virtue and vice are a result of fate, rolling onward throughout the universe. Thus he takes us full circle and tells us that our good or bad inner character – the shape of the cylinder, and the part we are supposed to take responsibility for – is fated, and therefore predetermined, and therefore not the sort of thing we should blame or praise. It's a bit messy.

It seems most likely, as Josiah B. Gould concludes in his *The Philosophy of Chrysippus*, that this prominent Stoic held two incompatible views of fate and alternated between them to draw the benefits from each. The first view was that the 'rigorous causal nexus' of fate provides a logical basis for the magical prophecies of the revered Delphic Oracle (in which the Stoics believed) and imparts a comforting sense of orderliness to the universe. On the other hand, the psychological experience of free will is necessary if we are to maintain the existence of moral responsibility. They do not sit well together, but, as Gould says:

> One cannot lightheartedly condemn Chrysippus, who was one of the first in the history of Western philosophy to become aware of the difficulties inherent in reconciling the principle of causality and moral responsibility, for having failed to solve a problem which has exercised thinkers to the present day.[59]

For our purposes, and despite these back and forth arguments, all we need draw from the Stoics' notion of fate is a helpful thought found repeated in various forms throughout Marcus's *Meditations*. We each constitute a tiny part of the universal whole. Each of us is like a limb that works with other limbs to create a functioning body. Or, if a different image helps us more: when things irritate us, or when we feel as if the universe is conspiring against us, we would do well to remember that we are better off seeing those irritants as the strewn shavings on the carpenter's floor and accepting that they are a natural by-product of a greater thing at work. There will always be people and events that get in the way of our plans. Thus we should not get too attached to our ambitions and realise that our tiny aims are an insignificant part of the myriad of plans, thwarted and realised, that make up the grand scheme of fortune as it continues to unravel itself.

We don't need to believe that there is wisdom or a *telos*

59 Josiah B. Gould, *The Philosophy of Chrysippus*

inherent in this unravelling. The model of evolutionary theory might prove more helpful. Random mutations occur; some by-products of that randomness that are conducive to survival stick around and are carried forward to the next round, and others don't. There is no grand meaning, no overall design, no fiery breath emanating from a Prime Mover. Yet there is a *principle* at work, and when we pit our mortal schemes against it, we might imagine we hear the hollow chuckle of the universe resounding back. Rhonda Byrne, whose Law of Attraction would like to reduce the mighty macrocosm to a pandering mail-order catalogue, might benefit from being more attuned to the reality of that cosmic indifference.

Amor fati

Marcus is reminding himself in his *Meditations*, and Nietzsche is telling us in the concept of eternal recurrence, to aim for the uncompromising acceptance of life *as it is*. To align ourselves with fortune; to cease trying to control it. This is the love of fate – *amor fati*. Neither philosopher would discourage improving our lot – 'Become who you are' was Nietzsche's rallying cry – or trying to ensure social change where it mattered. But these efforts notwithstanding, a key to living more happily is to simply decide that you are very happy with reality *per se*. We might as well be, because if we try to change things we cannot control, we are going to become angry and frustrated. Understanding we are only in control of our thoughts and actions, we can choose how to respond to events whenever they prove less than ideal, without making ourselves unhappy. It's fine that people are rude or ignorant. *It's fine*. If we were in their shoes, with their history and their current pressures, we would act the same way. We certainly shouldn't let them make *us* act rudely or ignorantly out of frustration.

It takes more than the words 'it's fine' to really *feel* that something is fine. We will be very eager to justify feeling angry. We most likely have, after all, a story in which we have been somehow slighted. It takes effort to let go of that. Rarely does our story reflect reality, remember; it is only our biased perception of a very complex conflict that has arisen between differing priorities held by people who are nervous about this or that. But take that thought – 'it's fine' – and let it drop into our stirred-up and agitated feelings. *It's fine*. It truly is. Feel what happens as you let it permeate through the story you have been telling yourself. Anything on the other side of the line – anything other than our thoughts and actions – we can safely decide is *fine*. We can ask ourselves: how is it fine? Why is it fine? Why is it OK to not try to fix or change this? What would happen if I left it? What terrible thing would occur? We can enjoy the warm glow of relief as our centre of gravity returns to a place located securely within us. We are not fooling ourselves – it truly *is fine* to let go of these things. Nothing bad happens if we stop trying to fix them. Of course some grievances are harder to let go than others. Occasionally we must act to protect ourselves from danger, and these are the thoughts and actions which we should seek to control. Beyond that, let us allow that *it's fine* to permeate where it can, and feel some prelude to the fuller relief it might eventually offer in time.

Each of us is born into a world where we know no better than to internalise every message we receive as being one about *us*. We learn patterns of behaviour to secure attention and to defend against feelings of abandonment or being overwhelmed. We move into life with those rigid patterns in place, while life swirls around us like a whirlwind of loose, constantly fluctuating possibilities. We desperately try to reduce it to something manageable, something that confirms the broken messages about ourselves we may have learnt in childhood and have institutionalised into our behaviour.

The Greeks understood this relationship between man and the machinations of the universe. Their tragedies taught us that we need to learn raw humility in the fickle face of fate. Tragic heroes marched out into the world full of pride, biased vision and a mighty capacity for self-deception. Fate ultimately brought them to their knees. The lesson for us is not that we are doomed but that we must reassess the control we think we wield.

☺

8

Applying Stoic Methods

I discovered the Stoics after reading Michel de Montaigne, the deeply influential French Renaissance philosopher who popularised the essay form and perhaps first explored what it truly is to be human. His writings explore every aspect of himself, from being in a friendship, through matters of happiness, to concerns regarding his penis. When Montaigne was a boy, his father instructed the family and its servants to address the child only in Latin, a pedagogical plan which was happily endured. Michel grew up to be a successful statesman and a vibrant, generous humanist. Eventually, and most appealingly, he retired at thirty-eight to write in his library, housed in a round tower in the family home. Across the edges of his bookshelves, he had the following declaration inscribed:

> In the year of Christ 1571, at the age of thirty-eight, on the last day of February, his birthday, Michel de Montaigne, long weary of the servitude of the court and of public employments, while still

> entire, retired to the bosom of the
> learned virgins, where in calm and free-
> dom from all cares he will spend what
> little remains of his life, now more than
> half run out. If the fates permit, he will
> complete this abode, this sweet ancestral
> retreat; and he has consecrated it to his
> freedom, tranquillity, and leisure.

Montaigne mentions Seneca frequently in his essays, which in turn form part of a general resurgence of interest in Stoicism during the sixteenth century. Curious as to who this Roman thinker and correspondent was, I left Montaigne and secured myself a copy of Seneca's letters, and discovered an approach to life that I was moved to realise resonated with my own; it assembled my own disparate thoughts like so many loose light bulbs that needed stringing together. When others inspire us, they tend to do so through the clear expression of these sketchy, adumbrated thoughts we ourselves have known but never had the perspicacity to formulate with certainty. I knew, for example, that I had always lacked ambition, never feeling a need to be famous. I knew I pretended to be excited by the idea of career success and viewing figures because that seemed to motivate the grown-ups I worked with. Reading Seneca on the wisdom of non-attachment to external things felt very powerful and encouraging: not only was it okay to not be fame-hungry, or to be wary of being better known, it might even be *preferable*.

The knowledge that a system has been thought through and holds up helps us more confidently put it to the test in our own lives. This first level of appreciation is not enough for a personal transformation, but it is a start. If these Stoic ideas feel deeply wrong to you – if, for example, you feel that happiness can only reside in our full surrender to the troughs and peaks of a wild emotional life – then no amount of advice as to how to best put them into practice will be of interest. If, on the other hand, they resonate at some level and seem to be worthy of at least a trial period, then we can look at some other ways we might make them part of our routine. Luckily, the Stoics were full of handy, practical means of applying their thinking and enjoying tranquillity.

Our aims, as we look at how to achieve this, are worth clarifying. Our goals may develop if the Stoic life continues to appeal, but for now at least we can recognise our principal objectives in the words of René Descartes, the philosopher who earlier featured in the story of the automaton. Over a thousand years after Stoicism reached its popular height, Descartes described that his ambition was:

> To try to conquer myself rather than fortune, and to change my desires rather than the order of the world, and generally to accustom myself to believing that there is nothing that is completely within our power except our thoughts, so that, after we have done our best regarding things external to us, everything that is lacking for us to succeed is, from our point of view, absolutely impossible.[60]

Marcus Aurelius offers us another thought that might help us to clarify our aims:

> Ambition means tying your well-being to what other people say or do.

60 René Descartes, *Discourse on Method and Meditations on First Philosophy*

> Self-indulgence means tying it to the things that
> happen to you.
> Sanity means tying it to your own actions.[61]

We are looking to tie our well-being to our *own* actions,
not those of others. The idea is simple, but its execution
can feel difficult. The Stoics have little sympathy for the
fact we are deeply social creatures, taking our cues from
our peers and routinely being made to act against our
values. So we can hold the image of the perfect Stoic sage
before us but also accept that he is all but fiction; the
Stoics did not believe him to actually exist (unlike
the Epicureans, who endowed their founder with near-
mystical qualities). Meanwhile, we should aim to do our
best, as Marcus reminded himself, and count our successes as they occur. Epictetus suggested:

> So is it possible to be altogether faultless? No, that
> is impracticable; but it is possible to strive continu-
> ously not to commit faults. For we shall have cause
> to be satisfied if, by never relaxing our attention,
> we shall escape at least a few faults.[62]

We shouldn't expect perfection in ourselves any more
than we should in the external world. Our final aim is, of
course, to lead a happier, more centred life, embracing the
kind of psychological robustness the Stoics called virtue.
But the Stoic path need not lead to a life that is *self*-
centred, despite the reputation the school has amongst its
critics. The fortitude that comes with only bothering
ourselves with those things within our control allows us

---

61 Marcus Aurelius, *Meditations*, vi. 51
62 Epictetus, *Discourses*, iv.12

to then reach out more widely into the world and experience it in a generous and selfless way. Despite this talk of paying attention only to what lies within *our* power, when we combine that thought with an attitude of openness, it will allow us to connect in the best possible way with the human race at large.

An entirely practical philosophy

The first point to consider when looking at how to apply Stoic thought to our real lives is that Stoicism, along with Epicureanism and the other major Hellenistic schools, were *entirely* concerned with the art of living. Even Aristotle, who arrived at the conclusion that a life of intellectual contemplation was the best way to live, was still talking about personal transformation and how to best engage with the few short years we have. Even the early Stoic discourses on matters of physics, ethics and logic were not merely theoretical pursuits for the classroom. The Stoics had no time for the type of philosopher who prided himself on his encyclopaedic knowledge, his polished rhetoric or his understanding of difficult abstract points. Theory *only* existed in the service of practical exercises.

If then, as described above, we find that the Stoic approach to fate leads to some inconsistencies, the matter need not be of great importance. What *does* matter is whether the models of fate we are given help us *psychologically* in achieving our aims. In one instance, it may serve us to see fate as rolling on throughout history without our involvement, and to accept that events in the world happen as they ought to. In another, it may benefit us more to know that our actions make a difference and that our choices do matter. We can hold both opposing models in our mind; it matters not if neither quite tells the full story, or the reality exists somewhere between or in some quantum space quite separate from the two.

Also, what might appear to be inconsistencies in thought will often emerge from the misunderstanding of the purpose of the extant texts. As modern people, we are tempted to read them as complete philosophical systems, but often these documents are mere notes to self (as in the case of Marcus), transcripts of conversations with students (as we see with Epictetus) or letters written to a specific student (Seneca). Information would have been presented differently to novice students than to those more invested in the teachings. Taken side by side they can seem confusing if we imagine they should always match. But they don't need to. When we remember that all that mattered was showing a listener how he might change for the better, we can understand that discrepancies might emerge, where the philosopher's priority as a communicator is to connect with the particular audience he has in mind.

Pierre Hadot, the late, though still hugely compelling, French philosopher and historian of philosophy, has written emphatically that the Stoic works must be read in their proper context as 'spiritual exercises'. He uses the word 'spiritual', acknowledging that we may baulk at it, to highlight the point that the Stoics were interested in bringing about a conversion, an entire transformation of the self and its relationship to the universe. Nowadays, it is hard to hear such language without thinking of flabby New Age practices and the flatulent cosmic mentality that pervades the fringes of modern society, as we try in our irreverent age to claw back an engagement with something greater than ourselves. Hence, when ancient philosophers talk about our souls, or the cosmos, we can easily switch off. To an extent, this may be justified by the fact that the world in which Stoicism developed is very different from ours. But we must be careful. The influential Swiss psychiatrist Paul Dubois (1848–1918) made the point:

> If we eliminate from ancient writings a few allusions that gave them local colour, we shall find the ideas of Socrates, Epictetus, Seneca and Marcus Aurelius absolutely modern and applicable to our times. In this field of ethical thought men remain the same.[63]

Hadot's point is that Stoic thinking was designed to be *life-changing*; neither merely intellectually interesting nor simply amounting to some suggestions for change in behaviour. What it offered was something profoundly transformative. It's worth noting that anyone who adopted these principles in the age we are considering was called a philosopher; the term referred to someone who *lived* in a certain way, not only to someone who spent his time contemplating or devising systems of thought. 'Such a transformation is not easy,' he writes, 'and it is precisely here that spiritual exercises come in. Little by little, they make possible the indispensible metamorphosis of our inner self.'[64]

Importantly, he is saying that living as a philosopher, or what we today would think of as living a considered life, can be difficult. This should encourage us, because it reflects the reality of that $x=y$ axis we have discussed. The philosopher of old was torn daily between living as a

63 Paul Dubois, *The Psychic Treatment of Nervous Disorders*
64 Pierre Hadot, *Philosophy as a Way of Life*

philosopher on the one hand and as a human being on the other, with the emotional and psychological demands of gritty, upsetting real life constantly clamouring for attention. We can acknowledge this and simply, as we have learnt from Marcus, do our best.

Of course, nowadays, philosophy means something different. How has the word come to have its current dry, academic feel? Hadot points out that as Christianity took hold, it first presented itself as a school of thought, adopting and assimilating the spiritual exercises of philosophical traditions such as Stoicism. But in medieval times, a period of scholasticism emerged, wherein Christian theology became the supreme science; all other forms of thought were divested of their transformative aspects, and philosophy became the mere 'handmaid of theology'. Philosophy's role was only to offer theoretical material that could be of use to Christian teaching.

The legacy of this period is that it has needed a few truly extraordinary characters such as Nietzsche to reclaim philosophy as something that should dramatically change lives; otherwise it has remained a largely theoretical business. Philosophers now very rarely work outside of the university system, which has only encouraged its language to become more technical and further disengaged from 'the soul's art of living'.

The Stoic approach is a formula for tranquillity. How, then, do we make sure it has real, practical, transformative value in our lives?

Start talking to yourself

The first, most fundamental decision we should make is to engage more often in a silent dialogue with ourselves. We need to be able to step back and recognise when we are making choices as to how to behave or think, or acknowledge when an unhelpful choice has been made and supply counter-arguments to remedy the situation. If we are feeling angry, upset or hurt, it's understandable, but we have forgotten ourselves. It may be unavoidable that we will feel some of these negative emotions, perhaps every day, but there is all the difference in the world between allowing them to take root (which comes from believing they are caused by external events and leads to us holding others accountable for our feelings) and accepting responsibility for them and seeing if we might correct them internally.

We know already the two big questions we might ask ourselves when we are feeling mad, bad or sad:

1. I am responsible for how I feel about external events. What am I doing to give myself this feeling?
2. Is this thing that's upsetting me something which lies under my control? If not, what if I were to decide it's fine and let it go?

We should ask these questions and pay attention to the honest answers. At first we might feel a fight: we still want to blame other things and other people for our problems. Until we have practised this, we may feel like there are things we don't wish to forget about and decide are 'fine'. But consider even the worst cases of, say, the effects of childhood abuse: if a survivor spent years in highly effective therapy and found herself finally rid of the debilitating legacy of such trauma, the key thought that will have allowed the healing to occur will be something along the lines of 'it's fine, now, to let it go'. At some level, this thought will release us. The only difference is how easy or difficult it is to let such a powerful thought take

root. If the seed needs planting deeply in those unconscious strata of which we are unaware, the chances are we
will need help from a professional to find the right spot.

Meanwhile, once we have opened ourselves to the
flood of relief that comes from relinquishing our annoyance at some external thing or person, it becomes a lot
easier to secure the next time.

We can be made aware of our own unhelpful tendencies when we listen to other people and make use of their
grumbles as a way of recognising how these unhelpful
thought patterns work in ourselves. It's much easier to
recognise when others fall into these traps, and in fact
we'll see it happens almost all the time. By being aware of
the unhelpful thinking that *others* fall prey to, we remind
ourselves of these important building blocks and are more
likely to remember to apply them to our *own* situation
when we need them most.

The aim, though, is not to criticise others for bad
thinking: that would be in itself a form of trying to control other people and how they operate, which are not
things within our sphere of influence. We might find that
gently offering forms of Stoic advice helps others who
find themselves in a fix, but our main concern for now is
to make sure that we are applying them in a way conducive to our *own* calm. And it is here that the ancients'
employment of pithy slogans and aphorisms is very helpful. Since the pre-Socratic days of Pythagoras, they knew
the value of a helpful formula. This technique, a kind of
auto-suggestion, has continued famously through our
times in the work of Émile Coué, the French psychologist
who gave us the daily mantra, 'Every day, in every way, I
am getting better and better.' This particular modern
example is not especially helpful, for it falls foul of
the problems of fetishising positive thinking and can

therefore leave us feeling like a failure (when things patently don't get better every day). Yet the fact that it *can* be damaging is in itself a testament to the power of internalising these sorts of apophthegm. We have to make sure we get them right, and the Greeks had a far better grasp of what works than we do nowadays, when we struggle to articulate ideas that were discovered and put to the test two thousand years ago.

Epicurus, we have seen, taught his philosophy through demanding a straightforward absorption of dogma – the opposite of Aristotle's insistence on rational discussion and private rumination to complete the process of teaching. Epicurus's approach relied on the memorisation of sayings that could then spring easily to mind when most needed. The Stoics, though keener on employing our rational faculties to bring us in line with a harmonious and robust life, also made sure that their ideas were clearly expressed and easy to bring before our mind's eye. Aside from the major building blocks we have considered, let's have a look at some other helpful techniques and points they offer us.

Don't add to first impressions

Here we are, every day navigating the world and the people in it from that unique point of view that we mistake for clear-sightedness. A neurotic or anxious person prides herself on being 'perceptive' when it comes to people, as if the legacy of a perennially unsettling childhood would be powers of observation as cool and perspicacious as Sherlock Holmes himself. We all operate from the vantage point of our own deep fears, and we stand guard against any threat to them. This wariness we mistake for insight; we thus decide from a place of insecurity what truth is and find evidence for it everywhere.

Thus Lover A asks Lover B if she is ever attracted to strangers; B pauses before assuring her nervous lover that she is not. A, searching for evidence to secure his fear that partners are fickle – a fear that compelled him to ask such a daft question – interprets the pause with neurotic discontent: as evidence that he will never be enough for his lover. Having found what he sought, he congratulates himself on his dizzying talent for seeing people for who they really are. Meanwhile, for B, the pause was an act of love: a hesitation while she decided how to answer an unfair question without hurting her partner's feelings.

The Stoics point out to us that we 'augment' our bad impressions of appearances 'with great wit'. We interpret and embellish, and make matters so much worse for ourselves.

The simple and beautiful alternative, as recommended by Marcus and Seneca, is to make sure we do our best to stick with our first impressions of things:

> Do not say more to yourself than the first impressions report. You have been told that someone speaks evil of you. This is what you have been told; you have not been told that you are injured. I see that the little child is ill; this is what I see, but that he is in danger I do not see. In this way then abide always by the first impressions and add nothing of your own from within, and that's the end of it.[65]

It is hard to stick to first impressions, perhaps because we think it makes us seem obtuse. People who just take things at face value and don't *think* more deeply about them

65 Marcus Aurelius, *Meditations*, viii. 49

hardly sound like role models. But we are not doing this out of a lack of imagination: quite the opposite, in fact. We are choosing when appropriate, because we can clearly see the advantages, to stick with our first impression and not embellish the story. When we do otherwise, we too easily work to consolidate and bolster our insecurities by confirming to ourselves our worst fears.

We might object that this instruction would have us ignore signs of a friend in distress. It need not. We can enquire about and feel sympathy for our friend's trouble, while making sure that we remain strong and appropriately distanced from the pain (and therefore of more help to such people who need our assistance). The Stoic advice is offered to reduce our anxiety, and therefore the answer to such objections is usually simple: apply the advice where it's useful.

Consider how easily we interpret silence or non-engagement – either face-to-face or via an unanswered communication – as a sign of dislike. We eagerly arrange events into a narrative in which someone is choosing to ignore us. We play vividly before ourselves a little movie of them reading our text or post, rolling their eyes and deliberately ignoring it. We see them as bored with us, disgusted with our attempts to impress, or whatever reaction best plays to our insecurities. We have turned *nothing* (silence) into *something* very hurtful, and the fact that we have frequently been guilty of non-response ourselves without harbouring any such motives is something we choose to ignore. We might commonly delay responding to a friend's text because we read it at a moment when it wasn't convenient to reply, and then as it disappeared from the bottom of our phone screens it slipped as blamelessly from our memory. We would find it strangely self-flagellating of our friend if he took it to mean we didn't like him. Yet we so readily assume such a motive when it seems to be aimed at us. We can benefit from remembering the words of the novelist David Foster Wallace: 'You will become way less concerned with what other people think of you when you realise how seldom they do.'[66]

Don't add to first impressions. It's difficult *not* to do something of course, once we have it in our mind. And in the same way we like to repeatedly press the button to call the lift when we're in a hurry, as if doing so will summon it any more quickly, we find it hard to sit back quietly if something is playing on our minds. So instead, we can accept it isn't within our control and decide it's *fine*. Once we've made that decision, our insecurity dissolves, and in the case of the text, they may come back to us to apologise for leaving it so long to reply. Meanwhile, if we had badgered them with further messages, we can almost guarantee that we *would* have infuriated them.

When our partner snaps at us, we can accept it as just that. He or she has had a hard day, or might be irritated by any one of a number of tiny factors that have nothing to do with us. Or, more likely, we have communicated a provocative emotion ourselves, and the curt reply is a reaction to that. We can communicate annoyance and impatience quite effectively even when we think we are hiding them. A is woken up by the postman after a very late night and drags herself to the front door, half-asleep, to accept the parcel. She sees in the front room, B, her partner or flatmate, who has been oblivious to the sound of the door as he is watching a video with his headphones on. A calls out to him; he doesn't hear. She calls again; still no response. Now she is annoyed, and the shouting

66 David Foster Wallace, *Infinite Jest*

has augmented her initial unhappy state by adding frustration to the mix. She walks into the front room with the parcel, interrupting B's field of vision, and drops the delivery on the table. He starts, removes his headphones and catches a look of annoyance in her eye. 'You had your headphones on,' she points out, trying to bury feelings of anger, aware that he hasn't really done anything wrong, despite how irritated she has become.

A expects an apology but instead receives a defensive response, 'Yeah, so?'

That's the last A sees of B before he goes to work. For the rest of the day, the scenario plays on her mind. Why did he react like that? Why couldn't he just say, 'Oh, sorry – I didn't hear the bell.' That's all she wanted to hear. Instead, his prickly riposte, which she now identifies as part of a general behavioural trait, annoying her even more, has ruined her morning. By the time he returns, she has been ruminating on it for most of the day. Yet she can't bring it up – it would seem bizarrely petty to draw attention to something so small that happened so long ago. So she sits on it for longer, until eventually, a week later, she finds a way of addressing it. Now she hears the other side of the story: B was annoyed because he could see A was annoyed. A insists she wasn't annoyed because she knows she was careful not to express anger.

You may be aware that an effective acting technique for communicating any state (drunkenness, anger, sadness) is to 'play against' it: that is to concentrate on displaying its *opposite*. An actor who simply 'plays' drunk will usually be an unconvincing caricature, whereas one who concentrates on desperately trying to appear sober (focusing very hard on placing a glass down without dropping it or getting a key in a lock, for example) will do a better job. Likewise, when we feel anger in a conversation we often try to hide it; we soften our voices and 'try' to seem calm. Our anger will, however, most likely be very evident indeed, and usually more impactful than a bellowing display.

B sensed A's anger or saw it flash across her face and, stung by it, did not think of apologising for the inconvenience but instead leapt to self-justification. So much anguish caused by not simply refusing to add to first impressions. A could just think, 'Okay, he has responded defensively. That's an understandable reaction.' B could think, 'She looked a bit annoyed.' Annoyance is understandable. That's fine too. Neither need to tell themselves a story where they emerge as the one in the right. It was an unfortunate and blameless situation, very common when people live together. We'll look more at anger later in this book, as it demands special attention, but so much pain can be avoided by not devising stories that further upset us. Thinking of that phrase 'Don't add to first impressions' may not always solve the problem, but it will help mitigate it. It might, for example, help us to talk about the incident or even laugh it off, without making the other person feel defensive or scared.

Do I have a problem right now?

So much of our unhappiness comes from ruminating over past events or worrying about possible future ones. Guilt, in particular, is very pervasive. Normally, I find, if I am annoyed at something for a long time, or if something someone has said is 'eating me up', it's because, if I'm honest with myself, I know I have done something wrong. That feeling of being 'caught out' creates in us all sorts of misplaced angry and defensive reactions. Guilt is attached to the past in the same way that fear is attached to the future. If we have let ourselves down, it is difficult, but highly therapeutic, to admit as much to ourselves and realise we could have done better; we make a mental note for next time, apologise if need be to the people concerned, and move on. We are fallible human beings and will make mistakes for the rest of our lives.

We may have been the victim of traumatic events in the past. Free-floating anger and misplaced feelings of guilt can have a lot to contribute. But they *are* in the past, and if we continue to fixate upon them in the present, and define ourselves by a story that casts us as a victim, we will not undo the damage done; we need to find a way to change that story and manage our feelings more productively.

Fears about the future fall into the same trap. We vividly anticipate upcoming events in which we know we are likely to feel uncomfortable. Or, already annoyed at someone, perhaps we imagine having a future conversation with them wherein they annoy us even more. We might play out to ourselves the terrible and annoying ways they might respond. Or we avoid the conversation because we fear an argument. These all create bad feelings *now*, about something that hasn't happened yet, or may not happen at all. Our capacity to think through possible future scenarios to work out the best course of action is a curse as well as a blessing. Seneca writes:

> Fear keeps pace with hope. Nor does their moving together surprise me; both belong to a mind in suspense, to a mind in a state of anxiety through looking into the future. Both are mainly due to projecting our thoughts far ahead of us instead of adapting ourselves to the present. Thus foresight, perhaps the greatest blessing given to humanity, is transformed into a curse. Wild animals run from

the dangers they actually see, and once they have escaped them worry no more. We however are tormented alike by what is past and what is to come. A number of our blessings do us harm, for memory brings back the agony of fear while foresight brings it on prematurely. No one confines his unhappiness to the present.[67]

When we find ourselves worrying or anxious, we might ask ourselves: 'Do I have a problem *right now*?' If not, and where possible, we could decide to worry about it if and when it happens, or learn something useful from it and consign it to the past.

As we continue to look at the Stoics' suggestions for dealing with a variety of threats to our peace of mind, we will find several thoughts of this kind. Bring them to mind as you need them, do your best to implement them and, even if you don't solve the problem entirely, note the difference that this kind of thinking makes.

This amounts to an attention paid to the self. The Stoics called it *prosoche*, and it comprises to their fundamental attitude. It distinguished them from the Epicureans: the Garden-dwellers aimed to take a simple joy in the natural pleasures of the moment, whereas the Stoics are more resolute, finding ways to guard against any threat to tranquillity. We should also therefore bear in mind that a certain amount of tenacity is demanded if we are to continue this dialogue with ourselves and achieve the Stoic take on *ataraxia*:

If you shall have lain down ten days, get up and attempt to make a long walk, and you will see how

67 Seneca, *Letters from a Stoic*, Letter V

your legs are weakened. Generally, then, if you
would make anything a habit, do it;[68]

Epictetus is saying that we need to practise. If we don't do
something for a long time, it is difficult to then do it when
we need to. And, likewise, failure is not important (for
everyone will fail as life and fortune sometimes prove too
much for us to virtuously handle); *tenacity* is the key.
'Getting back in the saddle' is how this thought has come
down to us over the millennia.

We will let ourselves down constantly as we try to utilise
these Stoic principles. Certain practices will get easier
over time as we get used to them, but new ones will
emerge that prove difficult. This is all part of the challenge and joy of a considered life. The important things
are not the individual successes or failures but the process
of learning and developing along the way.

You may have had the experience of stopping smoking and then three months later, after a stressful couple of
days, you smoke one cigarette again. You immediately
feel that you have failed. Within a week or two, you're
back to twenty a day. Epictetus's more helpful thought is
to embrace tenacity over perfection. One cigarette after
three months is a fantastic success after years of smoking
twenty a day. Maybe in *another* three months you'll have
another one. Perhaps *six* months after that, you'll have a
third. Perfection is not important, just *keeping going* is all
that matters.

Attention to ourselves is, then, the first step. Of
course this doesn't mean self-obsession or the kind
of attention-to-self prized by the neurotic. *Prosoche* is

paying attention and checking that we are remaining suitably in charge of ourselves. It restores our centre of gravity
to an internal point. It gives us distance from our negative
emotional responses, which is often all we need to avoid
being swept away by them. This kind of interior dialogue
allows us to question our attachment to positive feelings
too: new purchases and other people's flattery can feel
nice, but we have to treat them with the same dose of salt
that we would apply to negative 'externals' such as insults
and loss of property. By allowing this Stoic voice in our
head to speak up and hold us to account, we can take
some control over what we choose to accept. And when
we do feel bad, we have a wise interlocutor who can point
us towards helpful solutions instead of the more familiar
nagging voice that too often sends us into a spiral of ever-
deepening gloom by focusing us on what we lack.

Rational meditation

If we only use these techniques at the moments we most
need them, we are unlikely to make them part of the
fabric of our lives. Our aim, when we consider these Stoic
techniques, is to achieve a kind of tranquillity, and
through this to increase our happiness without making
the mistake of trying to chase it directly. Dealing with
bad feelings as they arise is a start, but not enough to be
most effective. Sometimes, this sort of intervention just
isn't enough: we might talk to ourselves, listen to that
sage-like voice, see how we should react, and *still* feel bad.

The key, then, is to get ahead of the game and make
sure we are experiencing life in such a way that makes
provision for such negative events before they arise.
Nothing prepares us like preparation itself. Marcus
Aurelius writes:

Say to yourself in the early morning: I shall meet today inquisitive, ungrateful, violent, treacherous, envious, uncharitable men. All these things have come upon them through ignorance of real good and ill. But I, because I have seen that the nature of good is the right, and of ill the wrong, and that the nature of man himself who does wrong is akin to my own . . . I cannot be harmed by any of them, for no man will involve me in wrong, nor can I be angry with my kinsman or hate him; for we have come into the world to work together, like feet, like hands, like eyelids, like the rows of upper and lower teeth. To work against one another therefore is to oppose Nature, and to be vexed with another or to turn away from him is to tend to antagonism.[69]

Marcus is reminding himself to look ahead each morning to the forthcoming day and imagine meeting the most unpleasant people possible. Dealing with those we don't like is at least as much a reality for us as it was for a Roman emperor two thousand years ago. But rather than merely trying to think himself out of the annoyance these people might provoke when it happens, he is doing his best to ensure that their irksome personalities don't bother him in the first place.

The passage might strike us as too pessimistic. Do we really want to venture into the world expecting people to be unpleasant? Might that even encourage us to see nastiness in people and miss the better natures we come across? Certainly it does not chime harmoniously with the notion of seeing the best in people. Are these lines just

69 Marcus Aurelius, *Meditations*, ii. 1

the ramblings of a miserable man and best ignored?

Pierre Hadot has reminded us that we should not read these lines as psychologically revealing self-expression. That was not the point of the book. Marcus was not writing down his feelings in quite the way one might express oneself in a modern journal. He is reminding himself to use Stoic exercises and to maintain the quality of psychological robustness through daily practice. The point is not to see the world as full of mean and ungrateful men and women. The point is that we *will* meet people we don't like, or people who are ignorant or rude, and if we can avoid being dragged down by those people, then we can be of better service to both them and ourselves.

Note that Marcus concludes by painting a very compassionate picture. We are all here to work together, he says, like parts of a body. We are all part of a whole. We need each other to function, and petty conflicts do not serve the greater good. His aim, then, is not to avoid those he doesn't like but to find a way around the clashing of personalities and achieve a harmonious relationship with all people. We must remember this if Stoicism ever seems detached and cold to us. Its ultimate aim is not an emotionless detachment from others but is rather about living in harmony with what the ancients called 'Nature' and being a productive part of humankind.

So prepare for the day ahead. The idea of spending the first five minutes of each morning considering our tasks for the day and anticipating possible areas where we could let ourselves down or run into trouble might seem alien to us, or too much of an effort. But consider the common alternative. We are normally awoken abruptly by an alarm clock when we could do with an extra hour of sleep, and if we have allowed ourselves a brief time to lie in bed and adjust to the morning, we tend to resort to that most banal of pastimes: browsing our phones. We check social media or see what emails have come through. One connects us with the rabble; the other starts our day with problems to which we are obliged to find solutions. Perhaps we check the news and again without realising we emerge into our day smothered by demands from the outside world, which root themselves unpleasantly in our groggy, too-malleable consciousness. We have prepared our psychological state for the day by laying the ground-work for envy (we see that a friend has bought a new gadget we want but can't afford) and by letting our barely sentient minds absorb the concerns of work communi-cated overnight to our inbox. Those first few moments of the day, when we are still suggestible enough to slip back into dreams unfinished, have been invaded by the outside world's blaring cries for our weary attention. And our brains, still spongy and soaked in semi-sleep, have had nothing of the preparation needed to distance themselves from the onslaught. Already by the time our shower has brought us into the fully waking world, it is too late: we have begun our day at the mercy of the crowds.

We could, instead, try the Stoic practice of premedi-tation. As we lie in bed and half doze, or even better, if we can allocate five undisturbed minutes to sit still as part of our morning regime, we might take the time to think ahead to the events we expect this day to bring. We know we are likely to meet certain types of people. As we con-sider them one by one, we note our emotional responses to their faces that flash up on our mental movie screen. A superior at work with whom we know we must have an awkward conversation today. The shy object of our crush we hope likes us but frustratingly says so little. The loud, self-centred man with whom we try to get on but always brings out the worst in us. Our partner or spouse, with whom we retired to bed last night dissatisfied and irritated after they embarrassed us over dinner with friends, an event that triggered an argument in the car on the way home and a miserable night without intimacy of any kind.

Upcoming events, too, might be a source of concern. That class or exam or presentation that always makes us panic. The meeting we always leave wishing we had handled it better. The series of tiny household chores we tend to forget and which then cause annoyance in our partner.

But now we can consider these people and events from a distance and while our centre of gravity is within us. What is in our control and what is not? Where, today, are we in danger of letting ourselves down and acting in a way that we would later regret? What are the alternatives, which we can mentally rehearse now and more easily employ when the time is right? Are we setting ourselves up for a fall? Demanding too much of others? Working with unrealistic expectations? How might it be absolutely fine if things don't go as planned? How much would it truly matter if the contract isn't secured, the meeting turns out to be unsuccessful, or the annoying loudmouth continues to act as he always does? Does having less demanding assumptions about how perfect our partner's behaviour should be, and acknowledging responsibility for our own emotional responses, help clear the murky waters of last night? How about imagining how we would really feel if we lost them altogether? Might that remind us what we value about them? Can we imagine a more admirable way of handling reliably tricky situations?

The word '*pre*meditation' might make us think of the more familiar practice of Buddhist meditation, or its currently very popular Westernised form, mindfulness meditation. Stoicism and Buddhism have common roots: Eastern philosophy mediated through the Persian Empire, seems to have influenced ancient Western thought (and therefore our own today). Stoicism could be seen as a kind of quarantine of Eastern spiritual ideas, systemised and intellectualised for Western tastes, until they later came to inform early Christianity. We have already touched upon the instruction to recognise the importance of the present moment, which is shared by both movements. Both Buddhists and Stoics also encourage us to rehearse 'non-attachment'. They share a goal of tranquillity, to be reached through detaching oneself from the passions that tie us to worldly cares. The Stoics, who wished to be active in the world rather than transcend it, tended to get more done. Both possess their wise sages who are deemed to have achieved this enlightened state, but the Stoic sage is not presumed to actually exist. He is instead a handy exemplary role model to bring to mind when most needed; this is what Seneca means when he writes: 'Without a ruler to do it against, you won't make the crooked straight.'[70]

In Stoic premeditation, we are not aiming to 'let go' of thoughts like the Buddhists; rather we want to rationally engage with them. While it will undoubtedly aid our premeditation to feel still and present, we are considering the future rather than learning how to let go of illusions of self and simply *be* in the passing moment. There is no need to talk of higher states of consciousness, and none of the language of half-borrowed, half-misunderstood spirituality favoured by our middle classes. We'll talk more about mindfulness in a later chapter, but for now it's enough to say that Stoic premeditation is no

70 Seneca, *Letters from a Stoic*, Letter XI

more than a matter of taking a quiet few minutes to consider the day ahead from the robust, yet open perspective that comes from absorbing their principles.

For those who experience nothing but an angry, thundering fit of pique in the antemeridian hours, until liberal quantities of quarantine and caffeine permit a begrudging acceptance of society and clear thinking some time around noon, Seneca provides an alternative approach to morning premeditation. For such people he suggests a *nightly review*: a retrospective alternative wherein we might drift more comfortably into sleep after considering our actions during the day just lived. Seneca describes the practice, attributing it to Sextius, a Pythagorean philosopher who we imagine taught it to his students:

> When the day was over and he had withdrawn to his room for his nightly rest, he questioned his soul: 'What evils have you cured yourself of today? What vices have you fought? In what sense are you better?' Is there anything better than to examine a whole day's conduct?[71]

The Pythagoreans had been instructed to 'never do anything without previous deliberation: in the morning forming a plan of what was to be done later, and at night to review the day's actions'.[72] Certainly, we can imagine that if we were to be bothered to practise both these morning previews and evening reviews, considering best approaches ahead of time and later holding ourselves to account, we would live and breathe these Stoic principles

71 Pierre Hadot, *What Is Ancient Philosophy?*
72 Iamblichus, *Life of Pythagoras*

more effectively than a person who merely brings them half-remembered to mind when it is too late to fully benefit from them. It sounds, though, like a lot of work. It might, however, start with a thirty-second reminder to be the best person we can be, to not attach our emotional well-being to things outside of us, to watch out for known trouble spots; likewise, we can round up the day with as brief a look back at how we behaved, whether we let ourselves down, if there's anything we should change tomorrow. It should be neither prescriptive nor arduous.

A regular period of quiet solitude helps create a bedrock of self-sufficiency that accompanies us into the social hours ahead. As the addictive pleasures and miseries of electronic communication and phone-browsing offer themselves to us every minute of the day and night, we forget the benefits of time spent calmly with and within ourselves. If we are able to find time and space each day to redress the balance, and if we use it to remind ourselves that so much of our life has nothing to do with us, and that it is only with our thoughts and actions that we need to concern ourselves, we will soon find that our centre of gravity returns to its correct place.

Third-person perspective

A technique which might help us, not described by the Stoics but I think implied in their descriptions, is to take a third-person perspective on the events we are looking forward or back to. If you bring to mind a recent event that makes you feel especially good or bad, you are likely to view it through your own eyes, as if it were happening still around you. The same applies to thinking about images that trigger phobic responses, such as spiders or snakes. In order to feel the emotions attached to these

254

thoughts, we represent them vividly to ourselves in a *first-person* perspective. It can therefore be very helpful, if we wish to gain some emotional distance from a memory or the thought of an upcoming event, to picture it as if it were being filmed with a CCTV camera up in the corner of the room. By seeing *ourselves* from the outside, we are a step removed from any feelings otherwise provoked by the scene. This practice of *distancing* is known amongst contemporary psychologists as a therapeutic technique. People who tend to be self-immersed frequently recall events in the first person and therefore more emotionally. The 'Brodmann Area 25' of the brain is linked to this sort of self-orientated perspective, and overactivity in this area has been linked to depression. When people change their perspective to that of a third person, they often find it easier to achieve insight and closure regarding traumatic events.[73]

Those familiar with neuro-linguistic programming will know of 'sub-modality changes', which amount to identifying all sorts of shifts within a person's perspective of a problem that might trigger a more helpful response. For example, a person with a fear of flying might notice that she imagines flying in the first person, in bright colour, high detail, and on a huge, panoramic, close-up screen in her mind's eye. This is a certain recipe for a strong emotional response. In contrast, if she pictures riding on a train, or something that does not make her feel anxious, she is likely to make a smaller picture, place it further away, with less colour and vibrancy. She is likely to *see herself* in the picture rather than view it from her

73 Özlem Ayduk and Ethan Kross, 'From A Distance: Implications of Spontaneous Self-Distancing for Adaptive Self-Reflection', *Journal of Personality and Social Psychology*, 98, Vol (5), 2010

own perspective. A classic NLP technique for relieving the emotional tension created by the thought of flying would be to practise re-envisioning the mental flight 'footage' to make it more resemble the train sequence.

NLP tends to borrow its techniques from pre-existing therapies; indeed, its cognitive slant can be traced back to Stoic thinking. Its use of distancing most likely owes a debt to developmental psychologists Bernard Kaplan and Heinz Werner.[74]

We might reap the benefits of both a first- and third-person perspective if we give the prospective morning meditation a try. To consider difficult upcoming events without feeling the anguish, try switching to that third-person, CCTV point of view. Then, when you come to rehearse a new, more positive response, resume the first-person perspective and view everything as you would through your own eyes, making it all as vivid as you can. This will give you a sense-memory of the new, desired way of behaving that will be more helpful when you then encounter the situation in real life.

We have now a few simple tools in place for ensuring that we can enjoy a little more of the psychological robustness in our lives that will lessen occasions of psychological disturbance and unhappiness. We can step back from a situation and decide not to add to our first impressions by concocting a story that makes us feel bad. We can bring to mind helpful and familiar thoughts or questions when we need them, such as 'Is this something in my control?' or 'Do I have a problem right now?' When we remember, we might even get ahead of the game by contemplating the day before it happens and/or holding ourselves to

74 Heinz Werner and Bernard Kaplan, *Symbol Formation: An Organismic-Developmental Approach to Language and the Expression of Thought*

account by reviewing our behaviour at night before we sleep.

Finding time

One of the more enduring and charming classics of self-help literature, Arnold Bennett's slim 1910 volume, *How to Live on 24 Hours a Day*, makes a plea for using time wisely:

> If one can't contrive to live on a certain income of money, one earns a little more – or steals it, or advertises for it . . . one braces the muscles . . . and balances the budget. But if one cannot arrange that an income of twenty-four hours a day shall exactly cover all proper items of expenditure, one does muddle one's life entirely. The supply of time, though gloriously regular, is cruelly restricted.

Bennett's message is to find time in the day that is normally wasted and allocate it to the pursuit of the self-improving. Words like 'waste', 'spend' and 'allocate' are examples of the economic language with which we describe time, yet we apply very little of the care we take when spending money to our disbursal of time. Most people (and Bennett was petitioning the large number of white-collar workers amongst his readers who had accrued since the Industrial Revolution) are less than enamoured with their jobs, yet consider time spent at work as 'the day'. The remaining hours of the day are seen as subservient, marginal; we get up with barely enough time to get ready and leave, and then after work we merely wind down, then 'think about going to bed' for nearly an hour before retiring. These remaining hours constitute the majority of our existence, yet still we denigrate them before the minority proportion that in itself brings us little true enjoyment.

For those who insist that after-work hours are neither numerous enough to devote to any sort of project nor provide the requisite energy to propel us into ardour, he offers a counterargument:

> But when you arrange to go to the theatre (especially with a pretty woman) what happens? You rush to the suburbs; you spare no toil to make yourself glorious in fine raiment; you rush back to town on another train; you keep yourself on the stretch for four hours if not five; you take her home; you take yourself home.

Twee but true: we have little trouble making time when the rewards (a great night out, the glimpse of a comely ankle) are highly motivating.

Bennett recommends an hour and a half to be stolen from each day and spent improving the mind. Novels are excluded from the provinces of the illuminating; instead, we are pointed towards anything we might find educative (though satisfyingly he does recommend Epictetus and Marcus Aurelius, saying he never travels without the latter). If we are untouched by his exigent Edwardian literary taste, we can still draw from his counsel regarding how we might go about making changes in the way we use our time. He understands that motivation is important, suggesting making small and manageable changes first. These will offer their own rewards and spur the seeker towards greater shifts. Any number of modern treatises on self-improvement make the same point: small changes lead to bigger ones. One step at a time. A friend even says he surmounts his reluctance to floss his teeth before bed by only aiming to attend to a single tooth. After having indulged that night's fortunate favoured denticle, he finds it as effortless to continue as to stop, and thus his nightly oral hygiene is assured. Now if only he would find a workable strategy for deodorant.

☺

9

Anger and Hurt

We don't know when he stopped making any noise. He – it – was being kept alive by regular feeding: just enough to prolong the agony and public humiliation that served principally as his punishment. Paraded around Athens, held high in a cage, this unfamiliar, blood-and-shit-encrusted creature was a monstrous perversion of the beautiful soldier he had once been: a lieutenant in the king's army and friend of the monarch himself.

King Lysimachus had ordered this most singular punishment upon his old friend Telesphorus after the latter made a remark at the expense of the king's wife. She, Arsinoe, was prone to vomiting, and when the valued soldier was heard during a banquet making a witty put-down regarding her condition, the king became incensed. He ordered Telesphorus to be mutilated, his ears and nose to be severed, so that he need never again be upset by the sound or smell of vomiting. His eyes were to be left intact in order that he could appreciate more fully the second part of his peculiar damnation: to be displayed in a cage like a beast and carried through the city until he died. Pitiful daily feeding extended this period so that he would not be too easily permitted the blessed relief of oblivion.

After his fury had subsided, the sovereign developed a most unkingly fear of his victim. The creature in the cage no longer resembled his fine soldier or indeed any human being; his once muscular body had become cadaverous through starvation and was covered in callouses and blisters from crawling on the floor of the cramped cage and rubbing against the bars. The layer of excrement that generously covered him afforded the only protection from the Athenian sun. The two long cavities where his strong nose had once protruded, and through which filth and slime now caked the interior of his head, made his wasted face resemble all the more that of a grinning skeleton. Transformed into a bogeyman, which disgusted and terrified those citizens whom he had once valiantly defended, he was no longer afforded even their pity. It was some time before the final point of dim light, deep within the monster, seemed to flicker and fail. Its emaciated cadaver was discarded, dead or at least appearing so, for the dogs to tear apart and salvage what little they could.

Thus ordered King Lysimachus. The ruler had himself, many years before, been thrown into a cage in order to be devoured by a lion. Alexander the Great, his close friend and ruler, to whom he had been bodyguard during the Persian campaigns, had issued this command. This was the same learned, admired Alexander, taught by Seneca, who, drunk and angry at a feast, had hurled a javelin through the heart of a dear companion he had known since childhood. The young Lysimachus had been more fortunate and somehow escaped the lion's jaws. Yet years later, in a moment of crimson fury, he would enact a perverse, nightmarish version of his punishment upon his own friend.

Anger is by far the most destructive and pervasive of the passions. It is also the ugliest. Seneca reminds us that:

> No other . . . surely has a worse expression . . . one moment rough and fierce, then pale when the blood has flowed back and been dispersed, then flushed and, it seems, gorged with blood, when all the heat and energy of the body has been directed to the face, with swollen veins, with eyes now restless and protruding, now fastened and rooted in one fixed stare.[75]

Plutarch, possibly the greatest essayist of the Greco-Roman era, noted:

> I was very upset to think that I might ever look so terrifying and unhinged to my friends, my wife, my daughters – not only fierce and unrecognisable in appearance, but also speaking in as rough and harsh a tone as I encountered in others of my acquaintance, when anger made them incapable of preserving their usual nature, appearance, pleasant conversation and persuasiveness and courtesy in company.[76]

Plutarch is a delight to read. He writes using vivid imagery rather than dry argument to drive home his points about the popular ethical concerns of his day: contentment, anger, how to distinguish a flatterer from a friend.

75 Seneca, *On Anger*, 3.4
76 Plutarch, *On the Avoidance of Anger*, [6] 455F

Later, in Victorian households, anthologies of his essays would be as ubiquitous as the corpulent Bibles that superintended homes with unsmiling jurisdiction. Classical historians, very much in vogue, raided his *Parallel Lives* for evidence of his times and of the prominent figures about whom he wrote. It was the eventual realisation that this major work was historically misleading that led the nineteenth century to discard Plutarch from the classical canon. Only recently have we re-evaluated him on his own terms, rather than as the chronicler he never claimed to be.

Plutarch was a self-defined Platonist, objecting to the irreligious atomistic stance of the Epicureans but generally sympathetic towards Stoic ethics. His *On the Avoidance of Anger* sits comfortably with Seneca's *On Anger*, as well as Epictetus's discourse on the same subject. Anger was a hot topic during these times. In a world where kings might parade their tortured friends in cages, and political and military uncertainty were rife, citizens would have been only too aware of the damage that fierce-tempered rulers could wield. Writers had much to say regarding how we might live a happier life and rid ourselves of the problems of an angry temperament. Even for those of us who rarely find ourselves truly angry, the same thoughts can be useful for dealing with frustration, which is a related, though generally weaker, passion, and another very common source of unwanted disturbance.

The consensus from these writers was that anger is an entirely negative, unmerited emotion. You may disagree. One dissenting thought that preceded theirs came from Aristotle: he believed that there is a use for anger, as long as it is correctly placed:

> Anybody can become angry – that is easy, but to be
> angry with the right person and to the right degree

and at the right time and for the right purpose, and
in the right way – that is not within everybody's
power and is not easy.[77]

His system of virtue, you may remember, was based on
achieving a mean between deficiency and excess in certain qualities. Too much anger and one becomes irascible;
too little and one is guilty of *aorgēsia*, a spineless lack of
spirit.

We might talk of a righteous indignation, directed
towards people who are acting profoundly unjustly. We
think of civil rights movements – how can social injustice
be combatted without anger? And if anger at that level is
justified, even necessary for important change, why
should it not be permissible or even encouraged at the
personal level?

Anger certainly seems to have an evolutionary basis.
It serves a social purpose: displays of anger encourage
others to change their behaviour and thus work to stop
people transgressing societal rules that keep us cohabiting
comfortably. If we neither felt nor exhibited annoyance,
we would become 'slavish', in Aristotle's words, and an
easy target for exploitation.

Our concerns here, as ever, are not theoretical but
practical. What matters is how we might be happier, and
part of that is addressing the role of anger in our lives. So
let's look at whether anger can be a positive force, with a
view to deciding what stance we would be best advised to
take in times of frustration or annoyance, and thus work
to make our lives as free from disturbance as possible.

One key matter is precisely what we mean by 'anger'.
Aristotle defined it as 'a longing, accompanied by pain,

77 Aristotle, *Nicomachean Ethics*, ii.9

for a real and apparent revenge for a real or apparent slight, affecting a man himself or one of his friends, when such a slight is undeserved'.[78] Perhaps we have never considered these two interesting issues that Aristotle raises. One is that anger is driven by a desire for revenge: to *harm* another person. As the American philosopher Martha Nussbaum has discussed,[79] that harm may be indirect (we might hope that, for example, an ex-spouse has a miserable time with her new partner) or mitigated by the nature of the relationship (a mother may be furious at her child but the desire to harm is suppressed into punishment, scolding or 'teaching the child a lesson'). The desire for retribution is, however, always present: without it, we are not really experiencing anger.

There is also that second element: that a *slight* has occurred. While this is sometimes a less valuable criterion, it is certainly a very common cause of anger. If we consider those times where we have become annoyed at the words or actions of another, it is usually because we perceive ourselves to have been slighted, ignored, disregarded or otherwise unfairly treated or perceived. Our private judgements, or what the Stoics would call our 'assents' to 'appearances' are hard at work here.

When we consider the anger we might wish to retain towards matters of grave social injustice, is it really our desire to harm or retaliate that will secure important changes? Or does a positive result depend not on the anger itself but how it is channelled? Nussbaum, in her lecture to the Law School of Chicago University in January 2014, points to the work of important social

78 Aristotle, *Rhetoric*, ii.2
79 Martha Nussbaum, *The Therapy of Desire: Theory and Practice in Hellenistic Ethics*

reformers such as Martin Luther King and Gandhi to illustrate the importance of what she calls 'the Transition'. Both figures, when motivating supporters against racial segregation in America and British colonial rule of India respectively, understood the strong undercurrent of anger created by such powerful injustice. Yet in the same breath they knew that fury and violence would not solve any of the problems being faced. Martin Luther King's 1963 'I Have a Dream' speech is a masterclass in transforming the anger of those black Americans into a future-orientated, constructive drive. He begins by describing the outrage that is felt by the black community as a debt owed, rather than a matter of criminal injustice: 'America has given the Negro people a bad check, a check which has come back marked "insufficient funds".' The speech moves on to famously motivate its audience to seek to realise a vision of equality, *not* to unleash wrath upon its oppressors. The incitement of aggression is masterfully avoided.

Perhaps, then, to feel anger is unavoidable but not in itself helpful; the key is turning it into something constructive. We are angry because we would like to change something in the world (or maybe in ourselves), something that seems to be unjust. A feeling of rage does very little to rectify the perceived injustice. An artist sees the world and notices a difference between how she feels it should be and how it actually is. The work of art she creates is a way of bridging the gap: a physical manifestation of that discrepancy. The emotions she experiences, which might of course be very pleasant and far from anger, are nonetheless channelled into something constructive, and the observer of the final piece might be challenged to pay attention to the issues in question and align himself with the artist's motivations. King is dealing with rawer, more volatile and highly charged emotions, but he and other motivators of non-violent protest are engaging in an essentially creative, visionary process.

The Stoic position, at least as detailed in Seneca's three-part work *On Anger*, is that this destructive passion is alien to the essentially sociable nature of human beings:

> What is gentler than the human being, when he is in a right state of mind? But what is more cruel than anger? What is more loving to others than the human being? What is more hostile than anger? The human being is born for mutual aid, anger for destruction.[80]

Seneca tells us that we do not require anger to motivate us: that the impulse towards duty and virtue should suffice. This is unlikely to feel satisfying to us; if a loved one is murdered, is it really only stirrings of virtue and duty that should motivate us to pursue the offender? Does this not suggest a rather inhuman model for us to imitate? And as Martha Nussbaum points out, if this wise person is strongly motivated (by duty and virtue) to punish an offender, is he not making the same judgement as a person feeling anger? And as the Stoics tell us that it is in our *judgements* that the passions lie, then surely that person *is* angry 'whether he foams at the mouth and rolls his eyes or not'.[81]

Seneca's response is to offer a motivation to punish that is different from anger: we should seek retribution in order to improve the offender. This is in some sense satisfying, but Nussbaum contrasts this medical model, typical of Stoic philosophy, with a report of the first member of

80 Seneca, *On Anger*, 1.5
81 Martha Nussbaum, *The Therapy of Desire*

the Allied forces entering a Nazi death camp. The officer in question entered the camp where the political activist Elie Wiesel was then being held as a child. 'Seeing what there was to be seen [this officer] began to curse, shouting at the top of his voice. And the child Wiesel thought, watching him, now humanity has come back. Now, with that anger, humanity has come back.'[82] It would seem strange to insist that the officer's first impulse should be to seek to rehabilitate and improve the Nazi offenders.

There is, as Nussbaum points out, an answer in Seneca to this, and it gives us a model of anger's place within human nature that is more satisfying and not only consistent with Stoic principles but reminds us that they should not be seen as an encouragement towards cold detachment. Seneca gives us a model where anger is pervasive and part of our lives, but not part of the propensities of our nature. We are born with instincts of love, openness and accord. As we grow, we tend to become attached to external goods and our own safety. Aggression results from this interplay between our natures and the circumstances in which we find ourselves: 'Life, if we attach ourselves to it, alienates us from our own humanity.'[83]

Anger, then, will often seem like a reasonable response to a situation, but we should reconsider. It pulls us from our natural state of openness and turns us against humanity. We should instead reconsider our attachments and, notwithstanding the importance of exerting just punishment, avoid acting out of anger. It's simply bad for us. The extirpation of this particular passion therefore realigns us with humanity and restores a gentleness and sociability that we should remember lie at the heart of Stoic thinking.

82 Ibid.
83 Ibid.

Causes of anger

What, then, actually annoys us? While triggers will vary wildly from person to person, we might identify some reliably provocative categories. Firstly, we are likely to feel angry when certain social rules are broken. You might have formulated a rule that it is wrong for a person, when sitting across a table from you, to browse his phone. Watching him do so might be infuriating. It might annoy us very much when our partners embarrass us in front of friends by airing private grievances they hold towards us, passive-aggressively disguising them as light-hearted jokes. This is a reliable trigger for me. I feel the sting of embarrassment, which is bolstered by the feeling that I cannot respond to the remark without becoming guilty of the same transgression myself. My thought process runs as follows:

1. WHAT? That's unfair. I do not ALWAYS leave my underwear lying around/neglect the parrot/forget to turn the lights off at night.

2. I *never* say 'You always . . .', because I know it's fallacious, unhelpful and aggravating. Why can't you ever offer the same courtesy? (I am of course contradicting myself here: an 'I never' formulation is no more a reflection of reality than 'You always'.)

3. You shouldn't be saying this in public, as it's humiliating and manipulative: you know I can't respond adequately. And you know if I bring this up later you can just say, 'God, it was just a joke', and I'll look like someone who can't take a joke about himself.

4. Perhaps I can find a way of bringing this up later. But no – that's such a boring pattern: the 'Why did you have to say that?' after a dinner party that leads to an

argument and creates misery for the rest of the night. So I'll sulk now (because I can't retaliate without being as bad as you or appearing argumentative), and I'll sulk later because it'll feel stupid to bring it up when we're home.

5. Why are we together?

A rule has been broken, and my rule is *you don't say those sorts of things in front of friends*. And there is a second category of trigger at play here: the perception of a personal slight. Aristotle, we remember, saw this as an important criterion of the feeling of anger, along with a desire to inflict harm on the offender. By my partner's indiscreet remark, I have been made to feel embarrassed: I neglect my pet; I strew my pants. This personal slighting is a common trigger for an angry response. I do, moreover, desire to inflict punishment on my partner for the affront. My wrath shall be mighty: I will become quiet and deny him the non-verbal language of affection. No eye contact. *That*'ll tell him.

A third source of annoyance stems from irritants. There is a hint of this in the above example: part of my annoyance comes from the feeling that my partner *always* makes those sorts of remarks. Aside from the remark itself, I am irritated by the fact that it seems to be a recurring pattern, like phone-browsing over dinner. Examples of irritants in their purest forms might be a screaming child or a barking dog: repeated disturbances that we try to ignore but cannot. My parrot Rasputin will occasionally enter a state of sudden distress and scream repeatedly at the top of his voice. He is somewhat highly strung, so this shrieking is normally caused by the sight of a possible predator through the window, such as a dog or a bicycle or a tree or a plant or a cloud. Other times, I imagine, the chilling caterwaul is an urgent response to an existential concern that his life in a taxidermy-stuffed townhouse in south London is not proceeding along a route as rewarding as it might amongst the lush viridescence of the Amazon rainforest. Faint antediluvian echoes of his ancestors' home probably play upon his tiny troubled brain and are dispelled only by an abrupt water spray and a conciliatory cashew.

Sometimes, I should add, he cannot be pacified. He will not be held, bribed, distracted or bathed. He will fly from lamp to computer to cage top to some stuffed creature, breathing heavily and warning the world about an invisible threat and annoying me profoundly. I read in an article that birds use different sounds to communicate the presence of particular predators: they will have one sound for a snake, another, say, for a bird of prey. This not only alerts the birds in the area to danger but can inform them as to what best action to take to avoid it. This subtle distinction between bird calls is fascinating to me. Even if I were equipped with the sensitivity of ear, the requisite ornithological knowledge, and had the finely tuned instruments of auditory recording and playback equipment necessary to identify and recognise the meanings of these precise shades of birdsong, I suspect I would still identify in this case no more than the avian equivalent of 'FUCKFUCKFUCKFUCKFUCK'.

Then there is our temperament. We know what reliably angers us, and what seems to bother others but leaves us undisturbed. We know if we are prone to anger or tend to bury or detach from our negative emotions. We can always trace this back to our past experience. We may imagine someone whose childhood took place in a home with a volatile parent, where shouting and rage were everyday occurrences. She is likely to have grown skilled at reading people and handling them sensitively. Her early need to judge when her mother was about to fly off the handle now serves her well and makes her very sensitive to when something is untoward with her friends. But she also learnt to meet her mother's anger with her own when she was little: often the only way to be heard was to scream back. Now, she remains on high alert. At the slightest sign of tension with her partner, adrenaline flows through her veins; she becomes unnecessarily anxious and highly sensitive to a threat that is no longer there. She is poised for the fight to which that familiar neural pathway still points her, ready to meet it with an aggression that is no longer needed. Her partner is usually left confused and exhausted.

Regardless of our temperament, it clearly serves us to be less bothered by irritants, displays of disrespect and transgressions of perceived rules. Being disturbed less leaves us happier. But there are other reasons why we might wish to avoid anger, and it will serve us well to know them if we are to feel motivated enough to try to reduce the frequency and intensity with which it grips us. Our aims are to increase happiness – why should we seek to avoid anger on these grounds?

Some good reasons to avoid anger

1. Not making the point

Plutarch and Seneca have offered us descriptions of the angry person. We have all seen one friend or another become angry, perhaps at some inferred slight. I remember watching a friend lose his cool at finding out that those of us who had worked with him the year before on some television projects felt that he had been rather lazy. What was fascinating was that his very human response of indignation undercut what would have seemed to him to be a reasonable protest. In his defensiveness (he was hurt not only at the idea that his effort and dedication would have been questioned but also that this had remained a sort of in-joke at his expense for an extended period of time), he lashed out and accused the person who had mentioned it of *also* having been lazy and how we had all joked about *that*. His eyes were wide and fuming, he had lost all grasp of his regular decorum, and the sight was uncharacteristically unpleasant. The visual phenomenon of his reaction, coupled with his angry verbal retaliation, completely overwhelmed his point that he may have been unfairly judged. Suddenly, with a horrified sort of amusement, we were just watching our friend being angry.

It was lucky in that situation that we had little emotional connection to the point we were making: we were very fond of this friend and had never held that criticism against him. His strengths in other areas and the delights of his company more than made up for it. Had we felt more emotionally charged, his outrage would have sparked a counter-defensive strike, and the results would have been far uglier. But I was left with the distinct impression that our open displays of anger completely distract from any point we might want to make. For it to serve its evolutionary purpose as well as possible, by letting people know they have offended and that they should reconsider their behaviour, it cannot emerge in its raw form. We knew intellectually that our friend disagreed, but we were not led to empathise with his disagreement and rethink our own stance, as the show of fury was simply distracting and fascinating. Instead, my only clear thought was how we had evidently hit a nerve.

In the sixteenth century, the essayist Michel de Montaigne bemoaned the unlovely, still all-too-familiar sight of a parent castigating a child in public. Modern images come to mind of parents, at the end of their tethers, bringing their children to supermarkets to smack them:

> How many times have I been tempted, among other things, to make a dramatic intervention so as to avenge some little boys whom I saw being bruised, knocked about and flayed alive by some frenzied father or mother beside themselves with anger. You can see fire and rage flashing in their eyes – *rabie jecur incendente, feruntur Præcipites, ut saxa jugis abrupta, quibis mons Subtrahitur, clivoque latus pendent recedit* [They are headlong borne with burning fury as great stones torn from the mountains, by which the steep sides are left naked and bare. – Juvenal, *The Satires*, xiv. 70] – they are carried away by burning wrath, like boulders wrenched free from the cliff crashing down the precipitous slope . . . as with shrill wounding voices, they scream at children who are often barely weaned.[84]

(One may wish to commit the Latin to memory with a view to reciting it for the edification of the next squalling matriarch one encounters in Argos.)

Anger, then, gets in the way of us making our point. We may feel desperately entitled to it, due to feelings of panic, or the outrage we feel in response to the story we have concocted about other people's motives and so on. But if given free rein, it will defeat our objective: to express ourselves convincingly.

84 Michel de Montaigne, *Of Anger*

2. Our inevitable regret

We may have punished or upset the people we wished to reprimand, but if we did so in anger, we will most likely experience contrition after the event. Anger destroys relationships and cuts through love of any sort. 'When anger is present, neither marriage nor friendship is endurable; but when anger is absent, even drunkenness is no burden.'[85] In fact, it tends to feed on the closeness of relationships; after all, we reserve our real fury for those people whom we have admitted into our most intimate circles. We can only feel betrayed by those whom we love and trust, and it is betrayal that often stings us the most. Whatever short-term pleasure is afforded by verbally or physically lashing out at a person who has upset us in this way, it will be greatly exceeded by the remorse we are likely to feel afterwards. Often a comment we have made in anger will bother us more after the event than at the time it will have upset the person to whom it was directed. He or she may have paid it little heed, but we might find ourselves guiltily obsessing over the remark as we chastise ourselves for being so short-tempered and worry at the damage we might have caused. This is better than being oblivious to the fact we have upset people but nonetheless creates a secondary source of misery.

Anger thus creates unhappiness for all involved, and in particular for the person who is angry. And as easy as it is to label a regularly angry person a 'monster', his frustration that he must be seen in that way can only intensify the cycle of anti-social behaviour. Seneca describes the person in the grip of anger as 'the executioner of those persons he holds most dear and destroyer of the things whose loss will soon make him weep'. 'Is this a passion,'

85 Plutarch, *On the Avoidance of Anger*, [13] 462B

he asks, 'that anyone can assign as a helper and companion to virtue [as Aristotle believed], when it makes havoc of the resolutions essential to virtue achieving anything?'[86]

3. No licence

When we are angry, we are driven by fury and make stupid decisions. Plutarch says that anger commits criminal acts 'after having replaced intelligence altogether, and shut it out of the house'.[87] He moves on to compare it to the experience of being trapped in a house fire, surrounded by smoke and chaos, unable to see or hear anything beneficial. We may feel, when angry, that we are giving people what they deserve, but we are fooling ourselves, as our intelligence has been banished when we are in the grip of anger. Seneca asks: 'Will someone call a man sane who, as if caught up in a tempest, does not walk but is driven along, and takes as his master a furious demon . . .?'[88]

Montaigne, too, is clear on this point, reminding us of the important link between anger and vengeance:

> No passion disturbs the soundness of our judgement as anger does. No one would hesitate to punish with death a judge who was led to condemn his man as a criminal out of anger: then why is it any more permissible for fathers and schoolmasters to punish and flog children in anger? That is no longer correction, it is vengeance. For a child punishment is medicine: would we tolerate a doctor who was animated by wrath against his patient?[89]

86 Seneca, *On Anger*, 3.3
87 Plutarch, *On the Avoidance of Anger*, [2] 453F
88 Seneca, *On Anger*, 3.3
89 Michel de Montaigne, *Of Anger*

The comedian Louis C. K., in his stellar stand-up show *Oh My God*, expresses his surprise at the extent of his own fury that can emerge behind the wheel of a car.

I waste a lot of time being angry with people I don't know . . . you know it's amazing how nasty we can get as people depending on the situation, like most people are okay, as long as they're okay, but if you put people in certain kinds of context they just change. Like when I'm in my car, I have a *different set of values*. I am the worst person I can be when I'm behind the wheel. Which is when I'm at my most dangerous. When you're driving, that's when you need to be the most compassionate and responsible of any time of your life, because you are fucking driving a *weapon . . . amongst weapons*, and yet it's the worst people get. And I am the worst. One time I was driving, and there was this guy ahead of me and he sort of, I don't know, kind of drifted into my lane for a second, and this came out of my mouth – I said, '*You worthless piece of shit!*'

What an indictment! What kind of a way is that to feel about another human being? *Worthless piece of shit!?* That's somebody's son! And the things that upset people – I was once driving and some guy in a pick-up truck did, I don't know, I don't remember even, and I yelled out my window, I said, 'Hey! FUCK YOU!' Where, outside of a car, is that even *nearly* okay? If you were in an elevator, and you were right next to a person's body, and – whatever – he like *leaned* into you a little bit – would you ever turn right to their face and go, 'Hey, FUCK YOU! . . . *You worthless piece of shit!*'?

No. Literally zero people would ever do that.

But put a couple of pieces of glass and some road between you, and there's nothing you would not say to them. 'I HOPE YOU DIE.' I said that to a person! I HOPE YOU DIE. Why? [*Angrily*] BECAUSE YOU MADE ME GO LIKE THIS [*mimes jiggling steering wheel*] FOR HALF A SECOND OF MY LIFE. YOU TESTED MY REFLEXES AND IT WORKED OUT FINE. SO NOW I HOPE YOUR KIDS GROW UP MOTHERLESS.

I mean – what am I capable of? I like to think that I'm a nice person. But I don't know, man . . .[90]

The term 'road rage' was popularised by the American news network KTLA in 1987–8 following a spate of shootings on the Los Angeles freeways. Ten years later, therapists were attempting to have this form of aggression classified as a mental disorder. I do not drive, given my enormous importance, but allow others the pleasure of having me as a passenger. I see then how the bad behaviour of other drivers – barely perceptible to me as someone unfamiliar with road etiquette – transforms otherwise affable and conciliatory friends into Seneca and Louis C. K.'s furious demons. Clearly we must remain in control of our cars and therefore are already operating from a starting point of tension. Unable to relieve that tension, and constrained not only by the rules of the road but also the dimensions of the car (and the less comfortable the car, I suspect, the more likely we are to be prone to aggression), it takes only a small territorial threat to trigger an aggressive response.

Much is happening all the time that is beyond our

90 Louis C. K., *Oh My God*, HBO (2013)

control, and, as the Stoics have told us, it is from that realm that most of our anxieties originate. The result on the road is a power struggle that is generally sublimated but can sometimes emerge to the fore as we prevent others from moving into our lane or somehow punish them for what we deem to be dangerous behaviour.

We have been slighted, and we wish to punish the offender. The two classic – and classical – elements of anger are present (harm done and harm wished). Certainly we can also identify the transgression of rules as an offensive element. The real culprit here, though, is our sense of entitlement. The tension that has already crept in to the driving situation before any seemingly aggressive act has taken place has already altered our perception of our relationship to others for the worse. It is very hard to be at our most compassionate, as Louis C. K. reminds us we should be, when we are navigating such dangerous territory; we must instead remain vigilant, looking out for ourselves. The result is that we feel a powerful sense of self-righteousness that not only makes us predisposed to interpret the bad driving of others as a malicious slur upon ourselves, but to feel that we are in a position of power and are entitled to punish those who have transgressed.

When we are in cars, we cannot communicate with any of the subtlety of a normal social situation. If road rage illustrates the startling ease with which we can regress to savages, we might take some comfort from the fact that the principal means of communication we have is what we do with fifteen hundred kilograms of metal. Its blinking indicators are a clumsy substitute for the myriad of social signals we can use in the rest of our lives. Consider what happens when we wish to jump ahead of a queue of people waiting at a ticket machine: feeling embarrassed, we are likely to adopt a pitiful body posture and a tone of voice that we hope provokes understanding and sympathy; we can explain with unassuming gestures that our train is about to leave and we have no choice but to rely on their goodwill and hope that they too are not in a desperate rush to let us alter the order in which a few people can approach and operate a machine. By contrast, if we are faced with a situation of similar urgency on the road, we are unable to utilise any of the subtle verbal and non-verbal signals that would be at our disposal in the ticket queue, and our intentions instead are communicated without finesse to a group already predisposed to take offence.

The result, as we drive our weapon amongst weapons, is that we retaliate without licence. It may be that we emphatically verbalise an eagerness for the other driver to auto-inseminate, or leave our vehicle to punch him in the throat; either way, these responses appear to us at the time to be perfectly justifiable. But the punishment will never be appropriate if it is issued from a place of anger (one's car or otherwise). Epictetus makes the point that we proudly seek accuracy in matters such as weight, measurement and scientific truth: 'we will never do anything by guessing'. Yet when it comes to how we judge appearances – the most fundamental building block of our happiness – our responses are haphazard:

> There we are only inconsiderate and rash. There is then nothing like scales, nothing like a rule, but some appearance if presented, and straightway I act according to it . . . And what is the name of those who follow every appearance? They are called madmen. Do we then act at all differently?[91]

91 Epictetus, *Discourses*, i.28

Anyone who – as a child or a childish adult – has returned a punch, slap or squirt of water with the words 'That was getting you back', will know how ineffective the revenge logic is to settling the score. The initial offender, now punished with his own medicine, only retaliates, usually to 'get you back for the last one'. The other protests: 'But that was getting you back for the first one!' before slapping the other again and making frantic 'game over' gestures or some such. Reaching agreement to stop such a game is very difficult and may provide a surprise fart attack many hours later when one is asleep.

The seductive logic of revenge creates a chain of escalating violence. We never accept a vengeful attack, or concur with a raised digit in the wing-mirror, whilst calmly accepting that we have been put in our place. Instead, we become angry again. The American counter-culture writer Kurt Vonnegut, in a 1999 lecture to the women of the graduating class of Agnes Scott College in Georgia, made the following point:

> What has gone wrong is that too many people, including high school kids and heads of state, are obeying the Code of Hammurabi, a King of Babylon who lived nearly four thousand years ago. And you can find his code echoed in the Old Testament, too. Are you ready for this?
> 'An eye for an eye and a tooth for a tooth.'
> A categorical imperative for all who live in obedience to the Code of Hammurabi, which includes heroes of every cowboy show and gangster show you ever saw, is this: Every injury, real or imagined, shall be avenged. Somebody's going to be really sorry.

Road rage, terrorism and Clint Eastwood: each linked by an unfortunate, ancient Babylonian code inscribed four millennia ago on a stone statue. Those who still adhere to its dictates when sitting in one of hundreds of thousands of cars trying their best to navigate our roads (or when fantasising over a specific act of vengeful arson) should remind themselves of paragraph twenty-one of the same code:

> If a man make a hole in the wall of a house, they shall put him to death in front of that hole and they shall thrust him therein.[92]

In for a penny.

Seven ways of removing anger

In the 1950s, an American psychoanalytic therapist severed his Freudian roots and turned to the Stoics to form a radically new form of therapy. Rather than plumbing the depths of the content of a problem and exploring how a stumbling block might relate to, say, one's early psycho-sexual development, Albert Ellis argued that we should look at whatever process sustains the issue in the *present*. The result was 'rational therapy', later known as 'rational emotive behaviour therapy' or REBT. Having had an interest in philosophy since his teenage years, Ellis explained: 'I really got my main theory that people largely upset themselves from ancient philosophers, some of the Asians, but also from the Greeks and Romans.'[93]

92 *The Code of Hammurabi* (1754 BCE)
93 Albert Ellis, *The Road to Tolerance: The Philosophy of Rational Emotive Behavior Therapy*

Ellis built on the work of Émile Coué, who had encouraged patients to work with his new science of 'conscious autosuggestion'. 'Every day in every way I'm getting better and better,' the French pharmacist encouraged his patients to tell themselves. But Ellis wasn't convinced. 'If she keeps saying to herself much louder and more often, "I'm really a shit; I'm no fucking good; I'll never possibly get better," all the positive thinking in the world is not going to help her.'[94]

Ellis's REBT eventually joined forces with the cognitive therapy of Aaron Beck, who had developed a groundbreaking means of treating depression. Beck had encouraged his patients to monitor and evaluate their negative thoughts and how they related to their feelings and actions. He helped them replace the unhelpful thoughts with more positive ones, through a rational process of sifting for evidence that could support or undermine the anxiety in question. Then the patient would apply the same process to deeper beliefs, which might be responsible for generating such negative thoughts in the first place. This is a truly cognitive model and recognisably a systematised version of the Stoic approach.

Together they formed cognitive behavioural therapy, or CBT, which has since become enormously popular. It claims to be evidence-based, and therefore highly effective, especially for anxiety-related issues. CBT practitioners often insist that traditional psychoanalysis remains a lengthy, expensive form of therapy with highly ambiguous, difficult-to-measure results. On the other hand, those preferring the longer form therapy of Freudian, Jungian and other schools often argue that the CBT approach merely deals with symptoms rather than root

94 Ibid.

causes. Most psychotherapists today offer an eclectic approach to suit the patient and the problems he or she brings to the office.

CBT certainly offers us a clear model of how anger arises. It is not only enormously helpful for untangling this and other oppressive, overpowering emotions but also follows logically from our understanding of the Stoic approach. Two thousand years after its conception, Stoicism has been taken up again as a form of therapy. The parallels between CBT and Stoicism remain remarkably striking; the only major difference, worth bearing in mind, is that CBT is about fixing certain troubles, whereas the key vision of Stoicism is the enhancement of an 'ordinary' life to connect more powerfully to one's fellow human beings and to move more in accord with the universe. There is a love-drive at the heart of the ancient school, which is not present in the problem-specific *raison d'être* of CBT.

Yet one can't help but feel that Seneca would have a keen interest in this modern therapy, and perhaps a sense of pride that his own letters and essays, through an accident of survival, have changed the lives of countless people for the better. In CBT, we find the Stoic insistence that it is our judgements that cause us problems, as opposed to events themselves; the instigation of more appropriate alternative judgements; and the instruction to systematically review one's work. Both have us question what is in our control and what is not, and remind us, when we are at the mercy of our over-imaginative narratives, to return to the present moment rather than fixate upon the past or future.

In the CBT model, anger begins with a *trigger*. Someone cuts us up on the motorway. An event occurs which, as we normally see it, *makes us angry*. But as the model continues along familiar Stoic lines, we see that of course the story is more complicated and gives us plenty of opportunity to elicit change.

1. After the trigger, we form a judgement. 'That self-ish prick,' we might conclude, 'just cut me up! He must be punished.'

2. The next factor that comes into play is that of our *inhibitions*. What do we feel it's okay to do to someone who has swerved in front of us? Should we merely glare, raise a middle finger or avow to avenge ourselves further along the road? Is it permissible to get out of the car and kick the other driver's car? What rules do we follow in this situation? Our inhibitions are a hugely important buffer between what we feel like doing and what we consider it appropriate to do.

3. Finally, we have the resulting *behaviour*. We shout, kick, sulk or, in the case of one man filmed in the grip of road rage and posted on YouTube, leap on to the bonnet of the offending moving car and smash straight through the windscreen with a fist before being thrown on to the road.

Here is our core process:

Trigger > judgement > inhibitions > behaviour.

There are other factors too, which bear upon the entire process. Our *core beliefs* about the world and what happens in it will play a huge part. If we believe that people are essentially selfish and out for themselves, then our judgements that follow a trigger event will be very different from those of someone who believes people to be essentially decent and good-natured. Likewise, if we believe that it is appropriate to hit a spouse if he or she deserves it, our inhibitions will affect us quite differently in a heated domestic argument from another person who follows a life rule that you never do such a thing. So our relevant beliefs might be about the world and other people, or they may relate to what we deem appropriate in our own behaviour. They can have an enormous effect on our judgements or our inhibitions.

Likewise, our *mood* at the time of these events will play a huge part in what happens along that line leading to the final behaviour. If I am hungry, I become irritable. I become snappy and joyless before I even realise that low blood sugar is the cause. A world that half an hour ago was populated by smiling, sexy and fascinating individuals is now full of people getting in my way. The joy I had previously found in my partner's silly and comical mood is now replaced with an impatience directed at his childish refusal to take urgent matters seriously.

Not infrequently, after a disturbed night of intermittent slumber, I have been delivered from sleep by the jarring electronic cacophony of my alarm clock and started the day in a foggy, fuming funk. Such mornings leave me poised for confrontation and, worse, cause me to mumble anything I need to say in a morose fashion that efficiently infects others with my wretchedness and irascibility as they struggle to understand me.

Thus factors such as our beliefs, moods, and our levels of tiredness and hunger, impact greatly upon that sequence of trigger > judgement > inhibition > behaviour. The Stoics and their admirers have left us with several interesting ways of making adjustments to one or more of these areas in order to interrupt what can otherwise become a tiring and destructive pattern. But we have, by absorbing the crux of Epictetus's teaching (that it is not events that cause our problems but our appraisal of them), already made the biggest and most important leap. By fully accepting the fact that *we* are responsible for our angry responses (and not those who anger us), we are crossing the wide river to more tranquil pastures, from which it is very difficult to return.

With that in mind, what other practical means might help us further assuage our anger and enjoy a calmer existence? Seneca wisely points out that there is no one answer to fit everyone: different remedies will work for different people.[95] Clients of a cognitive behavioural therapist are helped to study the specifics that propel them from experiencing a trigger to exhibiting anger (or anxiety, or any other undesired response). For our purposes, we can look at the suggestions given by the various thinkers we have encountered and find what works for us in particular situations. As we do this, we should keep in mind an analogy of Plutarch's: painters will step back from their work and periodically inspect it. 'Continuous familiarity hides the ways in which something might vary slightly from what is required; so by interrupting their viewing, they use repeated discrimination to keep the viewing fresh and more likely to catch minor variations.'[96]

Plutarch suggests we should ask friends for feedback as to how we are. We should make ourselves available 'for periodic inspection' to examine our habits and character, 'to see if over a period of time any good features have been added or bad ones subtracted'.[97]

His proposal that we should be open to this sort of criticism might be a challenge to us. It would be easy to build a straw man of this idea and suggest that if we listened to everyone's opinions about ourselves, then we would be living a life of trying to appeal to everyone and

95 Seneca, On Anger, 3.1
96 Plutarch, On the Avoidance of Anger, [1] 452F
97 Plutarch, On the Avoidance of Anger, [1] 452F

having no clear sense of who we really are. But this is not what Plutarch is suggesting. The valued opinions of a few friends who know us well could be of enormous benefit. Given the importance we tend to ascribe to how we come across to other people, it is astonishing that we are so hostile to honest feedback. Criticisms make us defensive or upset, and flattery sinks in too deeply. If we wish to make progress with a character trait, such as minimising anger, we would be well advised to start asking trusted friends how we're doing. There is surely no more direct route to self-deception than the avoidance of feedback.

Although different approaches will be suitable for different people, depending on the way their anger forms, and therefore where in their cognitive-behavioural chain the solution is to be found, the ancients offer plenty of advice that we might wish to take on board. There is a consensus, for example, that when anger flares up, the best time to intervene with the lessons of philosophy is *immediately*. Plutarch continues his fire metaphor: 'Anyone who doesn't fuel a fire puts it out, and anyone who doesn't feed anger in the early stages and doesn't get into a huff is being prudent and is eliminating anger.'[98] Seneca uses a military metaphor: we are talking about warfare and must make sure our frontier guards are alert. In true Stoic form, we must remain vigilant:

> The best course is to reject at once the first incite-
> ment to anger, to resist even its small beginnings,
> and to take pains to avoid falling into anger. For if
> it begins to lead us astray, the return to the safe path
> is difficult, since, if once we admit the emotion and
> by our own free will grant it any authority, reason

98 Plutarch, *On the Avoidance of Anger*, [4] 454F

becomes of no avail; after that it will do, not whatever you let it, but whatever it chooses. The enemy,
I repeat, must be stopped at the very frontier; for if
he has passed it, and advanced within the city gates, he
will not respect any bounds set by his captives.[99]

These are strong words. The kind of rational techniques
taught by the Stoics must be applied straight away before
anger gains any ground. From the point of view of narrative forming, we would wish to form a compelling but
helpful story about the event – that is, one that does not
make us angry – before we shape one that insists we
should be furious. Plutarch has a softer, alternative image:
when a father sees a child struggling to cut up his dinner
with a knife, he takes the knife from her in order to do
the job more effectively. The meat needs to be cut; the
child cannot do it well, so the grown-up takes over.
Likewise, if an event has made us angry, then it may be
that punishment should be executed and an injustice cor-
rected; however, our childish anger, knowing no licence,
cannot do that effectively. We should instead pass the
knife to our rational selves – before any damage is done
– in order to ensure that the job is carried out correctly.
Our aims are not merely to avoid anger; they are also to
deal with the situation at hand constructively and
appropriately.

Here, then, are some ways of undoing our fury before
it takes hold.

1. Wait
Perhaps the most widely recommended technique for
nipping anger in the bud is to simply *wait*. Time is a vital

99 Seneca, *On Anger*, 1.8

factor in allowing anger to dissipate. I came across a useful metaphor in *Overcoming Anger and Irritability*, William Davies's practical book of cognitive-behavioural techniques for those troubled or debilitated by this particular problem. He describes anger in terms of a leaky bucket: it gets filled, can overflow if we keep topping it up, but if we give it time, our anger will dribble away.

Today, we are sometimes advised to hold our tongue and count to ten when we feel angry. This modern stratagem is in origin a Stoic precaution: a not-terrible but rather weak solution that may not be adequate in some situations. But the instigation of delay was a highly recommended piece of ancient advice. 'Let the matter await your leisure,' Epictetus recommends in his *Handbook*.[100]

Seneca, in his *On Anger*, clarifies that we delay not to simply switch off from the issue at hand but so that we make better judgements as to how to act:

> The best corrective of anger lies in delay. Beg this concession from anger at the first, not in order that it may pardon, but in order that it may judge. Its first assaults are heavy; it will leave off if it waits.

Plutarch, too, emphasises this important reason for delaying. He finds the time by having people defend themselves, and listening to the reasons for their actions:

> Learning how to punish in a well-timed, moderate, beneficial and appropriate way will not stop one punishing altogether. So I try to quell my

100 Epictetus, *Enchiridion*, 34

anger above all by not denying the defendants the right to justify themselves, but by listening to what they have to say. This helps because time checks emotion and gives it space to dissolve, and also because rationality finds what method of punishment is appropriate, and how much is fitting.[101]

The Stoics' advice can seem rather cool for hot-headed situations. Plutarch, though, is right: if when angry with someone we first allow them to explain themselves, and if we actually *listen* to what they say, we can allow our anger to dissolve. We want to hang on to our anger because we feel we need it to effectively communicate something important. But this is wrong: it only gets in the way and makes people less likely to understand us. Perhaps it would help us to call anger by another name: panic.

Usually, when we are angry, we are scared. We are scared that someone's actions will leave us helpless, or in some way betrayed, overwhelmed or abandoned. We might be scared that we will lose our autonomy. We are angry with others for not doing their jobs properly, because we in turn are then forced to struggle even more under our own pressures. We are angry at bad service because we feel ourselves being undermined or unheard. I have said that we tend to suffer from one of two basic fears: the fear of abandonment or the fear of being overwhelmed. The former tends to make us meet stress with anxiety, the latter to retreat. With a little thought, we can normally identify which one rings most true for us: do we 'recharge' by being alone or by being in company?

In everyday reality, we might shift from one to the other as different situations present their own challenges.

101 Plutarch, *On the Avoidance of Anger*, [11] 459E

A fear of abandonment is evident in our feeling of rejection when our partner intimates he would rather spend an afternoon reading than come shopping with us. We need reassurance that he does not prefer his own company to ours. Or, conversely, we might like the idea of making a trip alone and feel overwhelmed when our partner is eager to accompany us. One person needs to hear of his partner's jealousy to know he is valued; another finds it stifling and exhausting. One yearns for space, his intimacy. Less obviously, a thousand daily situations bring us up against these fundamental fears, and the panic they engender often results in displays of anger. Waiting and listening allows the panic to subside.

The advice to wait is clearly effective in cases where one would otherwise strike out with ill-judged aggression, but it may ring rather hollow to those of us who are not prone to such outbursts. Some of us, hating the idea of snapping angrily at a partner and starting an argument, prefer to sulk. We are forcibly struck by the tendencies of those we love to express their moments of anger with abandon, with the sort of sarcastic comment or put-down that we feel (inaccurately) that we would *never* employ. Unable to reciprocate, as the idea of an argument makes us feel quietly anxious, we absorb it and silently play out our responses over the next twenty-four hours.

Firstly, we regret our partner's preparedness to make such hurtful comments. We consider all the kindnesses we thanklessly bestow upon them and consider that perhaps it is our lot to never be fully appreciated. Replaying to ourselves their hurtful comment, we grasp the anger we feel and from that emotional starting point engage in imaginary dialogues with our beloved, in which we bring up the subject at hand and they are entirely unapologetic.

293

As we play these fanciful conversations to ourselves, our anger increases. We are topping up that leaky bucket, seeing now a pattern of behaviour in the person dearest to us from which there is no escape.

Thus we fantasise about leaving them, finding the idea not so awful, and eventually work ourselves into such a state that we are now blaming them for provoking such an enormous amount of resentment. Why must they be so bloody-minded not to realise that a nasty comment can ruin our day? Then, still obsessing over the event a day later, we are aware that to bring it up would seem ridiculous: an admission of our exhausting neurotic tendencies and one that would probably start the argument we wish to avoid. So, finding ourselves caught unhappily between expressing our upset (which now seems silly and provocative) and continuing to sulk (but this has been going on for long enough that we should surely say something), we let our silent anger bubble and brew.

For those of us prone to this kind of stewing, it would do us good to remember that if our partners tend to blurt out their irritation with hurtful comments, then they are probably not doing so with the same intensity of feelings that it would take for us to do the same. *We* would only make those comments if we had been pushed to our limit. *They* don't: they most likely get it out of their system in an angry moment and then forget about it. We shouldn't presume that it is meant with the venom that *we* would have implied.

Perhaps, then, a proviso to the Stoic instruction to wait is in order. For those who become silently, privately angry, remember that the point of delay is to spare others a misjudged response, not an excuse to merely sulk. Such resentfulness spreads a potent poison through all other interactions with the person in question for no reason other than wounded pride. There is always the possibility to address lingering anger or resentment as long as one does it respectfully. 'You make me angry' or 'You are so weird' is neither respectful nor truthful, because the anger and sense of weirdness do *not* come from the other person, they come from the story *we* have made up.

To phrase our grudges in this accusatory way is to trigger fears within the other; to cause them to think 'I am incompatible with this person, I am not good enough, I am not normal.' Our unhelpful reaction, born of our *own* fear that things are not right, that our world is crumbling in some small but scary way, triggers reciprocal fear in the other person.

Instead, there is much power in simply stating how one feels as if it were one's own problem: 'I feel this way when you do that thing.' By respectfully avoiding the other person's fear triggers, and making no accusations, the thorny subject can usually be broached some time after the event without an argument ensuing. So we need wait only long enough to consider our phrasing and take responsibility for our feelings. To wait so long that we never bring up our concerns is likely to do both parties a disservice. Expressing our unhappiness in a sensitive way is one of the most productive things we can do in a relationship.

If we delay, what should we do in the meantime? The Stoics knew, we remember, that venting our anger only serves to make it worse. Plutarch acknowledges that venting unhappy feelings may sometimes be of use, but certainly not in the case of anger:

> It may be that mourners eliminate a lot of their grief as well as their tears in the release of crying and weeping; but anger is made considerably more

intense by the behaviour and speech of people in an angry state.[102]

Instead, Seneca suggests we do the opposite: hide our response with a display of serenity. If we simply refuse to give it expression, especially in those early moments, we have conquered it at the vital moment:

> Do battle with yourself: if you have the will to conquer anger, it cannot conquer you. Your conquest has begun if it is hidden away, if it is given no outlet. Let us conceal the signs of it, and as far as possible let us keep it hidden and secret. This will cost us a great deal of trouble (for it is eager to leap out and inflame the eyes and alter the face), but if it is allowed to display itself outside ourselves, it is then on top of us. In the lowest recesses of the heart let it be hidden away, and let it not drive, but be driven. Moreover, let us change all its symptoms into the opposite: let the expression on our faces be relaxed, our voices gentler, our steps measured; little by little outer features mould inner ones.[103]

Is Seneca right? Psychologists, as we have noted, have now reversed their 1970s' opinions and support this idea that venting our anger is not good for us. In fact, they have now empirically fortified the suggestion offered by Seneca (and observed in Socrates before him[104]) that we can affect our inner state by changing such outward features as our facial expression and our postures. I have

102 Plutarch, *On the Avoidance of Anger*, [5] 455C
103 Seneca, *On Anger*, 3.13
104 Ibid.

realised, by means of example, that my shoulders tend to roll forward. This can give me a somewhat hunched posture, created by an inordinate amount of time sitting on sofas reading or typing, precisely as I am now. My gym instructor suggested I correct this stance when I walk, and I soon noticed that by moving my shoulders back, creating a much more 'open' stance, I immediately felt a sense of authority and connection with others that I had hitherto not felt when out and about. Perhaps between a preference for not drawing attention to myself in public and the physical placement of my hunched shoulders, I had come to feel rather invisible on the street. The sudden shift in my mood engendered by this point of correction was startling to me, and a little unsettling, as I felt far more conspicuous. And I imagine I was: an open posture will attract the attention of people far more than a less-inviting, self-contained attitude. I have since returned to the slouch.

2. Resist curiosity

Another approach to not being disturbed by anger might be to entirely avoid it in the first place. The Stoic approach to dealing with this emotion is only necessary if we are forced into confronting it. Meanwhile:

> the best course is to look out for obstacles to our known weaknesses, and above all to order the mind in such a way that, even when struck by the most serious and sudden events, either it does not feel anger, or buries deep any anger arising from the gravity of so unforeseen an affront, or does not acknowledge that it has been hurt.[105]

105 Seneca, *On Anger*, 3.13

love is...

... letting him
let off steam.

One interesting means of avoiding anger altogether is suggested by both Seneca and Plutarch after him: *be less curious*. Seneca writes:

> Do you want to avoid losing your temper? Resist the impulse to be curious. The man who tries to find out what has been said against him, who seeks to unearth spiteful gossip, even when engaged in privately, is destroying his own peace of mind.[106]

Plutarch offers:

> I also try to cut back a bit on my nosiness. I mean, knowing every single detail about everything, investigating and eliciting a slave's every occupation, a friend's every action, a son's every pastime, a wife's every whisper – this leads to many outbursts of anger, one after another every day, and these in turn add up to habitual discontent and surliness.[107]

A vast number of us in the developed world spend our days connected to some incarnation of social media, both contributing to and drawing from a turgid stream of inconsequential facts concerning what our fondest friends and favourite celebutantes are up to from moment to moment. We are given technology that far surpasses that which put man on the moon, and use it to tweet spite from the toilet. Feeds alert us to the supposed urgency of every new message that comes through, and we might check news apps several times a day to make sure that our

106 Seneca, *On Anger*, 3.11
107 Plutarch, *On the Avoidance of Anger*, [16] 464A

levels of fear are artificially maintained from moment to moment. This obsession with current information forms the basis for our default state. If we are bored, we quickly turn to social media for the appeal of new information. Some of it may concern us or be of professional interest, some may be merely amusing, and most is of either no interest or ranges from the faintly irritating to the infuriating. But we still want to know: 'What are people saying?' And we want to know even more: 'What are people saying about us?'

For all of us who use social media (and I only skim its grimy surface) or read online comments about ourselves, this feeling will be familiar. During and after the broadcasts of my shows *Hero at 30,000 Feet* and *Apocalypse*, both participants turned to social media with forgivable curiosity to see what viewers made of their adventures. Having been through enormously uplifting and positive experiences, and excited to know how the show would be received, each found himself reading (albeit amongst a wealth of positive comments) any number of nasty remarks about every aspect of his behaviour or appearance. Many insisted the participants were either idiots to behave in the way they did, or more likely they were actors and the whole thing an insulting hoax.

After each show, I felt an enormous amount of sympathy for its hero. One blogger, having watched and presumably refused to believe that we would have gone to all the trouble we did for *Apocalypse*, published and distributed that Steven, its protagonist, was an actor. His evidence: he looked vaguely like an actor in an advertisement for noodles and had once half-filled out an online form for background extra work (undoubtedly the same urge that led him to apply for my programme). In the week between the two episodes that constituted the show, this story spread and was even picked up by *The Sun*, which reported 'Twitter Outrage at "Actor"' in its charming way that makes speculation read as fact. I told Steven to resist looking online at people's responses, but of course this was too much to expect. What should have been one of the most exciting weeks of Steven's life was thus reduced to a period of oscillating elation and disappointment. By the time the second episode aired, it was clear he couldn't be an imposter (for his family and friends who featured in the show would have had to have been actors too), quite aside from the legal impossibility of us claiming he was real if he wasn't. I also found the actor from the noodle advertisement and filmed the two of them together. Naturally, neither *The Sun* nor the blogger, entitled to his opinion of course, made an apology to Steven or anyone else.

Hero at 30,000 Feet's Matt, meanwhile, had been faced with a barrage of insults about his clothes, his voice, his relationship, his behaviour and his authenticity as an unwitting participant. The good work done by the show was in danger of being undone by the nastiness online. It was Matt's experience that led me to plead with Steven not to read any posts, but despite both of their efforts, the accusations of fakery still hurt. Their concern, very admirably, was primarily not for themselves (they were both pretty confident that they weren't actors) but for our production crew, who they knew had gone to such extraordinary lengths to ensure their adventures.

It is rare that we find ourselves in the position of overhearing people voicing their raw, unabashed opinions about us, unaware that we are listening. The act of eavesdropping brings with it a set of appropriate physiological responses that remind us we are doing something we shouldn't. Our heart rate may increase, our breathing is likely to shift to our chest, our palms might sweat. Our bodies are telling us to flee: we should be anywhere but here, doing this. We know that our continuing curiosity is dangerous: either we force ourselves to listen, or we move away from the door.

We *should* feel the same response when we read comments about ourselves online. The problem is, we don't. Irrespective of whether we are famous or otherwise, it is nowadays very easy to click or swipe and read what people are saying about us. When we secretly listen to a conversation from without, our guilty feelings let us know that we are doing wrong. In contrast, the ready accessibility of mentions, posts and online comments leaves us feeling that *our* actions are blameless. We can only direct our anger at those who have posted: *they* are idiots, probably spotty thirteen year olds whose opinion we would not care for if we met them in person; *they* are h8ers, anonymous cowards, trolls and bullies.

Some of the above may be the case. There is a strong argument for reconsidering the mask of anonymity in areas of the Internet prone to bullying and the classic symptoms of deindividuation. But the immediate problem is not the nastiness of the comments; it is the fact that *we are choosing to read them*. We should approach them with the apprehension we would have were we to approach a door and hear our name mentioned on the other side. We should remember and enact that same paralysing precaution.

It is the *curiosity* that directs us unflinchingly to read online comments about our work or ourselves, and the same curiosity that is responsible for the anger or hurt we feel when we find something nasty. While those who write these posts would be well advised to spare a thought for who might be reading them, we are wrong to blame them entirely. In cases of bullying, of course it is proper to track down and punish the perpetrators appropriately. But for most of the time, we might want to remember Seneca's and Plutarch's warning. 'Resist curiosity.'

The alternative is that we feel anger, and more often than not engage in an attempt to change the opinion of the person in question. Or simply argue back. We are now trying to control something *outside* of our control. This is likely only to augment our anger and lead to far greater disturbance. We need pay attention only to our own thoughts and actions. We can block, mute or take steps against those who unceasingly persist. On Twitter (I write in 2016), I happily mute anyone whom I find annoying: daily petitions for a reply (that is, to reply to nothing other than a request for a reply); exhausting, repeated declarations of love from the inveterately fixated; the bizarre accusations and outpourings that appear daily from those who are mentally ill. The person in question does not realise they have been muted and may carry on to their heart's content without it ever bothering me. Muting is a Stoic move: it makes no attempt to control what is beyond me and simply removes me from any feelings of irritation.

The instruction to resist curiosity, then, is a refinement of the rule to only concern yourself with what lies within your power. It not only translates well to our fumbling experience with new media, it also warns us not to enquire as persistently as to what our friends are up to or have been saying. Curiosity of any sort is concerned with how a subject relates to us. If I am curious about a subject – say the work of an artist – it is because I am ultimately seeking out how it might relate to me. We can enjoy being curious about other people and their lives and motivations when we meet them, or about their jobs and children. As we ask our questions, however, we are searching for points of interest where our two worlds connect. It is rare that we ask questions purely out of a disinterested motivation to see how the other person ticks or to understand a certain subject a little better, and even when we do we are doing so to enlarge our own world. But this self-interest is far more evident in the thornier quarters of our personal relationships, where the antennae of our deep fears become highly sensitive to anything that might involve us. *So and so was talking about you*: 'Really? What did they say?' *I had a long chat with a guy in the café today*: 'Did you? Was he cute?'

Resisting this curiosity is not to be dull-witted. It is to avoid pandering to our fears. It's enormously liberating to not feed the beast. When our ears prick up, practise resisting curiosity.

Consider how easy it is to become annoyed at what one friend tells us about how another has acted, even though it has nothing to do with us. Somewhere off in the distance, someone we know has done or said something which is now being told to us by someone else who has already edited the story to suit their own agenda. We hear this second-hand report and edit it *again* to enforce our own notions about the perpetrator's tendencies, and thus we become angry for no worthwhile reason at all.

Other Stoic suggestions for avoiding anger concern the way we form our judgements: those stories or beliefs that come into play to cause the bad feelings. Those judgements might concern the details of a specific situation, or they might inform our wider convictions about how the world works, which in turn affect our appraisals, inhibitions or behaviours across the board.

We should take on board, then, the following understanding: *we come to our anger.*

> Very many men manufacture complaints, either by
> suspecting what is untrue or by exaggerating the
> unimportant. Anger often comes to us, but more
> often we come to it. Never should we summon it;
> even when it falls on us, it should be cast off.[108]

To make this leap: to not flail and blame but acknowledge our responsibility for our emotions is not only a mark of maturity but the only path to relieving distress. As we have seen, we don't do this in order to let our perpetrators off the hook but to ensure we don't increase the damage caused by adding further distress, and perhaps to gain a clearer perspective of what punishment might be reasonable.

What mistakes do we make when we 'come to anger'? Seneca's expression is referring to that part of the cognitive-behavioural chain comprised of our judgement and inhibitions. This is where we do the 'thought' work: where we tell ourselves stories, draw from our beliefs, and make ourselves angry. Here are some classic errors we tend to make:

Selective perception. This is confirmation bias at work. We commonly pay attention to the things that confirm our pre-existing beliefs. If we are already convinced that a person is being unsupportive towards us, we will pay attention to any behaviour they exhibit which seems to confirm that. It's necessary of course that we do form these sort of patterns; we can't pay equal attention to every aspect of a person's communication, there are simply too many. However, we would do well to remember that we are selectively editing a much richer picture and probably missing evidence of support because it does not fit the belief we have already formed. We might think of what happens when we read a newspaper article that supports a view we already have versus one which argues against it. The former we read with the satisfaction that comes from reading good, well-researched journalism and a point well argued. The opposing one, however, will strike us as unworthy of our attention: badly investigated and lazy on every level. We effortlessly dismiss it from our ongoing catalogue of what is important in the world. Imagine how busy we must be as we make constant judgements about what to select as valuable from the infinite and shifting data source that surrounds us.

Mind-reading. If we momentarily package and stow my multi-award-winning, consistently envelope-pushing and hilariously lucrative performances neatly to one side, we must accept the conspicuous truth: we are terrible at reading each other's thoughts. Yet we consistently behave as if we have been endowed with this entirely handsome ability.

That person blanked us at the party because he was thinking, 'I'll ignore that idiot'. Our child repeatedly ignores our pleas to tidy her room because her thoughts are running as follows: 'Ha, I'll ignore Mum's instructions and it will really wind her up. I don't have to do anything she says'. Those who annoy us are *doing it deliberately*. Our boss is unsupportive because *he can't be bothered*. We just *know* what is going on in their heads. If selective perception gives us the pre-chosen data from which to form our stories, mind-reading is a common means of building the narrative itself. In order to make this mistake, we must replay an event (the blanking at the party) or run through an imagined scenario (our child alone in her room) and dub over a commentary. It may happen briefly, but we must construct something along these lines in order to create an angry feeling. The point is: we could form a *different* commentary if we wished. We are *choosing* a hurtful or irritating one. We are doing exactly what we would recommend if we were setting out a step-by-step guide of how to feel rotten. A person we admire and have met a few times walks past us at a party, making eye contact but not acknowledging us. That is an event entirely without moral content:

> Remove your judgement about the supposed hurt and make up your mind to dismiss it, and your anger is gone. How then will you remove it? By reflecting that what hurts you is not morally bad.[109]

To *make* it bad, we must 'add to first impressions' and supply a thought-track. And a specific one at that. From the variety of possible trains of thought we might wish to attribute to this person at the moment they passed us, including a vast number which tell tales of a mind simply distracted (perhaps they were absorbed in the lyrics of the song playing in the background), we are sure to find the most hurtful possible: that of a conscious, deliberate snub.

Catastrophising. Some people seem in a state of constant heightened emotional engagement with the world. A good friend of mine is one of those people. He tells a funny story and cries with laughter; he expresses incredulity at almost everything. I cannot imagine him ever disguising his feelings. This makes him enormously popular and rather different from me. The verso to this particular recto is that his reports of events tend to be told with a tone of such drama and catastrophe that it took me

109 Marcus Aurelius, *Meditations*, xii. 18

307

a long time to realise I didn't have to worry as much as his accounts encouraged me to.

We are of different temperaments, and I adore his in a way that I'm sure my detached, pedantic, grey-area nit-picking only irritates him. But occasionally I wonder about the brightly coloured, high-contrast world in which he must live. It must be different from mine. His judgements of events would seem to be starker than those I would form. Because we forget about the role of our appraisals and tend to ascribe our feelings to the events themselves and those who perpetrate them, two people with different judgements will live, by all accounts, in two different worlds.

Those beset by feelings of anxiety are of course most prone to catastrophising. Our loved one is to spend time with an attractive new client at work: clearly they will fall in love. We have a sore leg: we must have a ripped tendon, or worse. We have picked at a spot: we will always be scarred and more prone to skin cancer.

The language we use when we catastrophise becomes unnecessarily emotional, and contrasts become starker. Two experiences of being ignored at parties translates into 'I'm *always* blanked by people . . . I'll *never* find a partner because I'm just worthless'. We hear from Friend A that Friend B told Friend C that we are tiresome/too critical of others/a bad drunk, and this translates into 'B hates me'. Without ever finding out what was really said, we strike Friend B from our party invitation list and foster feelings of anger and betrayal under a guise of indifference. The friendship then suffers because of *us*, not our friend.

As anger feeds further anger, it is difficult to undo this process once it has started. We need some sense of detachment from the event in order to take a cooler look at what might have been happening, but our anger is being consistently topped up, and that leaky bucket isn't getting a chance to shed enough of its load. Instead, our exaggerated calamitous interpretation of events is offering us a fairy-tale depiction of good and evil, perhaps casting us as the pitiful victim of people's incompetence (like one cursed by a snubbed witch as a newborn, and who now stumbles pathetically through life doomed by a constitutional predilection to encounter the idiocy of others). What separates childish stories from real life is that the characters of fairy tales are impossibly one-dimensional; they tend to stand as potent symbols of forces that might figure in a child's psyche. The people with whom we share our lives, on the other hand, are as complex and contradictory as we are ourselves. Motivations are rarely black and white, and our futures are seldom, if ever, as drastically and obviously cast as we imagine.

We might wish to catch ourselves making these melodramatic leaps and see them for what they are. And when we use emotional or over-generalising language, either out loud or to ourselves – 'I'll never be able to do that/She always acts like that/I'm fucking useless/I'll never have a proper relationship' – we should make a point of correcting ourselves and drawing instead from a more discerning lexicon: ideally one that does not pre-suppose an extravagant world of imaginary beings and magical horizons.

3. Use imaginary friends

Let's continue with other means of avoiding anger. If you travel to Taormina in Sicily, you will most likely decide that it is worth your while to climb Mount Etna, the dark volcanic presence that hovers over the horizon and forms the backdrop to one of the most spectacularly placed

Greco-Roman theatres antiquity has left to us. To make the ascent, you take a cable car for the first part of the journey, before a minibus escorts you and fifteen or so other holidaymakers to a high plateau of 2,800 metres. There you can explore the red, desolate, near-Martian terrain.

I was travelling with a friend. In the queue awaiting our cable car, he voiced his fear of the journey ahead. He anticipated a rickety, creaking, swinging voyage high in the air, and his anxiety was evident in his irritability and restive attitude. He was determined to make the trip, as there was no other feasible way to reach the midway point. Or perhaps there was, but I had insisted on the cable car as I found the idea quite exciting. By the time we reached the front of the queue, his eyes were wide, his breathing short and high in his chest, as he nervously pointed out every flaw in the self-evidently ill-thought-through means of transport. Eventually, a car finally heaved its descent towards us, and we were ushered on by a worker; I cannot remember whether it stopped to allow us to get on or whether we had to step up while it was still moving.

Either way, we entered the loose, swaying cabin and found ourselves sitting opposite a Swedish woman and her husband. She held his arm tightly, and in the most agitated fashion turned her head first one way and then the other, keeping a vigilant lookout through the scratched plastic windows that surrounded us. As we lurched free of the pulley system beneath us and lifted high into the air, she began an antithetical descent into the depths of profound hysteria. She sobbed continuously, interrupting herself only to shriek and spread herself wide with every wobble like a cat held over a bath, while her husband flashed silent, apologetic looks at us two. We sat uncomfortably close, doing our British best to stare out of the window at the boundless horizon and pretend the urgent Nordic delirium was simply not happening.

Meanwhile, my concern was that this unfortunate woman would undo any attempts on my part to keep my friend calm. I would occasionally offer him a questioning look that wordlessly enquired as to his welfare; each time he blinked and looked away to register that no fuss should be made. Fascinatingly, the woman's hysteria had the opposite effect to that which I expected: faced with this display of frenzied terror, he drastically reappraised his view of himself as a cable-car traveller. Before, his narrative had cast him as the scared passenger in the upcoming cable-car flight. Now, sitting opposite someone who was having a far worse time than he had envisioned for himself, he assumed a different role. Now he was someone who was most certainly not going to act like *that*. This woman needed help and care: it would make no sense for him to be demanding the same; in fact, by remaining calm, he could even be available for assistance. It was as if a set of primal instincts took over; whether it was to be strong and at hand to help the suffering member of the group, or to be poised and ready for any event should she suddenly present a danger to her fellow passengers, my friend effortlessly transformed into a comfortable connoisseur of the cable car.

This struck me as a very useful experience. When faced with the distress of others, we tend to assume a calming role. Commonly, this happens when we talk to a friend who is facing difficulty. We see their concern, acknowledge their view of events, but calmly present a different, less worrisome view. Were we to be facing a similar difficulty, a friend would be likely to do the same. She would hopefully provide reasons not to fret and highlight certain pieces of positive evidence that would help us view things differently. Whether it is anxiety or anger that is the cause of the distress, these discussions serve to undo the chain of *trigger > judgement > inhibitions > behaviour* by focusing on the 'judgement' component and trying to shift it. 'It's *good* that bastard has left you: he was no good for you.' 'You'll be *fine* giving that presentation: you're well prepared and a few nerves are a good thing.'

In the case of the cable car, no discussion was needed, but a similar dynamic occurred. My friend's internal narrative just shifted; his role in the events was changed for him by the surprise addition of a person cast far more deservedly as 'scared passenger'. Although he didn't try to calm her through talking, he took the same view that we do when our friends are upset or angry: we see their distress as unnecessary and feel comparatively self-assured.

A couple of years later, I found myself sitting in a train carriage hurtling somewhere through England. I love train travel very much and always look forward to such journeys when I am to make them alone. On this particular occasion, I had secured my favourite sort of travelling spot – at a small two-seater table in a first-class quiet coach. The larger tables are less private, and the danger of someone asking to share with me is perpetually present. At a smaller table, I was less likely to be disturbed from the dreamy infusion of sleep and reading I had planned for the substantial journey to wherever it was. And then a woman sitting diagonally across the gangway from me started coughing.

This was not the sound of the sudden choking triggered when the airway of a train passenger is occluded by a wayward shard of reproduction ham. Neither was it the hollow hack of the inveterate smoker: the rattling, guttural clatter of catarrh and cancer and black-lunged death. Instead, this was that peculiar, soft, throaty *hmmmkhm*, whose opening gentle crescendo discloses that it is not triggered by pork-pricked throat or pitch-clad lungs but rather the *nervous desire* to cough: a satisfying tracheal tension release that dislodges nothing but the need itself. This was the muted, private cough of the compulsively habituated, which I recognised due to my own experience with similar tics.

Although I have never coughed in this way, I sniffed as a teenager with the ferocity and frequency necessary, for example, to clear a row at the Berlin Philharmonic during Alfred Brendel's recital of the Beethoven sonatas. I spent many years banging my knees together for no other reason than I could not dispel the desire to do so, to the extent that I was perpetually bruised and have most likely caused joint problems to which I can look forward in old age. Many people will find themselves prey to throaty tics or the obsessive ordering of stationery and remote controls; generally these are harmless habits, out of which we eventually grow. However, these impulses can expand into something powerfully debilitating when coupled with overwhelming anxiety; the miserable experience of the obsessive-compulsive is testament to how all-encompassing our capacity for auto-suggestion can become. And despite our kind efforts to 'relate', it's not helpful to tell a true OCD sufferer that we're a 'bit OCD' ourselves because we like to line up the remotes. One sufferer told me that it's like telling a person with diabetes that we don't eat sweets because we're a 'bit diabetic'.

On this note, one friend ruined an evening for himself and some companions by insisting they drive him across London so that he could tap his front door: the pain of leaving it untapped once the idea had taken hold, was too much to bear. Another friend, less severely afflicted, finds himself paralysed, running over thoughts, trying to recreate the *precise* feeling that was present when he had the thought previously, unable to continue with his day until a complete thought-feeling has been exactly recreated in its original form. Yet another cannot eat on days that contain a certain letter, and that offending letter can change from day to day. All have sought therapy to assuage this exhausting, fascinating and dismal condition, but realistic assistance seems to be limited to short-term solutions and tools to try to make it more manageable.

While I have never suffered from OCD, my tic-filled teenage years have lent me some experience of the thinnest end of that particular wedge, and I have only sympathy and fascination for it. To a large extent, we struggle to understand ourselves through others; we look at other people's behaviour and models of the world, and (perhaps too quickly) decide how they relate to ours. When someone reflects our own biases, we are happy and feel attraction; they have reinforced the peculiar script we are living out, and we need not, for a while, be quite so much on our guard. Sufferers of psychological conditions present rather more eccentric models of thinking yet are generally ruled by something that also stirs within *us* in embryonic form. Moreover, that 'something' might, given the right conditions, have emerged to take ownership of us too. Thus people with these conditions cause us to face our own fragility, and the extent to which we are comfortable with that tenuousness in ourselves makes the difference between whether we merely pretend to find them alien (or 'mental', 'attention- seeking'), or whether we feel empathy ('that could be me . . .') coupled with a guilty, healthy splash of relief ('thank God it isn't').

As I waited for the sound of coughing to repeat itself,

my senses snapped into the same state of hyper-alertness in which I had found myself every night for about three years when I lived above a tube station. Engineering works had to be carried out at night, and my bedroom wall was a convenient continuation of the very masonry into which they drilled and hammered intermittently most nights for that period. The first low moan of brace and bit began around 4 a.m. and was enough to heave me from sleep and leave me wide-eyed and open-eared waiting for the next. And the next. Sometimes they came; sometimes they did not. That extreme, adrenaline-fuelled attentiveness with which I anticipated each forthcoming disturbance was the same kind I felt now on this train, waiting to hear if she would cough again in the same way.

Hmmmmmmmmkhm.

My fears were confirmed: this throat-clearing would not stop any time soon. What had promised to be a long, rhapsodic journey now stretched before me as the loco-motive equivalent of sleepless misery at the grimy hands of London Transport's night staff. Infuriation rose and boiled scarlet before me. Should I collect coat and bag and book and laptop and move to a different carriage? Or could I ignore this woman?

Two quick thoughts flashed through my head. Firstly, how I might calm someone down who was infuriated at the coughing. Almost immediately thereafter the second: my friend on the cable car, having extirpated his fear, because someone else was having a far worse time. The solution offered itself: I imagined, sitting opposite me, the same friend, whom I knew to be a little prone to stress. I pictured him maddened by the coughing (*hmmmkhm*, there it came again), while I told him smilingly it was fine, to just let it float over him, to take note that the lady was quite sweet (I had looked at her: she was elderly and possibly embarrassed by her own habit) and that he didn't have to decide it was infuriating. The hyper-attentiveness, the inability to read or concentrate on anything else – this was the fault of a projection of frustration into the future, a story, a way of seeing the events, an unhelpful appraisal of how things would be. All trace of irritation left me. I returned to my book and some time later I presume she stopped coughing or got off the train.

The trick of bringing other people to mind is of enormous use in dispelling anger. It is tempting to hold on to our annoyance, to feel entitled to it and justified in every aspect of its expression. Yet, as we have discussed, it does us no favours; we might prefer to untangle our anger from the matter at hand to gain a clearer perspective on it. We might use a friend, an admired luminary, even a fictitious character, as a role model who can spring to mind when we find ourselves incensed. How might they deal with this situation? How would they coolly laugh it off or rise above it? This might give us some distance from our own story and offer a more helpful, convincing perspective. Or, if a friend were suffering with this particular problem, how would we advise them? Those calming words of wisdom we would offer – what would they be?

By imagining ourselves offering advice on the very topic that is perturbing us, we are made to engage in a different dialogue; our first take on events changes as we are made to consider a more phlegmatic and unruffled response. Having this imaginary conversation brings us out of ourselves, detaches us from the disturbances of those initial emotions, reminds us that our judgement is responsible for our anger and not the event itself, and is enormously effective at stopping the enemy 'at the very frontier'.

4. *Lower your self-belief*

> You ask what is the greatest failing in you? You
> keep accounts badly: you rate high what you have
> paid out but low what you have been paid.[110]

Perhaps the greatest cause of anger, not to mention frustration, is the fact that we have an inflated sense of our own entitlement. We believe we are entitled to happiness: the mistake discussed in the first part of this book is to see it as a birthright that we can righteously claim, some 'thing' out there that we can and should possess through sheer willpower. The overwhelming majority of self-help books, apotheosising that all-important first syllable, teach us to increase our self-esteem, our self-respect, our self-confidence. We set our sights too low, we are told; we absorb other people's negative appraisals of ourselves; we need to stand up, say no and decide we deserve more.

This message is now so ubiquitous that we never question it. For some, of course, who truly suffer from debilitating self-esteem, it can be an important intimation of hope and not to be belittled. But even in such cases, self-aggrandisement does not solve the problem. Our centre of gravity must be brought inside where it belongs; locating it in others is where we get into trouble, regardless of whether it results in shyness or a brash need to impress.

I remember meeting the mogul of a whisky conglomerate after a corporate gig some time back; the man was *immaculate*. His magnificent cologne wafted undoubted status; his manner was masterfully understated; every action, every inch of his appearance made

110 Seneca, *On Anger*, 3.31

me feel honoured to meet a man I had never heard of. Talking to me, he was utterly engaged and present, two hallmarks of charisma, and, like an actor playing a king, he let other people confer status upon him, playing none of it himself. When we are happy, we have won the game, and the fact is self-evident; there's no need to broadcast the victory.

All the difference in the world exists between that man and the other who *plays* high status for no reason other than inside he feels like a scrabbling, panicked child. I spend a lot of time amongst performers and am always struck by how much or little those who dazzle for a living need to impress in real life. Circus performers and acrobats, interestingly, seem to me to be most strikingly delightful and, as a rule, free from stifling egos. There is a true international camaraderie, which is patently lacking in, say, the magic scene. Perhaps that's because acrobats and jugglers and the like don't *cheat*, at least compared to conjurors. Amongst the latter group, undoubtedly fanned by the fear of being a fraud, egos are commonly as inflated as social skills are uncultivated. As a group, we magicians are prone to 'holding court': talking shop, telling anecdotes and keeping the focus on ourselves and our wearying, withering put-downs. Lacking the aerialist's confidence in his significant, quantifiable skills, magicians commonly lack the hallmark of the truly successful: quiet charm.

While the evolutionary advantages of status are self-evident, it's fascinating to me that despite our extraordinarily well-honed social radars, and the importance and appeal of getting on with people and being liked, we make such gross errors as thinking that being 'impressive' (in this least interesting sense) will make people like us. We make two common mistakes when we try to be liked:

we either try to impress or we try to be like the other person. Yet we know, from every day of our own experience of liking and disliking other people, that status and similarity are not especially attractive traits. The vast majority of us are drawn to basic qualities such as warmth and openness. The person eager to impress, on the other hand, might find it very difficult to freely compliment people, believing somewhere in his complicated, overwrought thinking process that to commend another would be to denigrate himself. Ironically, he misses that self-abnegation is a powerful key to social appeal. To whom are we drawn – the person who lets us know how fascinating he is, or the person who lets us know how fascinating we are? To the person who listens to what we say and converses about things that are important to us, or the person who lets us talk only to prepare what he is going to say next about himself? People who prioritise impressing people rather than letting *themselves* be impressed by others make it hard for those others to like them.

Meanwhile, for most of us who stride confidently enough through some areas of life and run and hide from others; who generally walk the natural $x=y$ diagonal, caught between lofty ideals and the cold hard ground of fortune, the message to believe more and more in ourselves is precisely what we need *less* of. When we consider things that make us angry – those judgements we make, not the things themselves – where does that fermentation process so often begin other than in the exaltation of the self?

It will be some time before titles such as 'Climb Out Of Your Own Arse' populate the shelves dedicated to self-improvement. Possibly, with a resurgence of interest in the lessons of ancient philosophy, we might one day realise that a large part of improving the 'self' is to shift the focus from 'self' to 'other'. As I have written elsewhere, the heart of true self-improvement surely lies in becoming kinder (from a place of strength).

When we are criticised, we usually snap into a spluttering defensiveness, which we would find ludicrous if we heard it from others. We can remind ourselves of how easily we can identify negative patterns in other people ('he's pretty arrogant, he talks too much, she tends to put other people down') but when such criticisms come our way, we object to the generalisation and insist on being given individual examples, each of which we can then explain away: 'When do I do that? Tell me one instance where I did that! Right, well, that was because . . .' The fury of Seneca's driving demon has us believe in our anger that we are entirely faultless. Perhaps we would admit our defects at *another* time in *another* conversation. Irrespective of what perfectly tranquil conditions we demand before we are prepared to acknowledge some fraction of those weaknesses that are so glaringly obvious to those who know us (to the extent that they undoubtedly make fun of us behind our back), we resort to snorting indignation just about every time they are pointed out.

And *of course* we do: living amongst others is a vulnerable business, and the fear of social exclusion cuts deep, doubtless haunting us from a prehistoric time when such ejection meant lack of vital protection and certain death. To suspect that our peers have identified our weaknesses is a troubling thing. Those narratives are again at play: *we* may have complex justifications for why we don't dance at weddings; to be told that we're simply 'boring' strikes us as plain wrong, and our initial impulse is to return that strike.

But we will not be cast out of the tribe. We won't be

left to wander the plains until we collapse and fall prey to the unhurried, fetid jaws of a passing carnivorous herd. We are still loved, despite every one of our laughably obvious foibles. Consider your friends: you have formed an affection for them despite their obvious points of deficiency, which you happily discuss when they are absent. These minor regrets, far from undermining your fondness, are in fact an important part of it; people's vulnerabilities are near impossible to untangle from their strengths. Psychologist and author Richard Wiseman, while we were discussing people's tendency to regret decisions in their lives, suggested the image of a jar of coloured threads: try to remove one and the whole bundle comes out with it. The same evocative image suits our purposes here: a friend's occasional spinelessness is impossible to untangle from his striking kindness of which we are so fond; another's occasional arrogance is commensurate with his appealing self-sufficiency and independence. Likewise, we can presume that if those we like point out a flaw in our character, they are likely to be justified and we needn't take it as a sign that they hate us. We can be reminded of Epictetus's point that we take enormous care to measure weights and quantities with accuracy but spend no time making sure our judgements are as close to the truth as possible. In the matter of how we appear to others, we tend to both care a great deal about doing so favourably, while simultaneously resisting the only yardstick we can use to ensure success: what others tell us.

When someone criticises us rudely, we can allow for the fact that their own annoyance will have led them to talk indelicately (as it would us), and even go so far as to decide that they are *entirely justified* in their annoyance. *We do not need to be right.* Much of the time we are likely to have misjudged, and the flawed or charged way another person points that out does not change the fact. As I have said, when resentment haunts us it is often because we feel a little guilty. The ongoing indignation we feel is a result of a conflict between our knowledge that we acted badly and our refusal to confess that fact to ourselves. Consider, next time you are plagued by irritation after an event, whether it might be guilt that you are feeling. This is anathema to many people. They would rather believe that they are blameless while those around them just act so *bizarrely*, so *unfairly*, so *selfishly*. They remain annoyed because they are refusing to admit that they themselves have acted in a way that could be seen as greedy, disrespectful, self-serving or unpleasant. By privately questioning whether guilt might be the reason for our ongoing disgruntlement, we give ourselves the opportunity to consider our faults, make amends where possible and then end the bitterness by letting ourselves off the hook. Life is much easier if we get off our high horses.

5. You have the same faults as those who annoy you

Allied to the above is a very helpful new belief we might like to try out when others annoy us: 'We're not so different.' The same genes that give us similar bodies also give us similar brains and therefore similar thoughts. 'If we are to be fair judges of all that happens,' writes Seneca, '. . . there is no justice in blaming the individual for a failing shared by all men'. He continues:

> All of us are inconsiderate and imprudent, all unreliable, dissatisfied, ambitious – why disguise with euphemism this sore that infects us all? – all of us are corrupt. Therefore, whatever fault he censures

in another man, every man will find residing in his own heart.[111]

Marcus notes a similar point to himself:

When you run against someone's wrong behaviour, go on at once to reflect what similar wrong act of your own there is.[112]

This thought was adopted into Christianity as the adage 'He that is without sin among you, let him first cast a stone.'[113] Drawn from the Stoics, this saying encapsulates a fundamental point for the philosophical school on the matter of anger. Seneca alerts us to how much anger can be avoided if we first say to ourselves in silence: 'I myself have also been guilty of this.'

It was customary for words to be written retrospectively into the mouths of historical figures such as Jesus decades after their deaths. This was in order that such erstwhile leaders could be seen to offer help to followers facing particular socio-political troubles in their own, later times. The Gospel of John (which contains the 'cast the first stone' precept) was written towards the end of the first century AD, a little while after Seneca's popular essay, but the relevant story of Jesus and the adulterous woman (known traditionally as the 'Pericope Adulterae') appeared later in the fourth and early fifth centuries. Presumably, then, the famous maxim had its origins in Seneca's less pithy:

111 Seneca, *On Anger*, 3.26
112 Marcus Aurelius, *Meditations*, x. 30
113 *The Bible*, John 8:7

> If we are willing in all matters to play the just
> judge, let us convince ourselves first of this – that
> no one of us is free from fault.[114]

Sadly, nothing could undermine the life-affirming point
of this Stoic advice more than its pious familiarity as a
religious aphorism. But by halting in our tracks the
moment we see the red light of flaring anger before us,
and considering that we too have been guilty of similar
behaviour, we can transform an ugly point of petty conflict into something of profound beauty. The Stoics, for
all their talk of rocks and fortifications, were ultimately
interested in a deep connection with their fellow human
beings. By employing a more modest, realistic approach
to self-appraisal, we connect with a community of flawed
fellow beings and turn aggression into its opposite: love.

6. Understanding the offender's motivation

Marcus offers us some further valuable thoughts that
can open us up to the possibility of a positive human
experience rather than that of aggression through self-
exaltation. We have looked at our own faults; now we
might wish to consider the incitements of the person who
has upset us.

> When people injure you, ask yourself what good or
> harm they thought would come of it. If you under-
> stand that, you'll feel sympathy rather than outrage
> or anger. Your sense of good and evil may be the
> same as theirs, or near it, in which case you'll
> have to excuse them. Or your sense of good and
> evil may differ from theirs. In which case they're

114 Seneca, *On Anger*, 2.28

misguided and deserve your compassion. Is that so hard?[115]

We make the same judgements. We can hardly blame others for acting in precisely the same way we would ourselves, Seneca writes:

> Some men, it is true, have not only just but honourable reasons for standing against us: one is protecting a father, another a brother, another his country, another a friend; however, we do not pardon these for doing the very thing which we would blame them for not doing.[116]

> No one says to himself, 'I myself have done or could have done the thing that is making me angry now'.[117]

We can't blame others for doing what we would most likely have done if we found ourselves in the same circumstances. If *we* had been that annoyed, or that protective, or felt cornered or scared to the same degree, we would have done the same thing. It doesn't matter if we think the other person has reacted over and above how we would; the point is that we, *under the same psychological conditions*, would have very likely done the same. It might have taken more to provoke us, but we know that we have the capacity, given the right circumstances, to be just as unpleasant or untoward.

Consider the fury we feel when we uncover a white lie that a friend has told. I recently made a friend, John,

115 Marcus Aurelius, *Meditations*, vii. 26
116 Seneca, *On Anger*, 3.28
117 Seneca, *On Anger*, 3.12

through another friend, Simon; both are actors. John and I got on well and decided to meet for lunch. Having seen each other in Simon's company a few times, it didn't seem wrong of John and I to arrange to meet on our own. However, the two of them were neighbours as well as close friends, and generally very aware of what each other were up to. John was concerned that Simon would at some point ask him what he had planned on the day we had arranged to meet and would certainly ask to come along if he heard we were hooking up. We fancied meeting on our own, so when Simon did indeed enquire as to his plans, John told a white lie to avoid hurting his feelings and pretended he was up to something else. We met for lunch as planned, but it turned out a friend of Simon's noticed us in the café and casually mentioned it to him the next day. Simon was angry with John; he couldn't care less that we had met, he said, but why, he complained, did John have to lie?

This is just one of many testosterone-fuelled adventures that might arise when one has actors as friends. But it is typical of many of our daily sources of annoyance and points to how it is our stories of events that principally create our grievances. Told from my perspective – a third person – we can see that John's motivations were perfectly understandable. We might feel that *ideally* he would have asked Simon if he minded, but even that might seem like a rather unnecessary gesture of courtesy. His motivation was out of affection for Simon; although we were both looking forward to getting to know each other one on one, neither of us wanted Simon to feel left out. If roles had been switched, I can imagine doing the same thing, and I'm sure Simon would too.

Yet from Simon's perspective, his grievance is clear cut. Any of us might think: 'John, my supposedly dear friend, wants to meet Derren, which is fine, of course, but lies to me about it. We've known each other for years. Did he lie because he really didn't want me there that much? Am I that unbearable?' And perhaps, beneath the protestations, a quieter voice asks, 'Are they going to like each other more than me? Is our friendship not as solid as I thought? I suppose I can be rather annoying . . . And John always does this. He's such a friend-thief . . .' If it were me, I would picture my two friends laughing and enjoying this me-free meal, perhaps the first of many, and I would feel a stab of jealousy. That emotion, unpleasant enough, would be worsened by the guilty conflict I would feel: 'Why does it bother me if my friends want to get to know each other without me? How pathetic to be saddened that they have their own lives.'

There is at the heart of this anger a pang of existential melancholy: we play only peripheral parts in the lives of our friends. They are the chief protagonists of their own dramas; to them, we are merely supporting cast. In the same way that the complexities of a minor character can never be fully explored, we too are reduced in the eyes of those who know us to a handful of clear-cut characteristics as predictable and easily categorised as our dress sense. Moreover, we only emerge in their minds in this diminished form on those brief occasions when they happen to think about us; for the vast majority of the time, our friends do not think of us at all. And when they do, our anger at the loving and considerate lie they tell us to spare our feelings is misplaced.

'You yourself . . . often do wrong,' Marcus tells us, and, referring to those who have offended us, 'You are not even sure that they actually do wrong.'[118] Many

118 Marcus Aurelius, *Meditations*, xi. 18

actions serve a purpose that may be hidden from us, and we would have to find out much more information about a person's motivations before we could decide with any certainty whether they were truly at fault. Marcus and other Stoics encourage a narrative understanding of the offender's predicament – asking us to approach them as fellow human beings. Epictetus likewise reminds us that we only ever act in accordance with our sense-impressions; we cannot act from any other standpoint other than what seems right to us (even if that means, on balance, deciding it is right to do something that goes against our instincts) any more than we can feel that day is night.[119] We are never crazy or illogical in our actions; we always act from clear internal logic. Others do the same. The psychiatrist-author Viktor E. Frankl, writing of his experiences in the concentration camp, finds this same truth in the most unthinkable circumstances, when he writes about the way in which prisoners placed in positions of authority granted meagre favours to their friends while others were denied:

> It is not for me to pass judgement on those prisoners who put their own above everyone else. Who can throw a stone at a man who favours his friends under circumstances when, sooner or later, it is a question of life or death? No man should judge unless he asks himself in absolute honesty whether in a similar situation he might not have done the same.[120]

It's a powerful thought. Understand where the person is coming from. Instead of fumbling for reasons to be

119 Epictetus, *Discourses*, i.28
120 Viktor E. Frankl, *Man's Search for Meaning*

annoyed, empathise with their behaviour. Let anger dissolve into love. Seneca tells us:

> It will be said that someone spoke ill of you; consider whether you spoke ill of him first, consider how many there are of whom you speak ill. Let us consider, I say, that some are not doing us an injury but repaying one, that others are acting for our good, that some are acting under compulsion, others in ignorance, that even those who are acting intentionally and wittingly do not, while injuring us, aim only at the injury; one slipped into it allured by his wit, another did something, not to obstruct us, but because he could not reach his own goal without pushing us back; often adulation, while it flatters, offends.[121]

A considered life involves looking at oneself in depth, and this encourages the same attitude towards others. By appreciating our own complex narratives and judgements, we can recognise that such things exist to the same degree in those who offend us, rather than perceiving only idiocy or evil. When we consider, in place of feeling angry with each other, that each of us operates only from the standpoint of what we know or have been told to be true; that we each are struggling to make sense of a vast number of conflicting priorities and nameless anxieties; only then can we begin to relinquish our loneliness and truly connect with each other as fellow human beings. We each live out our contortion of the same shared truth.

When a person is rude, or aggressive, or in some way riles us, we should, where we can find a moment of pause

121 Seneca, *On Anger*, 2.28

and wherewithal, appreciate they are acting from a place of pain. They are dragging around their own baggage, and right now is most likely a particularly bad time for them. We know how vile we can be when we are stressed, hungry, feeling abandoned or overwhelmed. At those moments, we have a desperate need for the world to slow down and appreciate that we are struggling. However strong people may appear, they struggle too, and when they upset us, they are very likely in pain.

In the moment of conflict or tension, we are likely to feel put down, even guilty for just being ourselves. But this is about our *own* pain; the message we are receiving is triggering a cluster of responses we have carried around since we were young. A dominant father used to make us feel insignificant, and as an adult we find that anytime someone – particularly an older male – suggests we are useless, we are flung back to the feelings of that pained child. We are hearing a frustrated expression of suffering from this other person and in the blink of an eye making it about our own afflictions. If we recognise this pattern, and take responsibility for it, we can, to some extent, be liberated from it. We can practise recognising the first flutter of pain, then relaxing as we pull our centre of gravity inwards towards us, and hearing hurtful words as what they are: a cry from a heart that has nothing to do with ours.

7. Lower your expectations
I was touring earlier this year and had a conversation with a girl about a famous pop star who lives in her city. When she was six and strawberry-blonde, the singer came to visit their house. Her father was a local artist, and the rock star (who had decided to become an art collector) wanted to purchase a piece of his. Clearly delighted to have

someone of such note in his home, the father offered him a seat and a cup of tea. The luminary accepted both, adding (and I struggle to do him the favour of imagining this was done nicely) that he only took tea from blue cups.

Blue cups? The artist had none. None hanging in the kitchen; none sitting turps-filled in his studio upstairs, paint-splattered without and ringed within, their kitchen days long behind them. So he sent his six-year-old daughter out into the streets to secure a blue cup for their illustrious guest. She knew nothing of the stranger who sat in their front room, nor why she had earlier been forced to help tidy, nor had she ever ventured into the busy city centre without the superintendence of a parent. Hurried into her coat and pushed out of the house before her tears showed, she made that first lone journey through the city to the Big Shops to buy a blue cup.

'Some people . . . having chosen one particular goblet or cup,' wrote Plutarch, some two thousand years before a famous singer was to implant such a miserable memory upon this girl, 'refuse to drink out of any other, even when they have plenty available.' At fault is 'a luxurious and enervating way of life' that leads to 'self-regard and discontent', and ultimately to 'continuous, constant feelings of anger, which gradually gather in the mind like a swarm of bees or wasps'. The person who demands his food to be just so, or leaves those who work for him distressed and trying to second-guess his every whim, 'is enslaved to a feeble, nit-picking, complaining way of life, and fails to realise that he is creating for his temper the kind of raw and oozing condition which a chronic cough or constantly bumping into things causes'.[122]

122 Plutarch, *On the Avoidance of Anger*, [13] 461A

We laugh at the near-mythical riders of American divas that demand a dressing room decked out in white lilies or M&M's of a single colour to be sourced and abundantly provided. Some may have a foundation in truth, others are undoubtedly the fiction of PR machinery or the neurotic stipulations of fawning management teams. Yet there is a gradual but sure slope of madness that starts with an everyday fussiness with food and climbs to these pastiche hallmarks of celebrity status. Along its way it passes the reception desks of progressively fine hotels, the corridors of workplaces where high-flyers talk to staff and personal assistants and secretaries, and winds through the tables of expensive restaurants, where the rich complain to increasingly servile maître d's about decreasingly worthwhile things.

An overstuffed pinstriped lawyer berating a waitress for bringing the wrong type of water sends shivers down our spines in a way that a guy moaning about a cold pizza never would. I have watched a wealthy restaurant owner dine with friends in his own establishment, bellowing vile remarks at his staff for any perceivable error such as the serving of water at an imperfect temperature, clearly doing so for no other reason than to impress his dinner guests (who in turn were ready to eat their own faces in embarrassment). Swaggering self-entitlement is chilling to behold and comes from an inflated level of expectation as to the extent to which others are likely to arrange every matter to one's complete satisfaction. The problem is that as we become successful, more and more people *do* begin to fuss around us, and embarrassed as we might be the first or second time this happens, we soon find ourselves making requests we would previously have never imagined could come from our lips. It is easy to grow accustomed to little luxuries and then soon generalise the experience and expect it elsewhere, at the restaurant tables and reception desks we encounter.

But exaggerated expectations do not belong exclusively to the privileged. Whenever we deal with a service industry, contractors or staff, we all find ourselves prone to the problems of unrealistically high expectations. A friend recently project-managed a house renovation and found himself consistently let down by his contractors. This being the first time he had undertaken such an enterprise, he had had no experience of companies and individuals within the construction industry who seem to pay little attention to customer service and who promise to turn up and repeatedly fail to do so. His frustration was not the self-entitlement of the spoilt brat; rather it was an anger most of us would share following a terrible experience as a customer. If we have not experienced it with builders, we have experienced it with call centres: the brain-boiling ordeal of trying to secure a normal human conversation within a nightmare world of blank apathy, responsibility-shirking and curtailed calls that would give Kafka a night of uneasy dreams. In the same way that we can adjust our desires in life to more accurately reflect what is available, we can also adjust our expectations of other people to mirror reality.

Seneca would ask us, 'Who said the builders would stick to their word? Whoever assured you the call-centre workers would do anything other than adhere to their script? Or that the note they made on your account would ever be read by the next person? And if you were assured of this, who's to say that they wouldn't be mistaken or something would stop it from happening?'

Sometimes people *will* be hugely disappointing. This is, in our graph, the *y* axis of life itself, the slings and arrows of outrageous fortune. Life, we are told when we are first refused a toy in a shop by a sensible parent, is not fair. It is fortune, not fairness that we meet, and we should not expect justice. Seneca says:

> Think of everything, expect everything; even in good characters some unevenness will appear. Human nature begets hearts that are deceitful, that are ungrateful, that are covetous, that are undutiful. When you are about to pass judgement on one single man's character, reflect upon the general mass.[123]

To lower our expectations is to greatly reduce our anger: if we don't expect things to work out brilliantly, we'll be less frustrated when they don't.

The Stoics introduced a qualification to be used when making plans, a proviso to be attached to any hopes for the future. This *exceptio*, or reserve clause, is another manifestation of the distinction between what we do and do not control. It is simply the mental addition of the thought, 'If nothing happens to the contrary' to the end of any statement concerning our intentions. Seneca describes this in action:

> The wise man considers both sides: he knows how great is the power of errors, how uncertain human affairs are, how many obstacles there are to the success of plans. Without committing himself, he awaits the doubtful and capricious issue of events, and weighs certainty of purpose against uncertainty of results. Here also, however, he is protected

123 Seneca, *On Anger*, 2.28

334

by that reserve clause, without which he decides
upon nothing and begins nothing.[124]

Outcomes lie beyond our control, within the realm of
externals, or indifferents. So we do well to remind ourselves, whenever we make plans, that things may turn out
contrary to the ideal. As we get excited about a planned
or expected future event, it's a good thing to remind ourselves – *unless it doesn't work out*.

We are mitigating any future disappointment. It
might sound pessimistic to qualify everything with such a
reserve clause, and in a sense it is. It is a very valuable and
life-enhancing form of pessimism. Of course it is harder
to get excited about a future event if we keep reminding
ourselves it might not happen. We're so indoctrinated
against the idea of pessimism that it might seem as if we
are actively *denying* ourselves a source of happiness through
this *exceptio*. But consider the alternative. When we
become very excited about a future event, we forget the
present and place ourselves in the future. We are at
the mercy of something outside of our control: whether
or not the event happens as we would wish. It may turn
out to be better than expected, or roughly the same, or
worse. The more excited we are, the more likely it is to
fail to meet our expectations, in the same way that something we dread is likely to not be half as bad as we feared.
The Stoics would not deny us feelings of excitement, but
they would encourage us to retain this little reminder that
we're not ultimately in control. And this is done with a
view to increasing our happiness. If the event turns out to
be a success, then that's a wonderful bonus. If it's less than
we might have otherwise hoped, we'll be pleased we kept

124 Seneca, *On Benefits*, quoted and modified by Donald Robertson

our expectations in check. And of course this reminder reflects the reality of that recurring diagonal: we may aim high but fate will do its own thing.

Epictetus summarises our best relationship to fate in the *Handbook*:

> Do not seek to have events happen to you as you want them to, but instead want them to happen as they do happen, and your life will go well.[125]

And to repeat myself, the Stoics are not promoting apathy, indifference and resignation. Their variety of non-attachment comes from a very engaged place. We are not being told to shrug like a recalcitrant teenager. The Stoics were movers and shakers.

The key is to remember that game of tennis. You still try to the best of your abilities. You play as well as you can. That realm of your thoughts and actions is under your control, and you are in charge. Whatever your role is – parent, sibling, citizen, worker, role model, president – you can do that thing in an exemplary fashion. Be the best you can be at what you are. Engage; inspire. Where there is injustice, and where it is under your control to make a difference, use your abilities to create change. But don't ultimately emotionally commit yourself to the outcome. That's out of your hands. You are not playing to necessarily *win*; you're just playing as well as you possibly can.

Marcus, one of the most powerful men and beloved rulers in history, writes to himself:

> Do your best to convince them. But act on your own, if justice requires it. If met with force, then

---

125 Epictetus, *Enchiridion*, 8

fall back on acceptance and peaceability. Use the setback to practise other virtues.

Remember that our efforts are subject to circumstances; you weren't aiming at the impossible.

Aiming to do what, then?

To try. And you succeeded. What you set out to do is accomplished.[126]

Marcus fought long, bloody battles against the Germanic tribes during his time as emperor; he was not in a position to merely let the world's events wash over him and his empire in a spirit of grand philosophical laissez-faire. But he tells us himself that when it comes to securing change in the world, we should only aim to try our best; all else is folly. So although he may have added a practical qualification to Epictetus's formula, reminding us that we can still try to make changes in the world, he would have agreed with its spirit: don't aim to achieve things outwith your control. Once that standpoint is secure, you can fight for the causes you champion if it seems just to do so, but you will not be so attached to the outcome as to either jeopardise your tactics or be devastated if you fail.

We can only guarantee success in trying our best. The desired outcome *in the world* may prove impossible, but having succeeded in our private aims, we won't be ruined by a feeling of crushing failure. The result we're aiming for has moved into *our* sphere of control (we aim to do our utmost), and therefore we are more likely to arrive at a pleasing outcome. And real-world success is also more likely, as we will not be hampered by the anxiety that comes from trying to control what we cannot. The Stoic stance brings a uniquely quiet,

126 Marcus Aurelius, *Meditations*, vii. 50

persistent resoluteness in the face of adversity.

This is a brilliant bit of thinking. We can aim high, seek to change the world, *yet always be satisfied with the outcome*. The Stoics have taken the reclusive Epicurean instruction to desire only what you already have, and allowed it to be active, engaged and vital.

The instruction of the Epicureans was to relax and not bother with engagement. Keep your desires natural and simple, and cut yourself off. It's appealing but a little lazy. In order to live, its followers needed to ask for handouts from the very society they shunned. The Stoics, on the other hand, tell us to *be on our guard*: against unhelpful attachments, against too-high expectations. With this armour in place, they send us out into the world to do our best.

What an extraordinary suggestion for life: *rein in your aims*. It plays against every goal-setting, positive-thinking, believe-in-yourself-and-you-can-achieve-anything mantra of modern life. We have to keep reminding ourselves that it isn't a recipe for motionless complacency. Yet with such modest expectations, we can still change the world. We do not need to fool ourselves into believing that we have control over uncontrollable fortune to go about trying to improve it.

Some people combine too-high expectations with a tendency to catastrophise. This amounts to feeling horrified at the fact that one's impracticable and distorted vision has not been realised. This is what happens when we see events as a 'nightmare', a constant struggle. Necessity, meanwhile, continues, and these people are dragged along like a reluctant dog behind a cart. In the image offered by the great early Stoics Zeno and Chrysippus, we have two choices: to pull and struggle against the rope and try to go in another direction, or to acknowledge the direction this cart is taking us and stop causing ourselves so much pain.

Of course the cart will sometimes need diverting. At that point, Martha Nussbaum's 'Transition' (which I described on page 267) must come into play: the channelling of unhelpful anger into a constructive means of advocating change. But aside from rare cases of true injustice (when we must move from anger to ensuring progress), we can be assured that most of our fuming and moaning is just that: noise. It is neither pleasant to listen to nor convincing. It is a symptom of gross self-orientation, of egocentricity. It may not come naturally in the moment, but our aim should be to abnegate this bloated, boorish self and move *towards* our apparent aggressor. Lowering our expectations of the people around us is not to live at their whim and let them 'get away with anything'; it is to stop obtruding our stories and priorities upon those of others and then whining when they don't match up. Anger is just proof of how unrealistic your expectations were.

Empathy and connectedness

What can we expect from making these changes? Philosophy exists to enhance every aspect of our lives, not just fix some parts that are broken. Above all, we can look forward to a greater feeling of connectedness with others when we make these shifts. No longer mistaking our judgements about events for the events themselves; being open to the complex narratives that lead to the imperfect behaviours of others; deflating our exalted sense of self to a more modest measure; letting our experience of others decide what's realistic to expect. These changes, of course easier to describe than to implement, can only culminate in an increased feeling of overall tranquillity and of warmth towards those whom we meet. Rather than feeling road rage, we might find it remarkable that a hundred thousand people driving a hundred thousand cars at varying speeds around a major city manage to successfully coexist and get where they want to *almost all of the time*.

'Composure, calmness and charity is nowhere near as kind and considerate and inoffensive to those who come across it as to those who possess it.'[127] We are ultimately made happier by being less angry, in fact happier than we'll make other people. Our aim is to improve our happiness; we needn't feel ashamed about this point. Psychologists have demonstrated that people gain more pleasure from acting altruistically than being on the receiving ends of such acts.[128] Far from undermining the point of kindness, this serves as a reminder that it's good for us. Being kind creates more pleasure for us than pain; Epicurus would take this as evidence that it is the wisest way to live, while the Stoics would embrace it for the fact that it is a rational consequence of living in undisturbed accordance with all things.

We are moving from blaming *others* (for their actions) to blaming *ourselves* (for our judgements) to blaming *no one*. Marcus writes: 'The gods [for which we can substitute 'fortune', or 'the onward momentum of all things'] are not to blame. They do nothing wrong, on purpose or by accident. Nor men either; they don't do it on purpose. No one is to blame.'[129] We do not lower our self-belief or even decide we deserve every insult in order to feel bad about ourselves. We can forgive ourselves every time we

127 Plutarch, *On the Avoidance of Anger*, [16] 464D

128 E. W. Dunn, L. B. Aknin and M. I. Norton, 'Spending Money on Others Promotes Happiness', *Science*, 319, 1687–1688, 2008

129 Marcus Aurelius, *Meditations*, xii. 12

act or think in old ways, while a happier and more toler-
ant connection to people is quietly and firmly attained.
Likewise, we substitute the optimism of modern positive
thinking with the disarming but prudent pessimism of
lowering our expectations in order to feel ultimately
happier. A rationally adjusted relationship with the world
creates less room for distress.

What acts as a barrier to accepting this? Once again,
our inflated egos. You may protest, 'I'm not going to
blame myself for other people's idiocy! I'm not going to
just settle for whatever comes my way! I deserve more
than that!' Well, then, you still miss the point. To talk in
terms of what you 'deserve' is meaningless and usually
leads to personal indignation, as what you feel you deserve
will most likely outstrip whatever you currently have or
can easily obtain. The Stoic ideas I am suggesting, remember, still allow for matters of justice to be considered and
carried out fairly, and for any important changes we wish
to make in the world to be constructed upon rock-solid
foundations.

Life is short.

> Soon we will spit out this little spirit. In the mean-
> time, while we have breath, while we are among
> our fellow men, let us behave as men should; let us
> not be a cause of fear or danger to anyone; let
> us despise losses, wrongs, insult and criticism, and
> let us tolerate with a great mind our short-lived
> misfortunes.[130]

While we admirably bear our brief inconveniences, we
have the opportunity to empathise with people around

130 Seneca, *On Anger*, 3.43

us. Kindness connects us; anger denies us all our humanity. 'Love is wise, hatred is foolish,' said the great British philosopher Bertrand Russell, as long ago as 1959:

> In this world which is getting more and more closely interconnected, we have to learn to tolerate each other, we have to learn to put up with the fact that some people say things that we don't like. We can only live together in that way – and if we are to live together and not die together, we must learn a kind of charity and a kind of tolerance, which is absolutely vital to the continuation of human life on this planet.[131]

Research in the early 1990s discovered a special type of neuron in the macaque monkey brain that is activated not only when the animal performs an action (such as picking up a nut) but also when it sees *another* monkey doing the same. They were named 'mirror neurons', and as research continued, other types of mirror neurons were discovered, such as those that work in the audio-visual sphere and which are fired not only by the *sight* of the action being performed but even by the *sound* of it. We, too, have these mirror neurons: when we see someone pick up an apple, or hear the familiar sound of a person slurping his tea, they fire in the same way they would as if we had carried out those actions ourselves. Findings in these areas have been valuable for research into autism, often characterised by the inability of the autistic individual to connect with or empathise with others at the most basic level. It seems in these special cases that the work of mirror neurons may be impaired or absent. Most of us, however, are

131 Bertrand Russell interview on *Face to Face*, BBC, April 1959

hard-wired empathics: something of enormous social and evolutionary importance. Despite this, we grossly *overestimate* our capacity to feel empathically about another person's situation and guess, for example, what she might do or feel under certain circumstances.

Let's say I believe that Jane is a kind person, and I wonder how she would react to someone pushing ahead of her in a queue. I would probably decide that she would say nothing and allow them their advantage. But I would be making an error. I would be calculating into my thinking her quality of kindness, which is not what *she* would be doing. You may consider yourself to be kind. But if you thought to yourself, 'I am a kind person – what will I do?' each time you were faced with a situation, you would be operating from a standpoint *outside* of kindness, which is arguably quite different from *being* kind. Jane might react in any number of ways to a person queue-jumping, as the cognitive-behavioural chain of events we've seen that produces anger would be hard at work. Her mood at the time it happened, as well as any number of specific inhibitions or beliefs she has about queue-jumping or the individual concerned, would ultimately decide her response, *not* the starting point of being a kind person.

Consider, as another example, the amount of presents you have been bought by friends who have clearly tried to think from your standpoint of taste. Their generally unsuccessful attempts show how erroneous this sort of empathic thinking can be. In fact, the offending gift tends to be so much *more* unlovable by virtue of being close to perfect but let down by a detail we could never endure. 'Yes, the colour of the T-shirt was nice, but no! Why ruin it with that logo? I could never wear it.' Or, 'Sweet of her to get me a notebook – must have been expensive – but, ugh, I could never use a notebook that actually had "Thoughts and Feelings" embossed on the front. What a waste.'

By contrast, notes philosopher-author Alain de Botton, a writer can make us feel he knows us personally by writing about his *own* foibles and complexities. A psychic might do something similar. You can give a very convincing psychic reading by describing the conflicts and insecurities you feel yourself and substituting 'You' for 'I'. If an author tried to think purely from the idiosyncratic standpoint of his readers in order to have them relate to his words, or were a psychic to attempt to form a reading from the *inside out* of her sitter, neither would be likely to produce anything particularly personal. It would most likely feel very shallow. Often what feels most intimate tends to be what we have most in common.

The Canadian philosopher Adam Morton (I used to sneak into his lectures when living as a graduate in Bristol and marvel at his academy-defying red socks) writes that we are prone to switching off our empathy when it would require us to relate to antisocial acts. He describes it as 'the blinkering effect of decency'[132], wherein we make it hard for ourselves to understand 'evil' acts of wrongdoers. This is disingenuous of us, because, as we have seen, we all act from standpoints that are logical to us, and we ourselves would very likely react in the same way if we found ourselves in entirely the same position. But to empathise in severe cases of 'evil', we would need to represent in vivid first-person perspective the commission of those acts by our own hands, and undoubtedly it is the offensiveness of such a representation that repels us. Thus we

132 Adam Morton, 'Empathy for the Devil', from *Empathy: Philosophical and Psychological Perspectives*

become angry rather than make any attempt to understand, as if trying to appreciate common ground were tantamount to the endorsing of or sympathising with the offending act.

I would extend the same thinking to matters of sexuality: it is easier to find unfamiliar sexual tastes repugnant than appreciate the common ground we all share in the complex development of our dispositions. Homophobia commonly belies conflicts felt by the aggressor regarding his or her own sexuality; if we shut off something within ourselves, we must expect it to noisily rattle its cage.

The abnegation of empathy in the case of something as complex and variable as sexual taste is a dangerous thing. The particular misfortune of the paedophile is not that he is a walking manifestation of evil but that his or her sexual development (as much subject to nature, nurture and questions of identity as any of ours) has resulted in a potentially very harmful and unacceptable attraction. We rightly call it a disorder because of these damaging effects, but merely reacting with horror will do little towards solving a complex and difficult issue stemming from a sexual drive as real and compulsive as any of us are used to.

So we can seek empathy but must not pretend that it allows us a special insight to others. We close down empathy where it might help us to understand atrocities, and we overestimate its power when we all-too fuzzily imagine what another person might do, want or feel. It is prone to wild inaccuracy and self-delusion, but to possess it inaccurately is better than not having it at all.

I feel I should mention the importance of empathic feelings, as they can so often be forgotten amidst the images of self-sufficiency and fortitude that the Stoics promote. The point, to repeat, of Stoic teaching is not to shut oneself off from life and other people by extirpating all emotions from one's existence. There is a certain *tension* to Stoicism that Pierre Hadot contrasts with the *relaxation* of Epicureanism, when he makes the point that an authentic life would involve a vacillation between both poles.[133] The Stoics tell us to be on guard; to be like a solid rock with the waves crashing against it; or to post sentries on watch for the invasion of angry and other unwanted feelings. Epicureans, conversely, merely sink into a simple life of natural pleasures, but they get less done.

It serves us to remember that total adherence to one school of thought or another is likely to deny the important and beneficial expression of part of our nature. To merely label oneself a 'Stoic' is to renounce one's own voice. A considered life should not, like the pious one, be a matter of subjugation to any label, under which all the 'consideration' has been previously done for you.

Stoicism can lead us to a powerful fellow feeling, but the journey is not infused with the rose scent of warm togetherness. So let's mix up our metaphors. If a large part of Stoicism is a comfortable alignment of oneself with the movements of fortune (the dog that trots along with the cart rather than pulls away and gets dragged), then we could as easily talk of a pebble on the seabed, rolling back and forth with the tide. That contrasts with the other Stoic image of a rock, unmoving against the lashing of the ocean waves. Of course, we must remember that this is a therapeutic philosophy, and we are offered an image so that it might help us, not because it perfectly illustrates the ideal state of man towards which we must dogmatically strive, or even remains consistent across the entire system. So we can be an unassailable rock some of the time and a

133 Pierre Hadot, *Philosophy as a Way of Life*

rolling pebble on other occasions. Whatever helps us the most.

Moreover, we relieve some of the Stoic tension by allowing the rocks of our analogies to be *porous*. This is Martha Nussbaum's recommended approach for a more permeable form of Stoicism,[134] and I think it is enormously helpful. We no longer seek to stand in defiance of others and the emotions they engender; instead, we can imagine an easy, free-flowing relationship with the rest of our race. The porous rock gives us an image of both strength *and* confluence, and as the water (of fortune and of others' influence) flows through us, we remain steady without a need for defiance.

Some activities might engender in us this state, and the result is invariably a happy one. I have a particular passion for street photography. To me, it is a thrilling way to take pictures, or to 'capture the decisive moment', a description ascribed to the pioneer of reportage photography, Henri Cartier-Bresson. One keeps an eye out for a particularly serendipitous arrangement of people and environment, and learns ways of securing one's shot unobtrusively.

Although I came to this form of photography through a love of portraiture, I soon realised that the appeal, for me (and I can only imagine for many more true talents), lies in noticing the poetry of the everyday. A sad-looking, long-haired man sits on a Southend sea wall, staring out into emptiness, smoking a cigarette; his aloneness is heightened by a family playing together far in the background. All else is straight lines; he forms the single curve of back and drooping head. To me, it's a touching image, and to get it I have to manually set my Leica camera to

134 Martha Nussbaum, *The Therapy of Desire*

what I deem to be the most appropriate setting, then sit on the wall near enough to the man for a minute or so. Then, whilst pretending to climb back off the wall, I have one chance to get the shot without him realising what I'm doing.

People, in relation to each other and their environments, can unwittingly create moments of poetry. When I carry out my novice efforts to capture these, I feel both *detached* from the world (as any observer might do – especially when looking at it through a viewfinder) yet feel very *connected* to people around me. I am paying far more attention to them than normal; I'm far more interested in life. I'm attracted to people and the snapshots of life that show through their postures and faces; I am drawn to the geometry of architecture and bodies. I become interested in the relationships between them and the possibilities of something lovely and serendipitous arising from that interplay (quite aside from whether or not I capture it with any success). My normal, regrettable practice of minimal eye contact and uncharitable pigeonholing is suspended in favour of a real fascination with everything human.

Regardless of how unsuccessfully my amateur photographs might live up to this promise, I find the experience very affecting. It has become a shortcut for me to this experience of *permeability* or porousness. There is the detachment, the centre-of-gravity-within-oneself that we are aiming for, but also an empathy and sense of free flow. It's normal, when taking street photographs, to wander Zen-like, getting lost, following whatever route one's instincts suggest, being open and available to whatever's happening around one. It's rooted in the moment, porous, yet centred.

While writing an earlier part of this chapter, I was

sitting in the lounge area of a hotel in Conwy, a small and achingly pretty Welsh town outside of Llandudno. The doors had been thrown open as the day was very hot; I had come inside to write after desiccating outside in the sun for an hour. The patio was small and probably needed some planters to cut off the view of the adjoining car park. But scattered around the few brown and yellow tables were families and small groups, and every fifteen minutes a bell rang from a nearby church identifying the quarter-hour, which lent the scene an unexpected Tuscan air.

I watched a slim woman in a white dress and a floral bandanna pour tea for herself and her husband. Another couple adjusted the position of a chair for an elderly man I presumed to be the father of one of them. A chap in his early thirties took off his hat, sat back in his chair and raised his face to the sun while his friend perused his phone. A poodle lay on its side in the sun, little curly legs outstretched. Two women chatted over white wine; the older one (whose face I could see) was about fifty and evidently very attentive to the successful arrangement of her bobbed blonde hair each morning; she must have enjoyed showing off her tanned arms with a sleeveless black dress.

With the fine weather and occasional bell tolls augmenting my appreciation, I suddenly felt a strong sense of delight in these people. Each had decided to put on *those* clothes this morning; to sit facing *that* way in the sun or shade; each expressed their affection for or ease with their companions in some different and touching way. Each was here, enjoying the same heat, sharing the same space, each, like the waitress who brought plates of risotto and crusted cod to her customers, was doing their very best to balance their responsibilities and desires, and navigate their life as well as possible. Each personality seemed strikingly distinct; every choice of shorts, sandals or hair-cut was suddenly rendered *perfect* for them: a moving signifier of how that person wished to portray him- or herself to the rest of the world. Each piece of exhibited, unconscious body language was an affecting window into private motivations and the delicate ballet of the particular interactions in which they found themselves.

I felt a joyful consequence of Nussbaum's porousness. Perhaps it was just the sun, but some invisible barrier dissolved, and I felt an enormous affection for my fellow hotel guests – a feeling that brought a great sense of happiness. And sitting here now a week later in a small private library in Nottingham, watching an old woman repeatedly wake herself up with her own farts, I again experience the flood of fond feeling from that afternoon and extend it towards the venerable and unhurried bookworms who are scattered here around me: crumple-faced reminders of extraordinary lives being lived, right here, right now.

☺

10

Fame

I blame Mary Pickford. On 24 June 1916, the actress signed the first million-dollar film contract in history. Somewhere amidst the media interest provoked by this event, celebrity took a historic new turn: a star's potential earnings were unshackled from the pedestrian considerations of whatever efforts they were likely to expend. 'The old reasonable correlation between what (and how) one did and what one received for doing it became tenuous (and, in the upper reaches of show biz, invisible).'[135]

Or maybe we should look further back and highlight the first time that early public-relations machinery purposefully created a sensation around a 'personality'. In 1910, an actress with the overripe name of Florence Lawrence was reported to have died in a tram accident. Her producer, who had himself released the story, roundly (and accurately) decried it as a fake and arranged for a high-profile appearance of the star, to much staged extolment.

135 Richard Schickel, *Intimate Strangers: The Culture of Celebrity in America*

Before these events, the private lives of actors and actresses were not a matter of public interest. 'There was no such thing as celebrity prior to the beginning of the twentieth century,' writes author and filmmaker Richard Schickel, rather boldly. Actors' lives and characters were only of interest to the extent that they served the films in which they appeared, and their perceived personalities were kept tightly in line with the sorts of characters they portrayed on screen. As the modern notion of a 'star' developed from this early, more modest notion of a 'picture personality', a power shift occurred in favour of the celebrated actors. They realised that the public might have an interest in them beyond the scope of their roles. At the same time, a media that had been hitherto eager to appear discreet and not overstep the bounds of good taste now created the popular gossip column. Very quickly an industry of manipulated information and star-creation was born.

Today, we are told that over half of our teenagers do not want a regular career, preferring instead to be famous. In a 2010 survey,[136] when young people were asked 'What would you like to do for your career?' 54 per cent answered 'Become a celebrity'. More than a fifth said they aimed to achieve this through appearing on a TV reality show, another 5 per cent through dating someone famous. But nearly 70 per cent of those who said they prioritised fame, when asked how they might achieve this goal, had no idea how to go about it.

It's easy to mock these ambitions and to hang our heads in shame. The implication is that kids know nothing about hard work; that an endless cloacal stream of television product like *Big Brother* (once so fresh and

136 *Independent*, 17 February 2010

fascinating) and any number of manipulative talent shows now disingenuously promise sparkling repute to our poor children who know no better. While that may be in part true, we need to separate a snobbish distaste for the popular from warranted despair. Shows that mawkishly exploit the young and ill educated, or parade posh caricatures, are of course going to horrify large swathes of the middle classes. But why shouldn't the young desire to be famous? It has become easier to be visible; even in 2003, when reality television was in its infancy and online fame entirely unknown, British television was estimated to have featured close to a quarter of a million 'ordinary people' a year on screen.[137] Why *not* grasp the opportunity with enthusiasm? Why would we not wish to be seen in the best possible light by the largest number of people? If it is human nature to worry unnecessarily about parts of ourselves, what could be lovelier than to feel adored? And if we can do so *just for being ourselves*, isn't that a kind of birthright we should all try to claim?

The commentator on celebrity Chris Rojek gives us three categories of celebrity.[138] Firstly, there is that which is *ascribed* through blood relations (to royalty or the American presidency, for example). Here, celebrity is *predetermined*. By contrast, it can be *achieved* through 'the perceived accomplishment of the individual in open competition'. Sportsmen, artists and musicians would be included in this category. Although such characters would have existed as 'items of discourse' throughout history, 'they did not carry the illusion of intimacy, the sense of being an exalted confrère, that is part of celebrity status in the age of mass media'. Finally, there is *attributed* celebrity,

137 Frances Bonner, *Ordinary Television: Analyzing Popular TV*
138 Chris Rojek, *Celebrity*

created principally by the very act of the popular media taking interest in that person. Rojek satisfyingly calls such people 'celetoids'; they are one-hit wonders invented, celebrated and destroyed by the media principally as a means to galvanise public attention and boost their own circulation or ratings.

It is this latter category that tends to attract the most virulent criticism. The celetoids concerned – lottery winners, YouTube and reality-show favourites – are promenaded provocatively in order to generate outrage, sympathy or interest that will keep the public returning *to the information source*. But whether the celebrities in question are the focus of passing, media-created fads and soon to be forgotten, or those whose fame is built around meritorious achievement, they may also be a surprisingly functional part of our capitalist society.

Rojek points out that the manufacturing of celebrity is conducive to our economic process. The key emotion that attaches us to celebrities is *desire*: we commonly want to be like them, to sleep with them, to *possess* them in some way. Because they are usually rich, sexy and glamorous (so few of us tick all three boxes and still have time for our extensive charity work), they broadcast a message of 'it is possible for people to succeed and have these things and this lifestyle'. Thus they continue to point the rest of the population in the direction of material aspirations. Celebrity serves as a helpful distraction from the material inequalities of real life. Thus the famous are commonly used to promote products; the desire we attach to them is harnessed and attached to objects that keep the wheels of industry spinning at higher and higher speeds.

At the same time, now that religion has lost its grasp on most of us, we have free-floating needs for intense attachment, powerful role models and immortal figures.

Our favourite stars (the celestial implication of the word is not coincidental) focus that need rather well. In a secular and capitalist culture, our new gods are rock stars and actors. Fan sites operate as churches where the devoted come together and pore over every utterance of their idols; individuals boast of or invent a personal relationship with the celebrity in question; 'rival churches' form, as a large fan base splinters into separate and faintly hostile factions, each of which likes to believe that it is most favoured by its particular god and knows the *correct* way to carry out its secular form of worship. Stars are suitably distant to not disappoint us with their human traits and foibles, and reach us only through the priesthood of PR and media machinery. Young, impressionable followers might fall into ecstatic states when they find themselves in the presence of those they worship, particularly at orchestrated, quasi-religious events such as rock concerts. Meanwhile, the best examples of celebrity, like Elvis, can posthumously transfigure into something close to divine.

We now live in a time where this holy realm is open, in ready-made form, to all. Once, the ancients saw the adoption of the wise, rational life as a kind of co-existence with the gods. These rational natures, they believed, constituted the deific part of us, and the philosophical life offered a route to transcend ordinary existence. It allowed us to glimpse those higher realms of divinity (according to Plato) or perhaps move in rational accordance with the flow of all things (which we recognise from the Stoics), depending on how mystically you like to think. Philosophy, as we have seen, then gave way to Christian theology, and rational enquiry became a servant to religion. The question of our relationship to the divine drastically changed and all questions were centrally and dogmatically dealt with; answers were certainly not to be found through any independent spirit of enquiry from the man on the street.

To live a godlike life nowadays is no longer a matter of living in rational harmony with the universe or contemplating the ideal forms. The elevation of one's life is now sought in terms of recognition and material wealth. If the celebrariat (to use Rojek's term) is now equivalent with our community of gods, then we are still seeking to join them, albeit via a very different route. As in ancient Greece and Rome, the desire to live amongst them arises from a wish to flourish. The question is, then: does it work? Does being famous increase your happiness?

Can't complain

This is a difficult section to write, because even as someone sort-of famous in one tiny corner of the world, it is enormously churlish to express anything other than gratitude and bewilderment in the face of one's success. We are happy with famous people when they tell interviewers that they feel so extraordinarily lucky to be where they are, and that they feel nothing but thankfulness to the fans who have got them there. We equally might enjoy the humility of a star who says she has a hard time dealing with some aspects of her success that feel to her undeserved, as long as she doesn't appear to whine about it. What we resolutely do *not* want to hear from her is what a pain it is to be hounded on the streets every day by fans. To be unable to go shopping in the high street without people attracting attention to her. 'Oh, you poor thing,' we can't help but think, 'must be shit being you with all your money and adoration. Those people who got you where you are, do they want a photo? How fucking awful for you.'

No one wants to hear any of that. But I hope you'll bear with me if I try to describe the tangled reality of an experience that seems to hold an unshakeable appeal for most people.

Because celebrities are largely dangled before us as a vision of success and affluence, and their perceived personalities managed through careful channels, we are usually keen to know what famous people are actually *like*. And any titbit of information is treated as a profound insight and amplified beyond reason. It's the first question I ask, and I suspect the vast majority of us do the same, when a friend says they have met someone well known. If stars are noticeably reluctant to have their photograph taken, don't stop for an autograph, or ignore having their name shouted in the street, then they are usually damned: they're not nice, or are up their own arse, or anywhere along that incriminating sliding scale. On the other hand, if they show some personal interest and don't play up to any sense of status, then they're utterly lovely, the nicest person you could meet. These too-hasty conclusions (drawn from such a brief encounter) presumably arise from the pleasure of having *any* opinion about a famous person: that in itself is a measure of status denied to most people. Clearly it's more impressive to say, 'Yeah, I met Angelina Jolie, she's lovely – a very nice lady' than it is to say 'I met her for a few moments but not long enough to form an opinion. She wasn't rude or anything; in fact, she probably just acted the way she usually does when she meets people who want to say hello. Nothing I could really base an informed opinion on.' Much nicer to use the language of *knowing* someone, which endows the speaker with a social cachet.

Because we like to form these opinions quite robustly, most famous people are careful to speak about fans in nothing but the most glowing terms. Any suggestion that a celebrity feels that his or her public can also be *tiresome* is likely to be hysterically amplified by the media. The immediate comeback from an insulted, indignant public to any such comment or insinuation from a celebrity tends to run along the following two lines:

1. It's your fans that have got you where you are.
2. If you don't like it, why are you being a big famous star? Don't court adoration and then whinge when you get it.

These are very natural responses. However, in having them, we have switched off any empathic understanding. This is easy to do, because the rich and famous may not, we feel, deserve our empathy. Our objections are made angrily because we feel slighted. We imagine that we might meet this person and she would be rude to our face, and this imaginary insult upsets us. It's confusing: we are used to loving an actress in her roles and now hear that we wouldn't like her if we met her in real life.

We emotionally invest in our stars and can become very sensitive to our affection not being reciprocated. This would happen with anyone we loved. Moreover, we place those who speak most deeply to us on a special pedestal and demand from them the additional peculiar quality of *authenticity*. Few disappointments compare to the experience of a favourite indie band or singer-song-writer selling out and going commercial. Such people become our sages, the articulators of our condition; when they deny us their integrity, it stings.

Just as in love, we create an image of these people based entirely on projection, which has nothing to do with who they really are (though unlike a lover, a public figure consciously courts this kind of image-conjuring on our part). And then we are horrified when we find that our investment and affection are misplaced. We have without realising made ourselves vulnerable in the face of this famous person. Proof of this is demonstrated by how blatheringly incompetent we become when we meet them face to face, and how we censure ourselves for a month thereafter (usually in the early hours while the rest of the world sleeps blamelessly) about how we so obviously uttered the *worst* thing imaginable upon meeting them.[139]

The problem, then, is not the star being ungrateful towards fans but that we are experiencing disappointment and even, at a deeper level, the rumblings of abandonment. When little bits of our world crumble (and this happens when we fear someone we love may not love us back), we feel exposed and scared, and commonly express our fear as anger or hurt.

Of course, a moment's consideration allows important qualifications to surface in the face of our complaints. It is unlikely to be the star's fans that 'got her where she is'. She might have struggled thanklessly for twenty years before she had her break. She may owe her success to a mixture of hard work, love for her craft, and a great manager. Fans might be now in part *sustaining* that popular success, but a long history of sustained effort (and luck) is likely to exist prior to her having any recognition at all. And, as for unalloyed gratitude, we all know what it is to

139 My mother met Martin Freeman, who like many an unassuming and charming star, introduced himself by name: 'Hi, I'm Martin.' My mother responded in a way that perhaps 90 per cent of people do to such a modest preamble, by smiling and saying, 'I know who you are.' It took her three months to get over that.

have too much of a good thing: just because it's nice to be liked doesn't mean that you want to be papped whenever you step outside your house.

It's just as wrong to say that the business of being famous is purely and simply about ego satisfaction. There are often other very important factors involved that can be unfairly sidelined by what one imagines must be a gross craving for adulation. A star may honestly derive a lot of satisfaction from pursuing creative goals, developing talent and doing his 'thing' as well as he can. Likewise, though of course some celebrities are clearly and understandably damaged, it would be unfair to typecast them as attention-seeking. Plenty – particularly the more established and talented – are surprisingly shy or self-effacing and see themselves as having a public job but no more. They don't crave adulation just because they are successful; they may well just want to do good work and sustain the career they love.

Now if we were to dig deeper into the reasons as to *why* a famous person derived satisfaction from doing a job well, we would most likely discover that wanting to be loved does indeed rank high amongst their motivating forces. Equally, the individual might feel – due to messages absorbed in childhood – that he needs to over-achieve to prove his worth. There might be a hundred other possibilities, but if we choose to isolate the desire for adulation, we should note that it is also shared by large numbers of people who are *not* remotely famous. Meanwhile, these performers may have *started out* from an exaggerated need to feel appreciated, or to seem impressive, but then in time that initial urge may have balanced out, leaving the individual to continue with what has simply become a deeply rewarding profession. To insist a famous performer must be motivated by an unbalanced need for admiration

– and therefore has no right to complain if he feels over-whelmed by it – is unfairly reductive. *How* and *to whom* he complains is another matter: to moan during an interview about the number of times he gets stopped on the street seems graceless and stupid by any standards.

Because we are interested in happiness; because the desire to be famous is apparently so prevalent now amongst young people; and because the chances are very high that these young people believe it will make them happy to achieve that fame, I would like to write openly and hon-estly about my experience of it and hope it will be useful for some.

Being famous

The overwhelming and blistering point I would like to make is that, aside from perhaps a few very rare cases, *fame does not make you happy*. Some of its aspects are of course very agreeable; others are very unpleasant. The appeal, though, surely comes from imagining a very intense and exciting elevation of ordinary life. Perhaps when we think about being famous, we might imagine a whirlwind of paparazzi, red carpets and autograph hunters – the *public* picture of fame (which won't ever correlate with your private experience). Intensity is a very appealing thing, and we search for it in many places in life. We need to find experiences of intensity in our lives, but ideally such exposure wouldn't come at the expense of what's good for us.

We imagine that intensity from outside a bubble, looking in. Our perspective fails to take into account a major point: once we're 'inside', once we're famous, it's still us looking back out. It's in some ways like that dream holiday: it's much less dreamy once we've arrived and realise we've brought ourselves with us. That person being photographed and lauded, for all the trappings of success, is still *us*. If we are dissatisfied in our lives (which is a given, if we strongly wish to be famous), then we will *still* be prone to dissatisfaction when famous. If we are fundamentally seeking some sense of accomplishment, that need probably won't go away.

One reason why the need doesn't disappear is that fame tends to come slowly. Consider Mike, a violinist that I know. He was burning for recognition, hugely competitive and insecure. He scraped by as a musician and could talk about little other than how other people succeeded who didn't deserve it and how he was constantly being passed over. After some years of this insecurity, he got some high-profile gigs through a new manager. I was delighted and expected him to feel finally recognised. But, trapped on that hedonic treadmill, he soon adapted to the general improvement in his position and felt the same hunger for greater success. A year or two later, he got some television work and developed a profile for himself in Europe. Gigs came flooding in, and he had a book deal. He was achieving everything he had hoped for a few years before, but his level of anxiety and frustration hadn't changed. TV brought new concerns and greater stresses, and just forced him to compare himself as resentfully to even more successful people. Nothing had changed; he had achieved what he had hoped for but *felt* no different.

Mike is the loveliest guy you could meet. He is not some whinging narcissist. It is simply that the drive to be more recognised cannot really be fulfilled. Fame and success tend to creep up, and because you quickly get used to each new stage, rarely do you feel any glow of satisfaction. The reality of it arriving is much more piecemeal and pedestrian than the intense experience you might imagine when you view it from afar. You don't usually have any clear indication of 'arrival'. Meanwhile, all the time, it's still you looking out. You will have adapted to all the changes along the way and still be seeking the same intensity if that's what's driving you.

Speaking for myself, I did not seek out television work; I have never been driven by anything that could be called ambition. My main aims have always been rooted in the present: whether or not things are organised *at the moment* in a way that seems right, or fun, or both. Meanwhile, I have a manager who I'm sure has a clearer idea of long-term career strategy than would interest me. I was very happy in Bristol, and the prospect of TV seemed like *fun*. I loved performing magic and mindreading, and the thought of doing it for a wider audience in this way seemed exciting. But I know I didn't *seek* greater exposure for its own sake. If you do, you are embarking on a journey with no destination. You are unlikely to reach that point of 'now I'm famous enough' or 'now I'm rich enough'.

Probably most performers *do* have that desire for fame, and many are ruined by success. If you unconsciously think that more money (or more exposure) will make you happier because it will bring you higher status, then you are basing your idea of happiness on what *other people feel*. Whilst being appreciated by other people is a pleasant part of life, it's also something we have no ultimate control over, and no clear or stable reference point to let us know we have achieved it. Likewise, fame is usually fleeting, and if a person feels a need to achieve it in the first place, that desire will only grow more neurotic as he or she struggles to keep hold of it. Other performers quickly become rivals, and witnessing their increasing success can lead to the most horrendous bitterness. A few magicians I know have been rendered intolerable by resentment after finding themselves hugely celebrated in the magic world but unable to make an impact on the wider public. I can only imagine it's a widespread experience.

Life can become a frantic chase after something that does not exist, a pursuit that can only be sustained by a refusal to confront important questions about yourself. The celebrity certainly has in place a very effective distraction from looking carefully at deeper personal issues: he has *another* self that purports to be at least as real as his true self. One successful British performer told me that she realised her need to act in Hollywood films was born of a desire to fulfil an image of success that was expected of her by others. Not surprisingly, this need for greater intensity, when coupled with a disorientating detachment from one's 'true self', can pave the way to addiction problems, as it did with her. Meanwhile, a recent television show has focused on the stories of pop-group members who were thrust into the limelight, promised fame and riches, then dumped overnight. It is heartbreaking to hear their tales of subsequent descent into drug addiction, severe depression, even prostitution. Worse, theirs is precisely the sort of instant recognition to which most fame-hungry young people seem attracted.

Schopenhauer and Seneca both made the point that fame is *relative*. It is diminished or increased by comparison: a British TV star might have a hugely dedicated following here but compared to a Hollywood luminary seems like a 'nobody'. 'A ship which looms large in the river seems tiny when on the ocean,'[140] writes Seneca. If

140 Seneca, *Letters from a Stoic,* Letter XLIII

you are not at all known, and you imagine being famous, you are likely to think of it as an absolute. It is not; it is relative, controlled by other people who populate the media industry and your fan base, and as such is prone to sudden disappearance. It would be mad to rely on it as a source of happiness.

Other people lend you renown and you rely on that – *something of theirs* – to be famous. It finds its home in the perceptions of other people, namely those who lend it to you, while the same damaged you peers out. It doesn't feel like *anything* to be famous, because that status is a product of something other people are doing. There are some comfortable by-products to enjoy and some uncomfortable ones to endure, but in and of itself, there is nothing in the middle you could describe as an *experience*, apart from, perhaps, a frequent urge to duck your head and avoid attention.

Being rich

You may object: 'Okay – but the money! Maybe fame won't make me any happier, but I'd love to be richer.' Indeed. Becoming richer *does* tend to make you happier, but only to the point of being financially comfortable. There is, as we've discussed, a yearly salary figure up to which people report themselves as incrementally happier. The amount depends on the cost of living, but importantly, when people earn higher than that 'comfortable' figure, they don't *continue* to grow happier. Again, we indirectly find happiness in the *absence* of a stressor (money troubles) not in the *having* of something. In a sense, much of this book concerns the value of understanding that distinction: we're switching our focus to removing needless frustrations, not chasing happiness. The belief that we would be extremely happy if we were extremely rich is so widespread that it's worth repeating: after the point of being financially comfortable, *more money does not make you happier*. Money constitutes a relationship, and like any relationship, we need a certain amount of mindfulness in place to get it right.

The relationship between fame and money is rarely as straightforward as it might appear. Speaking for myself, my first television show aired in December 2000 and I was paid five thousand pounds. My involvement in the show took perhaps three or four months, so that amount was by no means exorbitant. Until that point, I had been performing my brand of magic at occasional parties and events for a fee of three hundred pounds, having weaned myself off income support and housing benefit. After the show aired, I took to the bosom of a manager, who said I could now command a fee of three *thousand* pounds for an evening's work. This tenfold increase staggered me. Within a couple of weeks of the show airing, I had my first gig at that fee. The tip I received was five hundred pounds, significantly more than my fee would have been a month before. My life, it seemed, was about to change.

That gig turned out to be the only one of its kind that year. Although my television appearance meant my management could charge three thousand pounds to hire me out, clearly not enough people had seen the show to bring in any further bookings. Indeed, it was far from obvious to TV viewers that I *could* be hired as a performer. Prior to the show airing, I had got by on maybe two proper gigs a month. Now, despite being recognisable to some as a face from the television, I was facing an inability to support myself doing what I enjoyed. My manager even suggested that for the time being I get a different job.

Eventually – and I am lucky to have such a generous

man looking after my career – my manager lent me enough money to cover a difficult period, and I continued to take local bookings at three hundred pounds. I remember performing magic around the tables in a Bristol restaurant one night during that period and being told I was similar to 'that Darren Brown guy on TV'. When I smugly pointed out that I *was* that guy, they didn't believe me. It clearly made no sense to them that I could be on TV and still have to work tables in a restaurant: 'One step up from a rose-seller,' as a friend put it.

Yet I have no memories of being unhappy about money while in Bristol. My outgoings were very low: I lived in a student flat for my ten years of post-graduate *flâneuring* and black-cloaked preposterousness; my only expensive indulgence was a habit of dining alone in the finest restaurants the city could offer. My needs were modest and achievable (if sometimes hilariously self-conscious), which meant I was happy. Today, I earn significantly more, but the relationship between my desires and achievability has not changed, and thus my level of happiness has remained largely the same. My happiness seems to me no more attached to what I earn (once past that watershed point of not having money troubles) than it does to my wallpaper. And I know more than my fair share of wealthy people and they'll tell you the same.

A better strategy is to treat fame and riches as pleasant side effects. It may seem trite to stress the benefits of doing what one loves for a living, but for all the reasons given in this book, it works, if you're lucky or dedicated enough to find your way there. In my twenties, I enjoyed nothing more than crossing the Clifton Suspension Bridge in Bristol and walking through the fields of Ashton Court dreaming up magic tricks. As long as my life could continue roughly in that vein, it seemed to me I would remain very content. Of course one grows up and these priorities change, but not as much as one might imagine. I wished to spend my career performing magic, or doing something that would bring me a similar amount of freedom and pleasure, and I had reached a point where that desire was achievable and being lived out every day. I didn't know of Epictetus then, and I wasn't aware that I was aligning myself with his formula, yet my concerns were really only about my thoughts and actions: the things I could control. Money, fame and success exist on the *other* side of that line in the realm of external indifferents: nice to have, but outside of our jurisdiction. They may be rewarding by-products, but they will never prove gratifying if they are chased directly. When we focus instead on the activities we love and how we might tap into a market (which will always exist for someone who does something well), we keep our attention where it belongs: on the development of our talent and the energy we put into it. I'll talk more about that a little later.

It's important to recognise that we have a *relationship* with our money. This notion is very well explored in a little book called *How to Worry Less about Money* by the British philosopher John Armstrong. Simply having money is not good enough, in the same way that simply having a partner is not enough for a good relationship. The vital matter with any relationship is paying attention to what we ourselves might bring to it. If we have *worries* about money (as opposed to specific money *troubles*, which are about needing more cash to cover particular debts), then we might find that these floating concerns derive from feelings of low status, anxieties about achieving goals, or resenting others for having more than us. But money won't make those worries dissolve: many who are rich feel the same concerns when they compare

370

themselves to their own peer group. Money might represent to us all sorts of abstract, negative issues of which we are only half aware. Rather than let those ruin our relationship with money (our own money or other people's), we are better advised to look carefully at what those issues could be. We know that when we bring similar baggage to our human relationships, we soon get into trouble.

When a person decides to give up cigarettes, he is well advised to pay attention to the *reasons* he has for smoking. These will be well placed: smoking provides a means for relaxation; a way of rounding off a meal; it's something to do with the hands; it used to offer a subtle way of detaching in a social situation (at least it did when the smoker could puff out a literal smokescreen at a pub table between him and his companions). Today, it offers fresh air, a means of social connection and a hiatus from the rat race in the form of the back-door smoking break. These are all noble and important needs to which we should attend, and a non-smoker will usually have varied means for catering to them. To cut out cigarettes without looking for other ways of placating these requirements is going to make giving up very stressful.

Likewise with money: whenever something holds our attention in such a secure but misplaced way, we should pay attention to the needs behind its magnetic attraction. And the core reasons why we are drawn to money resonate far deeper than the requisites of a smoker. Looking past immediate and specific money troubles, the fantasy of wealth promises to change our lives for the better. The desire to transform into an improved version of ourselves is a valid and admirable urge to which we should all pay more attention. Money, however, is not a very effective means of securing the kind of improvement we truly seek; it too easily brings out the worst in us, and the acquirement of it can prove too distracting and empty a goal.

Wealth also seems to offer a means of elevating oneself above the parochial troubles of the ordinary and everyday, and to connect with something larger and more exciting. If we don't go to church (or even if we do), we may never find a means of incorporating wonder and largeness in our lives. In our modern age, so sceptical of myths or mystery, people still flock to psychics and cheap New Age spirituality because they seem to offer a tawdry semblance of transcendence.

These urges – to transform ourselves and connect with something larger than our familiar, humdrum lives – are primal longings to which religion once effectively paid heed. Today, these cries from the soul go largely unheard; hence we understandably attach them to the accumulation of wealth. Rather than daydream of riches or sneer enviously at media reports of strikingly young cyber-billionaires, however, we can acknowledge that such impotent activities arise from valid and noble cravings to improve ourselves and connect to a feeling of largeness. Opportunities may then present themselves for us to quietly enquire, within, as to how those needs might be more effectively honoured and met.

Armstrong, meanwhile, makes a refreshing point. He says we should pay attention to what we *need*. He emphatically does *not* mean by this that we should simply be frugal. Instead, as part of a considered life, he suggests we become more aware of what our priorities are: what we need to flourish. Some commodities will help us do that, and they may indeed be expensive or appear luxurious to others. Advertisers will tell us what we require to feel good about ourselves, but those things don't correlate with what we actually need to do ourselves justice.

Understanding what one's needs are in this sense – and then not bothering with the rest – sounds like a very liberating experience. I'm not sure if I've summoned the self-mastery necessary to think truly for myself and buy only what serves my priorities. But his point is a good one: we might require an expensive instrument if we wish to flourish as a musician or quality oils if we paint. If we really value late-night conversation with friends, we might decide that a nicely arranged room and certain furniture is of more importance to us than, say, the latest phone or some fancy sunglasses. What we *need* is neither the bare Epicurean basics (which for most of us would make flourishing difficult) nor the nicest newest version of everything the advertisers dangle before us. The latter invent needs for us; we can get ahead of that process by taking stock of what truly matters to us and making sure it is our *own* requirements that we're prioritising.

> We need to be more imaginative, more patient, more attentive to the lessons of our own experience, more serious about the things we care for, more canny, more independent in our judgements. But most importantly, we have to figure out what we actually need.[141]

Somehow, as we pay more of this kind of attention to what truly suits and elevates us, we might develop some resolve in this marketplace of snake oil and seduction. We could rediscover our personal taste within the confines of our means, think for ourselves and give our lives some style.

141 John Armstrong, *How to Worry Less about Money*

Being loved

Like the accumulation of money or reputation, being loved by people you don't know and are unlikely to meet is best treated as a *side effect* of doing what you enjoy. It is, however, such a profoundly touching and universally shared human requirement that we would do well to remember that it lingers behind many of the strange behaviours of the famous and connects all of us to such apparent weirdness. I've said it's unfair to presume that famous people are primarily interested in attention-seeking at a conscious level (when creative fulfilment – let alone earning potential – can play powerful roles too). Yet we can also, in the same breath, acknowledge the need to be loved as a more or less *unconscious* factor in their (and many high-flyers') careers: a need which all of us share at some level. When we appreciate that, we dispense with the cynicism we like to reserve for the highly successful and realise that we all come from similarly frightened and lonely places.

On a day that Justin Bieber lambasts a paparazzo or a star is incarcerated for self-destructive behaviour, we might wish to remember that they and others are scream-ing out to be loved. Their public personas may attract adoration, but the public face is not the true self. When the public face provokes so much idolisation, a sort of dis-sonance is likely to occur: it is as if the star has a twin who is receiving all the attention. The jaw-dropping mansion and fleet of cars cannot fill a gap left by an unnoticed and un-nurtured true self, which might have atrophied at a young age if fame arrived uncommonly early. In these cases, the fans who love you are not people *you* could ever connect with in real life; they respond to your mediated, orchestrated, grotesquely sexualised twin right on cue, whilst remaining the very people that the *real-life* you has to spend much of your time avoiding. Stars pout and flirt with the public enticingly from the pages of magazines or from the microphone on stage but obviously don't seek the intimacy they coyly suggest. A meticulously coordinated public image may suggest that the star truly adores her fans, or in some cases might even be sexually available to them, but the reality is that on most days she goes out of her way to steer clear of them and will cross the road to get away if she can.

Any love you might attract as a star is likely to be disproportionately intense and directed not at your 'true' self but your public face. Thus it easily feels misplaced and demented. Meanwhile, any hatred and cynicism cuts deep and seems to be directed very much at *you*. Such is our nature: it used to be a question of avoiding reviews; now one is best advised to steer clear of @replies on Twitter. A hundred kind comments never quite seem to make up for the one that cuts deeply.

Your twin is of course the favourite and renders you public property, even at private moments when you're in a restaurant or exhausted and trying to get out of a car without knickers. Your twin may be clean-cut and wholesome, which makes your real self eager to redress the balance by upsetting people's expectations through aggressive or objectionable acts. Sometimes this can be achieved harmoniously within the context of a career, and both twins can be kept on side: witness Kylie Minogue's famous transformation from benign teenybopper to sex kitten (my pop references are endearingly non-current). Few stars manage this balancing act so successfully. The fact that Kylie became not only a highly sexualised star but also presents herself as articulate, intelligent and is serious as an actor (she's magnificent in the bizarre movie *Holy Motors*), suggests that she became comfortable with such an admirable state of equilibrium. Who knows?

The private self is not honoured in our culture as it once was. We knew little of the personal lives of old Hollywood's stars, and that was part of their appeal. Today, the media invade and tap into our email and phone conversations, and reality stars attempt to display every facet of their lives in a seeming attempt to dissolve without remain into an entirely public sphere. The 'private life' of a public figure has come to mean something sinister, something synonymous with dirty secrets and having something to hide. Part of our dislike of hearing that a celebrity avoids her fans or didn't allow a photograph to be taken, comes from our poor tolerance of contradiction and ambiguity (we want them to behave at all times how we would expect from their performances), and a lingering distrust of the very notion of the private realm. And thus the experience of being famous, like that of being human, is most unpleasant when one cannot retreat to that private, inner space, or finds it violated.

Here we are, all of us permanently lost in translation, our verbal and physical language consistently failing to communicate quite what we mean to say or be. Our style choices both express our unique personalities and obscure them through cliché, reduction, and trivialisation; our conversations rarely do us justice, and the more we try to express who we 'really' are, the further that kernel retreats, indignant at our prosaic attempts to find the right means of bringing it into the light. We are not, we protest, quite the person others think we are. When our public face is larger than life, our private self will require more nurturing than ever.

Secrets, hypocrisy and duplicity are the nature of our

condition. The compassionate nurse occasionally fanta-
sises of extraordinary violence to her patients; the loving
parent of swerving her car with its wailing backseat cargo
into oncoming traffic; the terrifying boss harbours
thoughts so tender they would make you cry. The more
our media chase the private, human hypocrisies of the
famous (and for most female celebrities we must include
the further hypocrisy of a changing and imperfect body),
the more we reveal our fearful relationship with the con-
tradictions and shadows of our own irreconcilable natures.

All said, I find the experience of being known generally quite pleasant. Most people are respectful and friendly,
and it's up to me whether I focus on the positive or negative aspects. Meanwhile, it remains wrong to complain,
however double-edged the experience may be. Consider
the experience of people wanting a photograph with you
when you're out and about. How innocuous and flattering to imagine that someone might want a quick snap
with you, and how ungracious to suggest it could be anything less.

A conversation that commonly occurs between two
famous people if they happen to become friends is how
they deal with photographs on the street. Let's say you're
not in a particular rush to get anywhere and have the basic
manners to stop and chat if someone wants to say hello.
Chatting is usually very nice. Alternatively, you might be
having dinner somewhere and a chap apologetically (or
not) interrupts. Occasionally, someone might want you to
scribble an autograph; what could be more complimen-
tary? The heart of anyone well known does tend to sink,
however, when a photograph is requested in a public
place. Of course you agree and assume the customary
position. Now, a sequence commonly occurs (one which
has happened to me, in some form, several times).

The person wanting the photograph retrieves her phone or camera and appears to have forgotten how to use it. Meanwhile, you stand with your arm around her partner, aware that you are starting to attract attention. As the phone wielder apologises sweetly and jokes about her inability to use her own equipment, you can't help but notice passers-by (or other diners, if this happens when you're eating) are looking across to see who's taking a photograph of whom and why. We have a natural inclination to follow the direction of a photographer's lens to see what we might be missing; it seems to now be a hard-wired instinct. Plus it's fun to see what other people find interesting and always appealing to watch people standing, grinning happily and having their photo taken.

So now, while she takes the time to delete older pictures to make room for a few new ones, you are aware that another couple has clocked you and are now getting their *own* cameras ready. Trying to maintain a cheerful expression, you steel yourself for the second set of photos that you know will follow, while the first lady, having sorted her apparatus, now takes a photo of you with her boyfriend, before snapping two more identical pictures 'just in case' and then checking them with said boyfriend who complains that he looks awful and asks her to take it again. So she does it again, one with the flash by mistake, which she needs to delete to make room for another few, while the guy from the *second* couple (still waiting to take *their* picture) calls his friend who is shopping nearby to let him know that you are on the street and tells him to head over. Your first photographer now asks if she can be in one too, so she switches with her boyfriend, apologising kindly for taking up your time, saying that this is probably the last thing you want; she hands the camera to her partner and stands with her arm around you. He has less of an idea how to use the camera and asks her how to use it. She calls out instructions to him, attracting more attention to your little group. A few more people pause as they walk past; eventually one squints at you in half-recognition and stops, fishing in her red leather handbag for her camera phone. You wear your broad beam for the upcoming photograph, but by now you are dead inside.

Eventually the first couple are done, and you move to the second, who very kindly ask if you wouldn't mind a photograph with them too, and you smile and suggest maybe one with all three of you to save a bit of time. They agree – but where you meant a group selfie, they now ask *another* passer-by if he wouldn't mind taking a picture of them both with you. Because the guy making this request used your name, this passer-by looks at you, and his eyes widen in recognition; he agrees to take the picture and asks if he can get one too. Now the guy from that second couple whose phone is being used to take the photo has to explain its operation to this helpful pedestrian while you stand awkwardly with your arm around his girlfriend, watching the woman with the red handbag hovering on the periphery waiting to ask if she might get a photo too.

Throughout, you desperately want to give these people a nice experience of meeting you; at the same time you don't want to draw a small crowd and suddenly be the centre of attention when you're just out trying to buy some plasters. It's hard to know what to do.

Of course, when asked for a photo, you can never say no. 'He wouldn't let me take a photo! It's less than a second. What a dick.' Neither can you decline and offer an explanation. What can you say? 'It'll draw attention and other people will probably want one too and it becomes difficult to get away, or carry on having my lunch without feeling horribly self-conscious.' How to deal with this situation is a popular discussion point, and people will find their own strategies. One actor I know – far more likely to be photographed than me and genuinely one of the most impressively lovely people I have met – apologises and declines to have any photos taken at all. Evoking something of the Native American tradition, he explains with semi-seriousness that the taking of photos and prolific sharing of that image around the Internet steals one's soul.

The objection is an interesting one. Today, the proliferation of cameras makes it seem like you haven't really *had the experience* of meeting someone famous unless you have shared a photograph of the encounter online. It certainly can on occasions be oddly objectifying and uncomfortable, especially when passers-by shove a camera in your face without asking. People sometimes walk up to you and wordlessly snap pictures while their gaze never leaves their phone's screen, or they seize you presumptuously for a two-person selfie, or pretend to be texting while never-surreptitiously-enough taking your photograph in a shop or restaurant. I have sat in a restaurant while a group of teenagers walked back and forth outside fifteen, maybe twenty times, pretending to be on the phone while taking pictures. But I still hear you: 'Aww poor thing. Did the nasty people take pictures of the famous person whose career they're sustaining?' You can't, and probably shouldn't, ever utter a word of complaint. But equally it's infuriating. 'Oh, fuck off and eat your expensive restaurant lunch, you dick.'

For what it's worth, my advice to anyone in the position of frequently having his or her photograph taken in public is to take a breath and consciously *decide* to embrace and enjoy it in the moment. It is pointless trying to explain to someone why, with the best will in the world, it can draw attention you'd rather not have, and of course that irritation is only a consequence of your internal judgement. Take the phone from them and snap the picture yourself; you can take the photograph far more quickly and discreetly and, if you wish, focus the interaction on a pleasant conversation instead. Perhaps ask if the photo might be taken round a corner rather than in full view of passers-by. Refuse if you feel strongly of course – plenty of celebrities do, and they remain much loved – but above all to *resent* the request is, I think, simply a mistake. That counts even when it is discourteously made while you are eating or on the phone. Like Marcus Aurelius, we must expect to sometimes meet people with bad manners, and to be angered by them is a sign of too-high expectations. Decide that having your photograph taken is the most flattering and lovely thing, and refrain from communicating any whiff of reluctance. One day, no one will want your photograph; that inevitability does not automatically make the ritual more pleasant today when it escalates into a scene, but it might serve as a justification to discover enthusiasm when you feel none. Furthermore, although your job may be to entertain, act, or do what you do as well as you can (and *not*, you feel, to meet people or pose for photographs), you now have *another* role as a celebrity, which does involve such things, and you can do *that* as well as you can too.

However you feel about the fact, you will occasionally have come to mean a huge amount in the life of the person standing opposite you, who now fumbles with her camera. From time to time, you may have even, without realising, become something of a role model, or to some extent steered the course of her life. This does happen: I am often struck by how many people tell me they have chosen a career in psychology or magic or made other life decisions because of seeing my work. You may have played a role on TV or in film that moved her deeply and which represents to her something quite profound. For all you know, you may be for that person a pointer towards something larger and more exciting than everyday life, in the same way that certain people are or were for you. So take a moment, force a convincing smile if necessary, and respect these important machinations. W. B. Yeats warns us: 'Tread softly, because you tread on my dreams.'

I have focused on some of the more negative everyday aspects of the relationship between the famous and the public. I confess I have crossed roads and pretended to be on my phone more than my fair share of times,[142] but for me, the best consequence of having a little fame is that a lot of people seem to have decided they like me before I meet them. That's a very nice thing. Friendships usually need time and a certain environment in which to flourish, and for many adults it's not easy to find either of those things. Being well known cuts through a lot of that and much of the work is already done. (I don't, incidentally, have lots of *famous* friends. This is partly due to the fact that the well known tend to work hard and be difficult to see with any regularity, and partly due to the fact that I'd rather cut off my own balls with blunt bacon scissors than host a dinner party.)

Lovely as it can be to feel loved, I am aware that others will hate me for no reason other than they object to my work, face, or find me violently revolting in some vague but powerful way. I try to be as minimally

142 I'm also, after years of ending stage shows to the punctuated resolution of pyrotechnics, fairly deaf in one ear. So sometimes, when you yell out my name, I just don't hear.

annoying as possible by declining panel shows and only rarely (and when utterly obliged to) doing TV interviews. I don't emerge much in the press unless it relates to a specific project, though tabloids sometimes run or threaten to run stories that they know aren't true but serve the shit-stirring intuitions of their editors. I generally have an easy time with the media, perhaps because I don't court them in the way some others do. A story broke the other day about a member of a famous boy band smoking a joint on a car journey. Of course the band has to present a careful image to their young fans, but a back-seat toke caught on camera does no damage at all to anyone unless the media draw hysterical attention to it. Nowhere, to balance the mawkish *Schadenfreude* we derive from seeing a pop star embarrassed, do we read an article about the honest joy that the singer and his confrères spread at a gig the night before to tens of thousands of fans, or the positive role models the band members have proved to be for any number of hopeful young singers or devoted teenagers. A savvy journalist would point out that those stories *have* existed: at the start of the band's career they were media darlings, and now the time has come when they must expect to be treated with the requisite derision to balance out the earlier celebration. I fail to see how this is any more praiseworthy an attitude (particularly when the real motive for the story is to drive people to its media source), but such is the way it seems to be.

Rather than enjoy a star's embarrassment or complain about the hypocrisy of tabloids taking the moral high ground whilst they spread their muck, we might actually take some comfort in these kinds of stories. At the time of writing, the media have got hold of a piece of film showing Bieber making a racist joke to his friends. These stories of stars with a clean-cut image being caught indulging in wayward behaviour, whether mild and daft or dangerous and stupid, remind us that the ludicrous levels of fame achieved by some do not stop them being human. Life becomes perverse and extreme; how encouraging that, amidst the orgy of acclaim and money, they act in the far from admirable way we might ourselves, if *we* had arrived there with the same background behind us and under precisely the same conditions. Older stars – who will also have achieved more control over their careers – tend to find ways of honouring those deeper concerns and making life feel relatively normal. Some of the measures necessary to restore a sense of privacy may seem like madness to the outside world. Many step out of the Hollywood lifestyle altogether; an impressive few, like Daniel Day-Lewis, tread the bramble-strewn path of Thoreau and seem to achieve equilibrium in rural simplicity. However eccentric some of these choices seem, we know that we too would need to find sanity and balance amidst exaggerated public interest.

We've noted that when we are in our twenties, our urges are more iconoclastic; we have only recently emerged from the family unit and must quietly seek new role models while seemingly impressing the world with our fledgling independence. A good manager might partly fulfil those new parental roles for the young and famous, but usually the valuable star is pushed to 'dazzle the world' while truly nurturing mentors (who would stick around even in the case of career failure) are somewhat lacking. The public transgressions of the young and celebrated show us how difficult it must be to live authentically when one is adulated. Our natural instinct, unless we are fans, is to find it easier to deride rather than to love, as we see them as having everything and squandering it in a way we think we wouldn't. Fans may purport to adore the true person behind the public persona, but this is a pretence of intimacy, commonly a substitute for an intimate encounter that is unachievable, and still based on a mediated image. As I've said, it remains a love that doesn't satisfy or please the love-seeking star at all, commonly provoking horror rather than pleasure. That is because it can never truly please; it is an entirely *conditional* love. It is conditional because it depends on the star conforming more or less to his public's expectations. And unlike real love, it is one-sided. We might enjoy the feeling of being loved, but we will not be satisfied until we also learn the joys of giving it away. Love becomes far more fulfilling when we realise it in large part consists of sensitively accommodating our lover's inadequacies. A love that can only be *received* is barely worth bothering about. And the more a person is unconsciously driven to seek love on such a public scale, the less it will prove satisfactory. One's centre of gravity must be pulled within, where discussion with the self can occur to find healing, not thrown out to the four winds.

The publicised and very human transgressions of the famous remind us to engage our empathy in the most unlikely of cases. The famous are a group that many people on the one hand would like to join, and on the other resolutely feel do not deserve their sympathy. In fact, it takes the talent of Richard Curtis and a superior film-making team to make us sympathise with a fictional celebrity such as Julia Roberts' besieged character Anna Scott in *Notting Hill*. Were the real Roberts ever to be heard to complain in the same way as her character does, we would sneer and scoff, as if the rich and famous had forfeited any claim to real concerns. It might serve us better to take comfort in the fact that the gods are mortal after all; that they and we are in fact more similar than we imagine; that we would most likely do the same strange things if we found ourselves in their position; that our own insecurities might be exaggerated, not eliminated, by fame.

Madness and media

The most surprising part of receiving letters and emails at the start of my career was being on the receiving end of people's psychoses. I have a genuine interest in mental health (it feels odd to me *not* to; to have neither empathy nor curiosity in that direction would suggest a refusal to acknowledge the darker areas of our own minds that sometimes threaten to own each of us). There are currently several movements to de-stigmatise conditions and educate the public about the subject. My ex-partner joked with me that I have more friends with bipolar or obsessive-compulsive disorder than I do without, and it's probably true. These are two conditions that I find particularly fascinating, perhaps because of how very human yet very destructive they are. Most of us feel we can relate to the thinnest end of those particular wedges, but we cannot begin to imagine the spiralling horror of a life defined by them at the other. Perhaps, too, because both seem in part fuelled by auto-suggestion and the stories we tell ourselves, they remain hugely fascinating to me.

It is far harder to muster empathy and interest towards a sufferer when one serves as their psychotic fixation. The first letters from people who insisted, with disarming conviction, that I had caused them grave upset by doing something I knew I hadn't, were quite baffling. I replied to these poor souls, trying to explain that they had perhaps been the victim of some unfortunate prank or misunderstanding. It soon became clear that a deeper disturbance was the true source of the trouble. Now, after fifteen years on television, it has become a strange under-current of disquiet to the otherwise pleasant experience of people enjoying your work. There are people who like you way too much or despise you for some seemingly arbitrary reason upon which they have fixated.

As is normal and necessary, I have a manager, a pro-duction company and a personal assistant, who minimise the opportunity for disturbing correspondence to reach me directly. But over the years I have had to deal with stalkers of one form or another. My mother, the same evening after I had come out to her as gay, telephoned me to say that a lady was at her front door claiming to be my unfairly neglected wife. Other women have since made the same improbable claim. Those with whom I have had no connection other than appearing on their television screens have over the years screamed through social media that I have abused them, raped them or fathered their children and now refuse to accept responsibility for my actions. Friends and family have been plagued with hate mail and death threats from the tragically unbalanced. And sadly one can't simply go to the police; one might as well call up the tabloids directly and say that one is deny-ing such-and-such a horrendous claim. Such are the sad links between press and police in this country. Very rarely can one discreetly take the steps needed to secure an injunction, or, better, get such people sectioned for their own good. One just puts up with it until they cross what-ever line in the sand one has drawn, at which point one is forced to bite the bullet and approach the mental-health authorities. They in turn usually contact the person's family, and the disturbed individual might be taken to an institution.

It is only when you become known that you realise

how widespread these sorts of psychoses are, and how they always seem to relate to sex. There are any number of disturbed but less destructive women who still fail to grasp that one of the side effects of being a gay man is that you're not much into the ladies. Plenty of these lost souls are convinced that we are or have been in a romantic relationship, many believing that when I tweet or talk on TV, I am in fact expressing coded messages for them alone.

Stephen Fry has said that the best attitude to the drawbacks of fame is to treat them like wasps at a picnic. No matter how nice the picnic, there will be wasps, in the form of intrusive press or disturbed fans. These are analogous to Marcus Aurelius's cuttings on the workshop floor: an inevitable by-product of life. Such balancing analogies help.

I am only talking of my experience here, which, as I have said, is generally positive. These difficulties I am describing are personal and quite manageable in comparison to the devastation suffered by those whom the media gather to demonise. Asif Kapadia's documentary *Amy* charts the journey of Amy Winehouse, amply illustrating the mutually destructive forces of the media and machinations of fame on the one hand, and a plaintive, troubled soul on the other. Buzzwords like 'troubled' and 'tragic' abounded during her life and after her death, as do words like 'story' and 'journey' now that she's gone and supposedly left us a moral lesson. These are all reductive words that allow us to tidy up and make sense of something that could not be fairly reduced in real life. Tidy narratives are things we choose to apply; meanwhile, experience is messy and active and not reducible to these clean nouns and designations. Moralising is our attempt to distract from something complicated and painful in order to make it appear manageable, so that we can avoid feeling uncomfortably challenged (witness how the culpable media quickly turn to preaching in such cases in order to shirk their measure of responsibility). There may be lessons for us, but they are not the head-shaking, moral sermons delivered by the casually appalled.[143]

Another insight into the public horror that can come from being well known came via a veteran broadcaster friend who was blamelessly caught up in Operation Yewtree. Like several others, he had to live through a long period of no work and what felt like public shame. Where the police should surely be obliged to keep the identities of suspected people anonymous until the time of arrest, famous names are instead thrown to the press. Thus much noise is made by the police/press collaboration as these radio and TV figures are shamed to our mawkish dismay before evidence has even been assembled. Later, after months of misery, many of these poor figures are silently let go, pending 'no further action' (never proclaimed innocent; never are their names entirely cleared). This 'release' is normally orchestrated to coincide with the next high-profile arrest, ensuring that public attention is kept focused on the 'success' of the police and not their apparent failures. Naturally, the work of the police is desperately important here, but there is also an important balance to be achieved: anonymity until arrest would help secure that. Until then, the celebrity witch-hunt benefits the media and the police, while guiltless lives may be arbitrarily ruined.

*

---

143 The documentary honours this fact by not providing a voice-over (voice-overs deal in cause and effect, which organise messy reality into something artificial).

I hope I have made the point that all of the benefits one might imagine have their distinct disadvantages. Fame does not make you happier; instead, the nice things get nicer and the nasty things get far worse. The experience of fame is primarily one of widening the extremes between what is enjoyable and what is unpleasant, which does little to affect happiness.

Marcus Aurelius, presumably the most famous man of his time, repeatedly reminded himself that such glory was of little consequence. It comes and goes, as do all the people whose admiration you hope to secure. He compares one's public – those who 'applaud convincingly or on the contrary curse you or blame and rail beneath their breath'[144] – to leaves scattered in the wind. 'Brief life is the common portion of all, yet you avoid and pursue each thing as though it will be everlasting.'[145] We pursue fame and glory as if it will last forever, yet ultimately it passes quickly, as do those whom we want to adore us. Marcus elevates us to a position above the world and across time, reminding himself and the modern reader how many people will never have heard of us, regardless of how famous we might be, and ultimately how pointless is the endeavour of seeking renown. Consider, in today's age, what a small proportion of respected famous people remain so for even ten years. Very few of them, I would say, will have chased fame for its own sake. Those who have maintained a profile *and* found any happiness in it will all but unanimously have looked to creating good work as their priority.

Marcus's long view may not deter many of today's seekers after fame, but it might help the already celebrated

144 Marcus Aurelius, *Meditations*, x. 34
145 Ibid.

put their careers and goals into perspective. Meanwhile, we continue to seek renown because, perhaps, the accumulation of riches and popularity effectively distracts us from the fact that at some point we must give it all up and leave this Earth. At that point, our assembled goods will mean nothing to us, and we will face our exit from the world more or less alone. Lucretius, the Epicurean poet, knew this, writing that riches and honours make us feel further from death. Certainly for some, leaving a legacy becomes more important as they grow older; it is another means of reaching for immortality.

Fame seduces us with immortality, or so we like to think, despite the amply evident fact that it can be bestowed and brutally withdrawn in damagingly short bursts. As I have said, it represents a transcendent form of life in a post-religious society. There was a time when the vast masses of people who admired the famous – emperors, warriors, saints – knew they could never join their ranks. The poor did not aspire to great success. The gods with whom we may today aspire to co-exist are already stripped of much of their divine sheen; we no longer believe the airbrushed images of stars because we have seen them snapped by paps in unflattering beachwear or disfeatured by the absence of morning maquillage. Whereas once they only loomed large at us from cinema screens and the starry heights of billboards, they now seem to promise informal conversation on Twitter. Fans no longer hope for a signed picture or a glimpse of a favourite star at a publicly orchestrated event; they now hope to secure *dialogue*.

Yet for all the worldliness and availability of many of these modern immortals, we should still remember that part of their appeal lies in transcendence to some realm that only exists in our imagination. The reality of fame (from the inside) has nothing to do with the image of it from afar (outside), because prestige – again, like the king's status on stage – is played out only in how other people respond and react. When you enter its hallowed halls, the golden walls fall away and you realise it's still you, in the same world, looking out through the same eyes. I heard of a playwright who was shot to fame in a matter of weeks and found that the exciting bubble of celebrity burst miserably at a Broadway after-show party when he walked in on Whoopi Goldberg in the bathroom. As I understand, this minor accident thoroughly undid for him the exotic mystery of fame in an instant, exposed to him the all-too-human nature of celebrity, and left him depressed and confused for some time.

Palaces are most beautiful when viewed from afar, and stars shine most brightly from a distance.

The secret magical formula for success

There is a hitherto untold, mysterious recipe for success, known only to the favoured few. I share it with you now. You're welcome.

TALENT + ENERGY

That's it. I learnt it from my manager, Michael Vine, who is a rabbinical force in these and other matters. You can have all the talent in the world, but if you don't show it to a public and get it 'out there', it'll do you little good. Likewise, you can have all the self-promotional energy anyone could hope for, but if you have no real talent to back it up it won't get you very far. The development of your talent and the energy with which you approach that aspect of your life are of course two things that are under your control. Success itself is not.

Beyond the furthering of your aptitude and your stamina, you will of course need the coincidence of good fortune to secure recognition. You are not in control of that, and if you try to be (which is what concentrating on being famous amounts to), then you are likely to remain bitter and frustrated, *even if you succeed*. Aim to psychologically manoeuvre yourself into a position where developing your talent and balancing it with suitable energy provide you with enough enjoyment, happiness and money to get by. Fame and riches should only ever be seen as fortuitous side effects. But they are *more likely* to come if you focus on developing what *is* under your control: your talent and energy.

As a side note, Michael expanded on this point and gave the following formula for being a *star*:

STYLE + ATTITUDE

Stars are not merely successful. They are also in possession of a recognisable style *and* a certain attitude that surrounds them as a kind of aura. The 'style' may refer to the immediately identifiable, rapid-fire performance of one comic or the drawn-out delivery of another. It is the familiar sound of our favourite singer-songwriters; in almost all genres of entertainment, a performer's style is stolen or imitated the moment it is noticed and admired. 'Attitude', on the other hand, describes that powerful or withheld *something* that defines certain standout actors, as well as the confident swagger or passionate self-revelation of legendary rock stars; whichever way, there is always conviction and clarity and a singular voice that somehow transcends the work. Amy Winehouse had style *and* attitude and was a star; those who merely copy her sound are not. Look at any legendary singer-songwriter and a distinctive style and pervading attitude are usually very apparent.

In any form of entertainment or business, these formulae for success and stardom would seem to apply.

For performers: if you secure for yourself an agent, she is unlikely to do a lot for you unless you are already successful. Most performers whinge that their agent isn't good enough. 'She doesn't make enough calls or *publicise* me satisfactorily,' you'll moan, 'instead just takes a fee for work I have found myself.' That frustration is a symptom of too-high expectations and wishing to control something that you cannot. You *are*, however, in control of how visible you choose to remain to an agent who probably has much bigger and more profitable names to promote. You are in control of whether you just moan that she doesn't do enough, or whether you send flowers or champagne every time she does. You are in control of whether or not you are a pleasure to work with, and how much you keep yourself within her awareness.

If you are anxious, you are fixating on the uncertainties of the future. Focusing not on desired fame (which as something desired is always in the future) but on your developing talent and energy *now* will keep you rooted in the present and allow you to be open to opportunities without obsessing over where they might lead. You have chosen a job path that has the potential to offer great happiness, but this can only come from the experience of the journey (which, being in the areas of your talent and energy, is thankfully under your control) and not from the destination (which is unknown, ill defined and forever moving further away from you). Honour that potential by not confusing fulfilment and fame; the two look similar but are not related. You will have to treat fame very lightly if you secure it (to avoid being neurotic and repulsive), so you'd be well advised to start doing that now, because there's no clear moment when it suddenly arrives. This all keeps your centre of gravity within yourself.

A final piece of advice: recognise and beware the toxic blend of low self-esteem and grandiose self-regard known only to the truly damned.

☺

Part Three: **Happy Endings**

11
Debra

This part of the book is about death. Occasionally I tell people I am writing a book on happiness, and that I am turning my attention to death and dying. Their normal response is a half-laugh or snort into their flat whites, perhaps because abrupt contrasts are humorous. We relish any chance to make light of the dark, patient spectre of our own mortality. And isn't death a topic for sadness?

I want to look at the role that an awareness of death might play in our project of living more happily. Whilst self-help books typically focus on setting goals to fill your life with everything you want in order to find happiness, you'll understand by now my approach foregoes such questionable methods. We'll aim for something richer and less neurotic, exploring age-old advice that living well and dying well are two sides of the same proverbial coin. If we wish to enjoy a considered life, we must be able to step back and see an overall shape to our allotted span. Mortality provides that shape and can surprise us by being the wellspring of deep meaning, value and joy.

Most of my readers will be under forty, and thus few of them will think much about death, unless they happen to be gripped by morbid thoughts. Few might consider its role in the happy life. Nothing in our current culture recommends that we keep death present in our peripheral vision. When we are young, we have no reason to think about it. When we are older, we do so more frequently, but for the majority it remains a subject to be resolutely avoided. The sad result is that death becomes a terrifying business, and we miss out on its great lessons.

If you are still young, and have not seen your parents grow old, or even die, along with uncles and aunts; if aches are not yet constant companions and if your back and joints don't yet creak and moan every time you heave yourself from a chair, then you are very unlikely to in any way see your life shaped by a forthcoming end. If you are in your twenties, as we've discussed, you are most likely seeking out your place in the world. You may be beginning to find out who the real 'you' is, and as part of that will be looking for new role models to take the place of your parents. In your thirties, you may be aware of having moved past that first flush of self-involvement and are now keen to do something worthwhile in the world. You may have started a family. These are times of discovery and beginnings. And I worried for a while that devoting a chunk of this book to death would be lost on a significant proportion of its readership.

Yet younger people – teenagers perhaps especially – who find themselves growing up, or making a start in the world, are beginning existential journeys that others have largely forgotten about in middle age. Destinations become obscured or abandoned in the mugginess of grown-up responsibilities, and much of the vigour and faith needed for grand new undertakings feel hard to recapture. And thus younger people are often more vibrantly aware of the deep issues of life than the rest of us give them credit for. When a black-clad teenager styles her life around an alluring morbid fascination, she is articulating important concerns, which are unlikely to be sufficiently met by vampire sagas and entreaties from parents for her to cheer up. Youth can bring an inward-looking urgency regarding deep questions that might seem disproportionate from the outside, but deep questions they remain. And not surprisingly, many young people turn to Eastern spiritual teachings to meet those needs. Many will find solace there; the shame is only that our Western philosophical tradition, which as we've seen has offered millennia of rich advice to help us approach the span of our lives constructively, no longer appears to be relevant to the business of living or dying. It is now almost exclusively the meticulous, arid business of academics, and is regarded as largely inconsequential by younger people who may grapple hardest with the questions that once formed philosophy's lifeblood.

So bear with me, because I think there *is* something of real value in thinking about death, even if it has never occurred to you to do so. Consider the following, whatever stage of life you might be at. You are going to die. You know this, but consider for a moment what that means. The world you know is built upon your experiences. And you are the only person having those experiences. So your world is unique. When you look out at it, and the people in it, you do so through a filter that you don't share with anyone else. This is even more evident when you consider your past.

Consider your early memories. Snapshots within the house you lived in when you were young: the first pet, the picture on the wall in your bedroom, a pattern on the wallpaper or couch, cakes and cake tins. The times you got severely told off. Times of trauma. Brief moments from early birthday parties, dim images that flicker like candles, which you have confused with blurry photographs you've seen since. Old toys and TV shows, holidays, early lessons at school.

Then, as you remember how you grew up, you can trace the lines of experience that have more obviously formed the adult you are now. You notice aspects of your relationship with your parents that affect so much of your behaviour today. Moments you have shared with people along the way – early sexual experiences and infatuations, tough and great memories from school. From this tangle of events you have formed certain beliefs about the world. What is important and what is not. You've perhaps discovered some way of connecting with something bigger than yourself – through religion, through sport, music or art, or through some other endeavour that brings you out of your own head for a while and makes you feel that life can be rich and worthwhile. All this continues to feed into that filter that makes *your* world unique; that causes *you* to notice certain things and ignore others as you look across a room of people; that informs your beliefs, or set of priorities, or measuring stick by which you assess others, their behaviour and transgressions, and which allows you to arrive at the most obvious sense (to you) of what's normal. If you have children, you are consciously or unconsciously passing some of these values on to them; this is the legacy of learning and amassing thoughts and working things out and gradually becoming *you*, that particular individual who looks out on the world and views it as you do right now. Maybe you have a career that has allowed you to build some reputation or security. Perhaps you are, as an adult now, revered in some way by your community. Perhaps you are creatively gifted, perhaps you have fought to get where you are. Maybe you are young but are looking forward to a career trajectory and enjoy planning for success.

All of this and more constitutes your world. Let us then consider the harsh reality for a moment: it will all amount to nothing. Everything you have strived for, or intend to strive for, will cease to be. Your friends, family, your children will as good as disappear along with your world. The story of you, the framework of your world, will amount to nothing and most likely remain untold, without significance. That very self – that sense of *I* from which you are considering this right now – will be gone too.

'But life will continue without me,' you insist. My perspective will flicker and die but those of other people will persist. Seven billion or so other outlooks will continue, each supplying its owner with a particular slant on the world as uniquely inaccurate as yours was when it existed. In the worldviews of those who knew you, in which you were *never* the central character, a faint, semi-fictionalised version of you will exist as a set of memories and feelings that they attach to a mental picture of your face. If you happen to be one of the renowned few who establishes a legacy through a book or hospital wing that bears your name, then a sort of synthetic memory will kick around for a bit longer, before the work is no longer read or your hospital wing is renamed or knocked down. Meanwhile, those who remember your name or face will themselves come to breathe their last, and the final wisps of your posthumous presence will disappear as all recollection of you is snuffed out without trace or murmur.

'He is a collection of tissues and cells delicately and intricately conjoined and brought to life for only an instant. It will take just one sharp collision or a fall to render them inanimate again,' realises Rabih, the quiet hero of Alain de Botton's *The Course of Love*. 'He is only a visitor who has managed to confuse his self with the world. He had assumed he was yet another stable object, like the city of Edinburgh or a tree or a book, whereas he is more like a shadow or a sound.'

Only you carry your story in the world, and it must vanish with you. As the novelist Milan Kundera phrased it: 'What terrifies most about death is not the loss of the future but the loss of the past. In fact, the act of forgetting is a form of death always present within life.'[146]

Such is the finality of death. So how could that possibly help us or allow us to find happiness?

One of the bittersweet privileges of being well known is that now and then a terminally ill person – too often a young child – expresses a wish to meet you. Normally this request comes through a charity that has been set up to facilitate such get-togethers between the person suffering and someone they admire. As I tour for much of the year, this normally happens for me when I'm on the road: a kid comes to see the show with his parents and a charity official, and afterwards we all say hello. It's always extremely poignant. There is a strange atmosphere of buoyancy to these get-togethers. I hope that the event is fun for the boy or girl in question, and the burning questions I want to ask them about their ongoing experience do not feel appropriate at a time that is likely to be for the family a rare relief from the miserable drudge of treatment.

I was surprised one day to receive a request for a meeting from a son on behalf of his mother. It was a

146 Milan Kundera, *The Unbearable Lightness of Being*

reversal of the norm; I was on his mum's bucket list, and she hoped to say hello. It would have to be before the show, as she was not well enough to stay for the performance, and afterwards would be too late for her. So backstage at the Marlowe Theatre, Canterbury, in early July 2014, I met Debra Westwick, her son James and his partner Nik.

A room had been put aside for us to meet, and I arrived a little late; so when I walked in, they were already there. Debra was in a wheelchair and, aside from her seating arrangement, looked the picture of health. The three were in enormously good spirits, and it was clear that this was going to be a fun meeting. Debra had been a nurse for thirty years as well as a counsellor drawing from a range of therapeutic schools, including existential psychotherapy, which engages more explicitly than other traditions with our fear of death. I was relieved when Debra spoke of her cancer; it meant that conversation was going to be easier and more interesting than might have otherwise been the case. Her story was abominable. Commonly, stories of cancer seem to involve misdiagnoses and early assurances that everything will be okay, but Debra's tale was one of extraordinary medical negligence. To date, this is her cancer journey as described by James:

1. In 2006, Debra is diagnosed with a low-grade breast cancer with a very small chance of recurrence.
2. After surgery, she is told she will need chemo- and radiotherapy. Her surgeon and oncologist are diametrically opposed regarding treatment: the surgeon wants to carry out a full mastectomy, whereas the oncologist insists that this is wrong and that Debra is neurotic for requesting one following her surgeon's advice.

3. After a year of very little treatment, she has the mastectomy because she no longer trusts her oncologist. The surgery is a mess. The breast reconstruction fails (the transplant dies and falls off). Unbelievably, they leave three large dressings *inside* the wound, which become infected, and she nearly dies from septicaemia.

4. Debra speaks to a solicitor, and they find out she has been seriously undertreated. The notes show she should have had her lymph nodes removed and that she is now at a massive risk of the cancer returning. She takes the hospital to court.

5. The trial progresses; her 'oncologist lied a lot and tried to blame it all on Mum', and the contemporaneous notes kept by the Macmillan nurse show the true story. It turns out the doctor was already under supervision from the General Medical Council due to poor practice but wasn't being supervised in Debra's case at all. His name has now been removed from the register.

6. Six or seven years later, with the cancer seemingly in the past, Debra falls and breaks her arm. This time the scans show extensive bone metastases and deliver a clear verdict that she will die as a result. The Care Quality Commission, General Medical Council and the Parliamentary Ombudsman all find that her treatment had been appalling throughout and force the hospital trust to improve their oncology services.

As they told me the story, I was struck by how impressive her response to the malpractice had been. For her to take on the medical profession at such an exhausting, miserable time suggested an astonishing drive and resolve. Debra's knowledge of the medical world allowed her to fight her corner and hold the profession responsible where she could. Yet the tone in the room was not one of malice or bitterness. As I asked her about her feelings, it became clear that she had made her peace with the fact she was dying. Her life, in fact, somehow by virtue of being drastically shortened, had become *deeper*: richer, more vibrant, more compelling. After the uncertainty and back-and-forth of the early stages of her cancer, the final prognosis had provided a strange kind of relief. We must all die, and I can't imagine the horror of having a brief prognosis repeatedly dangled and then withdrawn in front of you. With the certain verdict of her extensive cancer finally proclaimed, she could at least acknowledge the fact that the inevitable was going to happen before long and that she was in the final period of her life. In a letter, she later described the feeling to me as follows:

> I had developed the most hideous, searing pain in my back between my shoulder blades. It was constant and unrelenting, and yet in a very perverse way, it was a relief to know what it was and also why I had been feeling very exhausted. Cancer is insidious, with its tendrils gradually invading the body like bindweed – slowly, steadily and stealthily entwining itself until its host is choked off. It was now unlikely that I would see my son qualify as a doctor, and [would] certainly not see any grandchildren, yet despite the deep sadness, I experienced a sense of liberation. The grim reaper was on his way, the cancer no longer an imaginary threat but rather a very present companion, which would impact not only me, but all those around me.

Her acceptance of death and her allowing it to transform her life for the better put me in mind of an extraordinary short film I had watched on YouTube about Philip Gould, entitled *When I Die: Lessons from the Death Zone*. Gould had been a prominent political consultant for Labour, advising on electoral strategy for nearly twenty years, and a key figure in the modernisation of the party. He developed cancer of the oesophagus and was eventually told he had three months to live.

In the short film, and in his small book of the same title (which was published posthumously with proceeds going to cancer charities), Gould describes his remaining time, very memorably, as the 'Death Zone'. Following his grim prognosis, he had told Andrew Marr in a 2011 BBC interview:

> This time it was clear. I was in a different place, a death zone, where there was such an intensity, such a power. And apparently this is normal. And so, even though obviously I'd, you know, rather not be in this position, it is the most extraordinary time of my life, certainly the most important time of my life.

The eight-minute YouTube film he has left us, made with director and photographer Adam Steirn, is very much worth watching. It delivers a powerful message: that that thing we fear most might not have to be frightening after all.

Philip Gould and Debra Westwick both 'stared death full in the face', to use Gould's expression, which Debra echoes. Fascinated to meet a woman who seemed to be 'owning' her death in a similar way Gould did, I was eager to talk more with her. She invited me to join her at her house for coffee later in the week, and I did.

I walked the few bright, warm miles from my hotel

in the centre of Canterbury to Debra's house in the leafy suburbs. I had with me my camera and tripod; she had said she didn't mind if I took a photo of her during my visit. The journey from town, over railway lines and past allotments, took me close to a churchyard chock-full of modest, mossy gravestones, and I went in to take some pictures. Later, Debra would tell me that it was used for burying lepers, and that it is now her burial place of choice.

When I reached her street, I was surprised to see Debra standing at her front door in the sunlight, lightly supported by the doorframe. We hugged and went in. Her cosy, charming house would strike anyone as the home of an intelligent woman with great taste. Surprisingly for me, there were no signs of medical equipment or the remedial compromises to easy grace one might expect in the house of a terminally ill person. She may have painted: I remember little pictures of local views dotted around her home. James and Nik were there too, and both seemed to know exactly the right amount to fuss over her: when to offer to help, when to roll their eyes or gently scold, and mostly to let Mum do as she wished. Like any great home, it was full of books, and James told me that his cancer-riddled mother had fallen from a small stepladder recently while trying to retrieve a volume from a high shelf. And here she was today, making me coffee in her cheery modern kitchen and telling me about how she and James had lost themselves in a fit of giggles over something on TV the day before.

The bedroom was the centre of social activity in the household, so we climbed the stairs with our coffees. Debra took her place on the bed; I sat on a small chair near its foot and to Debra's left. James sat on the window-sill opposite the bed; Nik propped herself to his right on a laundry basket or some such. And we talked about books and dying and how after her mastectomy the surgeons had left the dressings inside her. She recommended some books that she felt would interest me, most of which I didn't know, including *The Uses of Enchantment: The Meaning and Importance of Fairy Tales* by Bruno Bettelheim. She felt, along with the author, that fairy tales instil in us at an early age a sense of fairness that doesn't match with the real world. In her words:

> Very often as children we are set up for a fall . . . the downtrodden skivvy marries the prince, the wicked stepmother is defeated by the fairy god-mother, etc. I'm sure you get my drift. The general moral of the story is that the 'Goodies' always defeat the 'Baddies'.
>
> And how many of us, who are parents, are guilty of saying, 'If you're a good girl/boy you can have some sweets or a toy.' The subliminal ethos being subtly weaved is that good things happen to good people, and bad things happen to bad people. This is utter balderdash. The reality is that good and bad things happen to all people, death perhaps being the most extreme (and yet the most common) example. As the saying goes, 'Shit happens.' Therefore, when I was diagnosed, rather than thinking (as specified in the NHS leaflet), 'Why me, what have I done to deserve this?' I thought 'Why *not* me?'

Why not me? Debra and James spoke easily about her upcoming death. There was no veil of euphemism in their language, no avoidance of the truth or talk of 'passing', no mention of brave battles or beating the cancer or hanging on to the promise of cures found on the Internet. Death was accepted as an attendant, and now, for this extraordinary final period of her life, Debra lived with the vibrancy and a depth of feeling that can only come with an acute awareness that soon everything will be let go. She could, at the same time, both love her son more profoundly than ever and make peace with the idea that she was soon to say goodbye to him. Both she and James voiced one of the most extraordinary statements I had ever heard: that they wouldn't swap this time for anything.

Soon before I had arranged to leave, I texted a friend who was coming to collect me. Mark lives in a decommissioned church a small distance away with his wife and daughters. Not surprisingly for a couple who have chosen to live in such a place and whose young daughters play happily amongst the gravestones, they are the very picture of Psychobilly, that fifties-meets-seventies punk-horror Rockabilly subgenre. He sports a thinning, optimistic pompadour and vintage western shirt; his cuffed Wranglers are skull-belt-buckled above and end in high-gloss creepers below. She is at once Betties Crocker and Page: all fringe with side-flower, open-toed heels, polka dots and calf tattoos. As I sat with Debra, it suddenly dawned on me that Mark sometimes drives a hearse, and that he might come and pick me up in it.

The prospect of this spectre of death arriving imminently in his gory chariot outside Debra's front door was a sudden, paralysing concern. While we spoke in her bedroom about her cancer, I frantically texted Mark: 'R U DRIVING THE HEARSE? DON'T COME TO HOUSE. PULL UP ROUND THE CORNER AND TEXT ME IF SO.'

No reply. I took some photos of Debra on her bed and beside it, with and without James in shot. I had another coffee and waited for my phone to buzz in my pocket. Still no reply. I accepted fate and Mark's imminent arrival in his most inexpedient of runabouts. Perhaps it would be best to flag it up to Debra now.

'Um, I've just realised that my friend who's on his way to pick me up might well turn up in, well, turn up in a hearse. I realise that's, um, well, is that okay?'

It was better than okay; Debra was delighted. And disappointingly, Mark rolled up to collect me in his other car: a 1958 Oldsmobile Rocket 88.

Debra, James and I have kept in touch. They have emailed me with their ongoing experiences at my request, and I quote from their correspondence throughout this section. At the time of writing, it is two years later and Debra is still with us, currently fighting off the additional complications of septicaemia and pneumonia.

Her words often echo Philip Gould's. Speaking of living with an impending death, she says:

> As time and my illness have progressed, I now regard a terminal illness as a weird kind of privilege. Unlike the swift, brutal finality of a heart attack or road traffic accident, I have been granted the honour to plan and prepare both myself, and my family, for what is to come.

Gould writes in his book:

> I certainly do not think that a sudden, unexpected death – dropping dead, as they say – would be better than what confronts me. You would lose so much. Of course, it would be nice to avoid confronting death, nice to blunt that sharp edge. And

413

you would avoid a lot of pain, I suppose. But I
think those things are far outweighed by the things
you gain from knowing that you are going to die
and having the chance to act on that knowledge.

I can contrast the experience of Debra and Philip Gould
with that of the mother of a close friend who died recently
of cancer. She, too, was granted this period of reflection
and was able to die at home with her family. But in the
times that I saw her, she had not found this kind of peace.
She seemed to me to be scared of dying right up until the
end. Having met Debra and considered the themes I want
to explore in this chapter, it broke my heart. But when it
came to it, when I held her hand and she told me through
her pain that 'there was nothing I could say', I found she
was right. I could not sit there and explain to her that if
she stared it full in the face then she might find something
rich and good in the time that was left for her. Who was
I to say that? I later sent her husband a link to Gould's film
and thought he could decide whether or not she should
watch it. I don't suppose she did.

Debra, Gould and others who find peace with the
idea of death discover also, in the deepest sense, a good
'story' for themselves. One of the qualities of death is that
it does not bring with it any closure. It does not bring our
lives to an end in the way the last chapter of a novel or the
last scenes of a film wind up the story and give meaning
to the events that have come before. Death does not allow
our lives to come to some sort of fruition. It simply curtails life. It may stop it in its tracks quite suddenly, or we
might be permitted to hear the trundling of its dark carriage from a distance, but it does not complete the story
for us. That's for us to do, if we are given the chance.

Importantly, while the lessons from those like Philip

Gould and Debra are worth making available (through, say, support groups) to those who might benefit, there is a danger of adding to a person's misery by making them feel they are *supposed to* experience a terminal illness in a particular, positive way. The deeply personal question of coming to terms with sweeping metastases is reduced in some quarters to an evangelical slogan of 'Cancer Was The Best Thing That Happened To Me'. Debra has found a positive experience through facing death, but not through 'positive thinking'. We know the damage that such an approach can inflict: when we can't live up to its ideals, we blame ourselves. Barbara Ehrenreich writes in *Bright-Sided*, her treatise against the culture of positive thinking:

> There is a problem when positive thinking 'fails' and the cancer spreads or eludes treatment. Then the patient can only blame herself: she is not being positive enough; possibly it was her negative attitude that brought on the disease in the first place.

She goes on to quote a woman who had written to prominent alternative-medicine advocate Deepak Chopra after her breast cancer had spread to her lungs and bones:

> Even though I follow the treatments, have come a long way in unburdening myself of toxic feelings, have forgiven everyone, changed my lifestyle to include meditation, prayer, proper diet, exercise, and supplements, the cancer keeps coming back. Am I missing a lesson here that it keeps reoccurring? I am positive I am going to beat it, yet it does get harder with each diagnosis to keep a positive attitude.

Without adding to the pain and confusion that arise from the frantic 'unburdening' of 'toxic feelings' and the inevitable self-blame that accompany this kind of positive thinking, might there be an appropriate way to truly reappraise our fear of death? And can we learn from the powerful testimonies of those who face it unflinchingly?

☺

12

After Death

The soul

The nature of any fear you might have regarding death is likely to depend first and foremost upon your religious beliefs. I want to stay with this theme awhile, because such convictions can render further discussion about death redundant. If, for example, you are a Christian and believe you have an immortal soul, you presumably have some confidence that an eternity awaits you after your bodily death. Furthermore, you're fairly confident that this will take place in Heaven, although if you have unwittingly committed a lamentable doctrinal error, your destination may of course turn out to be the flames of Hell. (A point worth pondering, given that the particular branch of Christianity to which you belong will have been largely dictated by when and where and amongst whom you happen to live, and the 'rules' that dictate which of these destinations await you do vary considerably.)

Even if you do believe in the eternity of the soul, this does not disqualify you from having a fear of your earthly death, or from being interested in what we might learn from looking closely at the subject. These are generally compelling subjects regardless of what we believe happens *after* we die. We're going to look at the question of how we should think about death, and why or whether we should fear it, because our relationship to this question has a large impact upon our happiness, particularly in the second half of life. So let's talk about souls for a moment first.

A belief in souls certainly seems like one way of mitigating a fear of death. Should we then believe in them? When it comes to arguments for the existence of such things that we can't really measure or point to or see, we generally have to rely on something called 'inference to the best explanation'. This means that if a defender of souls (or ghosts or other unverifiable entities) wishes to be taken seriously, he has to be able to show that a soul is *the best explanation* for something that already exists (or 'X'). If an X can be found that necessitates the existence of a soul to explain it, then we have a good argument for the existence of souls. A soul (that we can't see) needs to be the *best explanation* for another phenomenon that we *can* see and appreciate.

For example, we can't see radiation as it passes through a piece of chicken at a frequency near 2.45 GHz, absorbing the energy in the poultry's water content. But we can point to the resulting piece of cooked chicken as evidence that our little oven does in fact work through microwaves. Likewise, a believer in souls (a 'dualist') would have to find an X that would *need* a soul to explain why it existed or occurred. Otherwise, there's no clear reason to believe in them, or at least no reason for non-believers to take the notion seriously. Unfortunately for the dualist, these soul-demanding phenomena (Xs), if they exist, are not making themselves evident. Pointing, as some do, to such qualities as creativity, personality, or the fact that we are animated creatures with wishes and desires does not work: these can all be explained without recourse to a soul.

A 'physicalist', in contrast to a dualist, holds that a functioning human being, with his or her brain working properly, contains all that is needed to be a 'person', without recourse to a mysterious soul to explain the things he or she can do. Most of us nowadays are physicalists, and we think of the body as a kind of amazing machine. When all is working as it should, it breathes and walks around and has experiences, but these are all signs that it's functioning properly, rather than evidence of some outside animating force.

But are the physicalists right? If I were a dualist searching for a soul-necessitating X, I would try to find a difference between what a well-functioning machine and an actual *person* can be said to 'experience', and use *that* to support my case. That could be my X. If I can find a clear difference between human experience and that which we can imagine attributing to some super-advanced sci-fi robot, I might have satisfied that criterion of inference to the best explanation and have good evidence for a soul.

We instinctively feel there would be a difference, and there may well be. A thought experiment that the dualist might point to is that of 'Mary's Room', which first appeared in 1982 in an article by Frank Jackson snappily entitled 'Epiphenomenal Qualia'. More recently it was discussed in the terrific AI movie *Ex Machina*, directed by Alex Garland. The scenario to consider is this:

> Mary is a brilliant scientist who is, for whatever reason, forced to investigate the world from a black-and-white room via a black-and-white

television monitor. She specializes in the neuro-physiology of vision and acquires, let us suppose, all the physical information there is to obtain about what goes on when we see ripe tomatoes, or the sky, and use terms like 'red', 'blue', and so on. She discovers, for example, just which wavelength combinations from the sky stimulate the retina, and exactly how this produces via the central nervous system the contraction of the vocal cords and expulsion of air from the lungs that results in the uttering of the sentence 'The sky is blue'. [. . .] What will happen when Mary is released from her black-and-white room or is given a color television monitor? Will she learn anything or not?[147]

Were she to walk out into the real world, and for the first time see colour *for real*, what would change for Mary? What, if anything would have been *added*?

Think about it. The thought experiment proposes that when Mary sees, say, the colour blue for the very first time, she learns something new about it – namely, what blue *looks like*. Or, if you like, what it *feels like* to see blue. This is the *qualitative* aspect of seeing blue. Do you agree? This qualitative aspect, if it exists, cannot come from her *study* of colour, only from her direct perception of it. Prior to stepping out, she already has *all physical knowledge* of colour in place. If she acquires something *new* when she steps out, it must mean that *not all knowledge is physical*. It is argued that if you believe that something is gained by experiencing colour for real, then you are proposing that there is more to being human – and specifically

147 Frank Jackson, 'Epiphenomenal Qualia', *Philosophical Quarterly*, 32: 127–136 (1982)

something non-physical – than an information-processing machine could ever be said to experience.

Thus Mary's room is used as a case against the physicalist. The dualist could point to the *qualitative* aspects of experience as evidence for the soul – as the 'X' that she was searching for. It *feels like* something to have experiences such as seeing colour, being hungry, or falling in love. While a machine might be programmed to carry out the behaviours we associate with desire, it can never feel those qualitative aspects – what desire actually *feels* like. In *Ex Machina*, Ava the humanoid robot understands everything about human experience but of course has no direct apprehension of it herself. She, like Mary at the start of the thought experiment, has never left her room. Are these qualitative aspects of an experience – known as qualia – what separates the 'knowledge' of an amazing machine from that of a human being? And is the existence of the soul the best explanation for these qualia? A computer might 'want' to beat you at poker through its programming, but it is not *feeling* that want. Does the soul-believer have a good case here?

Perhaps, but I'm not immediately convinced. It might mean that our modern 'machine' talk is just a metaphor limited by its time, in the same way that the 'steam engine' language we find in Freud offers an inadequate conceit for understanding the richness of the human mind. Ava might uncannily embody the 'person as machine', but she will still unquestionably be a robot, even if she could be pre-programmed to have these qualia when she steps out into the world. The fact that we can imagine a robot programmed to have qualia muddies the difference necessary for the dualist to preserve: if it's logically possible (i.e. we can imagine it without a contradiction) then, well, it might just be a matter of time and sufficiently advanced technology before machines *can* be said to have qualia. And if they did, would that make them 'as good as' humans? Maybe the machine/man comparison is a red herring.

Meanwhile, the human Mary's situation is more compelling. Does she really learn something new when she steps out? Possibly, but a number of philosophers have argued that she does not. If she were truly possessed with the full extent of physical knowledge of colour, argues the philosopher Daniel Dennett, such knowledge would *include* an understanding of how and why our neurology would give us the experience of qualia. Nothing *new* would be acquired when stepping out. Others have argued that she might gain a new *ability* when seeing a colour for the first time (to recognise it, imagine it or remember it) but that it's not correct to say that she has *learnt* any new knowledge. These intricate counter-arguments support physicalism and undermine the soul-defender's case.

It seems like qualia are certainly a puzzle point, and while they may be used to argue against the physicalist, they don't confidently *support* the existence of a soul either. How, we might ask, does a soul *explain* qualia? Ultimately, introducing the idea of a mysterious spirit doesn't seem to helpfully solve the mystery – it just cloaks one enigma in another.

Why we can't talk of an afterlife

When people talk of souls or the afterlife, they are normally trying to posit a deeper level to existence: that beneath (or above or outside) this world full of things that we can touch and name, there lies a spiritual dimension. This obscured realm would show us how things really 'are', if only we could apprehend it. It reminds us of

Plato's cave, and of how we are only looking at shadows on the wall, while we need guidance to recognise the 'real' dimension that exists behind us.

The positing of a spiritual plane sounds like a symptom of our very human wish that there must be more to this world than the everyday things that make up our lives. We want to be sure that somehow it must all add up and have some meaning not obvious to us now. Many atheists might proudly proclaim that our lives have no ultimate meaning, yet the business of finding significance in one's life is perhaps the most important part of being human. When we drift into a life without meaning, we soon become a pack of symptoms and pathologies; and without any feeling of significance, many choose to end their lives altogether. Meanwhile, the considered life upon which we are reflecting in this book hopes to give some clarity to our relationship with the matter of meaning, by offering criteria for sorting what's important from what is not. Meaning is not to be scoffed at. If we don't find it in some considered form, we commonly look for it in prescribed forms of spirituality. These tend to insufficiently articulate our yearnings, being either dogmatised (religion) or sentimentalised ('New Age' thinking), neither of which serves us or helps us grow.

A moment on this point. Religions sprang from highly charged moments in history that, at the time, connected people with a powerful sense of the transcendent. Certain suffused images spontaneously arose from these original events and gave people a pathway to a deep and vital sense of mystery. A culture would have assembled itself around these symbols and celebrated the force they still held, but over time of course this potency and import were lost. Later, with the original experience long gone from human memory, the culture came to create formal rituals or dogmas in an attempt to offer a symbolic connection to what made it so vibrant at the start. Eventually, the immediate, resonant experience of the transcendent was reduced to a mere *belief* and a set of practices. History was then rewritten and miracles and teachings ascribed to the hero saviour, who, instead of remaining a signpost to the transcendent, became himself the misplaced focus of worship.

The nexus of belief is institutionalised to preserve itself at all costs. Powerful and political, it needs to defend itself against rival faiths and perspectives. It employs fear to maintain its normative authority, and thus reduces and infantilises its followers, instead of doing its original job of connecting them to something large and mysterious. Today, in a scientific age, it is likely to use dubious historical proofs and bad science to make itself appear credible: witness the embarrassing offerings of creationism or pseudoarchaeology.[148]

Meanwhile, the perpetuating dogmas, rituals and images, once so richly symbolic and important, are of course mocked by disbelievers and shown to have no meaning in themselves. As if they were ever supposed to be anything other than pointers to the transcendent. Yet in the meantime these symbols have become forms of idolatry, mistaken by the religious for the *destination*, when they were only intended as *signposts*. 'God' becomes reduced to something with motivations we can have described to us by a pastor every Sunday, to this or that deity who revealed himself here or there. The deep experience of transcendence is lost once it is reduced to words

---

148 Or plain 'Arkeology'. Several expeditions have been led to unearth remains of Noah's Ark atop various mountains in Turkey, with a quite bewildering lack of success.

like 'God' (or for that matter 'transcendent'), let alone when it is personified in our image. What God might have once meant has long disappeared. Nietzsche's famous declaration that 'God is Dead' was lamenting this very issue.

By saying this, I'm making a psychological point: that we can still view spirituality (in regard to having a sense of meaning, and a conscious dialogue with what lies beneath) as an important internal experience, perhaps more important than ever in this age of addiction and distraction. It is an experience that has come to be overlooked since the Enlightenment project began, and which seems entirely disconnected from most of today's religious practices and the honeyed sentiments peddled in New Age bookshops.

I am describing a personal sense of meaning, which is quite different from talk of another realm where we might (or might not) connect with some ultimate truth. Ultimate truth is, I think, a point where many defenders of esoteric knowledge become unstuck. Let's then stay with matters of knowledge for a moment. It will take us to a tantalising conclusion: that there can in fact be no 'afterlife'. If we can challenge or tighten some of these preconceptions around the woollier mysteries of death, we might come to face it more securely.

Here around us is the world of people, tables and chairs: things that we perceive. I know this table is here because I am resting my laptop on it. That's the world I live in and navigate every day. So here I am, in this coffee shop in Swansea, perceiving this table. For me to do this, I know that *something is there that I'm perceiving.* I know this in the same way that I know that if I hear a cuckoo, there is actually a cuckoo somewhere (or at least something making a cuckoo sound). The sound isn't the actual cuckoo. It's just how I perceive that it's there. Likewise, I could smell a pizza and that would point to there being a pizza somewhere nearby. I can *see* and *touch* this table, but the representations I make through these senses are not identical to the table itself. They give me a depiction of the table, but they are not *it*. So, although on a normal day-to-day level, the information given to me by my senses is generally enough to get by, I can also appreciate there is a world *beyond my mere perception* of it.

However hard I looked, there would be more to this table than I could ever perceive. I might look at each square centimetre but there would always be more. That's because I'm surrounded by an infinite data source. I can always look more closely. I could examine every part of it with an electron microscope and still, in theory, I could go closer. I could also look more *widely*: I could use an apparatus that would allow me to perceive further up and down the electromagnetic spectrum than the thin narrow band we happen to look through and call light. A whole new dazzling world would burst into view that I miss every day, given the depleted visual range I am used to.

By this point I would probably be approached by a barista with a walkie-talkie and a calming fleece. But consider what I would be trying to do: I would be trying to perceive what's *actually* there, to get the entire picture. But I'd always, *always* be limited by my perspective. What would it mean to apprehend this table *directly*, outside of my perception? I know from my physics classes that if I looked closely enough, I'd see that it's mainly space and not solid at all. I know that there is something there beyond what I perceive, but I can't imagine what it is, and I would never be able to experience it without at the same time being blinkered by the limitations of my particular viewpoint.

The famed philosopher Immanuel Kant gave this language in the eighteenth century: he said we perceive the *phenomenal* world, with its various familiar phenomena such as tables, and that there is also the *other* level that we know must be there but can't experience: the *noumenal* world. 'Noumenal' comes from 'nous', in the sense of intuition; it describes the world we can intuit but not perceive – what lies beyond the reach of our senses. We can also talk of 'things-in-themselves' occupying this realm, rather than the ordinary 'things' that exist in our perceptions every day.

Now, in order for us to make sense of the day-to-day world that we perceive, we use certain organising language. This language allows us to take the vast array of things and events and form it into something manageable and vaguely predictable. To do this at the most basic level, we use the language of time and space. We say that something happens *after* something else, or that one person is *here* and another is *there*. We talk of *causation*: such and such happened, which made so-and-so react in a certain way. It's important to realise that this kind of language is only a way of describing the relationships between things, helping us edit and make sense (and stories) of what would otherwise be a random and overwhelming barrage of information.

Imagine if you had a mental illness that made it impossible for you to see relationships between things, like some of the patients described in neurologist Oliver Sacks' case studies. You would be unable to organise the world into before/after, here/there, first/second, why/because. Although this might be hard to picture, the fact that we *can* imagine it – or that it even makes sense to try to – confirms the important point that these sorts of relationships are just filters and tools we apply to the world.

They are not qualities *in* the world. If we could get a flash of the noumenal world of things-in-themselves, there would be no before and after, for example. That's because the very notion of time would change. 'Before' and 'After' are just labels we use to organise the things we perceive – they're not really 'out there'. Make sense?

We only perceive one slice of time from moment to moment. There's now . . . and now . . . and now. We treat *before* and *after* as aspects of the real world, whereas they are only bits of organisational *language*. Because of this mistake, we can play mental games that exploit the error. Are you exactly the same person you were when you were a baby? Will you be the same person when you are very old? What about tomorrow? Does it make sense to say that the person who will get out of your side of the bed tomorrow morning is the *same identical person* reading this page now? The fact that these questions can be puzzling hinges on the way we naturally see time (and our identity across time).

As three-dimensional creatures, we have a naturally restricted relationship to time, which exists in the *fourth* dimension. What does that even mean? Bear with me, because by adopting this fourth-dimensional perspective on time, we might not only find solace when we are heartbroken but can also dispel the classic notion of the afterlife. Plus it's a fun and dizzying mind game.

So to get our heads around the limitations of our three-dimensional perspective, let's drop down a level and see what a two-dimensional creature would miss about the world *we* live in. Consider a proposal in 1884 by Edwin A. Abbott in *Flatland: A Romance of Many Dimensions*. These beings live in an entirely 2D world. We can imagine these Flatlanders existing like animated cartoon characters on a thin, flat sheet of paper (a special paper that somehow supports moving pictures). Things have width and length but, like moving drawings, they have no *depth*. The limitations of their horizontal perspective are very clear to us. Now imagine an object from our three-dimensional world, like a balloon, entering Flatland. Picture this real, squidgy 3D object passing through the flat animated surface of the two-dimensional society. See the cartoon characters walking around on the paper and responding to what they see, while we push a real balloon through that wafer-thin surface and out the other side.

What would those Flatlanders perceive? They would not see 'up' and out of the paper and notice the towering balloon descending through their world, because they have no sense of depth, or anything that exists outside of their immediate, two-dimensional world. They would, instead, see a *circle*, starting small, opening up and shrinking again over time, as the balloon passed through the thin single cross-section of experience that made sense to them. The widest part of the balloon would make the largest circle, and its ends would be seen as the smaller ones. There would be no intuitive sense of the balloon as a whole, just a circle that starts small, grows larger and then diminishes again.

Now consider human beings. We live in a *three*-dimensional world. The fourth dimension (our equivalent of the balloon) is *time*; it's the next dimension up from us. So here, then, comes something *temporal* from the fourth dimension: a person's life from infancy to old age. It passes through our world like a balloon. We too, see one slice at a time. We begin by seeing a baby. Further down the line we see a child, later an adolescent: a series of snapshots of a person getting older. One moment of life to the next. If we could perceive the fourth dimension, we wouldn't see those single slices like the circles seen by the Flatlanders; we'd see a kind of wormy-balloony object that encapsulates the whole life in one go. At one end of the worm would be the newborn baby, at the other would be a very old person about to die, or perhaps even a corpse. That space-time worm is the person's life. We look at the toddler on its second birthday and the old man and say they're the same person, even though they look profoundly different. What connects them is a kind of metaphysical glue that keeps all the slices together and makes up the whole worm. With a real earthworm, we can point to different parts of it and know we are talking about the same object. Likewise, the young and old life-stages are in some ways different but also part of the same continuous person. But that four-dimensional worm passes through our three-dimensional world like a balloon passing through Flatland. We see only one slice, at whatever stage we find it.

Thus, if we could perceive things-in-themselves without the fetters of our three-dimensional experience, then time as we know it, in the sense of a series of sequential moments, would very quickly disappear. We would not see one thing happening after another, like circles on Flatland; we would instead be able to see the whole balloon in one go.

Even while we are somewhat limited by our current perspective, the thought game might help us when we find ourselves, for example, at the end of a relationship. It is so easy to see a break-up as the end of the story, whereas of course we are only experiencing one slice of a longer sequence of slices that tell a continuing narrative (one where we perhaps remain friends, reconvene, forgive, grow and learn, or retain a special place in each other's affections). We can mistake one 'now' slice for reality, like the Flatlanders mistaking a circle for a balloon, unaware that there's much more to come.

Once this makes sense, incidentally, we could go further. We are talking about one timeline, one life. What about the fifth dimension? If we included the fifth dimension, we would have to show *other possible* timelines for the same person. Instead of drawing a single worm for your life (which shows your journey from birth to death via the stages of your current life), we'd have to imagine a series of worm-lines coming from a central point like a star, showing all the *other possible lives* you could live. There's one when you become an actor, the one when you become a window cleaner, the one when you die young, and so on. The limitations of the *fourth*-dimensional perspective mean that we only perceive one particular space–time worm of a person's life . . . and as we move up through further dimensions it's just increasingly dizzying and wonderful.

Consider the basic point. Time and space are like filters we apply to the world to make sense of it. They describe the world of objects. This table is *here*, the lady making an espresso is over *there*. I was in my hotel room *before* I came here, I will be on stage soon *after* I leave. The person is an adult *after* he has been a child. We speak from the limitations of our perspective.

Now here's the problem for the idea of an afterlife. When people talk of it, to return to my original point, they are usually trying to articulate that level of reality that corresponds to the *noumenal* world beyond what we merely perceive: that of unknowable *things-in-themselves*. If you ask a person who believes in Heaven *where* precisely it is, or whether it's full of old people, she will most likely assure you that you're trivialising a spiritual existence by trying to make it concrete. Of course, she'll say, Heaven isn't really a place where people stand on clouds wearing togas. Instead, we'd expect her to insist, an afterlife will allow us to finally shed the limitations of human perception and 'experience' the unveiled world of noumenal things-in-themselves directly. The shroud of ordinary reality will be lifted. We will be outside the Matrix and see things as they really are.

But that's the problem. There is no 'after' outside the Matrix. 'After', again, is a word we use to describe how we organise the world of *everyday* things (which are contained inside the Matrix). There can be no 'afterlife', because there is no 'after' once we get into that noumenal world of things-in-themselves. Neither for that matter is there *causation*, so when we talk about 'true' reality it makes no sense to talk of God causing or 'creating' the world that we perceive. All spatial, temporal and causative language ceases to apply. Such words are just organisational terms we use to describe relationships between ordinary things.

If we are to talk of existing in any sense *after* we die, then the best we can do is to extend our sense of self – our space-time worm – to continue beyond the grave and incorporate how the atoms of our decomposing bodies feed into continuing life after we have breathed our last. Then we might say we have some sort of continuing existence. But this is unlikely to be meaningful to us, and certainly no consolation in the face of a fear of death. There is no sense here that our *personhood* has survived. Defenders of the afterlife want to have it both ways: on the one hand, they wish to describe a fundamental reality that operates beneath the everyday world we perceive. On the other, they wish to retain the everyday world's organisational language (and use ideas such as 'after') to describe it, as if such spatial or temporal concepts have any relevance to the world *beyond* what we perceive through space and time.

I've spent some time on this quite technical subject, mainly because I find it fascinating but also so that I can now continue without worrying about what comes after death. In any meaningful sense, and with all the finality I described at the start of this chapter, death brings us to an absolute end. Even if you maintain that we continue in some form afterwards, certainly life as you know it will be curtailed by your death. So should we fear this end?

☺

13

Fearing Death

We are frightened of things that we believe could cause us harm in some way. It may sound a mad question, but is death actually one of those things? Thomas Nagel, a modern philosopher, writes that we tend to have one of two views in reaction to this question: 'Either [death] is the worst thing for us as it denies us the one thing we have, or [it's] a symptom of confusion to say it's bad.'[149] Which is right? Is it the most natural and rational thing in the world to be afraid of death, or does it make no sense to fear it?

Most of us would instinctively feel it makes sense to be scared of our demise. Certainly we find ourselves with a convincing evolutionary prerogative to try to avoid it. Even someone who insists that death should not be feared is likely to jump out of the way if a car comes hurtling towards him.

The fear of death can make itself known in many ways. It may be overt at any time in life, leaving us with

149 Thomas Nagel, *Mortal Questions*

a sense of pointlessness that we cannot shake off. An older parent recovers from a stroke but we find that this first real confrontation with mortality leaves them bewilderingly resentful of their family. Or it can leak out into such things as an obsession with cosmetic surgery, a frantic chasing after youth, or even an anxiety regarding one's children growing up and becoming independent. We might come to feel with some panic that our lives are passing by unlived. Plenty of people, as they grow older, come to dread birthdays, school reunions and important anniversaries. For many, the murky waters of their impermanence can bubble and stir into a source of deep anxiety, while others barely give it a thought until old age.

And then, in one or another of its myriad forms, we will meet death: a progressive illness, a sudden accident, a quiet slipping away during a still night, or a slow mental deterioration that rids us of our personhood long before it finally brings our body to a grinding halt. We do not fear *that* we're going to die, not in the same way we might fear that we're going to get mugged if we walk down a sinister alley. Death is *definitely* going to happen. The fear we're discussing is more like a dread: that which accompanies the anticipation of something unwanted we know *will* happen to us.

Yet two arguments have endured through a couple of thousand years of Western philosophy, urging us to shed our fear of death. For those who accept one or both of them, it would appear that anyone else who worries about their own death is merely confused and falls into Nagel's second category. Is there anything to these arguments? Can they help us be happier? Why should we not fear what seems most natural to dread?

You won't be there when it happens

Our first argument against fearing death comes from Epicurus. We have of course met him already: he taught the simple life of relaxed pleasure and encouraged his followers to retreat from the troubles of the world. Where the Stoics took seriously a sense of duty and their role as citizens, the Epicureans chose to ignore any such pressures and define their own place for themselves at the periphery of society. Epicurus, you might remember, was also an atomist, one of the first to scoff at the notion of the afterlife, to insist there is no reason to fear the gods, and believe that we are made of swirling particles of matter and no more. His approach to death stems less from his attitude towards pleasure and more from this no-nonsense sense of our physicality. Here are the all-important words:

> So death, the most terrifying of ills, is nothing to us, since so long as we exist, death is not with us; but when death comes, then we do not exist. It does not concern either the living or the dead, since for the former it is not, and the latter are no more.[150]

While his words may not ring crystal clear, the message seems to be straightforward enough: death can't be bad for us, because we won't be around to experience it when it happens. By the time it comes, we are by definition unable to have *any* sort of experience, let alone a bad one.

Epicurus is pointing out to us a common mistake he thinks we make: that we tend to imagine ourselves as dead (rotting in the ground and so on) and feel fear or

150 Epicurus, *Letter to Menoeceus*

revulsion. But he says this is a silly error: we will have neither that experience of decomposition, nor of the flames of the crematorium. By the time it happens, we simply won't exist. We won't exist any more than Jessica, which was the name held in reserve if my younger brother had turned out to be a girl when he was born. If he had emerged as my baby *sister*, he'd have been Jessica ever since and not the Dominic I know and love and made eat a teabag when he was a toddler for fifty pence and then never paid him. Jessica Brown never existed. Should we feel sorry for her? No. She exists no more than you will after you die. It makes no sense to attribute to her any sort of experience. Of course she *never* existed, but that's neither here nor there. You will be non-existent to just the same extent as Jessica once you are dead. Non-existence can't be bad for you any more than it's bad for Jessica. So what on earth is there to fear?

We have all had experience of a kind of non-existence. Every night when we sleep deeply, we could be said to cease having any sense of personhood. Although our bodies continue some level of fundamental functioning, we might as well be dead as far as our on-going *experience* goes. The idea of a profound, dreamless sleep does not scare us. If we knew that everyone was going to go to sleep for a year and that we'd all wake up well and happy and free from bedsores, would we be scared of doing so? We'd have no obvious reason to feel fear. What if, then, we could sleep profoundly and dreamlessly for a trillion years and awaken with the brightest of eyes and bushiest of tails, the same age we were when we got into bed, with *nothing having changed*? All else being equal, there would be no reason to dread this happening; in fact, those of us who tour or have infant children might even welcome it. The trillion-year period of non-existence would make little difference to us; our concerns would only revolve around the conditions to which we would awaken. If you have objections to my suggestion that this trillion-year slumber wouldn't bother you, you are probably bothered by variables other than the sleep itself.

If this were a book designed merely to make us feel better about death, we might leave it there. But the argument is not entirely satisfying, is it? And I think it's worth getting to the heart of why it isn't quite right, because if we look deeper, we'll get richer answers: a sense of what it is about death that does disturb us, and therefore what we should learn to face. Such notions might permeate to the heart of our lives and our approach to happiness, rather than just serve as clever ideas that feel as if we're being tricked into believing something.

The first thought that might occur to you – as it always does to me – is something along the lines of, 'Okay, it's not death per se that bothers me, it's the process of dying. And that certainly can be a very unpleasant experience.' That's a sensible response. But if we pause there, does such an objection entirely do away with Epicurus's point? After all, the idea of dying makes no sense unless we presume that death will happen at the end of it. That's what dying is. So we may insist that it's the *dying* we fear, but would we really fear it if we knew we would emerge alive and well at the end? If not, aren't we then still talking about a fear of death itself?

So this common objection to Epicurus is not quite enough to undo his argument. Instead, to know whether he's right, we have to look more deeply at his line of logic. Something is only bad for you if you *exist*, he is implying, and when you are dead you don't exist. Therefore death isn't bad for you.

So we know something can't be bad for you if you've

never existed, like Jessica Brown. But what if you *have existed* at some time? This seems to be the key point. Imagine the death of a young girl. Surely it *would* make sense to say that the 'premature' death was bad for her. We would call it tragic. It would surely make sense to say her life would have been *better for her* had she lived to be eighty. Not just better for us in terms of how we would feel about her death but actually better for *her*. So dying young would constitute a harm. Even if she had lived until seventy, it would still, most likely, be *better for her* to live another ten years.

How is it bad for her if she's not around to experience being dead? Perhaps it's not enough just to say that a thing is harmful, we also need to say *when* it is. Epicurus is saying that death and the harm it's supposed to cause would have to happen at the same time. For this girl's early death to be bad for her, we have to allow for the harm of death to happen *while she's alive*.

Thomas Nagel picks up this argument as a response to Epicurus and asks whether we can have harm occur at a *different* time from the experience of it. If we can find examples of being harmed *without having a bad experience at the time*, then we can reject Epicurus's logic (which presumes they have to happen simultaneously). And if we can reject that logic, we can accept that there *is* something to fear about death, and in isolating it, learn how to face it squarely.

Imagine your long-term partner has been secretly cheating on you for the last five years. Worse, all your friends know about this ongoing infidelity and regularly get together with this partner of yours to joke about it and laugh at your expense. Now, no one has ever told you about any of this; in fact, imagine for the sake of argument that measures have been in place that made it impossible for you to have ever found out. It seems fair to say that harm has been happening to you for those five years, *even though you have been oblivious to it*. Now today, after five years, you suddenly find out. You now suffer the devastating experience of realising you have been not only cheated on but also been made a figure of ridicule. Would we say that the harm only occurs *today*, at this point of discovery? Surely it's better to say that you have discovered an *already* bad situation, not that the situation is bad *because* you have discovered it?

Nagel gives his example of betrayal as a harm done at a *different* time from the experience of it. The harm was done during those five years, even though you were blindly ignorant of the harm being done. This example is enough to make us question the seeming straightforwardness of Epicurus's argument. It's an objective idea of harm; it's as if a committee of people have been given all the facts and made the decision that, yes, harm has been done to you, even if you're not aware of it.

I don't think this has to be the full story: there is also the subjective view. If I don't *feel* harm, because I am ignorant of it, then how am I suffering it?

Perhaps the question of reputation helps us bring these two different models together and find some clarity. In the case of the five-year betrayal, which is carried out to the delight of your friends, of course harm is done to your reputation. Likewise, if lies are spread about you and are widely believed, then the 'you' is harmed in the sense that other people's image of 'you' has been damaged. But I would say there's an important difference between the sum of associations that people attach to their idea of you, the reader, and the 'actual' you that is now absorbing these words. This might betray my Stoic leanings, but surely the key factor is your attitude. If, upon discovery of the five-year betrayal, your reaction was not to feel devastated but to feel genuine amusement, or even relief, then were you really ever harmed? Does it really make sense to talk of harm occurring to you over the previous five years if you don't even experience it as negative when you find out?

These are subjective considerations, and they hinge on attitudinal differences. We are surely not our reputations. Our reputations are not in us; they are stories sustained in the minds of other people. When people fail to distinguish between who they are and their reputations, we make fun of them, saying they 'believe their own bullshit'. We intuit an important difference between the two. So I'm not convinced it's enough to hold up the ruining of a reputation (when the subject is unaware of it) as proof that we can be harmed without having a bad experience. The part that determines whether or not a thing is harmful seems to be the person's choice of attitude towards it, not the objective fact that the damage has occurred.

So although Nagel's objection is a good one for illustrating that Epicurus might be missing something, I'm not entirely convinced by Nagel either. My approach towards understanding unhappiness in life clearly tends towards the subjective, and thus I'd repeat Hamlet's maxim that a thing is good or bad only in as much as thinking makes it so. Nagel might insist that harm *was* objectively done, and the cuckolded victim has merely adopted a Stoic approach to distance himself from said harm, but harm it was. I'd say that the harm was only to his reputation, not to himself. An interesting alternative example would be to consider a worker who has been exposed to asbestos for years, unaware that it has been damaging his lungs. Eventually he is diagnosed with a terminal illness, but we would speak of the harm having already happened during the time that he was oblivious to the fact.

And as regards the child's early death, I think there is another way to understand why we want to say that it would be bad for her at such a young age, irrespective of her subjective experience. I'll discuss it in a moment, but first let's assess the second, classic Epicurean argument against the fear of death.

You've already been there

Lucretius, the Roman poet who brought Epicurus's ideas to his later audience, articulates this argument. He builds upon Epicurus's argument that death isn't bad for us precisely because we won't exist when it happens. Perhaps, then, with his new and improved version, he can give us good reason to not worry about our inevitable endings.

To understand the point of Lucretius's argument, imagine you know you are due to have a certain unusual experience, which we'll call *The Thing*. You know that *The Thing* is going to happen soon, and you find yourself nervous, unsure whether it's something to be worried about. Then you realise you've already experienced *The Thing* in the past. It's happened before and it was absolutely fine. *The Thing*, now you come to think about it, is something you've *never* had any bad feelings about, and when it did happen before, it caused you no problems at all. So, given all this, would it make any sense to be scared of the fact that you're going to have the experience of *The Thing* again? Clearly that would not seem to be a rational response. Even if you felt nervous about it, surely the knowledge that you've experienced it before quite happily should greatly mitigate your worries?

Lucretius says that the eternal non-existence of death is something we've already been through. It happened *before we were born*. We've been in the eternal abyss once before, and we don't feel any regret about it. So why fear returning?

This is known as the *symmetry argument*. What 'happens to us' after death symmetrically reflects what 'happened to us' before birth. Some examples come to mind that support Lucretius's point. If I think about going for a run, and find myself dreading the idea, it is helpful to have had previous experience of running that I can remember as positive, or at least *not* negative. I can't say that I have such pleasant memories of running myself (unless groin strain and self-hatred can be cited as plusses), but the idea holds.

Yet, rather like the earlier Epicurean point that you won't be around to experience death when it happens, Lucretius's symmetry argument is somehow not entirely satisfying. Few of us are likely to throw up our hands, roll our eyes and cry 'Of course!' vowing never again to consider death a negative. It might have some therapeutic value, of course, in the way that Epicurus's argument also reminds us at least that the state of *being* dead is not in itself something to be terrified of. And we shouldn't forget the important therapeutic underpinnings of Hellenistic philosophy: they were exercises to help us live well. The spirit of this kind of philosophy can be lost when an argument is pulled apart and every weak point highlighted. But in as much as they purport to show *rational* reasons not to fear death, we are allowed to respond by reaching for the cool clean scalpel of logic.

We looked at Epicurus's argument and what might be wrong with it. We're going to do the same with Lucretius, because I believe that he will unintentionally lead us to an understanding of why it *does* make sense to see death as a negative and, in doing so, make adjustments in our lives to increase our happiness.

If Epicurus's argument rests on the questionable but key presumption that harm and the experience of it have to happen simultaneously, Lucretius is taking as a given the idea that we treat the past and the future *in similar ways*. In other words, his argument only holds if we think of our previous negative experiences the same way we think of those yet to come. In our example of being reluctant to go for a run, the past might reliably inform our future. But is that the whole story?

It is one of the tasks of the philosopher to dig for examples to show that a presumption doesn't quite hold, and it is particularly useful in this case where again we probably feel that something isn't quite right. The modern philosopher Derek Parfit has found a good example that shows why the presumption of the symmetry argument is flawed.

Imagine that there is a horrendous operation that you have to undergo. It's particularly bad because it has to be carried out without anaesthetic, and it involves cutting into the most painful areas of the body. And it lasts for ten excruciating hours. Ten long hours of the most extreme, relentless torture. However, at the end, you are given a special pill that creates total amnesia for the operation: you won't remember any of it when it's over.

So you go to the hospital on Tuesday morning. The procedure is due to happen either that evening or on Wednesday afternoon, you don't know which.

Now mentally cut forward to Wednesday morning. You wake up, and as you look around the ward, you suddenly ask yourself: 'Did I have the operation last night?' Of course the pill would have removed your memory of it. You check your body for signs of the operation, but then remember the doctors telling you there'd be no sign of any procedure having happened. You have no way of knowing whether it's already happened (in which case the amnesia pill has caused you to forget it as expected) or whether you are still due to have the operation later that day. You ask a nurse to go and check your records and let you know.

As you lie in the bed awaiting her return, do you find yourself wishing the terrible operation has already happened, or would you prefer that it is yet to come? Presumably, if you have given this a moment's thought, you hope the operation is already over, that you've taken the amnesia pill and forgotten the whole painful business. The thought of still having to go through the ten hours of agony is horrible. In other words, we feel very differently about pain that has happened *in the past* and pain that is *yet to come*. Pain we prefer to be behind us, and positive experiences in our future. We have a certain 'future bias' that means we care more about what's yet to happen. An abyss of nothingness ahead of us, then, is *not the same to us* as one that's been and gone in the past.

And this bias is a good argument against Lucretius. His symmetry fails if past and future should not be treated the same. Our bias that wants anything bad to be in the past leads us to a good reason as to why it *is* rational after all to feel that death is a bad thing. And this reason holds an important key, I think, to how we might enhance our time while we're alive and well.

Death as deprivation

We have already spoken of the loss of the past when we die: Milan Kundera spoke of it as the source of our fear.

But now we have started to look at the loss of the future. We were non-existent for an eternity before we were born. We will likewise be non-existent for an eternity after we die. Yet they are not *psychologically* the same, because we feel and think differently about the future than we do about the past. And as we compare these pre-natal and post-mortem abysses, we will get a clearer grasp of why we do fear death. Armed with that information, it will be clear to us what we can do to minimise that fear and change our relationship with this pervasively ominous spectre.

We are creatures of desire. We engage in our world in such a way that means we are constantly involved in *projects*. That project might be to write a book, to raise a family, to see our grandchildren grow up, to watch a television series, to lose weight or just get food from the fridge because we're hungry. These projects point us towards the future. Death deprives us of seeing our projects come to some sort of fruition, and of engaging in fresh ones. Debra is unlikely to see James qualify as a medic, or meet her grandchildren. She cites such things as the most difficult parts of facing death. Yet even if her grandchildren had been born, it would doubtless be very hard to know she would never see them grow up.

For this reason, we are particularly sad when a star dies young or when their life or career seems to be on an upward trajectory. The death of a child, like the girl who dies young, is to us particularly horrendous because of the vast expanse of life and experience it wipes out so brutally.

Lucretius is trying to answer the deprivation account of death by pointing out that we don't feel deprived of the time we could have lived *before* we were born. But here is a difference: the deprivation that comes with death is something we can *imagine*. We know what we're being deprived of: grandchildren, our home, our loving relationships, even that sense of *I* that enjoys those things. It stings in a way that the prenatal abyss does not.

It's hard for us to imagine what our lives would have been like if we had been born earlier. If on the other hand we imagine dying *later*, we picture ourselves having a longer life and have a rough idea of what that might entail. Death deprives us of the benefit of those future years we can easily imagine, whereas we don't feel that prenatal non-existence dispossesses us of good in the same way. An answer to Lucretius, then, is to point to *deprivation*; it undoes his presumption of symmetry.

Or, well, at least it seems to. The trouble with a psychological answer (that we care more about the future than the past and prefer pain to happen securely in the latter) is that Lucretius can simply reply that we are *wrong* to feel that way, pointing again at his same argument. Our disagreement after all is not based on some deep metaphysics of time that undoes his thinking; we are merely stating that we tend to *feel* differently about the future than the past. Which may not be the best way of answering someone who is pointing out that those *very feelings* about death are misleading. Lucretius might say, 'Exactly – that's my point. Your point about deprivation is just another way of describing the fear of death. *My* point is that you have no reason to feel those things. Accept my symmetry argument and you'll see that your fears or worries about deprivation are unfounded.' Perhaps, then, it's unfair to say Lucretius's argument has been thwarted and better to admit that it still remains something of a puzzle for us. But the deprivation account is important, for it seems to clarify why we feel negatively about death.

We might also use the deprivation account to undo

Epicurus's point that death cannot harm us because when it happens it's too late for us to experience anything. It *can* harm us while we are alive, because we wish to continue our projects and extend our engagements into a continuing future, and death *thwarts those desires*. If you are ravenous and someone cruelly destroys all the food to which you have access, that person is causing you harm. So the deprivation inherent in death both harms us while we are alive (by obstructing what we would wish for in the future) and certainly weighs in far more heavily against any sense of being deprived of anything before we were born.

Although we're talking rather philosophically and at length about these aspects of death, we are arriving at something important. When we understand what we fear, we can untangle that fear and are more likely to be released from it. If the key to why we fear death is that it deprives us of furthering our projects and seeing them to completion, we might find some value in reassessing how much we value the completion of those projects.

Thus this discussion gives us the key to building answers we can incorporate into life, so that we might live (and die) more happily. So if deprivation is the key, let's consider first what would happen if there were *no* deprivation to worry about. What if we lived for ever?

A circle without a circumference

What if there were no deprivation and no death? If death is so bad because it deprives us of further life, does it follow that removing it entirely must be better? What would immortality mean for us?

Let's imagine that unlike the unfortunate Struldbrugs that Gulliver meets on his travels, who grow ever older and more decrepit into eternity, we can halt our ageing at any point we like. We can inhabit the healthy bodies of our young selves whilst continuing to learn and develop emotionally. Surely under such conditions, with death having been shown to be a bad thing, it must follow that we would be better off without it?

I've mentioned that Thomas Nagel argues *against* Lucretius, saying that our death *is* a bad thing, for all the reasons of future bias and deprivation I've mentioned. In response to Nagel, another modern philosopher, Bernard Williams, takes up the challenge to show that the *absence* of death would be utterly unbearable. In his 1976 essay 'The Makropulos Case: Reflections on the Tedium of Immortality', he takes the example of a fictitious character Elina Makropulos who secures immortality at the sustained age of forty-two after drinking a magical elixir. Three hundred years later, 'her unending life has come to a state of boredom, indifference and coldness. Everything is joyless.' Eventually she refuses to drink the elixir again and dies.

Still, my first inclination is to delight in the idea of the life indefinitely extended. I would have endless time to love, to pursue interests, to try different careers, to imbibe the endless delights of human life and possibility. I'd be a sort of vampire figure, and that appeals, especially if I could be one of the really hot ones (which I would be). And most of us would feel the same. If we like the idea of playing the piano, we could look forward to becoming master pianists. We would have all the time to learn how to play better than the greatest concert pianists we know today (remember we are dealing with *infinite* time, so, yes, we would absolutely, eventually, be able to achieve the position of Best Pianist In The World). We could read, learn and understand everything about the universe, and

satisfy every craving and curiosity we could ever have. Plus, unable to die, we would automatically be immune from any life-threatening harm or illness. We could never be killed (and neither could we kill, if we grant everyone else the same immortality). We could, given the sheer amount of endless time ahead of us, possess anything (or for that matter *anyone*) we could ever hope to. If you doubt how immortality would guarantee these achievements, consider the implications of eternity: eventually, without any effort on your part, *every possible situation* would occur. So at some point you'd eventually become the best pianist in the world even if you thought you had no interest in the piano . . .

This is a dizzying thought. The Argentine author Jorge Luis Borges vividly describes a mystical library in his story 'The Library of Babel'. It contains a vast number of interlinked hexagonal rooms, each lined with books. Now imagine this: each of these books contains 410 pages and together they bear *every possible random permutation* of alphabet characters and basic punctuation. Thus, the library contains, of course, mainly nonsense, but the inhabitants of the library are convinced that there is mysterious meaning in those pages, especially when they come across phrases or words that have arbitrarily fallen into place amongst the random combinations of letters.

The implications of such a library are fascinating. Consider what it means to have housed there every possible sequence of characters. Every book ever written, and every book that could *ever be* written, will be included there somewhere. Which means that *your autobiography* will be found on the shelves, along with the book that correctly predicts how you will die (as well as the book that tells you the steps to take to avoid that particular death). Of course, despite such information being occasionally and accidentally present in the library, the result of the almost endless random concoctions is only uselessness and despair. Cults spring up, and throughout history, sections of the library are destroyed by groups such as the 'Purifiers' who wish to rid the library of what they deem to be nonsense. Others believe that a book must exist somewhere on the shelves that contains the key to understanding the collection's contents, and they search for the messianic 'Man of the Book' who will have read it and can unlock the library's secrets.

Aside from the satisfying analogy to our search for mystical meaning amidst an arbitrary and meaningless universe, the joy of first reading the story comes from the vertiginous thought experiment proposed by the library's collection. Interestingly, the library is not infinite: the collection is limited to what arbitrary permutations can be contained within each book of a limited 410 pages. This perhaps suggests there is a point where everything that could happen in history will have been written. But again, the library is meaningless: when *every* permutation appears, it might as well contain nothing. The same conclusion is reached when we consider our immortality. When we know that we will come to experience every permutation of happpenstance (or near enough if we consider even a lifespan of a mere trillion years), and when *everything* that can happen eventually will, then that life starts to look strangely empty and pointless.

We do not have to look hard to see why any initial enthusiasm for the immortal life is misguided. True, our current projects and engagements could be fulfilled, even beyond our wildest dreams. We might relish becoming a successful and highly gifted concert pianist. Perhaps, if we are lucky, the joy we derive from the activity might last several decades. We could travel the world, enjoying public acclaim and all the deeper rewards of a period of time spent doing something we love. Eventually, however, that pleasure would have to cease. Fame would no longer excite us, and our enthusiasm would wane. We'd have played all the pieces that we enjoy and would lack the drive to seek out new ones. The lifestyle of the pianist would grow dull. We would start a new hobby. That could burgeon into a new career. And likewise in time, despite much success and enjoyment, we would become bored of that too, and switch focus to yet another. After a while, the very idea of starting a new project that we know will eventually bore us would lose its appeal. Even if it took a few hundred years to reach this point, this is barely the blink of an eye for someone who is to live *forever*. Then, in another perfunctory flicker of time, we'd find ourselves becoming a concert pianist again – life would have to repeat itself eventually, again and again, because time is never-ending for us. We would soon be unable to summon interest in what the world has to offer, like a child stuck for too long in a playroom with a bunch of toys he's played with before.

How many times would we have to fall in love before the prospect of yet another attachment filled us with tedium? How many friends would come and go before the very idea of making any social effort seemed pointless? When would we stop bothering?

I think there are two principal reasons why this overarching sense of futility would emerge. Firstly, because after a relatively short while we could look *back* and know that whatever we're facing has happened to us previously. Nothing would be new; everything would have come before. Without the surprise of novelty in our lives, there would be nothing to engage our interest.

The other reason is, I think, more interesting, and is

of use to us as we consider the question of happiness in our ordinary, mortal lives. We would not just look back and feel the dead weight of over-familiarity. Something in us, conscious or otherwise, would look *forward* and find that without the framework provided by precious finite time, *all engagements would be fruitless.*

What makes love so compelling? The fact that this is the one, short life we have and that we might spend a large part of it with this other person. That here is someone to cling to and grow with for our allotted lifespan. Here we are, broken and fraught in our own way, loving another who is broken and fraught in theirs, and who happens to love us too. But if we knew we were to have endless loves for eternity, there would be no reason to feel excited about *this* one. Love is a risk: we attach ourselves to someone and they to us, and we face the world together. Without death, any sense of urgency is lost; whether it be the urgency of love, piano playing or any pursuit we value. The very word 'pursuit' reveals the key to its appeal: it involves a chase and therefore a risk of failure. We may not reach what we are pursuing, it might not work out for us, we may not be any good, we might be wasting our money or our time. This risk, however slight, provides us with an important impetus and a feeling of intensity. Such feelings are important in life. They keep us engaged and tell us how we should value something. But what would risk mean to us if we were immortal? What could we risk? We can't risk *wasting our time*, as we have an eternity ahead of us. We can't risk death or, therefore, even injury, as they mean nothing to us. Therefore courage would be absent in our eternal lives. Failure would mean nothing, as we would find success again soon enough. We could master our craft, forget all our skills and then master it again a thousand times if we wished.

The philosopher Martha Nussbaum puts it like this:

> In general, the intensity and dedication with which
> very many human activities are pursued cannot be
> explained without reference to the awareness that
> our opportunities are finite, that we cannot choose
> these activities indefinitely many times. In raising a
> child, in cherishing a lover, in performing a
> demanding task of work or thought or artistic cre-
> ation, we are aware, at some level, of the thought
> that each of these efforts is structured and con-
> strained by finite time.[151]

Without any interests or engagements to define us, we
would presumably lose our sense of identity: we would
have nothing to separate us from others and give *our* life
its particular flavour. This is the inevitable consequence of
the unfathomable boredom that immortality would
impose on us. Everything worthwhile in your life draws
its meaning from the fact you will die. We need death in
order to live. 'The meaning of life,' wrote Kafka, re-
putedly, 'is that it stops.'

Rasputin, my Blue Quaker parakeet, would do better
than me if we both drank of the elixir of eternal life. His
plans do not extend beyond doing what is necessary to
steal a prawn from my lunch plate or a left-arrow cursor
key from the keyboard of my computer. Once he has
secured the miniature booty, he flies to his perch and
seems satisfied, until he realises he doesn't like prawns or
removable bits of keyboard and drops them behind the
radiator. It is easy enough to imagine similar creatures
that could remain so engaged in the present moment that

151 Martha Nussbaum, *The Therapy of Desire*

an eternity would remain compelling for them. But we're not made like that. Our engagements, rooted in the future, are part of our identity. If we had to exist as primitively and short-sightedly as a bird (and birds are very bright) in order to find immortality bearable, then we wouldn't be *us*, and we would have once again reached a point where this endless life has been stripped of meaning. Nussbaum points out that while we might find some sources of value in an immortal existence, 'its constructive conditions would be so entirely different from ours that we cannot really imagine what they would be'.[152] Todd May describes this in his book *Death*:

> For humans, an immortal life would be shapeless. It would be without borders or contours. Its colour would fade, and we could anticipate the fading from the outset. An immortal life would be impossible to make *my* life, or *your* life. Because it would drag on endlessly, it would, sooner or later, just be a string of events lacking all form. It would be impossible to distinguish background from foreground.

'A life without temporal boundaries,' writes the philosopher Samuel Scheffler, 'would be no more a life than a circle without a circumference would be a circle.'

Whichever route we take, we have arrived at a contradictory conclusion: death *is* harmful for us, but it is to be preferred in the face of its alternative: immortality. How can that make sense, other than to merely cast an inexorable doom over our lives? If we look into this seeming contradiction a little deeper, something positive

152 Martha Nussbaum, *The Therapy of Desire*

emerges from the balancing of these two statements.

Firstly, that immortality would be bad for us is a *fact*. There seems no way round that. The only way to retain an attitude of anything other than profound resignation in the face of utter meaninglessness would be to be stripped of all the qualities of engagement that make us human.

In the case of death, though, the subjectivity of harm is more apparent. Death is harmful *if* it thwarts our desires. But to what extent we *experience* it as harm depends on how attached we are to those desires. It harms us in that it deprives us of future life. But is that deprivation still harmful if we are *happy* to forego the future? While these harm-mitigating attitudes might be beyond the emotional reach of most of us (they are immediately recognisable as the qualities of the Stoic sage), we can certainly *imagine* a person having them. An anxiety-free attitude to one's eventual death seems to be logically possible (i.e. a notion we can coherently entertain) in a way that a meaningful immortal life does not seem to be. The harm of deprivation is subjective, the boredom of the immortal life is most likely not. So I would say that the scales tip slowly but definitely to one side: as long as we accept that we can harness our attitudes, death might not only lose its horror but balance out as a positive.

That conclusion may seem perverse, and of little comfort to someone who has lost a loved one or is herself caught in a miserable, painful death. Perhaps it is a meaningless conclusion, falling prey to the futility of what Scheffler calls 'metaphysics fighting fear'.

If it is of little help, it is because there is a difference between death being necessary or positive in the abstract, and feeling remotely positive for *us, now*, when it happens. There are all sorts of reasons why it's good *we* die: if not, the Earth would become impossibly overpopulated and immortality, as we have seen, would be unbearable. We may realise that death is good for us, but we don't ever want it when it comes: it almost always comes too soon. We can, if we step suitably far back, hang on to the idea that death is a positive, but when we reject that idea and find it horrible, we are almost certainly focusing on a particular concrete case that is known to us.

Now, I think I would also say that although we don't wish to die, we don't generally wish for immortality either. The either/or scenario is probably unfair. Bernard Williams (who showed us the tedium of immortality) criticises Nagel's conclusion that death must be bad by decrying its alternative, but perhaps he is constructing a straw man. Immortality may be the antithesis to death in the abstract, but it's not what we seek when we fear our own demise. We may be happy to die eventually, just not *now*. The famed French author Simone de Beauvoir wrote: 'There is no such thing as a natural death . . . all men must die: but for every man his death is an accident and, even if he knows it and consents to it, an unjustifiable violation.'[153]

So not *now*. Not for me. When, then? *Later.* Of course, that date never comes. It normally takes extreme circumstances in a person's life for him or her to be happy to die at a certain time. Sometimes a person might commit suicide when life becomes unbearable. Such an act might result from tragic desperation or it might be the product of clear-minded thinking. The late psychology professor Sandy Bem, for example, after finding out she had Alzheimer's resolved to take her own life when she reached a certain point in her mental decline. An

153 Simone de Beauvoir, *A Very Easy Death*

extraordinary 2015 *New York Times Magazine* article by Robin Marantz Henig tells her story and details the deeply touching business of how she was able to remain committed to her decision and make the necessary arrangements with her family to carry out her own death in a peaceful way. But such cases are rare.

For most of us, we expect this cry of 'Just not now', with its accompanying sense of unjustifiable violation, to become more urgent when the time approaches. We don't want it to arrive, although we have spent our lives needing it to happen, to provide our life with meaning, to provide a circumference to our circle.

Is there an escape route from this quandary at the personal, practical level? I think there is.

Freud's flower

The finite boundary death imposes on us provides fundamental meaning and structure to our daily endeavours. It makes us human. The very notion of transience is fundamental to human experience. Yet death seems bad for us because it deprives us of what we instinctively want: permanence. We want to extend our projects into the future, at least for now, at least until this or that is completed, and so on for as long as we take interest in anything we do. Yet the very fuel that gives those projects their impetus is the fact that they must end at some point. If we are looking for a therapeutic answer, we find it: *embrace transience* rather than fight it.

Epictetus suggested we bring to mind, as we kiss our daughter goodnight, that she might not be alive in the morning. What sounds at first like a morbid idea soon reveals its power as we consider it. By reminding ourselves that our loved ones are not immortal, and that they might be taken from us at any point, we not only mitigate the shock if and when they do die, but *we remember to value them more in the present*. We cannot take anything for granted when we consider that it will eventually cease to exist. How often do parents nostalgically reflect on their children when they were younger? It is easy to look at photographs and miss those cute, plump-faced, miniature versions of the gawky and resentful specimens they have become. How much more difficult it is to routinely take stock when they are infants or toddlers, to think, 'This is a special time. Here you are now. You will never be this age again.' When parents do this, they realise that the appeal and power of the moment is the fact that it will never return. Each period of a child's life, as it zips by at disarming speed, is likely to feel extraordinarily precious to a parent, and the fact each age will never be revisited makes it more significant. Things would feel different if we knew our children would *never* grow up. Surely it is the potential for future life and growth that we see in their wide, unabashed eyes that forms a substantial part of the magic?

Transience also opens the way to melancholy: a rich aspect of our experience that offers up a peculiar form of beauty. Melancholy is caught up with the passing of time, nostalgia, and a knowledge that all things must end. The Slovenian philosopher Slavoj Žižek cites melancholy as the starting point of philosophy: without disappointment we would have no reason to enquire or try to improve.

Music is perhaps the most obvious vessel for this melancholy richness, because music (unlike a painting) is inseparable from transience, in that it moves through time. Where the myriad distractions and addictions of life offer us pleasure and short-term happiness, melancholy gives sadness a place to comfortably sit. J. S. Bach's Cello

Suites, the *Aria* from the Goldberg Variations and the
'Erbarme Dich' from his *St Matthew Passion*; Chopin's
Nocturnes; Messiaen's *Quatour pour la Fin de Temps*;
Górecki's Third Symphony – composers have always
nourished the interlacing of beauty and sadness. Lyrics
only add more melancholy content: Richard Strauss's
'Morgen' and the *Vier Letzte Lieder*; Tom Waits' *Closing
Time* and the songs of Rufus Wainwright; Elgar's *The
Dream of Gerontius*; the strains and pains of sex and death
in Wagner's operas. The magic often happens by means of
counterpoint: a happy scene is made all the more beautiful for being described against a musical backdrop of
sadness. As Waits sees a woman across a bar, or Strauss's
lovers look forward to a kiss on the beach, the prolonged
tempo and minor key take hold of the moment and bring
it exquisitely, heartbreakingly out of time, making its
impermanence even more apparent. Such moments are
beautiful because they are tragic and must pass: the end,
again, gives the content its meaning.

We must somehow embrace transience and connect
where we can with the present moment in order to overcome our fear of death. Likewise, we must connect with
death in order to experience the richness of the here and
now. We fear an enemy that, perhaps more than anything
else, makes our lives significant. The will to see our projects extended makes us human and means that we are
likely to want to fight death when it comes. It's as if we
are attending a fantastic party and are told we have to
leave. We don't want to go. But neither, really, do we
want it to last forever. It would be unbearable if it did.
Part of what makes the party so good is that it comes to
an end. The metaphor of leaving a party has been a popular one: Socrates used it in a bid to convince us we
wouldn't want to outstay our welcome. Christopher

Hitchens used it in more recent times when discussing the prospect of an afterlife:

> It will happen to all of us that at some point you get tapped on the shoulder and told, not just that the party is over, but slightly worse: the party's going on but you have to leave. And it's going on without you. That's the reflection I think that most upsets people about their demise. All right then let's – because it might make us *feel* better – let's pretend the opposite. Instead, you'll get tapped on the shoulder and told: 'Great news: this party's going on forever, and you *can't* leave. You've *got* to stay. The boss says so and he also insists that you have a good time.'[154]

Sigmund Freud, out walking in the countryside with friends in 1915, was struck with how transience endows its subjects with a particular beauty. One of his companions was disturbed by the fact that the bucolic serenity of their surroundings was doomed to eventual decay or destruction. The other refused to accept that something so senseless could ever occur; he believed that somehow beauty must perennially persist. Freud found himself disagreeing with both stances, reacting against the notion that the value of a beautiful thing suffers a decrease where it must perish:

> On the contrary, an increase! Transience value is scarcity value in time. Limitation in the possibility

---

154 Christopher Hitchens, Los Angeles, (2011). In debate with Sam Harris, Rabbi David Wolpe and Rabbi Bradley Artson on the topic 'Is there an Afterlife?'

of an enjoyment raises the value of the enjoyment ... As regards the beauty of Nature, each time it is destroyed by winter it comes again next year, so that in relation to the length of our lives it can in fact be regarded as eternal ... A flower that blossoms only for a single night does not seem to us on that account less lovely.[155]

Freud, it must be said, did not remain convinced by his own optimism. But writing in the midst of the First World War, his assurance that new objects of delight would soon follow the destruction of those things we love would have been a powerful therapeutic message. Moreover, 'since the value of all this beauty and perfection is determined only by its significance for our own emotional lives, it has no need to survive us and is therefore independent of absolute duration'[156]. In other words, we value beautiful things because they have a certain emotional effect on us in the moment; they do not need to persist beyond that moment to be worthwhile. In fact, their value exists outside of time.

When we consider that these things we value are only here for a while and will eventually turn to dust, we both remind ourselves of their worth and align ourselves with Fortune. The Stoics tell us to think, when people die or things are destroyed, 'I gave them back.' What we have lost was never ours; we enjoyed them for a while and now they have returned to eternity. In the case of a broken vase, this may be a helpful thought; in the case of a lost loved one, perhaps it sounds like meagre comfort.

That isn't necessarily a fault of the thought (I think

155 Sigmund Freud, *On Transience*
156 Ibid.

it's a good one), it's just that the loss of a loved one can be so unbearable that any consolations tend to strike us as offensive and irrelevant. They are rarely any more effective than a funeral is effective in providing 'closure' for those closest to the deceased. And as Brandy Schillace describes in her book *Death's Summer Coat*, funerals can be pitifully inadequate when it comes to providing what mourners need:

> The greatest part of mourning really happens after the last cold clod of earth has been cast over the grave or the coffin sent to the cremation chamber; after the guests go home and back to their lives; after the silent car rolls down the silent driveway and you find yourself in the fuzzy dark of a long everafter. The dead have gone, we remain and we *remember*.

Anyone who has lost someone dear will testify to this. The pain of grief is often in part a feeling of aloneness; of wandering through a world populated by people that still laugh and go about their days and cannot understand what you are going through. Our brains still retain certain well-trodden neural pathways that trick us again and again: 'I must tell him about this . . . I should call her and see how she's doing . . . Oh, she'd like this . . .' Familiar lines of treacherous associations that repeatedly beckon us on until we collide with the cold hard wall of that person's devastating absence. Grieving does to a great extent pass, but it is of no service to assure those who grieve that time will heal. Rose Kennedy, the philanthropist mother of the assassinated Kennedys, is attributed with the following words: 'It has been said, "Time heals all wounds." I do not agree. The wounds remain. In time, the mind, protecting its sanity, covers them with scar tissue and the pain lessens. But it is never gone.'

We might never achieve, or even want to achieve, a feeling of detachment from our loved ones, especially after they die. Our grief, and the feeling of angry incomprehension with which we view a world that can go on smiling while we are in such pain, may feel superlatively important to hang on to. Grief is an honest expression of loss and of how much we treasured someone who has now gone. It can be painful, but it goes hand-in-hand with the things we value. The problem is not loss itself but that we are horrified by it and fight against it through whatever attempts to control we can muster. These are artificial means, and thus their inadequacy eventually comes back to bite us. We start our infant lives by losing the safest environment we will ever know, and encounter loss of the old and secure every time we bravely take on something new. Life is growth, and if it does not involve a perpetual passing away, then we can neither grow nor live in any meaningful sense. And eventually, by accepting this truth in our honest grief, we will be ready to let the first rays of light penetrate the darkness.

Eating the dead

When we are faced with death, we are left flailing without an instruction manual, and in our perplexity we are usually content to hand over control of the death story to the medical profession. And even here we are at a loss. In so many walks of life we are encouraged to make demands as consumers; now we try to do the same. We insist that the doctors do as we say and follow, as if we know best, our every frightened urging; yet we also demand they are infallible, godlike, in command. Amidst the tensions and terrors we flounder; whether it is our own death or that of a loved one, we know we face something important, and nothing rises out of the cold world of tests and medication and awkwardness to honour that significance.

Since the Enlightenment, the modern project has been to try to live without superstition and ritual, particularly so if it appears morbid. 'We think we can congratulate ourselves,' writes Carl Jung,

> on having already reached such a pinnacle of clarity, imagining that we have left all these phantasmal gods far behind. But what we have left behind are only verbal spectres, not the psychic facts that were responsible for the birth of the gods.[157]

We have moved on from the folklore, but not the deep stirrings that gave rise to the folklore in the first place. Religions warn us not to ignore the gods; if they have lost their lustre, we must now instead pay as much attention to the psychological needs that gave birth to them. Without this due care, we may suffer as the needs they represent re-emerge in pathological form. The poet Rainer Maria Rilke wrote around the turn of the twentieth century:

> *Gods: we project them first in the boldest of sketches,*
> *which sullen Fate keeps crumpling and tossing away.*
> *But for all that, the gods are immortal. Surely we may*
> *hear out the one who, in the end, will hear us.*[158]

157 Carl Jung, Commentary on *The Secret of the Golden Flower*
158 Rainer Maria Rilke, *Sonnets to Orpheus*, translation by Stephen Mitchell

And thus in exorcising the macabre from life, we have become strangers to death. Rather than living comfortably with our mortality, and growing acquainted with it as a nearby companion, we are suddenly forced into an intimate relationship with it when we are weak and unready.

Brandy Schillace describes a history of our relationship to death in *Death's Summer Coat*, beginning with the Black Plagues of the fourteenth and fifteenth centuries. Eruptions of plague swept through Europe and parts of Asia, killing a third of the population. The world became primarily focused on death, with some forms of plague killing their victims *within a few hours*. With priests and prostitutes falling alike, and religious systems collapsing all around, people stopped looking to Church authority to guide the traditions surrounding death. Texts such as the *Ars Moriendi* appeared, showing people how they might overcome temptation and die a good death without the need of the Church's stewardship.

The Protestant Reformation of the sixteenth and seventeenth centuries led to a breaking away from the highly ritualised Catholic procedures around death, which were still predominant. This disaffiliation included a denial of the Catholic concepts of purgatory and prayers for the dead, and an end to burial in 'hallowed ground', which was now deemed a Catholic superstition. The seventeenth century brought with it instead its emphasis on the physical aspects of death (coffins, monuments and deep burial, for example) and continued the shift away from the more spiritual, ritualised elements. The veneer of some Catholic rituals remained but without the value and significance they once had.

The Enlightenment of the eighteenth century ushered in a new role for the doctor. Our medicine was still

rooted in humoral theory, systemised in ancient Greece and blaming our ailments on imbalances in our levels of blood, phlegm and black and yellow bile (which in turn connected us with the four elements of earth, air, fire and water). The Enlightenment led the way to more rational investigation.

The business of doctors now became that of prolonging life. Schillace writes: 'Death began to be perceived as an untimely event and the middle-class employed doctors (and their methods) to hold death at bay.'[159] At the same time, the Enlightenment's denial of superstition and celebration of individuality highlighted the gap left by the comforts of ritual. Strange and foreign, death became 'possibly *more* terrifying than the old Catholic understanding of hellfire. The Enlightenment's gifts were decidedly two-edged'[160]. The public now saw the inevitable as something, in the individual instance at least, to be fought and defeated as an enemy.

Alongside this celebration of medicine and scientific knowledge, the story-forming part of us was left ungratified by the absence of meaningful ceremony. It was up to the Victorians to enthusiastically ritualise the *memorialisation* of the departed. The Industrial Revolution had set us about the fancy new business of shopping, allowing us to endow private grief with an elaborate public face. Queen Victoria set the scene: she is inseparable in our minds from the black 'weeds' she wore to mourn her husband, Albert. The nation's widows followed, as it were, suit. Locks of hair encapsulated in mourning jewellery, the use of the powerful new technology of photography to

---

159 Brandy Schillace, *Death's Summer Coat: What the History of Death and Dying Can Tell Us About Life and Living*
160 Ibid.

immortalise the dead in often unsettlingly life-like poses alongside the living, or any number of testaments to the departed allowed us to keep their memory alive and well after they were gone.

In 1848 in Hydesville, New York, the young Kate and Margaret Fox convinced their family and neighbours that the dead were able to produce 'rappings' in their home, in the country's first informal séance rooms. By the time they admitted the hoax (they had found a way to crack their toe joints to create the noise), the spiritualism craze had swept across America and England, and their confessions were ignored. Sir Arthur Conan Doyle (the creator of Sherlock Holmes, the very embodiment of cool rationality) had become an outspoken advocate of this new pseudo-science. The Fox sisters died penniless, shunned by the spiritualist movement they had created. But their legacy lived on, and today many people believe that the dead can haunt and communicate with us, and even inhabit specific objects and places. But increasingly and often hilariously, flash photography exposed the chicanery of the mediums in their dark salons. No more could the spiritualists fling their tambourines in the pitch-black, escape unseen from ropes and write on slates with chalk held between their toes. They were forced to shift their efforts to purely verbal deceptions, and their bequest is the wealth of modern mediums whose greasy promise of hope guarantees them audiences on TV and in theatres around the world. And tragically, with even the Victorian focus on memory-infused objects now seeming rather quaint and old-fashioned, the modern medium's offerings are one of the few ways our society provides any channel of meaning for those in mourning. Nothing, in truth, is signified; these camp conduits for the dead offer nothing but ambiguous, stuttering 'proofs' of the Happy

Summerland, and only then enough to lend the performance a dubious semblance of entertainment.

Rituals confer meaning, Schillace reminds us; we
have lost the power of the latter as we have come to scoff
at the apparent vacuity of the former. She points us to
other traditions that heavily ritualise death: the Toraja of
Indonesia who 'bury their dead in a variety of ways . . .
occasionally . . . keeping them at home. Life actually
revolves around death for the Torajans, and wealth is
amassed throughout life in order to ensure a properly aus-
picious send off at death.'[161] The dead are dressed up and
paraded through the village: 'a celebration and type of
extended family reunion'. The Wari, in the rainforests of
Brazil, practise necrophagy: they consume their dead. She
explains in her chapter 'Eating the Dead':

> The men of the village begin dismemberment,
> removing organs first and then severing the head
> and cutting the joints before placing limbs upon
> the roasting rack . . . The elders explain that only
> the cutting of the body is emotionally difficult – to
> eat the remains, on the other hand, is good and
> right . . . The living Wari explain that they would
> rather be incorporated into the living bodies of
> their kin than rot in the cold, wet ground.[162]

The point of these and other traditions is that death
becomes something communal and therefore familiar.
Today, the Day of the Dead celebrations in Mexico still
serve the same purpose: there is little room for fear when
death is so beautiful and colourful. These traditions, so

161 Brandy Schillace, *Death's Summer Coat*
162 Ibid.

different from ours, call the oddities of our own into question. 'Why do we call strangers to take care of the body?' Schillace asks. 'Why are the final preparations for burial done by non-family members, in a place far away from the home? Why do we embalm the body if we don't plan to preserve it? Why do we gather for viewings and wakes? Why flowers – or eulogies – or processionals?'[163]

We don't live with death as a companion, and so we fear it as an unwelcome, unbidden outsider when it comes. Without the cultural rituals in place to *give* death some form of meaning, and therefore to confer to the end of life a sense of closure (rather than simply see it curtailed absurdly and painfully), it is down to us to each identify and complete our own story. We ourselves have to take stock and see what has been important to us, what is undone, what can be healed, what needs to be said.

☺

163 Ibid.

14

How to Die Well

It's your death

So much of talk about death and transience in positive and abstract terms only brings to the fore the sharply contrasting realm of individual experience. We may accept that death is a good thing, certainly as opposed to immortality, but this seems of no comfort when we face our own death. So I'd like to look at the experience of dying and see what we can learn from it, because the act of facing it squarely can make us much happier while we are still young and healthy.

The mere fact that this sounds like an awkward topic for me to write about is, I think, a symptom of a striking, fundamental cultural problem about the experience of dying. Dying (and taxes, according to Woody Allen) is something we all must face. We are all heading there. And we all care enormously about how our loved ones will meet their end. Yet when that time comes, no one talks about it. A conspiracy of silence descends, and dying often becomes very, very lonely. Unwilling to upset or burden those she loves, the dying person does not speak about her fears to her family and friends. Horrified at the thought of saying the wrong thing or appearing to 'write off' their dying beloved, the living do everything to avoid mentioning it as well.

Instead, a new modern narrative is imposed on the situation, that of the 'brave battle'. This tale, in truth designed only to keep the living happy, can put further pressure on the person facing death and alienate her from the possibility of a deep richness that only acceptance can bring. As the cancer ate through her spine, Debra wrote to me:

> It is also unhelpful to be told enthusiastically to 'keep fighting', 'don't let it beat you' or, most annoyingly, 'don't give up!'. All that these inane, positive yet totally inappropriate comments do is to make the sufferer (me) feel they are lacking in moral fortitude or backbone (which I quite literally am nowadays). The insinuation is therefore that my current predicament is, somehow, my own fault. Taking an honest and authentic look at my situation, and in so doing, accepting that I am going to die, does not equal giving up; it means I don't waste time over petty things – life is too short, especially mine!

Oncology nurse Cynthia Rittenberg writes that positive thinking can:

> add an extra burden to an already devastated patient. By forcing 'positive mental attitude', health-care professionals are not allowing patients to face reality. Promoters of the 'cure' that comes with positive thinking are quoted, as well as authors

who question the promoters' intent and outcome. It is felt that 'positive thinking' may be appropriate as one of many successful coping strategies. To attribute more to it or, worse, to insist that patients believe in its power to cure may be courting emotional disaster.[164]

Death, we remember, does not round off a life with the satisfying ending of a novel or a film. It does not 'complete'; it curtails. It is up to *us* to bring the story to a close by recognising it as such. If a person knows she is dying, I would suggest that she needs from her loved ones every opportunity to take stock of her story and bring it to a meaningful end. Despite the fact that those of us who must watch them deteriorate are just doing our painful and miserable best to deal with the situation, it remains better for everyone that the dying person's story is given priority, and not that of the onlookers. Their experience is likely to be enriched too, if the deceased is able to leave with as much closure as possible.

If you are facing your own death, and have the clarity of mind and opportunity to make such choices, then realise that for you to *own* your death, to author it and to shape it, is tremendously important. You are the protagonist *and* the author. If you do not insist on this central role, you may find yourself reduced to a mere cameo. Others, stronger in body and in number, may take the leading role if you do not. Your death does not belong to your family or your doctors. They will have their important parts to play, but it is, I think, of ultimate importance that you insist, firmly and sensitively, and through discussion

164 Cynthia N. Rittenberg, 'Positive thinking: an unfair burden for cancer patients?' *Supportive Care in Cancer*

with everyone else, that your choices must steer the process.

Medical authors Atul Gawande and David Kuhl have both written beautiful books about death and the experience of dying patients. B. J. Miller, of the Zen Hospice Project in San Francisco, gives a truly magnificent TED talk on the subject. These and many others wish to bring a more humanistic perspective to the treatment of the dying. They warn of their medical profession aiming to merely extend life at all costs, with the issue of *quality* of life hazily relegated to a secondary or tertiary consideration. For Gawande and Kuhl (and others, as these new voices gain volume), a key to securing a dying person's quality of life at their end is for discussions to happen between the family and the person facing their death. These talks should take place in a suitable environment, with the specific aim of finding out what the dying person wants. When, for example, she might wish to move to palliative care at home. What aspects of herself she would want to retain before enough was enough. If this information is not known, if family and doctors are not on the same page, she will be unlikely to have the death she would want, once its imminence has become unavoidable and she may be too weak to effectively communicate her wishes.

This tension between the quality of life and mere extension of life was powerfully articulated in *A Very Easy Death*, a 1964 account by Simone de Beauvoir (from which I have already quoted) of her mother's death from cancer in hospital. Writing of her remorse at allowing an operation to be carried out on the older, frail woman, she notes that 'one is caught up in the wheels and dragged along, powerless in the face of specialists' diagnoses, their forecasts, their decisions. The patient becomes their property: get him away from them if you can!' Her mother, 'reduced by her capitulation to being a body and nothing more, hardly differed at all from a corpse – a poor defenceless carcass turned and manipulated by professional hands.'

In his devastating novella *The Death of Ivan Ilyich*, Tolstoy describes the prolonged death of a prominent government official. It is a compelling study of the shift in life priorities that comes with death, and of the differences in how the patient and his healthy attendants experience the process of dying. Ilyich has been very successful in life, in large part due to his prioritising how others might favourably perceive him. His marriage, however, is loveless, and his primary concern has remained to maintain the appearance of a successful and well-respected man. Obsessed with home furnishings, his life lacks the centre of a loving relationship and self-knowledge. His drawn-out death proves agonising and increasingly inconvenient for his wife and those around him. And while the 'brave battle' narrative was not prevalent in the nineteenth century, Tolstoy notes the not dissimilar, unhelpfully optimistic attitude of those around the dying man:

> The greatest torment Ivan Ilyich suffered was the lie – the lie which everybody accepted for some reason, which said that he was merely ill, not dying, and that all he had to do was keep calm and take the treatment, and then something very good would come out of it. Whereas he himself knew that whatever anybody did, nothing would come out of it except for even more excruciating torments, and death. And he was tormented by this lie; tormented by the fact that people didn't want

to acknowledge what they all knew, and he knew; they wanted to lie to him about his terrible situation, and wanted and compelled him to participate in the lie himself.[165]

What a dreadful form of social pressure this is. And how terribly easy it is to contribute to it ourselves as we desperately try to keep a mood of optimism prevalent. In one short passage, a fellow official visits Ilyich. Desperate as the dying man is for some fellow feeling and honesty, he cannot but play the professional role expected of him. We hear his profound, isolated, existential groan:

> Ivan Ilyich wants to weep, and wants to be caressed and wept over, and instead in comes his colleague Judge Shebek, and instead of weeping and being caressed, Ivan Ilyich puts on a serious, austere, profound expression, and from force of habit pronounces his opinion on the significance of a verdict by the Appeal Court, and stoutly defends this opinion. All these lies, around him and within him, did more than anything else to poison the last days of his life.[166]

Ilyich realises with great pain that he has lived pointlessly. As part of that process of self-awareness, he gains a new open-heartedness. Affectingly, it is his servant Gerasim who, in the final stages of Ilyich's decay, provides him with what he needs: human touch and simple sympathy devoid of self-centredness.

165 Leo Tolstoy, *The Death of Ivan Ilyich*
166 Ibid.

Here is the problem as I see it: we all want our loved ones to die peacefully, but we don't know what to do once their death becomes an imminent possibility. We will all die and all see others die, yet we are left frightened and flailing when it happens. If we have the opportunity to face our death and give our own story a meaningful ending, we should, we must, be given every opportunity to do so. But this demands that the dying person understand what such an ambition means, and that loved ones understand how to help them achieve it. Debra (an ex-nurse and therapist) and her son James (a medical student) have the experience and understanding to preserve what is necessary for a good death. They can ignore any unhelpful pressure for Debra to 'put up a good fight' when a fight is no longer an option. They can understand that entreaty for what it is: a way for people to make themselves feel more comfortable when faced with the death of another. It might be merely a way of avoiding an awkward subject, or a way of evading one's own fears about death, or a desperate clinging to a hope for a cure, but ultimately it serves only the living and denies the dying a chance to find some meaning in their final stages.

We do this because we don't know any better. There are a million handbooks for giving birth and raising an infant, and an obvious paucity of instructions for what matters most at death. Instead, the medical profession takes centre stage, and the narrative can become one of life-extension rather than preserving what people *want*. The post-Enlightenment medic's remit is extension of life. Now, to progress, we must place that medical knowledge in context and learn what *else* is important. And doctors may need to learn to face their own fears about death in order to communicate more helpfully and honestly with the dying.

It is as if our cultural obsession with goal-setting and optimism has blindly swum into waters far too deep and dark. 'Believe in yourself; you can beat this thing': the message is no different from any manual about achieving your ambitions. The same mistake is made in both cases: that upon which this book aims to throw some light. Our goals and aspirations only form half of the equation, only one axis of the graph. The other force at work is fortune, life, fate: everything that happens outside of our control. To try to control those things through indiscriminate self-belief or sheer aggression is likely to lead to failure and pain. And nowhere is this more evident than when a person is dying.

To align ourselves along that $x=y$ axis through life, shifting our expectations to work with reality, reminding ourselves that things may not work out as we expect, that we may lose the things we value, that things come and go: all this we know is to aim for a kind of tranquillity. This ideal not only serves us in life; it is also preparation for death. If we have throughout our life, here and there and within the limits of our ability, practised this easier relationship with fortune, it can place us in good stead for our final stages, greatly mitigate our fears and allow us, like Debra and many others, to experience the rich fullness of the present when it is offered to us most starkly. And from that open and robust starting point, we might take fuller control of our story in its final chapter.

Regrets

In 1943, the psychologist Abraham Maslow demonstrated that people are motivated to achieve their needs according to a certain hierarchy. At the bottom of the pyramid are the basic needs that we all possess (such as physiological, social, safety and love-related needs), and at the top, which only a small number of people fulfil, are the growth needs, or those of self-actualisation. As long as we continue to see our life spreading out widely and generously before us, our concerns move up the pyramid and we prioritise such high-end qualities as creative fulfilment. But as we sense our time on this Earth is getting shorter, our prime concerns 'descend' within the pyramid to the here and now: to relationships and everyday pleasures. This shift comes irrespective of age. It is not some mystical 'wisdom' of older people that tends to cause this shift, as younger people report a similar reappraisal of their wants if they develop a terminal illness. In fact, we can feel this change in what is most pressing if we merely imagine moving abroad.

As priorities change, regrets may surface. Bronnie Ware, an Australian nurse working in palliative care, recorded what she perceived to be the top five regrets of the dying. They were:

1. I wish I'd had the courage to live a life true to myself, not the life others expected of me.
2. I wish I hadn't worked so hard.
3. I wish I'd had the courage to express my feelings.
4. I wish I had stayed in touch with my friends.
5. I wish that I had let myself be happier.

It is hard to read this list without bringing our own choices into question. It's unlikely that we are going about our lives *now* in a way that will significantly mitigate our likely future regrets. 'Live each day as if it were your last,' we are sometimes told, as if such advice were truly helpful. But what would that mean? Should we sort out our financial affairs and make a will? Are we to devote ourselves to a gagging outdoor frenzy of terminal sex? Perhaps this bland and supposedly life-affirming instruction is no more than propaganda put about by the manufacturers of bungee cords. As if the thrill of death is something we should eagerly seek to court before we die.

The first point is, then, that we can forgive ourselves if our current priorities don't match those we will later wish we had; it is natural for our needs to be different when our life still extends brightly before us. The need for self-actualisation, for example, at the top of Maslow's pyramid, may demand certain sacrifices along the way, and may need time to come into fulfilment. *The needs of a present that has a future are different from one that does not*. We do have a future now, and all our projects grand and small depend on some kind of future, whether it comes three seconds or three centuries from now. So although the instruction to pay more attention to the present moment is helpful in a culture that teaches us to prioritise distant horizons of career success, we should also be wary of fetishising the here and now. It is not 'correct' to live in the moment, for the very reason that we are storytellers and right now is always part of a continuing narrative. We know from Kahneman's work on the remembering and experiencing selves that how you look back on this moment will be more conducive to deciding if it's a happy one than how you feel about it right now. We cannot merely instruct ourselves to be happy in the present moment, for we would need to return to our storytelling, time-orientated selves to decide if we had been successful.

However, being open to the opportunities of the present, at least sometimes and where appropriate and possible, does save us from leading a life that merely happens in the interim; one in which that same narrative drive keeps us lurching forward, while we worry where it's all going to end up.

Yet that fifth regret – 'I wish that I had let myself be happier' – does rather linger in the air, does it not? Here we are, convinced that our priority in life, in one form or another, is our happiness. We work hard to secure money to sustain a family and a home because we know they will make us happy. We endlessly buy things – often more than we can afford – because we are convinced they will make us happy too, at least for a while. We please others to avoid confrontation and 'keep everyone happy', including ourselves. One survey tells us we watch television for four times longer than we spend talking to people, and twenty times longer than we engage in religious activities, although we report that communication, worship and meditation make us far happier than TV.[167] Yet at the end, we are likely to feel a pang that we could have allowed ourselves to be happier. As if the idea had never occurred to us.

Again, there is no shame in working hard for a better quality of life in the future. 'You should live in the moment' is as unhelpful an imperative as 'You should believe in yourself and secure the future you want'. The only 'should' we need ever take on board is that we 'should' get on with our lives without hurting other people. Meanwhile, maybe, we can be aware of how we are likely to later judge our current actions and check that

---

167 Admittedly an American survey: 'American Time Use Survey' from the US Bureau of Labor Statistics. Exercise, sports and recreation (another great reported source of happiness) also comes in at one-tenth of time spent watching TV. Surfing the Net wasn't mentioned in the survey.

we're not wasting time with things that evidently do not matter. Maybe we do not need to work *so* hard. Maybe much of our work time is caught up with petty politics and pursuing meaningless things, and we could take stock and address that. Perhaps we should get back in contact with friends about whom we have almost forgotten, because one day they may matter a lot more to us than the other distractions that are stopping us from tracking them down today. And we can reconsider the wisdom of long-term goals that might now consume us needlessly.

As our priorities at the end shift towards the simple, the immediate and the social, naturally our other previous concerns may appear misguided. But this sounds like a product, again, of storytelling: it would be very easy to look back and see a story of missed opportunities, now that they are running out. It need not mean we were making mistakes at the time, when horizons were further away. The key to avoiding regret may lie as much in what story we choose to tell ourselves in the future as it does in what we do or don't do now. All we can do is try to anticipate that future narrative and let it gently guide some of our choices up front.

Paying attention to certain future regrets might genuinely enhance our lives in the here and now. When I carry out this thought exercise, some specifics come to mind (possibly they say more about me, but I think they're worth noting):

1. If you have something to 'come out' about, come out. If you carry a secret around with you, you learn to protect it in all sorts of ways that disconnect you from the rest of the world and the people in it. Meanwhile, the idea of your secret being discovered will come to

fill you with horror. But the huge deal you have turned it into is *not* a reflection of how big a deal it is in the eyes of other people. To them, it's just *some information* about you. Generally speaking, they don't care. They're far more likely to care if you're happy, and they'll certainly care if you're obviously hiding something (and it will be obvious), but they are unlikely to care about the thing itself (if it doesn't affect them). They don't think about you and what you get up to as much as you think they do. And when you come out, the bubble you have built around you bursts, and life suddenly becomes so much more delightful: it's like you've put down a heavy bag of rocks. You also realise that everyone else has his or her heavy bag of rocks, too. And you gain a much healthier perspective regarding how much people care about what you get up to.

2. You'll never regret falling in love. Do so over and over again. Lower your standards if necessary. It might lead to heartbreak now and then, but it'll always be worth it in the end.

3. If you work in a creative field, and you are faced with a choice of doing a job for the money or doing a job for the fun of it, take the fun one whenever you can. You'll rarely enjoy the work you do for money.

4. Don't be a dick. People around you are not there to make your life easier. The more successful you are, the harder it is to remember that, because you inevitably get used to people looking after you. Everyone is fighting a hard battle; everyone is just trying to do their best, *in the same way that you are*. If you remember this, and if, as much as you can, you treat people with compassion, you are likely to feel better and your life will be noticeably happier. You'll connect with more

people, and that's where good things and opportunities come from.[168] Open-heartedness feels good and is conducive to good things happening. Irritation with other people and the world only closes them off. People don't need to agree with you or see your viewpoint. We want people to agree with us because we are understandably threatened by a view of the world that contradicts ours. When they agree with us or reflect our views, our own identity is re-inforced. Growing up means tolerating different viewpoints and realising that you are not – like a baby screaming for its mother – the sole dictate of what's right and wrong. There is rarely a right and wrong. Most times there's just a jumble of viewpoints, and it's okay to grant others the validity you grant yours, and to tolerate the contradiction. Objecting to the differing viewpoints of others is a huge waste of time.

5. Look at what takes up your time and see what is worth doing and what is not. Think about what provides enjoyment, connectivity, a sense of fulfilment, and what, when you look back, will have been a waste of time or stifled you. Look for ways of removing those latter activities from your life. Not only does this offer the benefit of removing negative behaviours, it also engages you with the considered life. Suddenly you have a vantage point from which to view your behaviour, and from there you can give your life shape and meaning.

168 Richard Wiseman, *The Luck Factor: The Scientific Study of the Lucky Mind*

'Although the physicality of death destroys us, the idea of death saves us,'[169] writes the existential psychoanalyst Irvin D. Yalom. He points to a dialectic proposed by Martin Heidegger, the modern philosopher, to help make sense of this. Heidegger suggested there are two ways we can approach life: the *everyday* mode and the *ontological* mode. Most of the time, naturally, we exist in the everyday mode and might marvel at *how* things are in the world. However, in the ontological mode ('ontology' is the study of what it is to *be*), we stand back and look at the marvellous fact *that* things, and we, exist. Our attention is turned from the physical trappings of daily life to the deeper questions of being, and in this mode we are more likely to make worthwhile changes in our life. This, indeed, is part of the 'considered life' this book is talking about. Without stepping into this ontological mode, it will be hard to make sense of anything here. Yalom talks about the importance of this viewpoint in relation to dealing with a fear of death:

> You are prompted to grapple with your fundamental human responsibility to construct an authentic life of engagement, connectivity, meaning and self-fulfilment.
>
> Many reports of dramatic and lasting changes catalysed by a confrontation with death support this view. While working intensively over a ten-year period with patients facing death from cancer, I found that many of them, rather than succumb to numbing despair, were positively and dramatically transformed. They rearranged their life priorities by trivialising life's trivia. They assumed the power

169 Irvin D. Yalom, *Staring at the Sun: Overcoming the Terror of Death*

to choose *not* to do the things that they really did not wish to do. They communicated more deeply with those they loved, and appreciated more keenly the elemental facts of life – the changing seasons, the beauty of nature, the last Christmas or New Year.

Many reported a diminishment of their fears of other people, a greater willingness to take risks, and less concern about rejection. One of my patients . . . said to me, 'What a pity I had to wait until now, till my body was riddled with cancer, to learn how to live!'[170]

There are many ways to die, and plenty of them will deny any opportunity of self-discovery. Recently, as I write, my father has been diagnosed with early-onset Alzheimer's; he along with forty-four million others in the world will be denied any chance of ontological perspicacity. Others will not find time to reflect. I know of a young man who took a gentle cycle ride through the country, with his dog alongside him on a lead. The dog crossed in front of the bicycle, causing the bike to flip forward as it tangled on the lead, killing the cyclist instantly. Death, again, is merely a stoppage; we are very lucky if we can end our stories meaningfully. Meanwhile, we can learn from those who do, and use their revelations to reappraise our current priorities.

We might never rid ourselves of a lingering anxiety regarding our death; this is a kind of tax we pay in return for self-awareness. But, as with any fear that becomes inappropriately inflated, we can, like Debra and many others, learn to stare it in the face when it comes. With

170 Ibid.

further thought, we might even elevate our lives by accommodating ourselves to it right now, before it threatens to become urgent and terrifying. Death, perhaps uniquely amongst the objects of our dread, instructs us how to live.

☺

15

Living Now

Past, present and future

We generally feel defined by our past. Our past, however, is a story that we tell ourselves in the present. We create it every day when we accept the narratives we have developed about who we are and why we are who we are. 'I'm like this because this happened to me' is a common refrain in the modern world, where familiar fragments of psychoanalysis and flatulent bubbles of self-help advice have drifted into our popular culture. On the one hand it is a narrative, and on the other hand it is true. We are indeed governed here and there by little clusters of responses within our personality that leap into action whenever a situation in the present resembles the one in the past that caused this defensive stockpile.

A father repeatedly treated us dismissively as a child and now we have a particular pocket of activity within ourselves that is ready to feel miserable and self-justifying whenever a male authority figure does the same. We learnt to deal with a parent's flying rages by rising to anger ourselves first and meeting them on their own terms, and now we become incensed too quickly at frustrating situations in adulthood. Any number of situations, or even mere looks or turns of phrase can fling us back without any room for rational appraisal to those times when we suffered. *Now* feels like *then*, and without any conscious involvement on our part, the past and present pictures are compared and a close-enough match is found. Our unconscious selves, eager to protect us and working by analogy, set in motion the defence pattern we learnt as a child, and, although it feels reasonable to us when we are in its grip, it is of course a gross overreaction to what's happening to us as an adult in the present.

Our scripts are indeed written in our histories, but whatever our backgrounds, and however traumatic our pasts, the key to overcoming them is to stop telling ourselves the same unhelpful story today, to consciously own what has remained unconscious and therefore governed us, and to regain authorship ourselves. Some people never achieve this; others manage to do so through years of careful psychoanalysis, some through brief therapies or the sting of a sudden, shattering, shuddering revelation. It is the story we recreate and live out for ourselves every day that not only defines our past but also defines us, and stories are things we can change. The first step is to seek a perspective that allows us to see the story for what it is.

Naturally, our ability to adopt a new viewpoint – let alone what answers we find when we do – varies from person to person. Hence having a suitable figure such as a therapist or clear-minded friend or support group to gently suggest alternative viewpoints can be very helpful. This book aims to point us to the work of some people who have rigorously thought through what it is to live well. Without gaining something of a detached vantage point and identifying our stories for what they are, we will still remain prey to our deep-seated beliefs about who we are and how the world must work, mistake them for concrete reality and inflict them upon our loved ones and everyone else.

Whatever the past is, it has been and gone. If there are things you need to face in your past because they refuse to let you go, realise at least that they grip you not because they control you (they no longer exist), but because of the narrative they've left you with. You can't change what happened, but you can gain a little distance from it by reassessing your story about it. If certain behaviours from your partner or significant people routinely bother you and bring out the worst in you, ask yourself what their behaviour reminds you of from your past. Where were you made to feel the same? Identify where the anxiety is rooted and, in doing so, realise that you do not need to hold the person in the present accountable for something a particularly sensitive area of your personality is triggering. This man is *not* your father, this woman is *not* your mother; they may do this or that in the same way that your mum or dad did, but they have nothing to do with the actions of your parents. Your parents' behaviours were caused by their own clusters and frustrations, which in turn can be traced back to their *own* parents' points of brokenness. A fuller and happier life is going to involve recognising these clusters that still so over-eagerly leap into action and slowly allowing them to absolve their power.

One way to do that, having recognised the process for what it is, is to consciously note the way your unconscious machinations bring these old patterns to the fore, and then, where you can, quietly smile at them. Be grateful to your unconscious for looking out for you, while also acknowledging that it's being hilariously over-sensitive.

Each time you gently deny it its power by nipping it in the bud through your own amusement, and practise instead a new response (that may not at first come naturally but which encourages a richer and more sympathetic world-view), you break these old neural connections and form a new pathway. Vincent Deary in his lovely book on change, *How We Are*, talks about how pedestrians in his local park tended to avoid a provided path and instead cut across the grass to reach the shops. Eventually, a new path was formed by the repeated use of this shortcut. Buddhists talk of thoughts acting like drips of water on the brain: as the same thought is repeated over time, the resulting rivulet is fortified to etch a free-flowing new stream in the mind. Perhaps above all, by bringing an unconscious process into the light of conscious attention, we undo its power. It is those parts of us of which we are unaware that have us most firmly in their clutches.

The present moment, on the other hand, can be a more productive place to focus our attention. The here and now, we have seen, rarely contains problems; it is released from the tyranny of our imposing narratives. We might feel bad about events in the past or dread those yet to come, but rarely in the present – rarely *right now* – do we find ourselves in the middle of a serious difficulty. *Right now* we can gain some perspective by stepping back from our feelings and recognising that they are not *us*. *Right now* we can undo some of the grip of the past by recognising the patterns that rule over us. For those who find it difficult to switch off concerns about the past and the future, and who therefore suffer from anxiety (which often feeds off one or the other), any number of books are available teaching mindfulness meditation, an effective means of bringing one's focus back to the here and now. The practice aims to return your awareness to a standpoint *between* your thoughts, rather than where it normally is: caught up in their maelstrom. For the anxiously disposed, learning to simply 'be' in the present moment without trying to fix everything is a way of sidestepping the tyranny of anxieties created by the phantoms of the past and future.

Neuroscientist and author Sam Harris describes a greater engagement with the present moment as the antidote to a fear of death. When we are focused nonjudgementally on the present, we do not fret about growing old and dying. We are also freed from any obsessions with what we are trying to achieve in the future, and are likely to find that things around us become more compelling. The regrets of the dying point us repeatedly to the importance of the here and now. Despite the therapeutic value of learning to engage with the narrative-free present, we can remember it comes to pass *within the context of a contingent future*. As storytelling, project-forming beings, we would deny our humanity if we disregarded the yet-to-come, which, containing our eventual death, provides the circumference to our circle. But to be released from the grip of it, and to be more awake to opportunity and change where they help us, we will need to gently increase our attention to the present.

Getting old

Allied to the fear of death is a fear of ageing, which of course is exclusively tied up with the future. One cannot happen without the other. We easily equate ageing with becoming decrepit, lonely and invisible. When we talk of 'feeling our age', we are describing a kind of tiredness. Moreover, any number of cosmetic products promise 'anti-ageing' properties: the appearance of age is to be fought against at all costs; fine lines and wrinkles are an enemy to be obliterated. Disturbingly, these products are made and advertised for teenagers as well as adults, despite the fact that many are too strong for young people's skin (some can remove the outer layer of skin and increase sensitivity to the sun). Not surprisingly, the age at which young people worry about signs of ageing has dropped worryingly: as long ago as 2002, a survey revealed it was no longer uncommon for twenty year olds to fret about wrinkles, and one only imagines the age has lowered. Fear of being old is in large part fuelled by this meaningless, damaging, industry-driven neurosis.

Successfully growing old is portrayed as a kind of inevitable failure. It is a fight, and one ultimately to be lost. The road towards death must be one of loss and denigration. The elderly are seen as a race apart, despite the fact that there are now more people aged over sixty-five in the UK than there are under-sixteens, and soon, I read, there will be more over-eighties than under-fives. And ageism is a prejudice like any other, made more insidious and troubling by the marketing ploys of the beauty industries. But unlike, say, racial prejudice, gerontophobia has at its heart a bizarre paradox: 'They' are 'us', and although we might insist otherwise, *we want to be like them.*

We want to grow old, because the alternative is that we die. 'They' are what each one of us will be a number of years from now. If we feel a bias against the elderly, we are feeling it against our future selves. And, if we look at our lives as great space-time worms, we can forget the 'future' part of that description and see it as simply an aversion towards ourselves.

Anne Karpf has written a truly lovely book, *How to Age*, which works to undo this fear. We are ageing, she points out, all the time. We may live to be a hundred, so that's a very long time to be worrying about getting older. We have been ageing ever since we were born, and our experience of it has generally been positive, has it not? When we were four, we wanted to be five, and later, eighteen. Maybe we dreaded turning thirty, but once it arrived wasn't it surprisingly positive? Have we not accrued experience and a certain wisdom we would not want to lose? Ageing is an ongoing process synonymous with living. And our experience of ageing so far, on balance, is likely to have been positive. There is no reason to believe that it suddenly changes to being a negative one. We worry, as if a sudden discontinuity will occur around the time of retirement; that the experience of growing up, which we have *enjoyed* throughout life, will suddenly, drastically change into something unpleasant.

We do not somehow decline into a homogenous experience of 'oldness'. We don't start to resemble our peers more and more as we merge into a dusty, out-of-touch, grey-and-beige cliché: 'Age doesn't obliterate our individual traits and identities,' Karpf writes, 'on the contrary, it heightens them.'[171] And research suggests we are likely to become happier as we grow older, contrary to our usual expectations. Why is that? We have already discovered what we might broadly take to be the reason. As our horizons change, priorities shift towards 'present-moment' considerations (such as personal relationships), and when we are more engaged in the here and now, we have far fewer problems.

In the same way we might imagine travelling back in time to meet our younger self and giving him or her much-needed advice from the future, we can play the

171 Anne Karpf, *How to Age*

same game a different way around: what might our future, older self have to offer us now? How will we improve and learn in ways that will benefit us? And viewing our current and future lives as one worm-like entity that also includes our past, what traits might we start to learn now that will benefit us in the future? What qualities can we start to nurture now? 'We can think of ourselves like wine connoisseurs laying down bottles that will improve with age; similarly we can try to foster in ourselves qualities that deepen and enrich over the years.'[172]

Fearing old age by seeing it as something it patently isn't (a transformation into something discontinuous from our current experience of maturing), or neurotically fighting against it with a cosmetic or surgical regime, is another symptom of attempting to drag that $x=y$ diagonal towards an axis where it can never realistically remain. We need to recognise this fear as a modern madness that does nothing but make our own futures appear more dismal to us. In its place, we might remember to look beyond the unhelpful caricatures of the elderly and attribute to older people the same complex internal world that we possess. And, I might add, we'll always be exciting and sexy to someone.

A good-enough death

Donald Winnicott (1896–1971) was a British psychoanalyst and paediatrician. Writing at a time when Freud's ideas about child-raising were well known, he responded with a softer model for parenting that did not provoke the same sort of guilt amongst care-givers as his famous predecessor tended to. Winnicott, concerned at the threat of

172 Ibid.

professional intrusion into the lives of new parents and the ideal standards demanded by the Freudian schools, took into account the nurturing environment and accepted that a mother could never be perfect. This lack of perfection, in fact, would provide the basis of his model:

> The good-enough mother . . . starts off with an almost complete adaptation to her infant's needs, and as time proceeds she adapts less and less completely, gradually, according to the infant's growing ability to deal with her failure.[173]

His ideas became popular. As a mother (or the primary care-giver) gradually withdraws from her infant in well-timed doses, the baby learns in turn a certain independence. Done effectively, there is no shock for the child, as it moves from a place of illusion (that the mother will always be available) to that of necessary disillusionment (that this will not be the case), a dynamic that will allow it to get by in the social world. In essence, its expectations are gently lowered. Our too-high expectations of others (which the Stoics have told us to address) are a return to an infantile stage when we knew we could scream and get what we wanted.

Good enough. This releases new parents from the ideal that can otherwise easily be imposed upon them. Debra took this model of the early stages of life and applied it to the last. She wrote to me:

> I have extended the 'good-enough' theory to most of my life and now my death. We are, at times, so

173 Donald Winnicott, 'Transitional objects and transitional phenomena', *International Journal of Psychoanalysis* (1953)

often obsessed or feel pressurised into 'being the best at . . ., the fastest at . . ., the cleverest at . . .' I genuinely worry about all of this positive thinking/life coaching!

. . . It is undoubtedly excellent to strive to achieve one's maximum potential, but that should be to please ourselves, not be judged by others, and for me having led a 'good-enough' life with its share of wonders and disasters, I am content and so, ready for a 'good-enough' death.

These lessons in death apply as much to life. I hope very much you'll take some helpful ideas from this book, but if you strive anxiously to achieve a healthy perspective, or consider it an unachievable ideal, you miss the point. The advice of this book is there to take and use as it might benefit us, with an aim to live 'well enough'. The 'enough' reminds us of the $x=y$ diagonal of the healthy life: here are our aims, while here is the rest of life, which they used to call fortune, and we should aim to steer between the two. A mother must begin by sacrificing her independence for her newborn, but over time she can withdraw and safely teach the child that its desires will not always be fulfilled the instant it cries. The infant begins to learn about the $x=y$ balance, and if it does not, it is likely to carry imbalanced expectations into adult life.

Suggestions, then, of how to achieve a 'good death' must not be taken as another narrative to be imposed on the dying. 'No one knows what happens when we die, as it is an absolute and thus rather difficult thing to do by halves,' Debra continues, 'so, personally, I think dogma, from whatever point of view, is unnecessary. I think that I feel satisfied with a full life, well and, at times, adventurously lived.'

Echoing Yalom's patients and many others, she continues:

> I have reached a point of quiet acceptance, deep peace of mind and tranquillity. It is a beautiful place to be, in which I appreciate more fully the wondrous world in which I live, such as the simple pleasure of the vivid palate of colours and aromas that surround me. It is perhaps a shame that it has to take such a drastic event to open my eyes to that which has surrounded me all my life.

While reading on the subject of death on a summer's day in the garden of a hotel near Sheffield, I found my attention drifting from the page to a long-leafed, red-berried shrub next to me. For a while I considered: 'What if I knew I was to die tomorrow? How utterly beautiful this plant is. I have no idea what it is called, and I have never paid attention to one before. What a stunning thing. What if I knew I would never see a plant or a red berry again? I would be able to stare at this for hours. God, what a beautiful thing.'

Months later, in an excellent café in Norwich, I am now doing a similar thing. In front of me is a little brown sugar pot made of clay. A spoon sticks out of a hole at the side of the lid. Someone made this. It looks handmade, but even if it isn't, someone designed this to neatly hold sugar and a spoon, and to be a pleasing object. They made that, in a sense, *to please me*. There are rings around it where it seems with my limited knowledge of pottery that the glaze has been painted on while it span on the wheel. And now I see a little symbol-signature on one side, raised somehow in the clay. That person, who has represented him- or herself with the shape of a miniature hook and star, made this. And if I liked sugar in my tea or coffee, I would use it to make those things taste sweet, because the receptor sites on my tastebud cells, along with the fibres in my taste nerves and projection zones in my brain, would respond in conjunction with my opioid system to make me happy. How *amazing*. And the sugar pot sits on a knitted doily, of pleasing swirls and colours, in keeping with the bohemian style of this café. It serves no purpose I can fathom other than to look pleasant and to set off the little pot by circling it with a kind of home-hewn prettiness. It forms part of an overall aesthetic that makes this café extremely welcoming, which in turn – presuming its style and flavour coincide comfortably with your taste – makes you happy to come in and sit, to eat and drink things made to sustain and extend that pleasure.

I have just noticed that there is an adorable contrap-tion rigged up around the door: when someone opens it, a string is pulled that causes a realistic toy bird to simulate a short flight from its place in the entrance of a bird cage (almost hidden amongst the substantial plants that grow high in the window). Its brief attempts at escape will be forever thwarted by the maximum swing of the door: after about eighteen inches, its optimistic trajectory is reversed, and it returns to its starting point. It makes me think of Rasputin and his occasional attempts to leave the house when guests arrive through the front door.

Someone has climbed a ladder and screwed the hooks I now see into the ceiling and doorframe that allow this little animation to work. Thoughtful design and physical effort have gone into achieving this entirely trivial, easily missed effect. How extraordinary that we bother to please each other like this. It makes me think of a short film by the magicians Penn & Teller, in which human life is ultimately spared by aggressive, invading aliens. The invaders are bored with the mundane nature of human life and seek a reason why they should *not* destroy it. Appeals to the great achievements of man do not impress them. Eventually, however, they are won over by watching a magician performing a close-up levitation trick achieved by the secret use of finely spun thread, invisible to the naked eye. The fact that human beings would devote so much painstaking time and effort to secure such thread in order to carry out an activity so strikingly barren of consequence makes us unique and therefore noteworthy. It deeply impresses the hostile aliens, and our planet is thankfully spared.

I seem unable to entirely enjoy the bird contraption in the moment without falling prey to projecting into the future: my mind keeps drifting to the question of how and where I would assemble a similar contrivance in my home when I finish my tour. There seems to be only so long that I can stay present in the moment before my plan-making, future-fixated part comes to the fore. As we've said, this is probably as it should be; and after all, if we could truly remain in the present, immortality would present no problem to us. We are engaged creatures who project ourselves into a finite future.

The present is a fact; the future is contingent. While an antidote to a fear of death is to embrace the present, we cannot remain there for long. At some point we want to know what *use* the current objects of our attention are to us, or how they might affect us for better or for worse, or how they compare to what we have seen before; and with these new thoughts we disconnect from the now and give over to our imaginations. This is why we can only aim for 'good enough' when it comes to embracing the present, for short of somehow remaining in a state of permanent focused meditation, we will always need to look forwards.

To remind us (lest we become too fixated on living in the present), the intended result is a balancing act of the now and the yet-to-come. It is only awareness of the present moment that opens up a truly compelling experience outside of our daydreams and fantasies. Yet on the other hand, the temporally limited future permits us a framework and context that allows us to make use of the present and give it meaning. If, though, we become fixated on the future, we miss out on the tranquillity and richness of real experience. We achieve equilibrium by finding a 'good-enough' compromise. Embracing the present moment does not have to mean a brainless, passive giving of oneself over to the flow. It can be engaged and active.

I am writing this book here and now primarily for the enjoyment of doing so, but the pleasure I take in the process is inseparable from the fact that I am trying to communicate ideas, which means that you (as the future reader) and the physical object that this virtual typed document will eventually become, give shape to the enjoyment I am experiencing now. Yet I am only *concerned* with the current task of expressing an idea. If I expand my sense of the here and now, I think, 'Am I enjoying writing this book? How does it compare to my other projects? Should I do more writing and less TV? Would I enjoy that more? Have I found a nice place to write in today?' These thoughts remain fixed in a present more akin to a snapshot of life than the kind of elusive, fleeting instant upon which one seeks to come to rest in meditation classes. Meanwhile, I do not, for example, concern myself with worries of the future: 'How will this book further my career? How many people will read it? Will they want another book? What should I follow this with? Will they mess up the cover?' These are of no interest, although I do care very much about the cover.

We should live in the present while we plan for the future. Remembering the Stoic reserve clause of 'if things work out' (or 'God willing') we can make plans without investing ourselves with undue emotion in their outcomes. Achieving a balance will be good enough. This means we align ourselves with that $x=y$ diagonal as much as we can. We can wish, as much as we remember to do so, not for things to be exactly as they are per se, but for things to be *however they happen to be*. Thus the future can lie in our sights, but without the brute clarity and single-mindedness with which any number of self-help gurus tell us to picture it. We can save much of the clear-sighted engagement for the present.

Working on Winnicott's and Debra's 'good-enough' principle, we might reduce any terror surrounding death to at worst a residual anxiety and set ourselves in much better stead to face death squarely when it comes. If we have the opportunity, it allows us to live out our final time with the richness experienced by Debra and others when 'the path of the future narrows to the width of this bed'.[174]

Rethinking the afterlife

Schopenhauer said that when we die, the world disappears, as it can only ever exist in our perceptions. When we are no longer around to perceive it, it vanishes in the blink of an eye. It's an interesting thought to play with, but most of us would prefer to say that the world carries

174 A haunting turn of phrase from Christopher Isherwood's novel *A Single Man*.

on happily without us once we've gone. This is life *after* us: the 'after-life', no less. Not a personal afterlife, and in that sense nothing to bring us much comfort. But in some important sense, it can do. Even 'we' might be said to live on after our deaths in the sense that those who know us now will carry around their memory of us after we've gone. And what that will mean depends on how we affect others now while we are alive.

What legacy would we leave behind in the minds and hearts of others if we were to die right now? To stand any chance of leaving behind a positive footprint, we are well advised to see ourselves from an outside perspective. To do that, we need to remember the discrepancy between how we perceive our negative actions versus those we see in others. When other people annoy us, or are in some way rude, we often see it as part of a pattern of behaviour. Even for close friends, we can identify behaviour that is 'typical' of how badly they deal with stress, or behave after a drink, or reliably let themselves down in some other scenario. For others of whom we are not so fond, we might see negative patterns very readily across the board.

For ourselves, though, we do the opposite. If we bother to reflect on our behaviour when we have been rude, short-tempered or somehow let ourselves down, we see only exceptions and excuses. *He* acts like that because it's in his nature, whereas *I* acted like that in that instance only *because* of such and such. *He* acted from his nature; *my* behaviour was justified by exceptional circumstances. We rarely see negative traits in ourselves, only reasons that explain and excuse our behaviour on specific occasions. Rest assured that others see your negative behaviour as just as much a part of a reliable trait as you would in them.

If you tend to impose your emotional dramas on other people, for example, you're probably something of a nightmare to be around. And don't think, 'I'm not *really* a bitch when you get to know me, even if I act like one sometimes'; if you act like a bitch, you *are* a bitch. That's what being a bitch means. The need to manipulate others into making us feel good through emotional displays is the drive of the infant, who screams until he gets what he needs. Others – stronger people – will accommodate such demands and display what is needed, but they do so begrudgingly and their patience is not infinite. Growing up – and the lesson of the 'good-enough' parent – is in part a process of learning that our own desires are not the centre of anyone else's world. We can be needy and manipulative, bullying or seducing others into pandering to us, but we should expect to be resented for it.

Where our behaviour is positive and less self-centred, though, something very different can happen. Great people influence and change us. If we have a very generous and self-sufficient friend, we are likely to bring her image to mind on occasions and find ourselves emulating her. If a person's behaviour has touched us in some way, we are often keen to have the same effect on others.

Irvin D. Yalom calls this 'rippling': creating concentric circles of influence that 'can affect others for years, even for generations'. He cites it as a 'singularly powerful' means of countering patients' distress around the transience of life. He describes the experience of one patient, Barbara, who realises about herself:

> Perhaps death was not quite the annihilation she had thought. Perhaps it was not so essential that her person *or even memories of her person* survived. Perhaps the important thing was that her ripples

persist, ripples of some act or idea that would help others attain joy and virtue in life, ripples that would fill her with pride and act to counter the immorality, horror and violence monopolising the mass media and the outside world.[175]

When Barbara gives a short talk at her mother's funeral, she is reminded of one of her mother's favourite phrases: 'Look for her among her friends.'

This phrase had power: she knew that her mother's caring, gentleness and love of life lived inside her, her only child. As she delivered the talk and scanned the funeral assemblage, she could physically feel aspects of her mother that had rippled into her friends, who in turn would pass the ripples on to their children and children's children.[176]

The approach of death gives us a chance to pay attention to how our lives might affect those we know. We are dealing with the end of our story, and it is the end of the story that colours the rest. We remember that what happens in the final chapter of a book or the final scene of a movie is the key to how we feel about the entire tale. If we have the opportunity, we can make sure that despite the effect we may have had on a person in the past, we can finish the story well and ripple positively into that person. Knowing that life after our deaths will continue with positive memories of us in place might help us to engage richly and simply in our lives, and end our stories as satisfyingly as possible.

175 Irvin D. Yalom, *Staring at the Sun*
176 Ibid.

Meanwhile, as many of us will not have that opportunity when the time comes, we can choose to pay attention to this idea in the present and do our best to ripple positively now, where and while we can.

In the song 'Never Went To Church' by The Streets, Mike Skinner laments that he has nothing to remind him of his late father and is worried that his memory of the older man is slipping away. Then poignantly, towards the end, he realises:

> I guess then you did leave me something to
> remind me of you
> Every time I interrupt someone like you used to
> When I do something like you, you'll be on my
> mind or through
> Cause I forgot you left me behind to remind me
> of you.

The philosopher Samuel Scheffler points out a highly unexpected aspect of the 'collective afterlife' that remains after we have gone, in a series of 2012 lectures on the subject. These are brought together in a short, very enjoyable book called *Death and the Afterlife*. It's worth a mention here, so I shall do my best to summarise his argument.

We have seen that the framework provided by our own mortality is vital for our lives to retain shape and interest. Without it, it seems we would cease to value anything. Scheffler now draws our attention to the rest of humanity with two fascinating thought experiments.

Firstly, imagine that you were due for a normal lifespan, but you also knew all human life was due to be wiped out by an asteroid thirty days after you died. A month after your death, it is Doomsday. How would that affect your attitudes for the rest of your life? What would you do differently if you knew that such a fate awaited the world's population a few weeks after you'd gone?

Some familiar, though interesting thoughts emerge from Scheffler's 'Doomsday Scenario', which remind us of the formless fug of sluggishness implied by immortality. In the face of humanity's imminent extinction after our deaths, many of our life's engagements would quickly appear to be pointless. If we were involved in cancer research, for example, we would presumably curtail our efforts: without a future humanity to benefit from our work, such study would be rendered pointless. As we look closer, other activities also start to seem redundant given the upcoming end of human life. Many of our cultural engagements, for example, exist to keep traditions alive, and thus to place us within a sense of ongoing human history. Plenty of religious, artistic and intellectual pursuits would seem pointless now that confidence in a continuing cultural narrative is denied us. Other everyday pleasures would start to feel rather hollow. The previously noted notion of 'rippling' would be pointless: we would feel less need to positively affect others who we knew would not survive. Instilling positive values in our children, for example, would most likely seem a waste of effort.

Scheffler shows us that we like to imagine ourselves having some personal relationship to the future, even after our death. We value being remembered, and engage in cultural traditions that aim to preserve certain aspects of the present, for example. With no future for human life, our relationship to it vanishes, and the point of many of our projects and behaviours too.

We might feel that the doomsday scenario unsettles us because we can imagine those we love facing this horrendous early death by asteroid. To counter this distraction,

Scheffler puts forward a second scenario, described in the novel *The Children of Men* by P. D. James and later (in altered form) in the film directed by Alfonso Cuarón. In this alternative 'infertility scenario', we inhabit a world where everyone lives their normal lifespan, but babies are no longer born. We are in the final dwindling generation of the human species.

Now we need not worry about our loved ones dying prematurely. This scenario eradicates the future of humanity without the distraction of concern for those we know. Again we see the same engagements appearing pointless; the pursuit of knowledge as well as creative and cultural traditions lose their *raisons d'être*. Anything that tacitly depended on a certain future would become redundant. In James' novel, an ennui has settled over our race that resembles the profound boredom dissected in Williams' essay on immortality. James feels, as does Scheffler, that our understanding of human life as a whole 'relies on an implicit understanding of such a life as itself occupying a place in an ongoing human history, in a temporally extended chain of lives and generations'.[177] Without that wider context for our lives, it is not clear to what extent the ordinary pleasures of life would retain their appeal.

Scheffler, unlike Freud in his essay 'On Transience', argues that when we value something, we see reasons to preserve it over time. And in doing so, we project ourselves forward and invest in the future. Which means, by valuing something, we make a judgement about how an aspect of the future *should* be: that a certain thing should continue to exist in a certain way, for example. We presume a normative authority over time; in other words,

177 Samuel Scheffler, *Death and the Afterlife*

rather than succumb to its transitory nature, *we decide* what matters. Furthermore, by extending our values over time, we feel a certain stability in ourselves and our sense of identity. We like to imagine that if we were to find ourselves in the future, particular things we value would still be in place. When the future is removed from the equation, we lose this sense of confidence in what we value. And without values, our lives would be scarcely recognisable.

Of course this is all thought-play and conjecture. But if we are convinced by this idea that without a future for humanity we would lose interest in a wide range of our activities and confidence in what we value (much like in the immortality case), then we arrive at a startling conclusion. It is not merely enough that we have in place the temporal finitude provided by our *own* death to ensure our lives have meaning. It is not enough *that we die.* We also *need others to live on* after us and without us. We need to die *and* others need to live. Which means ultimately that *the continuing lives of others matter more to us than do our own.*

What an astonishing thought! And to be clear: those 'others' are *not* limited to those we love. They are also the unknown unborn, denied existence by the infertility scenario of *The Children of Men.* We don't realise how greatly we value future generations, Scheffler says, because we're used to taking for granted the fact that human life will continue after we die. We are not troubled by the alternative. In contrast, the prospect of our own deaths has the capacity to make us feel very anxious indeed, and we're used to giving it our attention. We don't notice that the more important factor (of the continuing survival of others) *is* more important, because we're not used to thinking about it.

Scheffler does not feel that this surprising conclusion

about our priorities is likely to reduce our fear about death. But he points out that where we cannot do anything about our own demise, there is much we *can* do about preserving the future of humanity (which, fortuitously, he has revealed to be more valuable to us than we thought). Rather than work to prevent climate change and other pressing environmental issues from a duty-bound place of begrudging responsibility, we can work to preserve future humanity for our *own* reasons, as we realise its survival matters more to us than we ever imagined.

☺

16

And in the End

On tour recently, I met at the stage door a man in his late fifties who asked for a picture and autograph. As I had ushered him inside and out of the cold, he now pressed me further. The worst thing imaginable had happened to him: he had suffered the death of his child. He described haltingly how his daughter had died the year before and wanted to know if I thought there was an afterlife.

My heart went out to him, and as he held back tears, I didn't know how to answer. I said as sympathetically as I could that I didn't think so, and sensing where his grief might take him, added that if there *were*, I was pretty sure that stage mediums were not a good way of connecting with it. He left, taking no comfort, and that night I changed a line in the show, which had offered good Stoic advice that it is only how we perceive events that causes our problems. I'm convinced that's true, but maybe some tragedies are so undeniable that they need special acknowledgement.

I didn't have an answer for him then, in the face of his loss, but I think I do now.

What does it mean for a person to survive his or her own death? The physical body may continue to exist for a while, but the *person* to whom we refer is no longer there. Neither should we invent an eternal spirit or soul in order to feel that the person continues in some ethereal form. So if not in the body and not in the soul, where is that person's 'self' housed?

Perhaps it is in their personality. In their consciousness. In their sense of 'I'. And what is that self? What form does it take? One way of thinking of it, as offered by the cognitive scientist Douglas Hofstadter, is as a looping pattern of abstractions. Our personality may be the most real thing in the world to each of us, but it is a fiction, a configuration, a way of thinking. It isn't found in the meat of our brains but rather in what our brains *do*.

If we accept this and think of ourselves – our consciousness – as *patterns* of thinking, then our 'self' is something that to one degree or other can be experienced by other people too. Let's say I know you very well: I know your 'story', I'm well versed in your tastes, preferences and your ways of thinking. Then, if for a while I think and feel like you (perhaps while looking at a photograph of you or contemplating how you would behave in a certain situation), I am approximating in my body *your* brain pattern, at least a rough version of *your* 'self'. It won't ever be *quite* you, but I can be you with, Hofstadter would say, a 'Derren' accent. It's like a translation of a book: my copy of Kafka's story *Metamorphosis*, translated from the German, is undoubtedly the *same* story as the original *Die Verwandlung*, but it's lost something. It's got an accent, it's an approximation, but as it's still essentially the same pattern of thoughts and ideas and symbols, we can say it's the same thing.

If I were to lose a daughter, and every day I found

myself reminded of her, and if I were to think about what she would say or do about this or that, then *my* pattern for a while becomes *hers*. And thus her consciousness – her *pattern* – her *self* – is recreated in me for a while. It's sadly a coarse, grainy, much-reduced version of her, but it is, in some sense, her.

It's like the 'rippling' we've spoken of. Hofstadter writes:

> When someone dies, they leave a glowing corona behind them, an afterglow in the souls of those who were close to them. Inevitably, as time passes, the afterglow fades and finally goes out, but it takes many years for that to happen. When, eventually, all those close ones have died as well, then all the embers will have gone cool, and at that point, it's 'ashes to ashes and dust to dust'.[178]

It reminds me of the Mexican tradition of the three deaths, described by neuroscientist and author David Eagleman:

> There are three deaths. The first is when the body ceases to function. The second is when the body is consigned to the grave. The third is that moment, sometime in the future, when your name is spoken for the last time.[179]

We resurrect our loved ones whenever we find ourselves thinking and feeling like them. We carry them with us, in that blueprint of how to think and feel that they have

178 Douglas Hofstadter, *I am a Strange Loop*
179 David Eagleman, *Sum: Forty Tales from the Afterlives*

left behind. And the closer we are to them, the more we understand them, the more accurate that blueprint will be. It turns out, then, to be the positive connections between people that provide the mechanism for our 'self' to survive death in any meaningful way. It turns out to be love.

☺

17

And Now

The Stoics have given us a means of increasing our happiness by avoiding disturbance and embracing what they called 'virtue'. Through taking to heart their pithily expressed maxims, echoed in future generations by subsequent philosophers, we might move in greater accordance with fate and align ourselves more realistically with the $x=y$ diagonal of real life, where our aims and fortune wrestle with each other constantly. We have seen the wisdom of not trying to control what we cannot, and of taking responsibility for our judgements. Otherwise, we harm ourselves and others by becoming anxious, hurtful or intolerable. We have learnt to approach happiness indirectly, concentrating instead upon removing hindrances and disturbances and achieving a certain psychological robustness.

We have also seen that there is no magical route to happiness. There is no single philosophy – including Stoicism – that will provide all the answers, because when we think we will find all our answers in one place, we are projecting a fantasy. In matters of love, we see there is no single perfect partner who will give us everything we need, because we project those needs upon them, placing upon them impossible demands, unless our expectations are brought in check. Only a deep dialogue with ourselves will untangle those needs, never the never-enough behaviour of those upon whom we cast our projections. Likewise, as we saw at the start of our book, no single life-goal will ever prove enough for us in its attainment, because we are once again projecting our needs upon the unworthy. Even as we reject God in his Heaven, we moderns seem obsessed with seeking Him everywhere else. We find the Almighty in single, magical 'others' and systems that we expect to provide all our answers for us. Such a God is not forthcoming, and neither are his myriad secular or romantic counterparts. These mysterious, romanticised or celebrated panaceas only infantilise us. Life is not simple; there is rarely a right and wrong; the good guys do not always win and the bad guys are not always punished. Such logic is the stuff of fairy tales, read to us when we were children. And the expectation that some person or thing will be there for us to answer all our needs or prayers is a deeply childish one. We only have to watch a child in the street screaming in defiance of some perceived unfairness to see how painfully infantile this urge is. Our 'good-enough' parents teach us to expect disappointment as well as fulfilment, and thus we learn to grow up.

It is the same inane urge that has us expect easy answers. Politics tends to infantilise us, as do the media that communicate news to us. We are told that answers are black and white; that there are good guys and bad guys. We are not educated and nurtured to tolerate grown-up complexity and ambiguity. In an ideal society, a politician would explain to us where a matter at hand is multi-faceted and difficult. 'Here are the issues to be aware of on the one side,' she would tell us, 'and then we have to take into account these on the other. Somehow we must make sense of those conflicts and subtleties with patience and compassion and intelligence.' We are infantilised when they use fairy-tale logic or fear to manipulate us or sell a story of events that serves their ends. In politics, we find merely one example of how we are reduced; our maturity is denied in many areas of life. We prefer the illusion of black-and-white thinking to the real-life complexities of the grey in-betweens. We guzzle down sugary drinks and food rather than develop a sensitive and subtle palate; we play endless games and seek increasingly convincing virtual realities in favour of seeking actual growth. We look to be spiritually coddled, to avoid what is difficult, to be attended to each time we cry in the night. To grow up is to endure the equivocal, to permit the ambiguous.

Stoicism offers us great lessons and helpful threads to weave through our lives. As I hope I've shown, it is at its best neither cool nor detached but rather open, porous and connected easily to life. Yet if we have a lingering doubt about its all-encompassing wisdom, it is perhaps because some part of us remains unmoved. It may seem an odd question to ask at this point in the book, but *is happiness truly what we should seek?* And if so, is it in its richest form synonymous with an avoidance of disturbance? Having perhaps convinced you of those things, I'd like to leave you by undoing those convictions.

Remember, we begin our brief stay in this world by internalising everything as a message about ourselves. We live in our world with lingering background fears, usually centring around being abandoned or being overwhelmed. We grow up, editing and reducing the infinite data source of the present world to a repeating pattern that reinforces the biases that were instilled at an early age. We spin a tale of how the world works, a story that supports those historical maxims inevitably laid down by even the most well-meaning parents. That tale is, to us, 'reality', and it unconsciously governs our choices into adulthood. What we learn about the world, our role in it, and ourselves, we recreate and reinforce wherever we can. Hence the person who thinks lovers are never faithful suffers a long string of relationships with partners who always seem to turn out that way. Likewise, it is not at all uncommon for therapists, nurses and people who help others for a living to have learnt this urge early on, when they perhaps had to subjugate their own needs to a demanding parent.

This is our condition. Here on the one hand is the world, full of rich and mysterious things, experiences and people; and here on the other is our need to navigate it, and the only compass we know how to use has been battered and misaligned long ago. To forge ahead and do our best, we have to turn an ambiguous world into a set of easily navigable certainties. Thus we name the unnameable so we can identify it, tick it off and move forward. To get our bearings, we glibly label those things that remain eternally unresolved. We overgeneralise and reduce in order to make sense of the world and our place in it.

Concepts fall prey to our projections, which reduce rich ideas to what we'd like them to be; these projections are often illuminated by our fears. Happiness is one of those concepts. We've seen it has been diminished already by a society that tells us we are owed happiness and can achieve it simply by believing in ourselves (and assembling fancy goods along the way). But it is also reduced every time we use the word 'Happiness', because it is not a thing like a chair or a table that can be labelled so easily.

Instead, happiness shows itself to be a kind of activity, something that happens through our fluctuating relationship to life, others, fortune and ourselves. Prior to Plato, we saw the world as a state of flux. Heraclitus told us: 'No man ever steps in the same river twice, for it's not the same river and he's not the same man.'[180] Plato replaced this model with that of ideal forms, a shimmering nirvana of consummate examples of every quality, which could only be reached through hard work and contemplation. And thus fluid activities like happiness became *things*.

When we reduce complex ideas to nouns and categories in order to navigate swiftly through them, we start to become mindless. The important notion of transcendence, for example, is reduced to words like 'God' that no longer stand for anything and can be easily discredited. In the meantime, we might turn to addictive behaviour or waste our time on diversions because deep down we lack a sense of meaning, or a connection to something larger than ourselves. It's the equivalent of pigeonholing people: whenever we do this, we sever any chance of connection, discovery or surprise. We do the same every time we pigeonhole an idea with a glib term. It's a mindless form of autopilot that steers us forward, ever forward, reinforcing our core biases and fears in an ever-repeating pattern.

Mind*ful*ness, on the other hand, when it is summoned, keeps us engaged firmly in the present and brings with it the riches that come from paying attention. Mindfulness has been adopted by the world of meditation, but it is *not* meditation, though meditation is one popular tool, suited to some, to increase it. Mindfulness is just paying deliberate attention in the present: noticing

180 Thus Plato puts Heraclitus' law. See *Cratylus*, 402a.

things. When we are mindful, we turn off our autopilot and switch back on. Suddenly the world blooms before us. In matters of health, for example, rather than simply saying we suffer from an illness or condition, we might pay attention to how and when it flares up, and notice that some of the time it isn't much of a problem at all. We might even (the psychologist Ellen J. Langer points out in the most recent edition of her seminal book *Mindfulness*) be able to then recreate those contexts where we don't feel the pain, and come to alleviate much of our suffering. Two hundred and seventy-seven performances of my secular faith-healing show *Miracle* have convinced me of the psychological component of many debilitating afflictions, and the power that can come from harnessing the stories we tell ourselves about them.

Mindfulness challenges the stories we tell ourselves by having us pay attention to the larger picture, which is only accessible in the here and now. A greater dose of mindfulness would have allowed you to unscramble the last anagram at the start of this book if you could not before, rather than fall prey to the 'story' of learned helplessness. Paying attention to the present moment is our most effective means of undoing the harmful and perpetuating narratives by which we live, by challenging them with the counter-evidence we notice around us.

In old age, mindfulness can increase health by saving us from a diminishing sense of authorship of our stories. In a 1976 experiment by Langer and her colleagues, a number of elderly residents in a nursing home were given houseplants to look after and water. They were also encouraged to make decisions for themselves, such as where to receive visitors, and when movie night would occur on their floor. Meanwhile, a second control group was also given plants, but this time it was the nurses who looked after them and made decisions about visitors and movie showings. Three weeks later, the first group, who had been given responsibility, was happier and healthier. Eighteen months later, they were *still* significantly more active and sociable. But most astonishingly, this group *lived longer.* The mortality rate was twice as high in the group that had all their decisions made for them. Being granted authorship of our stories, and experiencing mindfulness rather than mindlessness, makes for happier and healthier lives.

In matters of love, a mature relationship involves celebrating the mystery and wholeness of one's partner. It is standing in appreciation of their otherness, not neurotically attempting to obliterate it because at some level their separation from us might trigger responses we once had to a fallible, unavailable parent. It is realising that we are each of us alone, that no one is ever entirely right for us because we are all broken, and that we can only open our broken aloneness to that of another. A good relationship, like a good parent or a good death, need only be 'good enough', consisting of two people navigating each other's inadequacies with kindness and sympathy. At its best, the poet Rainer Maria Rilke tells us, it 'consists in two solitudes protecting, defining, and welcoming one another'.[181] Likewise, a mature life, and a flourishing one, involves standing in toleration and acknowledgement of ambiguity rather than greeting it with disappointment.

The Stoic approach is effective for ensuring greater levels of tranquillity, and for most of the time that's likely to be enough. But not all of the time. For if we live a diminished life driven by a fear that tells us we are in some sense unworthy, our concept of happiness may

181 Rainer Maria Rilke, *Letters to a Young Poet*

remain similarly limited. The Stoics tell us to 'remove disturbances', but for some this might come to mean 'hiding away safely' where nothing can harm them. This is a meagre substitute for flourishing. Our ultimate aim is maybe *not* so much to be happy as to live fully and make sure we are moving *forward*. Rilke suggests 'imagining an individual's experience as a larger or smaller room . . . most people are only acquainted with one corner of their particular room, a place by the window, a little area to pace up and down'.[182]

Wholeness cannot be found in the mere avoidance of troubling feelings, however helpful the tools of the Stoics are for reassessing attachments and finding one's centre of gravity. To live without anxiety is to live without growth. We shouldn't try to control what we cannot, and we must take responsibility for our feelings. But the reason for this is to walk out into the world with strength, not to hide from danger.

If you feel anxiety, let it sit. See if it is amenable to the lessons we have learnt from the Stoics. You don't need to fix things that lie outside of your control. You also don't need to *fix* the anxiety: it is a feeling *that you have*; it is therefore not *you*. The need to fix, to control is what fuels the anxiety in the first place. Let it be, and it will lose its excessive force. Then, once you are no longer running away with it, or trying to remove it, you might even welcome it.

Why? Because the Stoics can't always be right. We cannot demand from them a formula for our happiness, because no such formula exists; happiness is messy and fuzzy and active. Can disturbance be a good thing? Why would we not wish to pay attention to these disturbances

182 Ibid.

if they have something to teach us? Anxiety is a signal that we are not in harmony with ourselves. Who is? It is good to detach from worthless sources of worry but also vital for our flourishing to listen to those rumblings and see from whence they arise. What does this disturbing feeling remind us of from our past? What fear lies half-hidden behind this dread? What part of myself am I closing off? Why is this obviously important?

Very few people find a better partner without the pain of breaking up with a previous one. We don't change our career without first letting our current job get us down. We don't start anything new without the pain of ending the old or the frustration of enduring it. Disturbance, then, can be a signal that we are moving in the right direction: namely, out of our comfort zone. To remain tranquil and comfortable would deny us our growth. To remain happy would stop us from flourishing. We can manage our anxiety in the ways we have discussed, but when it stirs, it is likely to be a helpful signal from an untended part of us that wishes now to be heard. If we shut our ears to these voices, they will come in time to own us, because the things that remain unconscious are always in charge. Jung called them 'offended gods', by which he meant energy-charged aspects of our personality (such as the erotic, the creative, the aggressive) that if not honoured will wreak their revenge.

Rather than seek to expunge all sadness, we might know when to pay attention to what it offers. After sadness passes, Rilke says:

> one might easily suppose that nothing had happened, but we have altered the way a house alters when a guest enters it. We cannot say who has come, perhaps we will never know, but there are

indications that it is the future that enters into us like this, in order to be transformed within us, long before it actually occurs.[183]

We might sometimes pay patient heed to our sorrow, allow it to penetrate into us, knowing that it is an important articulation of what was already there. It is showing us that something demands our attention. We do not need to fear the world, or treat it with suspicion. Any monsters that dwell there are our own.

The final call, then, is not to merely seek tranquillity but, from its strong shores, to welcome its opposite. It is a strong society that encourages dialogue with its enemies, and a fearful one that promulgates reductive nouns and categories (such as 'Terror') to demonise and avoid the unsettling complexities of active, untidy reality. We, too, must seek the same conversation within ourselves. And do so before the forces we repress rage against us.

☺

183 Rainer Maria Rilke, *Letters to a Young Poet*

List of Books Cited

Aristotle, *Nicomachean Ethics*
Aristotle, *Rhetoric*
Armstrong, John, *How to Worry Less about Money*
Aurelius, Marcus, *Meditations*
Beauvoir, Simone de, *A Very Easy Death*
Bennett, Arnold, *How to Live on 24 Hours a Day*
Bettelheim, Bruno, *The Uses of Enchantment: The Meaning and Importance of Fairy Tales*
Bonner, Frances, *Ordinary Television: Analyzing Popular TV*
Borges, Jorge Luis, 'The Library of Babel' (short story)
Brown, Tom, *Amusements*
Byrne, Rhonda, *The Secret*
Cain, Susan, *Quiet: The Power of Introverts in a World That Can't Stop Talking*
Chomsky, Noam, *The Common Good*
Clarke, Arthur C., *Profiles of the Future*
Darwin, Charles, *The Descent of Man*
Davies, William, *Overcoming Anger and Irritability*
Deary, Vincent, *How We Are*
de Botton, Alain, *The Art of Travel*
de Botton, Alain, *The Course of Love*

Descartes, René, *Discourse on Method and Meditations on First Philosophy*

Dubois, Paul, *The Psychic Treatment of Nervous Disorders*

Eagleman, David, *Sum: Forty Tales from the Afterlives*

Ehrenreich, Barbara, *Bright-Sided: How Positive Thinking Is Undermining America*

Eliot, T. S., *Four Quartets*

Ellis, Albert, *Reason and Emotion in Psychotherapy: A Comprehensive Method of Treating Human Disturbances*

Ellis, Albert, *The Road to Tolerance: The Philosophy of Rational Emotive Behavior Therapy*

Epictetus, *Discourses and Selected Writings*

Epictetus, *Enchiridion*

Epictetus, *The Golden Sayings of Epictetus*

Epicurus, *The Essential Epicurus: Letters, Principal Doctrines, Vatican Sayings, and Fragments*, translated by Eugene Michael O'Connor

Evans, Jules, *Philosophy For Life: And Other Dangerous Situations*

Foster Wallace, David, *Infinite Jest*

Frankl, Viktor E., *Man's Search for Meaning*

Freud, Sigmund, *The Standard Edition of the Complete Psychological Works of Sigmund Freud Volume XIV (1914–1916): On the History of the Psycho-Analytic Movement, Papers on Metapsychology and Other Works*

Goethe, Johann Wolfgang von, *The Sorrows of Young Werther*

Gould, Josiah B., *The Philosophy of Chrysippus*

Gould, Philip, *When I Die: Lessons from the Death Zone*

Grosz, Stephen, *The Examined Life: How We Lose and Find Ourselves*

Hadot, Pierre, *Philosophy as a Way of Life*

Hadot, Pierre, *What Is Ancient Philosophy?*

Hammurabi, *The Code of Hammurabi*

Harris, Sam, *Waking Up: Searching for Spirituality Without Religion*

Hofstadter, Douglas, *I am a Strange Loop*

Hume, David, *A Treatise of Human Nature*

Hutcheson, Francis, *An Inquiry into the Original of Our Ideas of Beauty and Virtue*

Huxley, Aldous, *Brave New World*

Iamblichus, *Life of Pythagoras*

Irvine, William B., *A Guide to the Good Life: The Ancient Art of Stoic Joy*

Irvine, William B., *On Desire: Why We Want What We Want*

Isherwood, Christopher, *A Single Man*

James, P. D., *The Children of Men*

Jung, Carl, Commentary on *The Secret of the Golden Flower*

Kafka, Franz, *Die Verwandlung (The Metamorphosis)*

Kahneman, Daniel, *Thinking, Fast and Slow*

Karpf, Anne, *How to Age*

Kundera, Milan, *The Unbearable Lightness of Being*

Langer, Ellen J., *Mindfulness*

Lipsius, Justus, *On Constancy*

McMahon, Darrin, *The Pursuit of Happiness: A History from the Greeks to the Present*

McRaney, David, *You Are Not So Smart*

May, Todd, *Death (The Art of Living)*

Mill, John Stuart, *On Liberty*

Montaigne, Michel de, *Of Anger*

Nagel, Thomas, *Mortal Questions*

Nietzsche, Friedrich, *On the Genealogy of Morality*

Nietzsche, Friedrich, *The Birth of Tragedy*

Nietzsche, Friedrich, *The Gay Science*

Nussbaum, Martha C., *The Therapy of Desire: Theory and Practice in Hellenistic Ethics*

Plato, *Cratylus*

Plutarch, *On the Avoidance of Anger*

Plutarch, *Parallel Lives*

Randi, James, *The Faith Healers*

Rilke, Rainer Maria, *Letters to a Young Poet*

Rilke, Rainer Maria, *Sonnets to Orpheus*

Robertson, Donald, *The Philosophy of Cognitive-Behavioural Therapy (CBT): Stoic Philosophy as Rational and Cognitive Psychotherapy*

Rojek, Chris, *Celebrity*

Rousseau, Jean-Jacques, *Emile*

Rousseau, Jean-Jacques, *The Social Contract*

Scheffler, Samuel, *Death and the Afterlife*

Schickel, Richard, *Intimate Strangers: The Culture of Celebrity in America*

Schillace, Brandy, *Death's Summer Coat: What the History of Death and Dying Can Tell Us About Life and Living*

Schopenhauer, Arthur, *Aphorisms on the Wisdom of Life: What a Man Has*

Schopenhauer, Arthur, *Counsels and Maxims*

Schopenhauer, Arthur, *On the Basis of Morality*

Schopenhauer, Arthur, *Parerga and Paralipomena*

Schopenhauer, Arthur, *Studies in Pessimism*

Schopenhauer, Arthur, *The World as Will and Representation*

Seneca, *Letters from a Stoic*

Seneca, *On Anger*

Seneca, *On Benefits*

Tocqueville, Alexis de, *Democracy in America*

Tolstoy, Leo, *The Death of Ivan Ilyich*

Watts, Alan W., *The Wisdom of Insecurity: A Message for an Age of Anxiety*

Werner, Heinz and Kaplan, Bernard, *Symbol Formation: An Organismic-Developmental Approach to Language and the Expression of Thought*

Wiseman, Richard, *The Luck Factor: The Scientific Study of the Lucky Mind*

Wood, Gaby, *Living Dolls: The Return of Sexism*

Wroth, Warwick, *The London Pleasure Gardens of the Eighteenth Century*

Yalom, Irvin D., *Love's Executioner and Other Tales of Psychotherapy*

Yalom, Irvin D., *Momma and the Meaning of Life*

Yalom, Irvin D., *Staring at the Sun: Overcoming the Terror of Death*

Acknowledgements

Talking to people about happiness is a delightful thing; it leads to especially life-affirming results. So a deep and heartfelt thank you to all those who have been part of that discussion, and to the people who have expanded or challenged my understanding of happiness over the last few years.

Thank you to the Piglace for all the joy you give to me and everyone you meet; to my parents and brother for shaping me this way; to the phenomenal trio of Debra Westwick, James and Nik and their happiness to be part of this book; to A. C. Grayling, Alain de Botton and Stephen Fry for their brilliance and generosity; to Chrisses Goto-Jones and Mason. Thank you to Coops who works every day to make my life easier and keep things as tranquil as possible for me; to Michael Vine and Andrew O'Connor who have guided my career through happy pastures and Andy Nyman and Sharkey with whom I have shared in and dreamt up so many happy adventures. A generous golden shower of love upon the rest of my touring pals – Dodds, Ollie, James, Matt, Beth, MJ, Matt, Lauren – with whom for the last three years I could never go hill-walking or go-karting because I was writing. And to all the rest of my dear friends because it makes me so happy to be with you, perhaps with special mention to Cleo Roccos who breathes happiness out to the frilly edges of the universe through every one of her particles.

Finally to Doug Young, Viv, and the team at Transworld; and to Greg Day for PRing the fuck out of this book.

List of Illustrations

Index

TRICKS OF THE MIND
Derren Brown

DERREN BROWN'S TELEVISION AND stage performances have entranced and dumbfounded millions. His baffling illusions and stunning set pieces – such as *The Séance, Russian Roulette* and *The Heist* – have set new standards of what's possible, as well as causing more than their fair share of controversy. Now, for the first time, he reveals the secrets behind his craft, what makes him tick and just why he grew that beard.

Tricks of the Mind takes you on a journey into the structure and psychology of magic. Derren also takes a long hard look at the paranormal industry, and looks at why some of us feel the need to believe in it in the first place. Alternately hilarious, controversial and challenging, *Tricks of the Mind* is essential reading for Derren's legions of fans, and pretty bloody irresistible even for those who don't like him that much . . .

'Reveals a surprising amount about his art . . . there is much to enlighten, entertain and put into use!'
Psychologies

'Will delight anyone with an interest in the weirder things people think and why they think them.'
Independent on Sunday

CONFESSIONS OF A CONJUROR
Derren Brown

IN *CONFESSIONS OF A CONJUROR*, Derren Brown invites you on a whimsical journey through his unusual mind. Structured around the various stages of a conjuring trick, performed by his younger self in a crowded restaurant, Derren's endlessly engaging narrative takes you from the history of magic, to speculations on the manufacturing of Monster Munch and the correct way to poach an egg, via discussions about psychology, what he hums while cleaning his teeth and the social niceties surrounding Parmesan cheese.

Hugely revealing, hilarious and unlike anything you've read before, *Confessions of a Conjuror* is a refreshing alternative to autobiography that will charm and delight you.

> 'Weird, whimsical and, at times, uproarious . . . Brown
> takes us on a meandering pleasure cruise downriver.
> It is worth the journey.'
> *Sunday Times*

> 'It combines a playfully baroque prose style with pinpoint
> observation and almost excruciating levels of self-examination,
> if not loathing. It's a fascinating experience.'
> AL Kennedy, *Guardian,* Books of the Year